D1241906

International Handbook
on
Social Work Education

International Handbook
—————— on ——————
Social Work Education

Edited by
Thomas D. Watts, Doreen Elliott,
and Nazneen S. Mayadas

Foreword by Katherine A. Kendall

Greenwood Press
Westport, Connecticut • London

Library of Congress Cataloging-in-Publication Data

International handbook on social work education / edited by Thomas D.
  Watts, Doreen Elliott, and Nazneen S. Mayadas ; foreword by
  Katherine A. Kendall.
      p.   cm.
    Includes bibliographical references and index.
    ISBN 0–313–27915–2 (alk. paper)
      1. Social work education—Handbooks, manuals, etc.   I. Watts,
    Thomas D.   II. Elliott, Doreen.   III. Mayadas, Nazneen S. (Nazneen
  Sada)
  HV11.I565   1995
  361.3'2'07—dc20   95–6674

British Library Cataloguing in Publication Data is available.

Library of Congress Catalog Card Number: 95–6674
ISBN: 0–313–27915–2

First published in 1995

Greenwood Press, 88 Post Road West, Westport, CT 06881
An imprint of Greenwood Publishing Group, Inc.

Printed in the United States of America

 # 32133499

The paper used in this book complies with the
Permanent Paper Standard issued by the National
Information Standards Organization (Z39.48–1984).

10 9 8 7 6 5 4 3 2 1

Nam et ipsa scientia potestas est. (Frances Bacon)

Dedicated to all social workers and social work educators worldwide, especially to the contributors to this volume, whose sharing of international knowledge empowers our profession.

Also dedicated by co-editor Thomas D. Watts to Rebecca Watts Crawford and Dean M. Crawford; and to Carol, Leonard, Daniel and Jeffrey Morrison, Suzanne Morrison Condon, and their families.

CONTENTS

LIST OF TABLES AND FIGURES

Table

Figure

ACKNOWLEDGMENTS

We have many people to thank for their contributions to the preparation of this book for publication. First we wish to thank Sue Anderson, who contributed her considerable computer and word processing knowledge and skill, and who helped with the completion of the script and with the indexing. Special thanks go to Cathryn Martin for her extensive and skilled work in preparing the typescript for camera-ready copy. We wish to thank other support staff who helped at different stages: Roberta K. Dotterer, Judy A. Linville, Donna D. Turner, Marion Britten, Melissa Jane Adair, and Carolyn Miller.

We would like to thank our contributers for their scholarship and their participation in this project. They have been gracious despite delays in publication and difficulties in communicating at a distance.

Finally, the co-operation, expertise and consistent support of the editors at the Greenwood Press, Mildred Vasan and Ann Newman, made this project possible.

FOREWORD

Katherine A. Kendall

The challenge of global interdependence to social work education was thoroughly explored at the 16th International Congress of Schools of Social Work held in July 1992 in Washington, D.C. The full impact of political upheaval and global change has clearly not yet been felt, but what was clear to educators from around the world was the extent to which the problems with which social workers deal transcend all national boundaries. The recital of worldwide social problems seemed endless: poverty; hunger; Acquired Immunodeficiency Syndrome; substance abuse; street children and the homeless; new waves of refugees, migrants, and displaced persons; environmental deterioration; and many more.

The chapters in this book reflect the global nature not only of social problems but of the functions served by the social work profession. For social work educators, an outstanding feature of the historical events of recent years was the discovery by Eastern European countries of social work and its methods of professional preparation as a positive force for social betterment. This has led to new possibilities for educators to undertake foreign assignments, notably in Eastern Europe and even in communist China, where social work training programs have been reestablished after a hiatus of thirty-six years. American educators are among those who eagerly seek to take advantage of such opportunities.

This awakens memories, not generally known, of the involvement of American social work educators in many ground-breaking firsts in international cooperation specifically related to social work education or social welfare services. The U.S. Congress in 1939 passed its first law on international cooperation, establishing a program of bilateral exchange with Latin America. The first "participant" training of any kind conducted under the new legislation involved the development of trained people for the social welfare field. A series of ongoing projects, planned cooperatively with Latin American directors of schools of social work, was conducted by the Inter American Unit of the U.S. Children's Bureau in cooperation with the American Association of Schools of Social Work (now the Council on Social Work Education). After World War II, the Inter-American Unit was renamed the International Service, with a greatly extended program of educational exchange, involving experienced or intending social workers from many parts of the world as visitors and students. American social workers were also recruited by the Children's Bureau as consultants and advisers overseas. For the first and only time, the State Department appointed social welfare attachés, who were accredited to American embassies in India and Brazil.

In the United Nations, as well as in the United States, there were other firsts that can, with pride, be attributed to social work and social welfare. The vast network of technical assistance services that became available through the United Nations to the emerging new nations had its origins in the social welfare advisory services taken over from the United Nations Relief and Rehabilitation Administration (UNRRA) in 1946. Social work education was given high priority with scores of Western consultants, preponderantly American, assigned to developing countries around the world to establish schools of social work.

These international activities, much admired at the time, have since been described and denigrated as professional imperialism. While there were indeed some unfortunate consequences of well-meaning efforts to establish high quality programs of professional education, critics have forgotten or are not aware of the spirit of the times. After World War II and with the launching of the Truman Point IV program and the Marshall Plan, everything American was seen as good and worthy of emulation. Developing countries seeking technical assistance wanted the best for their peoples. If, as was generally assumed, the American pattern of social work education was superior to that of other countries, why shouldn't they aspire to the same standard of excellence? It was much later, when American influence had waned and U.S. programs of foreign aid had lost much of their humanitarian flavor, that questions arose within the regional and international branches of the profession about the suitability of the fit for developing countries of Western models of social work education and practice.

Those questions arise anew as social work educators and other social work advisers from the West flock to the aid of the newly liberated Eastern bloc countries in their efforts to adopt new patterns of human service. What has been learned about international cooperation in the past fifty years should effectively guard against professionalism, but there is still the danger of professional myopia, with culture-bound assumptions about the universal applicability of one's own pattern of professional education. Myopia, fortunately, is more easily corrected than imperialism. The worldwide examination of social work education in this volume should go far to correct shortsighted views. It should also have the salutary effect of contributing to a much needed international perspective in social work education. And the volume appears at a time when the challenge of global interdependence cries out for comparative study, cooperative research, and collegial sharing of professional knowledge and experience about how best to tackle social problems that are worldwide in their impact. This challenge is best met in social work education that includes

relevant international content and provides learning experiences which encompass a worldview as essential to the mission of the profession.

In any profession, however, a worldview is more easily expressed than
achieved. The major objective of programs of professional education is to
prepare practitioners for the tasks mandated by a particular society. This often
leads to a parochial and culture-bound selection of the subject matter to be
included in the curriculum. Faculty members may also resist teaching in an area
for which they feel inadequately prepared. The press of courses required for
practice in the domestic setting tends as well to exclude international content as
marginal and therefore expendable in a crowded program.

This handbook with its broad coverage of nations in every continent should
serve as an excellent resource for social work educators seeking to become
knowledgeable about the international dimensions of their profession. The
range of functions described in these accounts of social welfare services in both
industrialized and developing countries underlines the importance of schools of
social work opening their windows on the world. Universals can be readily
identified. Just as important, but less obvious, are the social, cultural, and
economic differences that shape social welfare policies and programs. In all
regions, the family as a social institution is undergoing tremendous change, but
how the family, its forms and functions are viewed may vary greatly in different
cultures. In all societies, there is special concern for children, with poverty
putting many children at very great risk. Most societies, too, must reckon with
the inevitability of an aging population, although the problems posed may differ
from country to country. Disability and health issues have compelling social
consequences everywhere. Racism and ethnic conflict are searing problems in
many countries. While there are marked differences in the status and role of
women in diverse cultures, commonalties have also been clearly identified in
international and regional conferences. These examples-and many more could
be noted-hint at how much can be learned of benefit to one's own country
through knowledge gained of how other countries deal with social problems and
issues common to all. How to communicate this knowledge is the task of social
work education.

Because one cannot teach what one doesn't know, it is important for faculty
members to have ready access to research reports and other information that will
make them sufficiently knowledgeable about international developments to add
that dimension to their teaching. Fortunately, a wealth of documentation is
available from sources that are well known, if not sufficiently mined. The
United Nations, its Regional Commissions and Specialized Agencies produce
quantities of material that is relevant for teaching and research and available free
or for purchase through United Nations offices or related outlets in most
countries. While the reports and other documents produced by UNICEF, the
Economic and Social Council of the United Nations, and other UN bodies
provide the most extensive and useful teaching material for the field of social

welfare, other international governmental organizations such as the World Bank and the European Organization for Economic Cooperation and Development publish excellent reports on subjects such as poverty and development, with considerable attention in recent years to women in development.

Quantities of teaching material can also be found in the publications of international nongovernmental organizations. The proceedings of international conferences, seminars, and workshops sponsored by the International Council on Social Welfare, the International Association of Schools of Social Work, and the International Federation of Social Workers along with reports on intercountry projects and research offer definitive information on many subjects that lend themselves to an international perspective in social work education. *International Social Work*, the official journal of the three international social welfare bodies, is designed to extend knowledge and promote communication in the international field. Many other international journals, bibliographies, and publications of organizations with worldwide social programs could be mentioned, but enough has been said to indicate that lack of material is no barrier to the inclusion of international content in the social work curriculum.

What is needed, then, is a strong desire of a social work faculty to broaden the educational experience of students and the will to undertake study of current curriculum goals, with a view to their revision to include international content. The infusion of such content into already existing courses is perhaps the most productive approach in the study of a national social welfare system, for example, content on more comprehensive policies and services from another country or countries would sharpen the ability of students to analyze the programs with which they will be involved as practitioners. In the study of human behavior, the significance of cultural factors as seen in content from other cultures would lead to a more sensitive awareness and understanding of difference in all their professional relationships and particularly in their work with minorities and ethnically diverse peoples. In social work practice, the range of possibilities is enormous, with illuminating material available on, for example, the family, child welfare, the elderly, poverty, refugees, and many other subjects with which students must be familiar if they are to become competent practitioners.

As noted, inclusion of content in already existing courses is the most effective way to develop an international perspective, but it is not always possible to persuade all the faculty members involved to take the time or make the effort to search out relevant material from other countries. Special courses on specific international subjects given by knowledgeable and committed faculty members could then become the preferred way to begin. Examples might include the wide-ranging social welfare activities of the United Nations and other international governmental and nongovernmental organizations; an overview of high-priority global social problems such as hunger, poverty,

Aquired Immunnodeficiency Syndrome, and   drug abuse, and approaches to their solution; or comparative research on social policy issues.

Whatever the approach, the important considerations to keep in mind are the international scope of the social work profession and the global nature of the problems with which social workers deal in our interdependent world. This book underlines the necessity for all schools of social work in all countries to take heed of this global interdependence and, at the same time, offers much needed help in developing an international perspective in social work education.

International Handbook
on
Social Work Education

AN INTRODUCTION TO THE WORLD OF SOCIAL WORK EDUCATION

Thomas D. Watts

The purpose of this book is to provide an overview of social work education around the world, so that the reader might well have a handy compendium and analysis of social work education as it is carried out in diverse country settings. Social work education has many faces across the six continents represented here. This introduction serves to introduce the book, and briefly discuss a few concepts central to its concerns.

Increasingly, we live in a "global village." "The earth has become so small and the peoples of the world so intimately cross-joined," notes Hartman (1990: 291), "that all of us are deeply affected by events occurring in distant corners of the world, and people in those corners are affected by us." Most noticeable to all of us is the increasingly internationalized economy. What happens in the Japanese or German economies, or other economies, has effects on all of us. It is difficult, if not impossible, to be an "isolationist" in such an environment. Since we already live in an internationalized economy, can internationalized social work and social work education be far behind? It probably has dragged behind. Mayadas and Elliott (1990: 293) note, "Education policies worldwide have failed to foster a 'world view' of social problems." Healy did find some bright spots in a survey that she conducted, but still observed that it "is probably safe to assert that while some educational programmes address international issues, deliberate and comprehensive treatment of the international dimension of social work is rare in all parts of the world" (Healy, 1986: 144). It is difficult to move from the local to the global, but it is rewarding and beneficial to do so. This book is predicated upon the notion that when we examine social work education in other countries we learn a great deal about that work but about social work education elsewhere and in our country as well. Through comparisons come insight and new knowledge about the familiar social institutions which surround us. We may, through this process, glean some fresh ideas on social work education. Perhaps an idea or program in another country could be adapted for use in ours. Perhaps other countries could learn from the experience we have had. Learning is mutual, ongoing, and dynamic and can help us to advance the human condition.

Social science and can resemble a quagmire at times. Definitions of some key terms in social science and social welfare terminology are in order. Comparative social welfare "is concerned with the structural differences of various social welfare systems. The study of similarities and differences forms a logical basis for the classification, analysis, and conceptual synthesis of differential systems" (Mohan, 1987: 957).   Barker (1991: 44) notes that comparative social welfare is the "analysis of by reviewing how different societies have addressed the same objectives." Comparative Social Welfare incorporates an emphasis on comparing and learning. One could make a strong case that the history of civilization itself centers on these two concepts. After the wheel was invented about five thousand years ago near the eastern end of the Mediterranean Sea, other socienties followed suit. Civilizations that could learn and adapt from other civilizations thrive, while others could not. "Comparative analysis promoted through international cooperation," Mohan (1987: 967) notes, "has tremendous potential to lubricate the rusty mechanism of international relations." Comparative analysis can help us gain new insights into our own familiar social welfare institutions, new ideas about how to change those institutions for the better.

International social welfare is an "inter-disciplinary effort focusing on a range of services, resources, educational and research activities in the human services field, that cut across national and regional boundaries, with ongoing concern for the development of social provisions that are necessary to deal with the human consequences of social, political, and economic developments" (Sanders & Pedersen, 1984: xv). They go on to point to some of the differences between "international" and "comparative" social welfare (1984: xv), such as the fact that the term comparative refers to a methodological tool of comparative analysis, whereas international refers to the content that is taught. The term international social work could be defined as a "focus on the profession and practice in different parts of the world, especially the place of the organized profession in different countries, the different roles that social workers perform, the practice methods they use, the problems they deal with, and the many chal-lenges they face. It may also sometimes refer to the practice of social work in international agencies or programs" (Hokenstad et al., 1992: 4).

Social work education seeks to provide information, knowledge and skills to people who wish to work in the field of social work. Social work is a helping profession, and as such is a practice profession. The International Code of Ethics for the Professional Social Worker (International Federation of Social Workers.1976) discusses social work as follows:

Social work originates variously from humanitarian, religious and democratic ideals and philosophies and has universal application to meet human needs arising from personal-societal interactions and to develop human potential. Professional Social Workers are dedicated to service for the welfare and self-fulfillment of human beings; to the development and disciplined use of scientific knowledge regarding human and societal behavior; to the development of resources to meet individual, group, national and international needs and aspirations; and to the achievement of social justice.

A social work student is learning about social welfare and social work, while learning about the "how" of working with people (and organizations) toward human betterment. Social work education, like nursing education, like teacher education, is "how" focused, or methods focused. This presents a particular challenge to social work educators, for the imparting of skills about the helping process is no easy matter.

There seems to be a limitless amount of diversity in social work education worldwide. Kendall (1987: 988) has stated that there is "no universal pattern of social work education, and even within countries a variety of models may coexist comfortably." Social work education is so diverse because social work itself is a multifaceted field from country to country. Whereas in some countries like the United States "private practice" social work takes place, in other's social work is looked upon as almost exclusively a "public" or governmentally based field, that is, social workers as agents of the welfare state (Britain, etc.), though, we do see a growth of privatization in Britain (Elliott, 1990) which may change this. Even within one country, social work can occupy so many occupational roles that one is hard-put to figure out what it is that social work does not do, what social work is. In the United States, for example, social workers are working in private practice, in psychotherapy, in public welfare administration, in employee assistance programs in business and industry, in hospitals, schools, child welfare, and many other areas. Social workers are now working in personnel departments in business and industry. The future areas of social work involvement seem at times to reach so far out that it becomes more difficult to answer the question of what is social work. This presents distinct challenges to social work education, for it is difficult indeed to satisfy all educational needs under such a wide occupational umbrella.

Social work education in Third World countries presents a different picture, as it does in other areas of the world. There are similarities as well as differences in social work education world wide. But there are certainly similarities, for Kendall points out (1987: 995) that historically social work education programs, "no matter how they are organized, are informed by humanistic values and encompass knowledge of social ills and social provision, understanding of individuals and society in interaction, and methods of intervention into social and human problems." Mayadas and Lasan (1984: 42,43) assert that social work as a profession has long had a commitment to the larger environment in which clients are located and philosophically committed to disadvantaged populations. There are those who question whether social work is as committed to the needs of the disadvantaged as it should be.

Elliott (1993) has proposed a model for social work that combines social development theory and general systems theory. This kind of perspective would pave the way for large-scale prevention efforts, so badly needed; would place the oppressed and the disadvantaged at the forefront of social work education's concerns; and would do so in a systems context. Let us add to that mixure the comparative and international context and we have at hand a model that will help us considerably.

The orientation of the editors of this volume is developmental, comparative and international, and systems anchored. The developmental perspective is delineated partly as follows (United Nations, 1986: 3):

It is predicated on the maximization of human potential and based on the mobilization of all segments of the population for the resolution of social problems and the attainment of social progress. This new vision of social welfare contrasts sharply with earlier formulations, which focused on enabling certain population groups to overcome what were primarily perceived as individual or group shortcomings.

It should be noted that an "unprecedented interest in questions of social development is evident in the decision to convene a World Summit for Social Development in 1995 (General Assembly resolution 47/92)" (United Nations, 1993: iii). The timely publication of a volume on introducing social development content in the social work curriculum (Healy, 1992) is indicative of a growing concern that social work education be responsive to the need for incorporating this valuable perspective.

The developmental perspective is prevention oriented. Anticipating problems is considered a fundamental social welfare activity. But yet another dimension should be mentioned here, and that is going beyond a problem perspective altogether, attempting to ensure decent conditions for human growth and development in a wide context.

Social work education can be in the driver's seat to assure that there is a wider vision in social work. One of the major goals of this book is to contribute in some small way to enlarging that vision. Countries have been selected for inclusion on the basis of a wide range of criteria: size and importance of the country, adequate representation of various regions in the world, presence of social work education in a given country (or, in the case of Russia, an emerging presence), and availability in respect to authorship and other variables. This last variable of author availability represented a particular challenge, as did the difficulties in communication with authors living in various regions of the world.

Lastly, the editors make no pretense at total comprehensiveness of coverage (if, indeed, this would be possible). Some countries are not included because of editorial commitments we have made in respect of the overall length of the manuscript.

We have attempted to offer a systematic examination of social work education worldwide, as manifested in many different countries, enabling students and scholars of social work education and related fields to draw some parallels, to compare and contrast, and to analyze issues beyond the conventional boundaries of studies on social work education.

REFERENCES

Barker, Robert L. (1991). *Social Work Dictionary*, 2nd ed. Silver Spring, Md: National Association of Social Workers

Elliott, Doreen. (1990) Social welfare in Britain. In Elliott, Doreen, Mayadas, Nazneen S.; & Watts, Thomas D., (Eds.) *The World of Social Welfare: Social Welfare and Services in an International Context*. Springfield, Ill.: Charles C. Thomas, pp. 91-109.

Elliott, Doreen. (1993). Social work and social development: towards an integrative model for social work practice *International Social Work*, *36*(1), 21–36.

Hartman, Ann. (1990). Our global village *Social Work*, *35*(4), 291–292.

Healy, Lynne M. 1(986). The international dimension in social work education: current efforts, future challenges *International Social Work*, *29*(2), 135–147.

Healy, Lynne M. (1992). *Introducing International Development Content in the Social Work Curriculum*. Silver Spring, Md: National Association of Social Workers

Hokenstad, M. C., Khinduka, S. K., & Midgley, James (1992). The world of international social work. In M. C. Hokenstad, S. K. Khinduka, & James Midgley (Eds.). *Profiles in International Social Work*. Washington, D.C.: National Association of Social Workers Press, pp. 1–11.

International Federation of Social Workers. (1976.) *International Code of Ethics for the Professional Social Worker*. Geneva, Switzerland.

Kendall, Katherine A. (1987). International social work education In *Encyclopedia of Social Work*, 18th ed. Silver Spring, Md: National Association of Social Workers, pp. 987–996.

Mayadas, Nazneen S. & Elliott, Doreen. (1990.) Refugees: an introductory case study in international social welfare. In Elliott, Doreen, Mayadas, Nazneen S. & Watts, Thomas D., (Eds.) *The World of Social Welfare: Social Welfare and Services in an International Context*, Springfield, Ill.: Charles C. Thomas, pp. 281-295.

Mayadas, Nazneen & Lasan, Delores B. (1984). Integrating refugees into alien cultures. In Guzzetta, Charles, Katz, Arthur J. & English, Richard A. (Eds.). *Education for Social Work Practice: Selected International Models*. New York, Council on Social Work Education, pp. 39–49.

Mohan, Brij. (1987) International social welfare: comparative systems. In *Encyclopedia of Social Work*, 18th ed. Silver Spring, Md: National Association of Social Workers, pp. 957–969.

Sanders, Daniel S. & Pedersen, Paul. (1984). Introduction. In Sanders, Daniel S. & Pedersen, Paul (Eds.). *Education for International Social Welfare*. Honolulu, University of Hawaii, School of Social Work, pp. xi–xxvi.

United Nations. (1986). *Developmental Social Welfare: A Global Survey of Issues and Priorities Since 1968.* New York: UN Department of International Economic and Social Affairs

United Nations. (1993.) *Report on the World Social Situation 1993.* New York: UN Department of Economic and Social Development

I

NORTH AMERICA AND SOUTH AMERICA

1

UNITED STATES

L. Diane Bernard

INTRODUCTION

Social work education in the United States has a relatively short academic history since it was introduced less than one hundred years ago. On a less formal basis it has been evolving from the time of the earliest colonies. The sick, indigent, orphaned, elderly and destitute have been with us from the start. The initial settlers brought with them from England a set of policies identified as the Elizabethan Poor Laws which basically called for each locality to be responsible for its poor, old and handicapped. These laws were imposed by elected or more usually appointed governmental functionaries who executed them on the basis of their own judgment. The treatment of those in need ranged from cruel to humane depending upon the qualities and capacities of those responsible for administering the law.

Because the population was small and the resources were plentiful in the beginning years, poverty and dependency were viewed as both unusual and temporary. Almshouses and workhouses became the warehouses for all those who either could not or would not be productive. Before long it became apparent that this was neither an effective nor a profitable solution. Voluntary societies emerging primarily from religious groups were developed for the relief of various categories of the poor and unproductive. With very limited public provision, the number and variety of these voluntary organizations became extensive. The religious influence combined with the beginning of the scientific method led to the emergence of a new agency for every social problem.

An attempt to bring some order and organization to this philanthropic impetus led to the development of the Charity Organization Society. The philosophy of this organization was based on giving all people a chance to achieve self-sufficiency. Individuals were classified as either the deserving or the undeserving (those not willing to help themselves) poor onthe basis of the judgments of the workers, who were volunteers. The Charity Organization Society movement coincided with the Settlement movement, which attempted to educate people to their responsibilities as citizens. During this period it was the more economically fortunate who volunteered to "rehabilitate" the poor through the power of personal influence.

As the complexity of economic and social problems expanded, the social agencies developed institutes and training programs for salaried employees who gradually replaced the volunteers or so–called friendly visitors. Initially the apprenticeship method borrowed from the older professions of law and medicine was the system of professional indoctrination. This gave way to a six week summer training program at the New York School of Philanthropy founded by the Charity Organization Society of New York in 1898. This initial effort became a full academic year by 1904 and by 1910 a two year program. The New York School of Philanthropy became the New York School of Social Work and, since 1962, the Columbia University School of Social Work.

HISTORICAL DEVELOPMENT

After the establishment of an academic year in 1904, some fifteen different schools developed educational programs for social work, and by 1919 they came together and established the Association of Training Schools for Professional Social Work. This association was the forerunner of the American Association of Schools of Social Work (AASSW), which was established in 1927 to formulate and maintain educational standards for all schools. By 1932 a minimum curriculum was developed requiring at least one academic year of professional education which included both class and field education. The milestone for formal accreditation was thereby established.

This early period encompassed programs within universities as well as those under the auspices of private welfare agencies. By 1935 AASSW ruled that only those programs established within institutions of higher education accredited by the Association of American Universities could be accredited. By 1939 AASSW instituted the requirement of a two year program leading to the master's degree as a condition of membership.

During the 1930s and the 1940s another group consisting of public institutions of higher education developed a different model. To meet the demand for trained personnel in a variety of programs these institutions combined four years of undergraduate education with one year of graduate training leading to a master's degree. These programs did not meet the minimum standards set by AASSW and organized separately in 1942 as the National Association of Schools of Social Administration (NASSA).

Both AASSW and NASSA established standards for membership, leading to considerable confusion regarding necessary and sufficient preparation for professional social work. In 1946 a National Council on Social Work Education brought both groups together to resolve the conflict created by two sets of standards. The Carnegie Corporation provided a grant to study social work education in 1951. A unification of educational standards and a merger of AASSW and NASSA in the Council on Social Work Education (CSWE) in 1952 resulted. Since then, CSWE has been the primary national organization responsible for social work education. Major functions of CSWE include continuous review and reformulation of educational standards; accreditation of newly established programs; periodic review and evaluation of existing programs; development and distribution of publications related to social work education; initiation of meetings and workshops on various aspects of social work education; consultation to schools planning to develop social work programs; maintenance of working relationships with national and regional accrediting organizations; organization of annual program meetings for CSWE members, members of the National Association of Social Workers (NASW) and other professional affiliates, and the general public; participation in programs of international exchange and cooperation; and provision of information about social work education for universities, faculty, students, agencies and the general public. In addition, CSWE maintains a governmental watch and provides members with current information regarding significant legislation impacting human service programs with emphasis on available training, teaching, and research funding for social work education.

The Commission on Accreditation of CSWE is the sole accrediting body for social work education in the United States. Its authority to accredit is recognized by the U.S. Office of Education and the Council on Postsecondary Accreditation (COPA). The latter is the organization to which all postsecondary educational organizations belong. Prior to 1970 the commission was the exclusive accrediting agent for both the United States and Canada. Since then the Canadian Association of Schools of Social Work has developed an independent system. The two organizations maintain a cooperative arrangement.

The accreditation process includes a variety of standards, policies and criteria based on policies approved by the CSWE Board of Directors. Responsibility for enforcement is carried by the Commission on Accreditation, which is a semiautonomous body appointed by the president of the board. The *Manual of Accrediting Standards* incorporates criteria dealing with the accredited status of the sponsoring educational institution; the educational resources of the institution; the position of the social work program within the institution; personnel policies; financial adequacy; qualifications of the executive officer; recruitment, size, qualifications, and responsibilities of faculty; selective admissions of students; faculty and student governance; curriculum development and evaluation; correlation between stated program objectives and curriculum; advising and grading policies; and physical facilities, including the library. While specific standards appropriate for both the BSW and MSW are identified, each of the areas mentioned is included in the accreditation process for both levels.

At this writing, there are presently 368 accredited BSW programs with 32 more in the candidacy process, and 111 accredited MSW programs with 8 in candidacy.

LEVELS OF SOCIAL WORK EDUCATION

By the regulations of COPA, the national organization responsible for granting accrediting status to all postsecondary education in the United States, only those programs providing the entry level to a profession can be accredited. Since social work education provides for professional entry at both the BSW and MSW levels, the Council on Social Work Education petitioned and was granted the opportunity to accredit at both levels.

However, social work education encompasses four levels of degree programs, which include the associate and doctoral degrees as well as continuing education that may be provided for those holding any or all of the degree credentials. The associate level is provided by community or junior colleges to prepare students for community and social service technician or preprofessional tasks. The doctorate is provided in graduate schools of social work to prepare students for leadership roles in administration and policy, more advanced and specialized practice, research, and teaching.

While these various levels exist there is no orderly progression between them. As each level has developed it has affected all the other levels and changed the identification of practice tasks considered appropriate for each educational attainment. The general objectives of social work education, which encompass imbuing the student with the value system of the profession, providing basic knowledge, and developing skills and competence to perform in social work roles, have remained constant.

After World War II the impact of social problems increased the demand for social work personnel. A number of baccalaureate and associate degree programs were developed to meet human power demands. During the 1960s many additional social forces converged to reinforce this trend. Student interest in social reform and academic relevancy stimulated expansion of educational opportunities in the human and applied social services. Increased sensitivity to client rights and greater recognition of the needs and contributions of ethnic minorities began to include the involvement of indigenous and paraprofessional workers. Government support for antipoverty programs along with increased interest in career related training gave further impetus to expanding the levels of social work education.

The Council on Social Work Education prepared a guide in 1962 to suggest content and learning experiences appropriate for undergraduate education being provided by undergraduate departments in accredited colleges and universities. This followed the CSWE sponsorship and publication in 1959 of a thirteen volume study coordinated by Professor Werner W. Boehm which recommended the distribution of social work education content over an undergraduate-graduate continuum. Despite this effort, prior to the 1970s the MSW degree provided by graduate schools of social work was the only professional accredited degree in social work education. By 1970 CSWE was granting approval status to programs fulfilling the suggested content and learning requirements prior to gaining permission from COPA to accredit at more than one professional entry level. The need for beginning level practitioners had been recognized by many social welfare agencies and institutions, and in 1970, NASW admitted to full professional membership those practicing in social welfare agencies who held baccalaureate degrees from approved CSWE programs. This growing recognition of the baccalaureate as the first professional degree led to intensified concerns for quality control and professional accountability. Authority was granted by the U.S. Office of Education and COPA after the upgrading of the existing approval status into formal accrediting standards in 1974. Even before the official accreditation of BSW programs, the Commission on Accreditation adopted a new standard in 1971 permitting advanced standing up to one year for students holding the BSW from CSWE approved programs. A special CSWE Committee to Study the Length of Graduate Social Work Education, as well as a joint CSWE-NASW Committee on Manpower Issues, recommended this action. A major consideration supporting this move was the need to reduce redundancies in the educational process and recognize the linkage between levels.

Undergraduate programs follow a variety of structural patterns. Some are located within the same administrative structure as a graduate school of social work; many are located within undergraduate colleges with independent department status; others are part of an existing department that provides for a separate major or concentration. All of these patterns are currently acceptable as long as the social work program is specifically identified and described in the college catalogue and the transcript indicates that the student has successfully completed the program preparing for beginning social work practice.

Prior to 1950 doctoral education in social work was only available in two programs, namely, Bryn Mawr College and the University of Chicago. Education beyond the MSW occurred primarily in third year programs focused on advanced practice in a particular method or problem area. As the professional schools gained academic recognition the demand for those who could contribute to theory development and knowledge building increased, as did the demand for more faculty for the expanding levels of social work education.

Two types of doctoral programs are offered, the PhD and the DSW. The different titles reflect institutional preference rather than a real difference between these degrees. Almost all doctoral programs prepare for research and teaching, and many provide for social planning, policy analysis and administration. Advanced direct practice is available in a few programs but it is not the current norm for doctoral level education in social work.

At this writing there are fifty doctoral programs in social work. There is no separate accreditation procedure for these programs since all, with the exception of one, at Brandeis University, are affiliated with an accredited MSW. The U.S. Office of Education and COPA permit accreditation solely at the entry level of a profession. Special permission was granted to social work since one gains full professional membership upon the successful completion of the BSW or MSW from an accredited program. Since the doctoral degree is essentially an academic rather than a practice degree it does not provide for professional entry. Doctoral education is considered part of the overall institutional accreditation process by the regional accrediting organizations. When the MSW program is reviewed by CSWE the site team is required to ensure that resources provided for the doctoral program do not detract from or infringe upon the integrity of the master's program. An independent, nonaccrediting organization, the Group for the Advancement of Doctoral Education (GADE), has maintained relationships with schools offering the doctorate and has held regular national meetings for the exchange of curriculum and trends occurring at this level of social work education. They also list all programs in a directory which can be obtained from CSWE.

RELATION TO PRACTICE

Since the primary purpose of professional education is preparation for practice, there is an essential connection between practice and education in social work. A considerable proportion of the curriculum in the BSW and MSW programs occurs in the required field instruction component, which takes place in agency settings. The mutual dependency and accountability of these two systems have created an arena for both cooperation and tension. Changing patterns of financial support over the years have at times occasioned disparate goals and expectations. Preparation for future practice, apart from the difficulty of projecting the future, does not always serve the existing needs and the reality of present practice. Despite disagreements and frustrations, the overriding commitment to students and the profession has established continuous dialogue and mutual accommodation.

While CSWE and NASW are separate, autonomous organizations, they work together nationally through standing and ad hoc committee structures, and NASW is represented on the CSWE Commission on Accreditation. Modifications and changes in the educational system affect practice, and the standard setting and licensing functions of NASW seriously impact social work education. As more states move toward licensure, it is anticipated that even closer collaboration between CSWE and NASW will develop.

INTERNATIONAL SOCIAL WORK EDUCATION

Biennial meetings of the International Association of Schools of Social Work, held just before the International Conference on Social Welfare at different locations around the world, provide a forum for the exchange of ideas and issues related to social work education. Despite the unique styles and solutions emerging from the cultural differences, educational problems provide a focus for common concerns. Mutual understanding and stimulation promoted by interaction can lead to the development of creative solutions.

U.S. social work educators have participated abroad in social welfare programs and social work schools as Fulbright scholars, State Department specialists, and United Nations consultants and through CSWE arrangements. Comparable programs sponsored by other countries have introduced foreign expertise and interest into U.S. programs.

Student exchange programs and U.S. university based centers in foreign countries have added to knowledge and enriched the learning opportunities for students. Consortia arrangements between U.S. schools and selected foreign institutions have provided an additional means for exchanging ideas, students, faculty, and teaching materials.

The evaluation of foreign academic credentials to determine their equivalency to accredited U.S. programs is provided by the Foreign Equivalency Determination Service of the Council on Social Work Education. Such equivalency determinations are essential to establish qualifications for employment, school admissions, NASW membership, and state licensing or certification eligibility.

PROCESS OF RENEWAL AND REVISION

Prior to the establishment of CSWE in 1952 a number of national studies regarding social work education were undertaken at approximately ten year intervals. Four of these early studies are worthy of note. In 1921, Dr. James H. Tufts studied social work education and wrote *Education and Training for Social Work*. The study coincided with the move from the system of vocational training within voluntary agencies to colleges and universities following World War I. Tufts believed that social work should not only attempt to aid individuals in need of assistance, but examine the fabric of society and initiate social reforms. Tufts identified the differences between education and training and believed both were of importance. He strenuously favored quality as opposed to quantity and argued for raising standards for those entering the field. Responses to this study led to the recommendation that schools of social work be considered professional schools meeting certain requirements of autonomy within the institution of higher education. A further recommendation was that all professional education be at the graduate level. In 1931, James Edward Hagerty wrote *The Training of Social Workers*. This study reflected developments in the West and Midwest, where social work had begun to pass from private to public support and where state universities had begun to establish social work educational programs. Hagerty recommended theoretical training at the undergraduate level followed by a year of graduate work leading to a master's degree. This represented a revolt against the privately funded colleges and universities in the East. The trend toward public sponsorship identified by Hagerty became a reality after the passage of the Social Security Act in 1935. This produced a tremendous need for large numbers of social workers to implement the programs of public assistance, child welfare, old age insurance, unemployment insurance, and employment services. The level of content and training for such personnel and the role of social work education in meeting these needs became vitally significant. This led to the third study in 1942 sponsored by the AASSW, *Education for the Public Social Services: A Report of the Study Committee*. The impetus for such a study arose because the 1939 amendments to the Social Security Act had introduced the principle of merit selection of personnel, making it essential to develop standards of education for such personnel. The study recommended joint planning by schools and public services to meet the needs of the public field and to familiarize faculties with the significance of the expansion of public social and health services. Recognition was also given to the need to train students in the management and administration of public services. Efforts were made to add public welfare administration courses, thereby broadening the curriculum of schools of social work. After World War II there was further expansion of the public social services and by 1946, the bulk of social services in the United States originated in the public sector. While professional social work education in the eastern part of the United States was being provided through two year graduate degrees at private universities, considerable social welfare content was being provided at the undergraduate level in state universities, primarily in the midwestern and western regions of the country. This led to the fourth major study, undertaken in 1951 by Ernest B. Hollis and Alice L. Taylor, *Social Work Education in the United States*. The purpose of the study was to establish some specifics regarding the nature, scope, status and direction of social work education. Among the recommendations were the establishment of a national organization for education and accreditation and the development of a four year generic program in social work education. The first two of these years were to take place at the undergraduate level to provide general education and social work content offering preparation for beginning social work practice and for graduate study. The next two years were to be taken at the graduate level. The first of these years was to focus on the principles, policies, processes, and concepts of social work, with the second year devoted to preparation for advanced practice in several specialized areas. While the recommendations for social work education were not implemented for some time, at the national level the recommended organizational changes did occur. The Council on Social Work Education as the standard setting and accrediting body was established in 1952, and several membership organizations of social work practitioners merged in 1955 to become the National Association of Social Workers.

Since 1952 studies regarding social work education have been under the purview of CSWE. A comprehensive examination of the social work curriculum was undertaken in 1955 under the direction and coordination of Professor Werner W. Boehm, *Objectives for the Social Work Curriculum of the Future.* The study produced some thirteen volumes in areas encompassing human growth and behavior; social welfare policy and services; social casework; social group work; undergraduate curriculum; community organization; administration; research; values and ethics; and education related to specific fields of practice. Aside from attempting to delineate the nature of social work as a profession and identifying educational objectives, the study explicated the need for clear articulation between the undergraduate and graduate levels based on the principles of continuity, sequence, and integration. After publication of the study in 1959, CSWE formulated a revised curriculum policy; it has taken more than a decade to implement all the recommendations.

Each decade has seen revised curriculum policy statements to reflect changes in the profession as well as society. Early on, the required curriculum for accreditation was based on the inclusion of eight subject areas. These components, known as the basic eight, were social casework, social group work, community organization, social administration, public welfare, social research, medical information and psychiatric information. These theoretical subjects were balanced by required time in field placement under the supervision of a qualified professional social worker. During the late 1950s, many programs began combining the traditional methods courses in generic skills courses with emphases on developing sound practice skills not confined by old boundaries. In addition, classroom content began to move away from settings, or agency identification toward a broader problem orientation as the focus of intervention. The new policy statement included social work methods, human behavior and the social environment, social welfare history and policy, and research along with field instruction. During the 1960s more social science concepts were incorporated and there was increased demand for practitioners with management and planning skills. Curriculum designs developed along the lines of direct service (micro), supervision, consultation and staff development (mezzo), and administration, planning, analysis and evaluation (macro). In addition, there was increased awareness regarding regional differences, the role of ethnic minorities and the need for schools to identify their own objectives and philosophy. Programs became less standardized in an effort to permit greater sensitiv-

ity to changing social conditions and allow for more experimentation and innovation in the ever changing role of the professional social worker. During the
1970s new standards required special efforts to ensure racial and cultural diversity in the student body, faculty, staff, and curriculum content. A new standard reflected the increased awareness of the changing role of women, and all
aspects of the program have been mandated to eliminate mechanisms and
stereotypes that negatively affect any particular group. During the 1980s the
emphasis was on continued clarification of the undergraduate-graduate continuum and inclusion of more policy initiatives in response to societal pressure for
greater professional accountability. A revised curriculum policy statement came
out in 1994 reinforcing the undergraduate-graduate continuum, and emphazing
that students from acccredited social work bacculereate programs should not be
required to take foundation courses in master's programs.

The *Manual of Accrediting Standards* for both BSW and MSW programs
includes the most recently accepted curriculum policy statement. As mentioned
previously, accreditation is officially a function assigned to the Council on Social Work Education by the national Council on Postsecondary Education and
by the accreditation and institutional eligibility auspices of the U.S. Department
of Education. Schools and programs meeting minimum standards are accredited, providing quality assurance and consumer protection for students. Accreditation also affords eligibility for publicly funded grants and only students in
accredited schools or programs can receive financial assistance from these
grants. Acceptance into the National Association of Social Workers requires a
degree from an accredited BSW or MSW program which also determines eligibility for taking state examinations in states with licensing and certification
laws. Accreditation is widely accepted in the profession, and, although it poses
certain limitations in adhering to a national curriculum policy, it assures
maintenance of professional standards. The constant monitoring of schools and
programs, reviewed on a ten year cycle, contributes to the strengthening of
many programs and the elimination of inadequate ones.

FUTURE DIRECTIONS

To the extent that one can predict or estimate changing social, political and
economic circumstances or trends, it is possible to determine the potential impact on social work education, whose purpose is to provide human power for the
delivery of social services. With this in mind, it is likely that there will be
increased emphasis on the employment of women and ethnic minorities as well
as the furthering of curriculum content in this and other areas which extend
awareness of cultural diversity. As economic growth and expansion contract
along with career obsolescence, increasing numbers of older people may be en-

tering the profession and they, along with women and ethnic minorities, may require more part time and off campus programs.

New service settings are always developing, requiring practitioners with specific knowledge. The aging of our population will require greater emphasis and training in gerontology and health maintenance. Mounting problems associated with substance abuse and the acquired immunodeficiency syndrome (AIDS) epidemic require many more workers with specialized knowledge. Other expanding areas in birth technology, genetics, health, industry and the justice system further the trend toward increased specialization. In addition, ecological concerns will undoubtedly generate new areas focused on our relationship to other planetary inhabitants. As the service delivery system diversifies, requiring more competent and varied practitioners, there will be a recognition that no time limited curriculum will be able to encompass the range of specialization demanded. This in turn should lead to the expansion of more staff development and continuing education opportunities with more certification programs and standards.

The issue of specialist versus generalist orientation will require revisiting. While it is clear that new areas are constantly emerging which require specialized knowledge and commitment, there is a concurrent need for more independent, autonomous practitioners with a broad service perspective. The present trend of moving from the generalist orientation (undergraduate and first year graduate education) toward specialization (second year graduate) may give way to more experimentation and different patterns. For those employed in vastly underserviced areas or those charged with primary planning, evaluating and administrating tasks, a more extended generalized emphasis may be required at advanced levels. The increased complexity of the service delivery system may demand ever more flexibility and variety of the social work educational system.

CURRENT ISSUES AND DILEMMAS

The BSW-MSW Continuum

As the background history indicates, the development and legitimating of the BSW as the first professional degree were originally envisioned as a means of providing trained personnel for the social service delivery system, primarily the public social services. The 1960s was a time of considerable social ferment with concern focused on improving social conditions nationally. The government was spending money on the human services both directly and in terms of training funds. Students were demanding more relevant education and moving from more traditional disciplines into the social services.

By the time the profession was able to gear up and develop national standards for the BSW and gain approval of COPA to accredit at more than one entry level for the profession, the mood of the country had changed. The BSW degree, which had achieved approval status by 1972 and accredited status by 1974, was turning out graduates by the mid-1970s. The government was no longer focused on the social services, funding had dried up, professional training for the public social services was no longer considered essential, and positions were being declassified. As the newly emerging BSW graduates quickly learned, there was no market for their employment. Concurrently, the national emphasis on education was focused on future employability while the educational system was being taken to task about the redundancy of courses and duplication. Social work responded to these concerns with the development of the continuum. BSW graduates from CSWE accredited programs could be granted advanced standing in pursuit of the MSW since the BSW is considered the equivalent of the first generalist year of the master's degree. Although there are different patterns and time frames and all accredited graduate programs are required to provide the standard two year MSW degree, the majority of schools are permitting BSW graduates to accelerate and obtain the MSW in less than two years.

Critics have raised serious objections to the continuum on the basis of age, lack of life experiences, reduction of liberal arts education, and the marketplace mentality erosion of the value of higher education. The heavy emphasis on BSW preparation has not encouraged further development of the MSW except for the recognition of the second year as the time for specialization.

The final chapter in resolving this dilemma has yet to be written. There are those who anticipate the demise of the MSW altogether, with some movement toward a three year post-BSW degree leading to a practice doctorate in the future. The rationale for this is threefold: emerging content in the areas of greater emphasis on diverse populations, genetics, acquired immunodeficiency syndrome (AIDS), medical ethics, ecology, and our rapidly increasing aged population, and so on, can hardly be contained in one year of specialized education; the MSW is no longer considered the terminal degree in social work; doctoral level education in social work is expanding exponentially.

Given the continued growth of MSW programs it is very unlikely that the degree will be phased out despite being overtaken by the even greater expansion of BSW and doctoral programs in recent years. The BSW is not clearly recognized as the degree preparing for beginning professional practice, and the doctoral degree is identified as preparing for teaching, research and/or leadership in administrative and social policy arenas. The MSW has lost educational turf to both these burgeoning programs and status with respect to no longer being considered the terminal professional degree. Although it is viewed as the program preparing for advanced practice through specialization, it has become obvious that the accreditation requirement of a foundation year for those entering without the BSW has reduced such emphasis to one year. As a result, to some extent the MSW is suffering a credibility crisis along with some erosion of degree clarity. While some social work educators continue to rail against the viability of baccalaureate social work education it is now a well established reality.

One future possibility would be to affirm the MSW clearly as the degree providing for specialized advanced practice, requiring the full two years to achieve such purpose. In such an eventuality the BSW would become a requirement for entry into the MSW or applicants would have to acquire the equivalent before become eligible, in the same way that pre-medical courses are a requirement for medical school.

Another alternative, to extend the MSW program to a third year, raises serious economic and other constraints. A variation on this possibility is the reintroduction of third year certificate programs for advanced practice. The potential interest in either of these arrangements has been limited by the increased priority and prevalence of doctoral education.

One other notion regarding the MSW has gained some advocates. Since studies have indicated that those with graduate degrees move quickly out of direct service to positions of middle management or administration (unless they pursue private practice), the second graduate year should build on the first generalist direct practice emphasis by providing a generalist macro orientation. This arrangement would then require that specialization be obtained through certification or third year programs.

Other suggestions and patterns will no doubt emerge as the dialogue about the continuum continues, but one thing is clear: the timing for professional education in social work will be extended either through the established degree route or through some formal continuing education procedure.

Generalist/Specialist and Micro/Macro Issues

These issues are closely related to those identified in the previous discussion but raise some additional concerns. The BSW-MSW continuum has structured a mind–set of beginning professional education as generalist and graduate education as specialized. While it is clear that the social service system is desperately in need of highly trained and knowledgeable practitioner specialists in myriad areas, there are extensive geographical areas with limited facilities requiring practitioners with a wide range of knowledge and skills. This has given rise to a new specialization, primarily in rural and underserved areas, called advanced generalist as a focus for the second year of graduate education. Concern is being expressed about whether one year or eighteen months of graduate education following the BSW degree can meet the need for either of these types of specialization.

The micro-macro issue is closely related but not precisely the same. As the need has grown for greater clinical expertise in a wide range of specializations, there is increasingly less emphasis on social reform and major system change in the whole service delivery enterprise. The pressure on social work education to meet the demand for specialized practitioners has moved it ever further from issues addressing the need to change the social system. Indirectly, it has led more and more trained practitioners away from public and broader concerns into private and narrower fields. Where demand is greater, so is financial compensation, adding to the imbalance currently observable of increasing numbers of graduate social workers in the private sector, leaving the public arena almost entirely to the BSW graduates. The problem is compounded by the recognition that BSW education by design is focused on beginning generalist direct practice. In short, there is currently little emphasis at either the BSW or MSW level of social work education on preparation for the public sector or on the impact on the present social system.

Extension/Off-Campus/Satellite Programs

The demand for more social workers, the expansion of educational opportunities, and the strained economy have given rise to the provision of programs away from the main campus facility. Arguments in favor of this trend range from the self-serving opportunity for programs to maintain enrollments through such outreach possibilities, to provision of education to those who cannot leave families and employment for prolonged periods. The positives in this trend are the provision of education to outlying and rural areas desperately in need of upgrading services, reaching the nontraditional, older, committed workers who are place bound and ensuring the growth of professionally educated service providers. The negatives include a more limited educational experience, poorer facilities with respect to the potential quality of adjunct faculty, limited libraries and reduced exposure to diversity and peer learning opportunities. The monitoring of these off–campus arrangements has made for increased accreditation problems and has raised serious concern regarding the maintenance of standards.

Academe-Practice Impasse

Social work is, and has been, a practice profession. The basis for social work education has been to train people to work in the social service delivery system. Initially, those employed to teach were primarily individuals with extensive experience or an outstanding background in the provision of social services as practitioners. As social work education has moved into the academy, it has come to serve the needs of a host agency with its own system of expectations and rewards. In order to survive in academe, teachers no longer receive recognition on the basis of their practice knowledge or expertise. To remain within the academic environment, one must meet academic standards which go far beyond the capacity to teach practice skills. Faculties are expected to hold doctorate degrees; add to knowledge through research; benefit the program through the acquisition of grants; and most of all publish books or scholarly articles with some regularity. As more faculty are recruited and retained on the basis of these academic credentials, many offering extensive practice backgrounds are either overlooked in the hiring process or lost because they are unable or unwilling to meet such expectations. Many new doctorates are employed on faculties showing promise of meeting academic standards with little or no practice experience. There are no currently enforced standards requiring those entering doctoral programs to have even minimal practice backgrounds and it is possible to be admitted into some social work doctoral programs without prior social work education at either the BSW or MSW level. In other words, the DSW or PhD can in some instances be an entry level to the profession, circumventing the practice expectation. Since COPA only provides for two entry points, the doctoral level does not undergo the accreditation scrutiny of meeting the standards expected of the BSW and MSW degree programs. With the expansion of more and more BSW and MSW programs under academic auspices, the demand for those holding doctoral degrees is burgeoning at all levels. This has raised serious concern about the capacity of social work education to provide adequately for the practice component of the profession. The only safeguard is the requirement by CSWE that the methods courses be taught by faculty holding an MSW degree in addition to any others. For those entering a doctoral program almost immediately upon obtaining an MSW this still does not guarantee practice experience beyond the requisite field practicum.

There are many other problems facing social work education, but these are among the most pressing issues currently being debated in the United States at the close of the twentieth century.

REFERENCES

Annual Reports to the Board of Directors from Commissions and Committees of the Council on Social Work Education. (1991). Alexandria, Va.: Council on Social Work Education.

Baer, Betty L. & Frederico, Ronald L. (Eds.). (1971). *Educating the Baccalaureate Social Worker*, Vols 1 and 2. Cambridge, Mass.: Ballenger.

Bernard, L. Diane. (1971). Education for social work. *Encyclopedia of Social Work.* New York: National Association of Social Workers.

Bernard, L. Diane. (1977). Professional Associations: Council on Social Work Education. In *Encyclopedia of Social Work*: Washington, D.C.: National Association of Social Workers.

Bernard, L. Diane. (1987). Social work in academe - for better or worse. Invitational presentation, annual program meeting, Council on Social Work Education, St. Louis.

Boehm, Werner M. (1959). Objectives of the social work curriculum of the future. In *Social Work Curriculum Study*, Vol. 1. New York: Council on Social Work Education.

Boehm, Werner M. (1971). Education for social work: studies. In *Encyclopedia of Social Workers*. New York: National Association of Social Workers *Colleges and Universities with Accredited Social Work Degree Programs*. Council on Social Work Education: (1991). Alexandria, Va.

Hollis, Ernest V. & Taylor, Alice L. (1951). *Social Work Education in the United States*. New York: Columbia University Press.

Rubin, Allen. (1986). Current statistical trends in social work education: issues and implications. In *Social Work Education Monograph Series*. Austin: School of Social Work, The University of Texas at Austin.

Sheafor, Bradford & Shank, Barbara W. (1986). Undergraduate social work education: a survivor in a changing profession. In *Social Work Education Monograph Series*. Austin: School of Social Work, The University of Texas at Austin.

2

CANADA

Estelle Hopmeyer, M. Dennis Kimberly and Frank R. Hawkins

INTRODUCTION

Social work education and social welfare in Canada may be better understood if some dimensions related to the social context of the nation are appreciated. While Canada is the second largest country in the world in terms of land mass, it ranks thirty first in population size. The population estimate for 1989 was 26,218,500 (Statistics Canada, 1991). The 1986 Census estimated that 61 percent of the population identify English as their first language, while 24 percent select French. Another 11 percent identify a language other than English or French. Canada has a typically British system of government, with a bicameral system: an elected parliament and an appointed senate.

Canada has a long history of publicly supported health, personal, and social service programs; universal Medicare, established in 1968, is one such example. Most programs are jointly funded by federal and provincial governments. Of current significance is the changing demographic profile, especially with respect to a rapidly increasing aged population, one of the highest in the Western world. In 1988, according to federal government data (Statistics Canada, 1991), 13.1 percent of individuals in Canada lived below the "low income cutoff," which is a euphemism for poverty. Elderly and single-parent families are overrepresented among the poor. While the level of employment is high, the last two decades have seen an increase in both the unemployment level and job insecurity. A recent phenomenon has been increased reporting of incidents of family violence and child abuse, which has given rise to legislative and program initiatives across the country.

Investment in education is one of Canada's priorities, as evidenced by the fact that expenditures represent 7 percent of the gross domestic product (Statistics Canada, 1991). Until the end of the 1960s there was continuous and significant growth in education services, including universities and community colleges. University degrees are held by 9.6 percent of the population (Statistics Canada, 1991); this is double the 1971 figure. However, under the domination of the conservative governments of the past decade, there has been a significantly reduced commitment both to higher education and to related research and development, even in the face of increased demands for university education, including social work education. The level of support has been reduced to the point where university class sizes have increased dramatically. Many qualified students are not able to gain entry to the programs of their choice-especially professional programs such as social work.

In Canada, there is no uniform system for education at any level since the responsibility for education is vested in each of the ten provinces. However, with respect to higher education, the provinces are dependent on the federal government for financial support. Additionally, the Canadian Charter of Rights and Freedoms guarantees equal status to French and English, and also to minority language education where numbers warrant. With reference to professional education for social work, there are two overlapping and significant traditions: anglophone and francophone.

HISTORICAL CONTEXT OF SOCIAL WORK EDUCATION: THE ENGLISH AND FRENCH TRADITIONS

Before the establishment of Canada as a nation in 1867, social care in English Canada evidenced two major thrusts, an Elizabethan Poor Law–type orientation in Maritime Canada and in Upper Canada (now the province of Ontario), a relief system which saw responsibility resting with individuals, families, and private charities. The movement toward public intervention in the interest of social justice and social well-being did not gain momentum until the late 1800s and early 1900s. Of special concern were child protection, public education, and public health-within a philosophy of a "social minimum" and a beginning concept of social justice. The beginning of the professionalization of social work services and education in the early 1900s was associated with a move in the country toward accepting more government intervention in the lives of individuals and communities (Millar, 1990). Professionalization of social work and social services was further supported by a national policy of equalization in the quality of services, in part related to legislation establishing programs to support veterans returning after the First World War. During the 1920s Canada's longest-serving prime minister, the late Honorable William Lyon Mackenzie King (Prime Minister 1921–1930; 1935–1948), was a social caseworker at Hull House in Chicago, serving under the pioneer social worker Jane Adams (Rowe, 1991). He was apparently also influenced by the British social development tradition (Ramsey, 1984). These influences may account for the progress of social legislation during King's tenure as Prime Minister. Thus, by the 1940s Canada had adopted significant income security programs, including minimum wage legislation, old age security, family allowances, and unemployment insurance. By the 1960s the most important pieces of social legislation created up to that time were a universal medical care program and a comprehensive and integrated social assistance program known as the Canada Assistance Plan (1966).

The 1970s and 1980s saw some "tinkering" with existing social benefits and programs, but there was no notable progress in social legislation during this period. As Canada enters the final decade of this century, all evidence indicates that the federal government and some provincial governments are systematically eroding health care, social care, and correctional services. The federal government's actions are clearly directed toward the devolution of the burden of responsibility to the provinces; some provinces, in turn, are attempting to devolve responsibility to the municipalities. The dominant theme is rational economic, with the principal slogan being "more with less." Within this context, the profession of social work is confronted with an obvious ambivalence. On the one hand, government is apparently interested in the professionalization of social services, as expressed in their concern for quality of services. On the other hand, their obvious resistance to professionalization is reflected in a frequent willingness to employ untrained individuals in positions that clearly require professionally qualified social workers. In some instances this is intended to promote a philosophy of privatization, while in other cases it is clearly using social work positions to support political patronage (Kimberley & Rowe, 1991).

The preparation of personnel for social service positions in Canada reflects a range of educational opportunities from in-service "on the job" training to community college and university education. These levels of education are presented in Figure 2-1 (Lacompte, 1981: 309).

Figure 2-1
Levels of Education

Education Programs		Education Levels
University programs	→	PhD or DSW
		Advanced Diploma
		MSW
		Advanced Diploma
		BSW
Community college programs	→	Diploma or certificate
In-training programs	→	No formal degree

In Canada, the development of social work education at the university level and the development of the profession are inextricably linked. The first professional courses of social work in Canada were offered at the University of

Toronto in 1914; the first francophone program in Canada was established in Québec at the Université de Montréal in 1942. The Canadian Association of Social Workers was established in 1926.

Developments in social work and social work education received considerable support from the Government of Canada and the provincial governments, as well as from a number of prominent Canadians (including two prime ministers, St. Laurent and Mackenzie King. The models for education that developed drew heavily upon the British and American traditions of social work. It is noteworthy of the board and that as early as 1897 Mary Richmond gave a presentation on social work at the University of Toronto. Included in the active supporters of Canada's first program in social work at this university were British social workers. Canadian social work curricula reflect a dual focus which draws upon both the British model (social administration) and the U.S. model (practice and methods). These ties to Britain and the United States are further reflected in the early use of curriculum materials from these countries. As well, Canadian programs (including some francophone programs) at first applied for accredited status to the United States's Council on Social Work Education.

The Province of Québec exemplifies French Canadian developments in social care and social programs. The best examples are seen in health, education, and social services, which developed from a French Catholic tradition. In this tradition the responsibility for service and charity rested with the church and various institutions it chose to create (Millar, 1990). Francophone services within Québec were organized on the basis of language and religion. English services in Québec were modeled on those in English Canada and evolved quickly into social work services associated with the professionalization of practice and developments in social work education. The professionalization of francophone services and social work education came later, associated with the needs of French Catholic charities which supported the first francophone schools of social work. Initially, French-speaking social work faculty members were educated in English Canadian programs (primarily at the Montréal School of Social Work, which became McGill University, and at the University of Toronto) and in English-speaking Catholic programs based in the United States (Groulx, 1990). It took three decades for literature in French to evolve to the point where it could provide an alternative to English North American theories, concepts, and practice. Unlike England, France was not able to provide social work education literature useful to Québec.

The first francophone program was developed at the Université de Montréal in 1942. This was the last evolutionary stage derived from two private programs, one located at L'Institut des Söeurs de Nôtre Dame du Bon Conseil (1939) and the other at L'École Catholique de Service Social (1940). The Université de Laval (in Québec City) began their francophone program in 1943. They saw their mandate as providing professionally trained workers (largely women) for Catholic social services. The first programs offered were diploma programs. They quickly adopted the American two year master's program model which offered courses in methods, policy, and research–adapted, of course, to the Québecois milieu. By the midsixties there were three additional francophone Schools of Social Work in Québec, and one in the province of New Brunswick (to serve French-speaking Acadians). Canada's only bilingual program was established in northern Ontario at Laurentian University. A new French MSW program has recently been approved at the University of Ottawa. Most francophone programs adopted the Canadian model for social work education where the first degree (BSW) is followed by a graduate one year degree program (MSW). In 1985 the Université de Laval was granted permission by the Government of Quebec to offer a doctoral (PhD) program in social work–the first in the French-speaking world (Paré, 1988). Given that many doctoral-level degrees held by professors of social work in francophone schools were in cognate disciplines, this doctoral program in social work is an extremely important development. The Laval program also publishes Service Social, a francophone periodical devoted to practice and education.

There is a special structural and financial arrangement between the Québec Schools of Social Work and the Canadian Association of Schools of Social Work (CASSW). The Québec association was established in the late seventies to enable these schools to deal collectively with the provincial government on matters of educational policy and programming. It also provided a forum whereby the francophone schools could ensure that the CASSW was sensitive to their needs–particularly with respect to educational policy and accreditation matters. In an effort to address these needs, the CASSW Board of Accreditation is co-chaired by a francophone and an anglophone and pays particular attention to the bilingual ability of potential members other standing committees of the CASSW. To formalize this thrust, a formal accord between the CASSW and the Québec schools was approved in 1985 and is still in effect.

THE PROFESSION IN CANADA

The Canadian Association of Social Workers (CASW) was established in 1926. The CASW has a federated structure which includes ten provincial and one territorial association. Cooperation and collaboration among the CASW, various provincial associations, and the schools of social work in Canada occurs largely at the provincial level. However, consultation at the national level does take place, particularly between the CASW and the CASSW on matters pertaining to national policy. An example is in establishing standards for BSW programs. Additional cooperative efforts include a joint study and review of continuing education for the profession, and the joint hosting of the IFSW, IASSW and ICSW international conferences in Montréal in 1984.

Of particular significance to the professionalization of social work in Canada was the role played by social work leaders in the 1940s and 1950s in convincing the federal government of the need for professional social workers in social services. They were also successful in making the case for professional education that was accessible in all regions of the country, complemented by a policy of equalization of services, to ensure that professional social work education standards were established for the nation. These directions were further supported when the Canadian Association for Education in the Social Services (the precursor of the Canadian Association of Schools of Social Work) promoted the establishment of a Welfare Grants Division within the National Department of Health and Welfare (1962). This division gave support to the establishment of the Canadian Association of Schools of Social Work/Association Canadienne des Écoles de Service Social (CASSW/ACESS). As the number of educational programs in Canada increased in the 1960s, the CASSW took over the program accreditation function, which until 1970 had been assumed by the Council on Social Work Education in the U.S.

In the interests of quality control, equalization, and public protection, educational standards governing the accreditation of BSW and MSW programs were established in 1972. Of significance was the commitment given to policies that accommodate official bilingualism (English and French), acknowledge regional differences, and promote the importance of regional relevance in the development of social work education programs. Accreditation by the twelve member board of the CASSW is normally for a period of up to seven years. While BSW and MSW programs are candidates for accreditation status, doctoral programs are not currently accredited.

Schools of social work have both a professional and an academic identity. The professional identity is grounded in standards for practice which promote quality control and public protection. The academic identity is tied to membership in the university community, which includes affiliation with the Learned Societies through membership in the CASSW. The Learned Societies is a coalition of most academic bodies in Canada. Under its auspices the CASSW conducts an annual business meeting and scholarly conference for social work educators and students. The structure of the CASSW is such that it promotes opportunities for interdisciplinary exchange among academics. The annual Learned Societies meetings provide an important opportunity for exchange and debate in the advancement of knowledge, scholarship, and research for social work education, policies, and practices.

Another avenue for scholarship which is promoted by the CASSW is their publication of the journal *The Canadian Social Work Review/Revue Canadienne de Service Social*. While this publication is viewed quite positively by social work scholars in Canada and elsewhere, it has primarily attracted a scholastic readership (approximately two-hundred and fifty academics). This journal is complemented by *The Social Worker/Le Travailleur Social*, which is published by the professional organization (CASW) and draws upon a much larger membership (more than thirteen-thousand).

An important thrust in the professionalization of social work is controlling who can practice social work and who can use the title "social worker." Regulation of professions is a provincial matter.   While the Canadian Association of Social Workers adopted a national code of ethics and recommended national standards of practice, it was left to the provincial associations to promote and develop mandatory regulations for social work title and practice.   At present, seven of Canada's ten provinces[1] have regulations governing social work practice which may be described as "voluntary."   Only two provinces, namely New Brunswick and Québec, have "mandatory" regulation, the latter being legislated protection of title.   The tenth province, Newfoundland, has no regulation of practice although legislation is expected within the next year.   Finally, it is important to acknowledge that while many social work educators have taken part in establishing a code of ethics and have supported the development of standards of practice, there have been others whose energies have been directed to subverting efforts to professionalize services and social work education, including initiatives toward mandatory regulation.

BACCALAUREATE AS THE FIRST PROFESSIONAL DEGREE

Baccalaureate programs in social work appeared for the first time in Canada in the late 1960s. The first MSW program was initiated in 1947; the first BSW offered as a professional degree was in 1966 at the University of Windsor.[2] The architects of these programs were social workers, whose intention was to build programs that were both academically sound and distinctly professional. Community college programs in social service, while increasingly popular, were not seen as professional programs. Community colleges serve the needs of an expanding market for case aids and social service technicians. A study on social welfare personnel needs in 1967 confirmed the need for professional education for social workers at the undergraduate level (Association of Universities and Colleges of Canada, 1967). Graduate level studies in social work, available at the time, did not adequately meet the need for professionally trained personnel in the country. Thus, the province of Alberta hired its first professional social worker as late as 1958; in 1965 New Brunswick had a total of twenty 20 trained social workers in the entire province, while Newfoundland had only three.

The decade of the 1970s saw the development and formal accreditation of twelve baccalaureate programs across Canada. By 1984, 2781 students were enrolled in twenty-one BSW programs. While the number of BSW programs has not significantly increased since then, the number of BSW enrollees has increased dramatically (see Table 2-1).

Table 2-1

Registration and Graduation by Type of Program: 1990

	BSW*	MSW** DSW***	PhD	Total
Full Time registration	3496	793	63	4352
Part-time registration	1607	749	21	2376
Total	5103	1542	84	6728
Total degrees granted	1351	538	10	1899

* These figures are taken from a total of 22 BSW programs (one program includes UQAC, an extension of UQAM). To allow for meaningful comparisons, all BSW programs have been considered of three year duration.

** These figures are from a total of 16 MSW and one MA program.

*** These figures are from a total of 3 DSW or PhD programs.

University programs at the baccalaureate level in social work combine a balance of academic courses in the social sciences/humanities with a range of professional courses in social work. While there is some variation in BSW programs across the country, the typical program is made up of forty one-semester courses, with twenty being taken as general arts, sciences, and humanities, and the remainder being taken as professional courses.[3] The courses designated as field practice are normally taken in the last two "professional" years and, on average, account for seven hundred hours of supervised practice. In addition to the traditional core curriculum (intervention, social administration, research, human growth and social development, etc.), Canadian schools have generally been quick to respond to new practice concerns. Examples are seen in the introduction of courses on multiculturalism, sexual abuse of children, family violence, the legal system, and Acquired Immunodeficiency Syndrome (AIDS).

The expected graduate of these programs is a professional who is broadly educated, is prepared for "general practice," and demonstrates "at least beginning competence with respect to direct professional intervention with clients" (CASSW, 1988). Graduates are expected to have "an ability to arrive at professional judgments and actions, based on an integration of theory and practice within the context of professional values" (CASSW, 1988).

Despite the success of these programs, one unresolved dilemma is the gap between the aspirations and competencies of graduates and the expectations of employers in the work setting. The majority of BSW graduates are employed in public sector (government funded) organizations where cases are increasingly complex, outcomes uncertain, and resources inadequate to meet the clients' needs. More specifically these gaps may be seen in the following dichotomies:

Table 2-2
Gaps in the Dichotomies

Professional Social Work Values	← →	Bureaucratic Expectations
Semiautonomous Workers	← →	Bureaucratic Control
Generalist Training	← →	Specialised Practice Demands
Personal-Structural Problem Analysis/Intervention	← →	Personal Crisis and Short-Term Intervention

This would seem to suggest that many social work graduates at the BSW level in Canada, unlike MSW graduates, experience some conflict between what they have learned through professional education and their experiences with the realities of practice.

GRADUATE EDUCATION FOR SOCIAL WORK

Canada has eighteen graduate level university programs in social work, seventeen leading to the MSW degree and one to the MA in social policy. Only three of these programs are of two academic years duration,[4] all located in the province of Ontario. The remaining fifteen programs are of approximately twelve months' duration. In 1990 there were more than 1542 Canadian students registered in full- and part-time graduate study. In this same year, of the 538 graduate level degrees granted in Canada, 287 or 53.3 percent were conferred by the three Ontario universities mentioned.

Consistent with the educational policy of the Canadian Association of Schools of Social Work, graduate programs in Canada are expected to respond to regional interests and needs, while promoting specialized study that will ensure academic excellence, promote critical professional judgment, and deepen professional competence and analytic skills. At the same time it is recognized that Canadian schools of social work represent a variety of ideological positions related to the purpose, nature, and function of social work education. Some schools have chosen a "structural" framework for analysis and intervention, while others have adopted an "eclectic" model (both to be discussed later). A distinguishing feature of all graduate level programs in Canada is the expectation that systematic inquiry be a part of the curriculum.

The one year MSW program requiring the BSW for entrance assumes that students have a reasonably standardized background for graduate studies in social work. While this permits considerable variation across the country in curriculum design, most programs are developed around a specialization, either in a methods concentration or a field of practice. As noted, research is a requirement in all programs.

Programs designed on the basis of two years of study require a baccalaureate degree for entry, although all allow BSW graduates entrance with advanced standing. While universities with two year programs had some initial reservations, it quickly became apparent that BSW graduates compared favorably with the regular two year MSW graduate (Thomlison, 1982). Interestingly, educators in the United States raised similar questions regarding the efficacy of granting "advanced standing" to baccalaureate graduates. Their research pointed to serious differences in the performance of these students as compared to "regular" master's students (Dedmon, Farel, Salinsky and Henley as reported by Lacompte, 1981). Possible explanations for these differences between Canada and the United States may be found in the accreditation standards related to curriculum and the location of "programs" within the university. In Canada all baccalaureate programs developed as distinct departments or schools, with well developed curriculum expectations, particularly with respect to practice methods and professionally supervised field practice. This helped to establish a distinct professional identity within the various university communities. American programs, on the other hand, present a variety of models, some established as separate programs, others located in social science departments (where it may have been more difficult to establish professional programs).

A number of educational issues at the graduate level face Canadian schools of social work. The first relates to the place and form of systematic inquiry. Considerable debate has occurred regarding the thesis requirement. Schools with "low completion rates" have typically identified the thesis requirement as the problem. Some schools have been reluctant to drop the requirement, because of university academic expectations at the graduate level; others have introduced a thesis option for the same reason.

Field requirements in social work are not mandatory in the one year programs in Canada. This remains a contentious issue. Central to this debate is the academic/knowledge model versus the practice/knowledge competence model. Related to this are the student's personal expectations regarding the purpose and function of graduate studies. Some students are desirous of more in-depth specialization, which can be problematic in one year programs with multiple curriculum demands on the student. Many Canadian schools are finding that large numbers of students are expressing a clear preference for courses and field work in advanced clinical practice. This is seen as the result of both a lack of job opportunities for policy/administration graduates and the increasing attractiveness of independent clinical practice as a career option (Levin & Leginsky, 1989).

Canadian graduate programs in social work have not increased significantly in recent years, in spite of the desire of some schools to introduce studies at this level. While they have been given approval at the level of the university, support and funding have not been forthcoming from the respective governments. This has exacerbated the problem of accessibility, particularly for those who cannot relocate for family or financial reasons.

The limits of the "specialization model" have led to the development of new and flexible graduate level studies combining social work and other related disciplines. A recent example is seen in program developments at McGill University, where students are able to pursue a combined law and social work degree. Wilfrid Laurier University offers a post-MSW diploma in social welfare policy or social administration. Finally, some graduates of MSW programs have used their professional education as a platform for advanced studies in related areas such as law, business administration and medicine.

DOCTORAL STUDIES

As the profession developed in Canada, a need for individuals with doctoral level qualifications in social work was identified. The need was strongest for social work educators, social policy analysts, and specialists with the skills to do applied research and evaluation, and to give direction to social policy formulation and social program improvements. The federal government has given support to doctoral studies in social work through the provision of doctoral fellowships and funding support for research and development in social work and social programs. Part of the rationale for these initiatives has been the concern that social workers, particularly university teachers, were pursuing their doctoral studies in cognate disciplines.

A survey of Canadian schools of social work in 1989 confirmed the need for expanded opportunities for doctoral education in social work (Holosko & Erickson, 1989). The findings revealed that the majority of full-time social work faculty would be reaching retirement age by the turn of the century.

Until recently, the only social work doctoral program in Canada (begun in 1952) was at the University of Toronto. While three universities[5] offered multidisciplinary studies that included social work (1980), it was not until 1987 that two more programs were established. A social work doctorate developed at Université de Laval with a research concentration and interdisciplinary focus was designed to serve both a national and an international francophone community. A DSW program introduced at Wilfrid Laurier emphasized the preparation of doctoral graduates who could provide leadership in professional education, research, and specialized practice.

Some findings on doctoral qualification in Canada are interesting to note. In the 1960s and the 1970s males were overrepresented among social workers with doctorates. As the 1980s ended the number of females pursuing doctorates in social work increased. Current trends indicate that Canadian women will soon equal the number of men with doctorates represented in the profession.

In the early 1980s, nearly 45% percent of Canadian social workers went to the U.S. to pursue doctoral studies, nearly 50% percent attended the University of Toronto, while the remainder went to Europe, in particular, Great Britain (Gripton, 1982). In the 1990s, more programs are becoming available within Canada. Four new doctoral programs are planned, a bilingual program in Montréal,[6] an Atlantic program in Newfoundland,[7] and two programs in the West (University of Manitoba and University of Calgary). In the future it appears that a higher proportion of Canadian doctoral graduates will be "home grown." Key issues facing doctoral social work education are seen to be the lack of clear and agreed-upon objectives for programs, the need for financial support for doctoral students and the establishment of criteria for academic excellence (Yelaja, 1991).

NATIVE SOCIAL WORK EDUCATION

The constitution of Canada identifies aboriginal peoples as consisting of three distinct groups: Indians, Métis, and Inuit (formerly known as Eskimos). According to the 1986 Census (Statistics Canada, 1991) 711,725 individuals (3 percent of the total population of Canada reported having at least one parent of aboriginal origin. Indians have been governed by the Indian Act, which was passed in 1876. Throughout the 1970s and the 1980s Indians obtained various forms of self-government and social and economic responsibilities. The Constitution Act of 1982 entrenched aboriginal and treaty rights for Canada's Native peoples, ensuring them guarantees in terms of self-governance and self-determination. A Parliamentary Committee of the Government of Canada on "Indian Self Government" in 1983 recommended the reorganization of human services to bring them under the authority and control of Native communities. Recognition has been given to the disproportionately large number of Native people represented in the clientele served by social services, particularly in the area of child welfare. Castellano, Stalwick and Wien (1986: 173) state that Native people have been "largely unrepresented in the ranks of social work students and human services personnel." Educational initiatives to address this, among other concerns, are seen in a number of programs in various regions of the country. Using twelve programs, these authors develop a typology representing four models in Native social work education:

1. *Autonomous*–program designed and implemented by Native community; self-determined with own authority
2. *Affiliated Autonomous*–Native program designed and administered by *Native controlled* education organization or public agency in affiliation with an existing educational institution
3. *Special Native*–program administered and implemented by faculty/school of social work, in addition to "regular" social work programs
4. *Conventional*–modest adaptation of core curriculum to accommodate Native students in regular program; this may include consultation with Native community (Castellano, Stalwick and Wien, 1986: 179–80)

Concern with the issues related to Native education for social work practice was seen in the 1987 CASSW resolution on Native social work education. The resolution highlights six criteria: Native rights, Native program initiation and management, ongoing university commitment, adaptation for student needs, employment of Native faculty, and incorporation of Indian history and culture (Pace & Smith, 1990). Whether Canada's Native programs meet all of these criteria is not clear. It is recognized that the more autonomous programs have a higher completion rate for Native students. While this is clearly of benefit to Native students, it does not resolve an inherent "bi-cultural" tension. This has two dimensions–the failure of white students to learn from their Native peers, and vice versa. The second disadvantage is that "segregated" programs for Natives may limit their employment options.

An additional dilemma relates to the geographical location of the program. If programs are located in the North, the cost to Native students and the sponsoring institution is substantially less; thus, when relocation for study is necessary, student living costs need to be incorporated into operating budgets. Some programs have identified faculty recruitment and retention as problematic in the North. In the affiliated programs there is the additional concern of faculty travel costs. However, if these programs are moved out of the North, students are less likely to return there to work.

A final dilemma is the obvious difficulty of maintaining a balance between the concerns for "quality and standards" and the need for programs that are culturally affirming and relevant to Native people. This, however, is possible, as the CASSW Board of Accreditation has just granted two year accreditation to the Saskatchewan Indian Federated College–the first Native program to receive accredited status in Canada.

DIRECTIONS IN CONTINUING EDUCATION

Adult education is the most rapidly growing sector of Canadian education (Statistics Canada, 1991: 58). Given this reality, the CASW and the CASSW, supported by Health and Welfare Canada, have just completed a series of studies and Canada-wide consultations on continuing education for the profession of social work. These national consultations have supported the development of model certificate programs in child welfare, discharge planning, field teaching and ethics in social work (Browning, 1991).

Most Canadian schools of social work and professional associations are involved, to varying degrees, in continuing education, giving direction to new opportunities and meeting various community needs. Continuing professional education is often the forum where new concepts and knowledge are tested and where practice wisdom may be translated into learning and field-tested material. Continuing education offerings include presentations for the general public, cross-discipline offerings, field instructor preparation, "specialized" training for BSW graduates and "upgrading" for other graduates, many of whom have an interest in private practice.

One dimension of the Canadian reality is the immense geographic distances; many social workers are employed in relatively isolated rural and northern areas. As a result, some schools of social work have experimented with providing continuing education course offerings through distance methods such as teleconferencing.

While the profession is moving toward a philosophy of "lifelong learning," it is important to acknowledge that the success of continuing education offerings for the profession is largely market-driven. There is an increasing demand for courses that offer credit, certification, or specialty diploma courses (Bernard, 1977). As more provinces adopt legislation to control the title and practice of social work, it is expected that Canada will move toward a model which requires continuing education credits for the maintenance of "good standing" as a professional.

TRENDS AND ISSUES: TOWARD THE YEAR 2000

There are many issues and trends in Canadian social work, social service, and social work education that are of potential interest to the international community. Given the limitations of space, the authors have decided to present an analysis of three issues/trends of current importance. Others, while of no less importance, are simply identified.

IDEOLOGICAL CONFLICT

Since the late 1970s the Canadian social work education community has experienced an ideological division. On the one hand, following from a social humanist and scientific tradition, defined as the cornerstone for social work by the IFSW (Ramsey, 1984) are faculties of social work that are basically eclectic and practice oriented. They emphasize "critical thinking" to evaluate personal and professional observations, judgments, and actions, as well as "truths" related to client systems; they have a bias toward intervention based on evaluating persons in social context. This bias evaluates the impact of structural, systemic, contextual, and social situational realities. It bases professional assessment on an ethical base derived from humanism (valuing critical independent thinking and collegial consultation), an observational base derived from an empirically based practice scientific information perspective, and a judgmental base derived from formal logic (Gambrill, 1990). Liberal feminists are most likely to identify with this orientation. The greatest strength of this perspective is in preparing students for practice with individuals, families, and social groups (including community groups); its greatest weakness, according to Carniol (1984), is that it places too much faith in the social worker's professional expertise to overcome problems that are basically structural and systemic. From an educational point of view, social work educators operating from the eclectic general practice perspective are likely to subscribe to a traditional concept of the university as a place to teach knowledge and to promote critical thought—emphasizing how to think over what to think. They are most supportive of the professionalization of social work including control of title and practice.

On the other side are faculties who ascribe to "critical analysis" and who place the word *radical* before words like *humanism* and *structuralism* (for example, Carniol, 1984). They promote practice based on an ideology which begins with a political–economic critique of society. Marxist concepts and analyses are embedded in their interpretations of the profession, of policy, programs, and practice. Radical feminists are most likely to identify with this orientation. The critical analytic school's greatest strength, the critique of social work methods, is also its greatest weakness. It offers no new direction to transformative skills and competencies; these have already been well described within the eclectic practice and general practice perspectives, particularly with reference to traditional social work methods of advocacy, community organization, social action, and alternative services (all of which are presented by Carniol (1987) as if specific to critical analytic practice). Other social work skills and competencies are neglected, at best, and "critically analyzed" as part of the problem, at worst.

That this perspective rarely rises beyond rhetoric to truly new intervention strategies is not surprising, as the critical analytic network is overrepresented by persons with doctorates in cognate disciplines such as sociology, political science, and political economy, or by persons with a doctorate in social work who specialized in social administration. Their approach to university education is oriented toward an ideological analysis that emphasizes oppression and alienation when teaching their critiques of society; they desire social work education to be "essentially moral education–to train to develop the skills of critique and moral judgment" (Leonard & Ralph, 1990: 6–7). They are most likely to support deprofessionalization (of all professions), and to challenge professional registration by labeling such ", at worst (Ralph, 1990: 6).

The differences between the two orientations were orientations as elitist, at best, or by describing social workers as "pimps debated in mutually tolerant and usually respectful dialogue in the 1970s; the unfortunate reality of the 1980s and early 1990s is that the level of acrimony has increased. Radical groups have tried to suppress open discussion and debate between the two factions, on the basis of a rigid and absolutist orientation currently labeled "politically correct thinking." This defines radical analysis as the only interpretation of reality that is able to construct the truth. One would hope that respect for interpersonal dignity will prevail over "group-think."

MULTICULTURALISM

The theme of multiculturalism in Canada finds its roots in a history of cultural and ethnic diversity originating from the many immigrant groups who came to this country over the last century. More recently, significant legislative and policy milestones highlight the importance that Canada has given to the many diverse groups that make up its population. In 1971 the Canadian government adopted a formal policy of multiculturalism which was designed both to recognize and support to our cultural diversity. This was followed in 1981 by the Canadian Charter of Rights and Freedoms, which moved multiculturalism from a cultural interest sphere to formalized social policy. In 1988 further emphasis was given to multiculturalism in the Canadian Multiculturalism Act. Here recognition was given to individual and civil rights and the need to promote full and equitable participation of individuals from all ethnic and cultural origins.

Multiculturalism as an issue of concern to professional social workers, while not new, is seen as being often neglected. Boucher (1990) raises the question of the profession's interest and concern in this area and states that "in spite of the increasing number of awareness conferences, there is still little research and training in social work dealing with intervention in inter-cultural, inter-ethnic and inter-racial settings" (p. 155). Such concerns are shared by educators who acknowledge the need to prepare students to work effectively with diverse ethnic, cultural, and racial populations.

In 1987 the Canadian Association of Schools of Social Work established the Task Force on Multicultural and Multiracial Issues in Social Work Education. It was given the mandate to study relevant issues; to recommend revisions to current educational policy related to accreditation standards for schools of social work in Canada; and to recommend future directions and organizational forms to continue the emphasis on multicultural and multiracial issues. Released in 1991, the report points to the inadequacy of response of educational programs across the country. Four areas, among others, were identified as being of particular concern: the lack of knowledge and "expertise" both in the classroom and in field teaching; the lack of support for minority students; the absence of "ethnic" faculty members in university teaching positions; the need for expanded partnerships with the community to allow participation of available ethnic resources. This comprehensive report poses a challenge to the profession, particularly to social work educators, to "dare to take the road leading to change and growth in social work education" (CASSW/ACESS, 1988: iii). Ultimately this will be seen in the ability of the CASSW to formalize these concerns in standards for accreditation that balance its value for relevance with due respect for knowledge, skills, and competence.

CORPORATE IDEOLOGY

A major problem facing Canadian social workers is the increased bureaucratization of social services. The general problem is that "corporate" decision rules, based on rational economics and political expediency, are displacing "professional" decision rules in medicine and social work based on standards of care and professional ethics. The management norm is the illusion of "more with less"; the professional norm is "more to do better." Many social work positions are filled by the untrained. When the incumbents are unable to do the job properly (for example, when rural people demand equal quality professional services), provincial governments demand quick degrees–quick fixes to problems of their own making. Some provincial governments are also "end running" legislation to protect title by reclassifying and deprofessionalizing social work positions. Challenging the corporatist ideology will be a major preoccupation for educators and professionals as the year 2000 draws near.

CONCLUSION

This review of social work education in Canada has described the current and historical context of Canadian society, English and French traditions in social work, new directions in education for Native social work, the Canadian model of social work education (including continuing education), and an analysis of selected issues and directions. As we approach the year 2000, there are many challenges and opportunities for social work in this country. Schools of Social Work in Canada are facing these challenges as reflected in current developments such as the following:

• Increased numbers of faculty who have achieved doctoral degrees, particularly social work doctorates;
  • Increased scholarly output and research by faculty;
  • Improved status and gender balance for women faculty in Schools of Social Work;
  • Curriculum materials and courses for social work practice in northern settings;
  • Distance education and distance support programs for social workers;
  • Improved awareness and course content regarding gender issues;
  • A national curriculum on AIDS for Schools of Social Work.

The building strength of the profession and education for social work during this first century bodes well for continued progress in the twenty-first century.

NOTES

All three authors have contributed equally in the preparation of this manuscript.

1. Prince Edward Island, Nova Scotia, Ontario, Manitoba, Saskatchewan, Alberta, and British Columbia.
2. In fact, this was the first such professional program in North America. While some Canadian universities awarded a BSW for completion of the first year of the two year MSW program, this was not recognized as the first professional degree. Similarly, a BS with a social welfare major as offered since the early 1950s was not recognized or considered a professional degree.
3. Baccalaureate programs typically require five years for completion (from high school leaving), meaning in some provinces that studies extend one year beyond the requirements for a baccalaureate in an academic discipline.
4. Toronto, Carleton, and Wilfrid Laurier.
5. McGill (in Québec), the University of British Columbia, and the University of Calgary (in Alberta).
6. This is a joint program of McGill University and l'Université de Montréal.
7. At the Memorial University of Newfoundland, in St. John's.

REFERENCES

Adachi, R. (1990). Multiculturalism and social work. *The Social Worker/Le Travailleur Social*, 58(4), 166–168.

Association of Universities and Colleges of Canada. (1967). Manpower needs in the field of social welfare. Paper presented at a conference of the Association of Universities and Colleges of Canada, Ottawa, November 1966.

Bernard, L. (1977). Education for social work. *Encyclopedia of Social Work*, 1(17). Washington, D.C: National Association of Social Workers.

Boucher, N. (1990). Are social workers concerned with Canadian immigration and multiculturalism policies? *The Social Worker/Le Travailleur Social*, 58(4), 153–156.

Browning, R. (1991). Personal communication with D. Kimberley. Canadian Association of Social Workers and the Canadian Association of Schools of Social Work, Ottawa, July 29.

Carniol, B. (1984). Clash of ideologies in social work education. *Canadian Social Work Review/Revue Canadienne de Service Social*, 184–199.

Carniol, B. (1987). *Case Critical: The Dilemma of Social Work in Canada*. Toronto: Between the Lines Publishers.

C.A.S.S.W./A.C.E.S.S. (1988). *Manual of Standards and Procedures for the Accreditation of Programmes of Social Work Education: Educational Policy Statement*. Ottawa.

Castellano, M., Stalwick, H., & Wien, F. (1986). Native social work education in Canada. *Canadian Social Work Review/Revue Canadienne de Service Social*, 166–184.

Gambrill, E. (1990). *Critical Thinking for Clinical Practice*. San Francisco: Jossey-Bass.

Gripton, G. (1982). Canadian doctorates in social work: a survey report. *Canadian Journal of Social Work Education*, 8(1, 2), 59–74.

Groulx, L. (1990). Cinquantennaire de l'école de service social. In *Les Naissances Successives de L'école de Service Social* Montréal: Université De Montréal, pp. 2–5.

Hawkins, F. (1986). Invitational address to the annual program meeting. St. Louis: Council on Social Work Education.

Holosko, M.J., & Erickson, G. (1989). Faculty needs survey of Canadian schools of social work. Paper presented at the Annual Meeting of the Canadian Deans and Directors of Schools of Social Work. Québec City, Canada: Université De Laval.

Kimberley, M., & Rowe, W. (1991). Mount Cashel: What Went Wrong? Part 1: Issues for the profession. *The Social Worker/Le Travailleur Social, 59(2)*, 85–90.

Kimberley, M. (1984). Trends and issues in education for the profession of social work: a Canadian perspective. In Kimberley, M. (Ed.), *Beyond National Boundaries: Canadian Contributions to International Social Work and Social Welfare*. Ottawa: Canadian Association of Schools of Social Work.

Lacompte, R. (1981). The education of social work personnel. In Turner, J. & Turner, F. (Eds.), *Canadian Social Welfare*. Don Mills, Canada: Collier Macmillan Canada.

Leonard, P., & Ralph, D. (1990). Accountability and dialogical education. Board discussion paper, Ottawa. Canadian Association of Schools of Social Work.

Levin, R., & Leginsky, P. (1989). Independent social work practice in Canada: an initial profile. *The Social Worker/Le Travailleur Social, 57(3)*, 155–159.

McKenzie, B., & Mitchinson, K. (1989). Social work education for empowerment: the Manitoba experience. *Canadian Social Work Review/Revue Canadienne de Service Social, 6,* 112–125.

Millar, K. (1990). Social welfare in Canada. In Elliott, D., Mayadas, N., & Watts, T. (Eds.), *The World of Social Welfare.* Springfield, Ill: Charles C. Thomas, pp. 35–52.

Pace, J., & Smith, A. (1990s). Native social work education: Struggling to meet the need. *Canadian Social Work Review/Revue Canadienne De Service Social, 7,* 109–119.

Paré, S. (1988). L'école de service social. In Faucher, Dans A. (Ed.), *Cinquante Ans de Sciences Sociales à l'Université de Laval.* Québec: Faculté des Services Sociales, Université de Laval, pp. 219–247.

Ralph, D. (1990). Issues of accountability in social work: the role of the C.A.S.S.W. past, present, and future. Consultation Meeting, C.A.S.S.W. Task Force on Multicultural and Multi-racial Issues in Social Work Education, Ottawa, February 24.

Ramsey, R. (1984). Social work in Canada: Snapshots of practice in the twentieth century. *The Social Worker/Le Travailleur Social, 52,* 11–16.

Rowe, W. (1991). Personal communication with D. Kimberley. July 29.

Stalwick, H. (1991). Personal communication with E. Hopmeyer. May 29.

Statistics Canada. (1991*). Canada: A Portrait.* Ottawa.

Thomlinson, R. (1982). Regular and advanced standing status: M.S.W. students after graduation: a follow-up. *Canadian Journal of Social Work Education, 8*(1, 2), 45–57.

Yelaja, S.A. (1991). Doctoral social work education: a Canadian perspective. *ARETE–Journal of the College of Social Work, 16(1).*

3

MEXICO AND CENTRAL AMERICA

Marian A. Aguilar

INTRODUCTION

The literature related to social work education in Central America in the English language is very sparse. While material in Spanish is available in a few libraries, the publications are limited and are not current. Even travel to Central America to obtain data does not guarantee access to recent information. Most developing countries do not have the resources to maintain and upgrade their data collection methods and publications. The professionalization of social work education in Mexico and Central America has enhanced the social development of these countries. Although professional social workers have contributed to changes in the social order through their practice, little is known of their work.

The purpose of this chapter is to add to our knowledge of social work education in the developing countries of Mexico and Central America. The chapter focuses on Mexico and secondarily on the Central American countries of Costa Rica, Honduras, Panama, Nicaragua, El Salvador, and Guatemala. The chapter includes information on the historical development of social work as an academic discipline; the influence of culture, values and religion on social work education; the structure and range of social programs; the client groups served; the form of program funding; the training qualifications, the evaluation process used for gatekeeping; the role of the political climate and government in the profession, the curriculum decision makers; and the role of research.

HISTORY OF SOCIAL WORK EDUCATION

The early origins of social work education in Mexico and Central America can be viewed in the context of the historical development of Latin America. It began in Latin America with the founding of the first school, Alejandro Del Rio, in Chile, which based its curricular structure on the European model of that era (Torres Diaz, 1987).

According to Torres Diaz (1987), schools of social work in Latin America have gone through three identifiable phases of development. During the first phase, which lasted from the founding of the first school in Chile in 1925 until 1940, the curriculum of many schools was influenced by the ideology of schools in Belgium, France, Germany and less so by American schools of social work. The course of study followed a conceptual framework which emphasized the role of the worker as a technician who provided charity or assistance benefits according to a medical/juridical model of practice (Torres Diaz, 1987). The typical program took three years to complete and ended with the conferral of the title of social assistant on individuals meeting the requirements. During the second phase, 1941–1965, social work continued to evolve as a profession, and more schools were established. The curriculum of the programs was now greatly influenced by schools in the United States, by Pan American Conferences, and by the professionals (Torres Diaz, 1987; Ander Egg, 1985). At this time the term *social service* replaced the term *social assistance* in some of the academic and professional settings. Torres Diaz refers to the conceptual framework as antiseptic technology, in which the main preoccupation was with scientific skills and psychological theories. According to Ander Egg (1985), the first phase maintained the traditional social work model; the second sought to modernize what existed. The third phase, from 1966 to the present, sought radically to transform what existed. A number of models using a variation based on Paulo Freire's *Pedagogy of the Oppressed*, which provides a conceptual framework for the transformation of society through a reflection-action of the political and social reality of the country, were adopted in the curriculums of schools of social work.

Social work as a discipline was strongly influenced by forces external to Latin America until 1966, when Chile took the lead to create and implement a curriculum which reflected the Latin American reality of colonialism and oppression. This third phase integrated a native ideology which added a revolutionary and consciousness raising dimension to social work education and practice in Latin America (Torres Diaz, 1987; Ander Egg, 1985). During this period of implementing a reality based curriculum *social work* became the term of preference for the profession.

The first schools of social work in South America pre-date those of Central America except in Mexico, Puerto Rico, and Cuba, whose first schools came into existence in the 1930s. The other schools in Central America began during the second and third phases of the development of the profession in Latin America. It is important to note that this distinction indicates the different social, economic, and political reality of the country in which the Central American schools came into existence. Though both the South and Central American schools were established in Spanish speaking, highly Catholic countries, their founding and development reflect a Central American reality distinct from the South American reality (Torres Diaz, 1987).

Schools of social work in Mexico and Central America sometimes use different terms to distinguish academic programs from those housed under the auspices of a ministry of the government or independent institute of learning. The term *faculties* is used to designate a school associated with a university; the term *school* generally refers to a program with a good academic curriculum which may or may not be affiliated with a university. Faculties generally issue either license or *titulo* (title) (Ander Egg, 1985). Most schools and institutes confer a technical title which is equivalent to an associate degree. Only a few confer licensure, as can be abstracted from Table 3-1. The term *school of social work* will be used to identify all of these schools for the purpose of this chapter.

Table 3-1

Status of Schools of Social Work
Mexico and Central America

Country	Year of Founding of First School	Number of Schools	Years of Study
Mexico	1933	107	3-5
Costa Rica	1942	3	5
Panama	1947	1	5
Guatemala	1949	5	4
El Salvador	1953	6	2-4
Honduras	1957	1	4
Nicaragua	1961	1	4

Sources: Ander Egg, 1985; Torres Diaz, 1987; Aguirre, 1984

Mexico

Mexico is a vast country with a population of over 87 million people living in thirty-three states. There are currently over one hundred schools of social work interspersed throughout these states. The first was officially recognized in 1933 and was known as the Center for Technological Studies No. 7 (Aguirre, 1984). The School of Domestic Learning incorporated it to become the School of Social Work and Domestic Learning. In 1936 a course was offered by the National University for those working with minors. In 1938 faculty of the National Autonomous University of Mexico (UNAM) proposed a three year course of study in social work which was adopted and located in the School of

Law and Social Sciences. In 1940 the University Council approved the creation of the career of social work at the technical level under the same department. In 1969 the School of Social Work at the National Autonomous University of Mexico and the school at the Autonomous University of Nuevo Leon received approval to confer licensure upon those completing their baccalaureate and requirements of the School of Social Work (Aguirre, 1984). Finally, in 1973 the university council approved the creation of the school of social work independent of the school of Law and Social Sciences. In 1974, it appointed Dr. Manuel Sanchez Rosado as its first director (Torres Diaz, 1987; Universidad Nacional Autonoma de Mexico, 1982).

From the inception of the first school until the end of the 1960s, schools of social work grew slowly, there were only twelve. With the democratization of education came growth. The profession was legally recognized and listed in the Directory of Professions. Then between 1970 and 1976, with the support of the first lady of the country, schools multiplied. The government felt that trained social workers would help with the economic development of the country by reducing social problems (Torres Diaz, 1987).

Today there are over one hundred schools of social work throughout the thirty-three Mexican states. Some are located in independent departments of a University, others are under schools of law, health sciences or, social science and administration. Some of the schools are state-operated or under the federal department of health. Still others are affiliated with the school of social work at a university.

In 1986, over eighty-six schools were offering either a technical title or licensure. Over 70 percent were offering a technical degree when data were collected in 1979. According to Aguirre (1984), Queretaro, Chiapas, Campeche, Yucatan and Quintana Roo did not have schools at that time. Table 3-2 provides a profile of schools offering licensure.

Table 3-2

Schools of Social Work in Mexico Offering Licensure

Name of School	Semesters Required
Escuela de Trabajo Social de Tijuana	9
Escuela de Trabajo Social "Profesora Guadalupe de Araiza"	10
Facultad de Trabajo Social de la Universidad Autonoma de Tamaulipas	12
Escuela de Trabajo Social de la Universidad Autonoma de Coahuila	9
Escuela de Trabajo Social Centro Universitario de Estudios Superiores	9
Escuela de Trabajo Social "Miguel Hidalgo" Ciudad Madero	9
Escuela Nacional de Trabajo Social de la Universidad Nacional Autonoma de Mexico	9
Escuela "Vasco de Quiroga"	9
Escuela de Trabajo Social de Zacatec	9
Centro Interdiciplinario de Ciencias de la Salus IPN	8
Departmento de Trabajo Social de la Universidad Autonoma de Tlaxcala	8
Instituto Tecnologico Regional de Tlalnepantla	8
Facultad de Trabajo Social de la Universidad Veracruzana Poza Rica, Veracruz	10
Facultad de Trabajo Social de la Universidad Veracuzana Minatitlan, Veracruz	8

Source: Aguirre, 1984.

A greater percentage of the schools are found in the central region of the country, which includes Mexico City. The southern region has the fewest (Aguirre, 1984). Only the University of Nuevo Leon in Monterrey offers a post graduate degree. The Center for Social And Economic Studies of Mexico (CESEM) is now offering a postgraduate degree. The program offers specializations in medical social work, family therapy, school social work, and industrial social work. In 1991, the National School of Social Work at the Autonomous University of Mexico approved a new curriculum which includes a postgraduate program in medical social work.

Only two schools in Mexico were founded in the 1930s. The majority were established around the same period as those of Central America, as is seen in the sections which follow. The first school in Central America was established in Costa Rica in 1942, followed by Panama in 1947, Guatemala in 1949, El Salvador in 1953, Honduras in 1957, and Nicaragua in 1961 (Torres Diaz, 1987; Ander Egg, 1985)

Costa Rica

Costa Rica is the only Central American country which has a democratic history and a relatively stable economy. The economy is based on two agricultural exports: bananas and coffee (*Culturgram for the '90s: Republic of Costa Rica*, 1991).

Costa Rica was the first Central American country to establish a social security system. It has the highest literacy rate and the most students enrolled in higher education. The war of 1948 opened the way for reforms which allowed for what is termed "a dynamic process of material development." The other factor which has allowed Costa Rica to continue developing or maintaining a basic standard of living for its citizens is that the country does not possess a regular army (Osorio, 1986; Rodriguez & Tesch, 1978).

Public funds have been channeled toward development, health and education. Costa Rica, like many export dependent countries, has endured economic crises, high inflation, unemployment, and poverty. In addition, the country is impacted by the economy of the countries to which it exports, such as the United States (Osorio, 1986; Rodriguez & Tesch, 1978).

Rodriguez and Tesch (1978) note that the emergence of social work as a profession coincided with the establishment of the "Welfare State" in Costa Rica in 1942. The first school came into existence the same year with support from the United Nations with the initial objective of training individuals who were already in the field (Ander Egg, 1985; Rodriguez & Tesch, 1978). A three year curriculum was implemented in 1943, and in 1946 the program was annexed to the Department of Economic Sciences. In 1956 the program was given approval to establish itself as a school in its own right. Eventually the school, known as San Jose, established three off–campus sites throughout Costa Rica: (1) Centro Universitario de Occidente, (2) Centro Universitario de Guanacaste, and (3) Centro Universitario del Atlantico (Rodriguez & Tesch, 1978). Two of the centers offer baccalaureate level education and licensure. One of the centers trains auxiliary or social work assistants and volunteers (Rodriguez & Tesch, 1978).

Panama

Panama has had a unique history of colonization by and dependence upon the United States because of the Panama Canal. This nation suffers from structural, economic, and agricultural problems. The migration of the population from rural to urban areas has added to the economic and social problems of the cities. Over 50 percent of the population resides along the Canal Zone. The country has good schools, and the literacy rate is 90 percent. although the rate is lower in the rural areas. Most people have access to basic health care, which is part of the national social security system (*Culturgram for the '90s: Republic of Panama, 1991*). Panama has two institutions of higher learning, the National University, established in 1935, and the Catholic University (Rodriguez & Tesch, 1978; *Culturgram for the '90s: Republic of Panama*, 1991).

Although social work activities in Panama were conducted as early as 1937, the establishment of a School of Social Service at the University of Panama did not take place until 1947. Initially, the school grew slowly, but today it boasts three centers: one in the Sede Central, the second in Provincia de Chiriqui, and the third in Provincia de Colon. The school is under the Department of Administration and Commerce. The United Nations intervened to establish this school, and the United States offered technical assistance (Ander Egg, 1985; Rodriguez & Tesch, 1978). Students graduating from the program are conferred licensure.

Guatemala

Like most Central American countries, Guatemala is economically dependent on its agricultural exports. It is a relatively poor country. Historically, military leaders maintained control of the country, and some feel that the lack of social and economic progress is the result of turmoil from frequently changing military juntas. Though recently inflation has dropped and the economy has experienced growth, the illiteracy rate is high and health care services are limited (*Culturgram for the '90s: Republic of Guatamala, 1991*; Rodriguez & Tesch, 1978).

Within the context of a frequently changing government, social work as a profession was born with the founding of the Instituto Guatemalteco de Seguridad Social (IGSS) in 1949. In 1947, the United Nations offered assistance to the institute and several physicians were sent to Medellin, Colombia to attend the Latin American Seminar on Social Well Being in which an American, Walter Petit, was one of the chief participants (Ander Egg, 1985; Rodriguez & Tesch, 1978).

Shortly after this event, the United Nations sent Walter Petit to Guatemala to conduct a study and found a school of social work. Contact was established with the University of San Carlos. The University of San Carlos delayed making a response and the Guatemalan Institute of Social Security took advantage of that delay to found its own school. The school remained under the auspices and supervision of the United Nations until 1953, when native graduates took charge (Rodriguez & Tesch, 1978).

Only after much pressure did the Council of the University of San Carlos approve the formation of a school of social work in 1975. This school later replaced the one founded by the Institute of Social Security (Rodriguez & Tesch, 1978). The term *substitute* was used to reflect the transfer of the program to the university. Historians still list five schools (Ander Egg, 1985, Rodriguez & Tesch, 1978; Alayon, 1982). What is not clear is whether the initial program is still a separate entity or has become a part of the school at San Carlos.

In 1959 efforts to found a school to train workers to provide leadership in rural community development were initiated in Quetzaltenango. The school remained under the direction of the University of San Carlos until 1971, when it was integrated with the Division of Humanities and Social Sciences of the university, where the school of social work is located.

The Catholic University Rafael Landivar founded a school of Social Service in 1963 and in 1964 received financial assistance from a German Catholic organization, Misereor. The major objective of the school was to train workers for either the rural or urban camps (ie., rural or urban fields or settings) (Rodriguez & Tesch, 1978).

Several years later in 1976, the Feminine Institute for Superior Studies established its own school of social work and received financial support from the Catholic organization Opus Dei. Most of its graduates work in the business and industry sectors (Rodriguez & Tesch, 1978). All four schools offer the technical title of social worker (which is equivalent to an associates degree) and continue to work toward licensure which is equivalent to a bachelors in social work plus one more year of course work for a total of five years of study in most schools affiliated with a university where the *licenciatura* is awarded.

El Salvador

El Salvador is a country which has been plagued with civil wars, internal strife and military dictatorships since its declaration as an independent republic in 1841 and most recently since 1979. Compared to those of most of the Latin American countries, its economy is very weak. Unemployment is high. The literacy rate in the rural areas is only 30 percent. The infant mortality rate remains high in spite of efforts to improve public health services. Health care to the rural population is almost nonexistent or limited to whatever medicine troops can hand out (*Culturgram for the '90s: Republic of El Salvador*, 1991).

More positively, in the 1950s industrial development took place as a result of the injection of foreign capital and advanced technology. In 1973 the government introduced a plan for the country's development. Its objectives included the elevation of the quality of life for its people; better wages; social services; promotion of growth of production in agriculture, industry, and construction; integration of the nation; and diversification of exports. For a while much progress was made in these areas, but war has virtually stalled progress. The University of Salvador has seen its doors closed more than once, and the Catholic University has been attacked by the military because of its position.

There are conflicting reports on the number of schools of social work in El Salvador. Ander Egg (1985) and Alayon (1982) cite the existence of one school of social work; Torres Diaz (1987) reports six; Martin–Baro (1985) reports five. For our purposes, the number six will be used, since that figure is found in the most recent source.

With industrial development came the need for social workers. In 1951 the minister of education asked the United Nations for assistance in establishing a school of Social Work. In 1952 a Chilean, Raquel Zamora Morales, arrived to study and carry out the plans for a school. The project was inaugurated in 1953. The school offered three years of training, was classified as an institute providing "nonuniversity superior studies," and was placed under the Ministry of Education (Rodriguez & Tesch, 1978).

Today there is only one school of social work at the university level. The others are considered institutes, such as the Instituto Nacional Francisco Menendez (Martin-Baro, 1985).

Honduras

Like its Central American neighbors, Honduras is very poor, yet its economy is growing. Honduras is dependent on agriculture for economic growth. Over 60 percent of the population is employed in agriculture, although only 14 percent of the land is suitable for cultivation (*Culturgram for the '90s, Republic of Honduras*, 1991).

Currently, Honduras has a relatively stable government, low inflation, a high poverty rate, a 56 percent literacy rate in the urban areas and a much lower rate in the rural areas. Few health services are available outside cities.

During the 1950s Honduras experienced a series of economic and political changes which led to the diversification of production and the development of industry. In 1954, a strike by the laborers employed by banana companies not only led to some improvement in labor conditions and wages but for the first time created a voice for this segment of the working class (Mendez et al., 1985).

In 1957 a decree was issued by the Junta Militar de Gobierno and the school of social work emerged from this social and political context. The school was placed under the Ministry of Labor and Social Assistance (Donaire et al., 1985). Mendez, Flores and Amaya (1985) assert that placing the school under the Ministry of Labor was not a coincidence. The workers were demanding changes, services, and programs, the school was one way of meeting labor's demand. Along with changes in the the commitment of the University to social transformation allowed the School of Social Work the opportunity to reconceptualize its program so that it would be more in keeping with the social reality of the people of Honduras. Up to this time, both the United States and the Latin American countries had influenced the Central American curriculum. With reconceptualization, some traditional social work methods were abandoned in favor of others law which were favorable to the worker, a public agency, the National Council for Social Well Being, was created around the same time. This agency became one of the principal employers of social workers (Mendez et al., 1985).

In 1973, due to pressure from faculty and students, the University Council established social work as one of the academic disciplines. Furthermore, the transfer of the school from the Ministry of labor to the University allowed for program revamping. The climate was right. The faculty of the Autonomous University of Honduras held their First Encounter of the University Community, in which the role of the university was redefined to add social transformation as one of its functions (Mendez et al., 1985; Palacios, 1985). The incorporation of the school and which would contribute to social transformation (Palacios, 1985; Mendez et al., 1985).

Nicaragua

Nicaragua has had civil strife for many years. The United States has intervened by sending marines, cutting off economic aid or providing arms. From the 1930s the Somoza family determined the political and economic conditions of the country. Much of Nicaragua's financial resources was directed to the ruling family's personal coffers. In 1973 the economy was shattered and the industrial infrastructure almost destroyed. The Central American Common Market failed when Honduras and El Salvador went to war, aggravating the economic situation in Nicaragua.

During the years of civil war, 26,000 died, 250,000 were displaced, and thousands of young people were disabled or orphaned. In 1988, a hurricane destroyed a large percentage of the crops and left many homeless (Zellin & Tick, 1990). The United States suspended economic aid in 1981, and in 1984 imposed a trade embargo which severely crippled the economy. In 1990, with the country's economy shattered, high inflation and workers demanding higher wages, Violeta Chamorro was elected president. The United States backed her candidacy and promised to restore economic aid (*Culturgram for the 90s: Republic of Nicaragua*, 1991).

With the establishment of the Institute of Social Security came the need to prepare social workers for jobs in the institute. The Department of Housing also recognized the need to train social workers. With the financial backing of both the Institute of Social Security and the Ministry of Labor, the School of Social Service was established in 1961. The United Nations supported the institute's efforts. A woman identified only as Mrs. Gutierrez in documents, became the director of the school. In 1965 the school was placed under the Department of the Humanities of the National University of Nicaragua. Financing by the Institute of Social Security continued until 1973. Social workers who complete their studies at the university receive the title of *licenciado* (Rodriguez & Tesch, 1978).

Historically, Nicaraguan social workers have not been highly visible, but their involvement aiding the victims of several national disasters has added to the profession's recognition. Unfortunately, social workers are recognized solely as providers of social assistance. Unlike in the other Central American countries, the ideas related to reconceptualizing social work to reflect the country's reality have been slow to take root. Now with new peace efforts, social workers see the need to develop those skills needed to work within the social, economic and political reality of their country (Rodriguez & Tesch, 1978; Zellin & Tick, 1990).

CULTURE/VALUES/RELIGION

The schools of social work in Central America and Mexico exist in countries which are developing, are predominantly Catholic, have economies that are highly impacted by the developed countries, have populations which live primarily in rural areas, have cities congested with the marginalized who moved into the urban areas for jobs when the respective country developed industry, and have had foreign ideologies imposed on them (Ander Egg, 1985; Torres Diaz, 1987). Originally, the schools of social work in Mexico and Central America integrated both the European and U.S. history of the development of social work in their curricula along with some of their own ideology and value base. Since the mid-1960s, however, they have incorporated more of the cultural, social, and political realities of their respective countries in the content on social work practice.

In an anthology (1989) compiled by members of the faculty of the National School of Social Work of Mexico, several chapters address conflictual issues related to traditional social work ideology and values (*Conceptualizacion Del Trabajo Social: Antologia*, Pena et. al., 1989; Hill, 1989; Estruch, 1989). In one chapter, Ander Egg (1985) reviews the interpretation by various authors and organizations of social work principles and summarizes them as (1) the respect for the value and dignity of the individual; (2) the potential of all persons to overcome their situation though they may lack the means; (3) the rejection of paternalistic tendencies, favor of a search for the latent potential for individual, group, or community development; (4) the assumption of an integral or holistic view which takes into account all dimensions of a person including spiritual and cultural values and material and economic circumstances (Pena et al., 1989).

Historically, three major factors have influenced the values and principles taught in schools of social work in Mexico and Central America. The first was the support for the establishment of schools offered by the United States through the United Nations; the second was the training in the United States and Puerto Rico of the first social work academics: the third was the infusion by these academics of U.S. social work values and principles into the Mexican and Central American social work curricula.

In the 1960s when the Catholic University of Chile changed its curriculum to reflect the social reality of the country, a whole era of reconceptualization of social work began in Latin America. Academics used the term *intellectual colonization* to describe the imposition of one country's reality on another country through the curriculum. According to an article in the anthology (1989: 187) the approach to the solution of economic and political oppression is not through the social work values of self-determination and the participation of the client in decision making, as these are not derived from the concrete social reality of the Latin American countries. These values only impact individual performance and do not address the country's social problems, which prevent individuals from achieving self-determination.

The Judeo-Christian values have not been in conflict as the Latin American countries have a high percentage of Catholics. Judeo-Christian values are social in nature. They support the liberation of people from oppressive systems as part of loving one's neighbor. These values support the process of reconceptualization upon which many of the schools have embarked. Conscientization, liberation, oppression, praxis, critical thinking, subjective and objective reality, dialogue, transformation, equality, universality, participation, decentralization and solidarity constitute the basis of social work values in Latin America. The values of self-determination and self-actualization are important, but they cannot always be realistically pursued in countries where social systems would need to be transformed to allow them to be. Most of the schools of social work actually teach the traditional U.S. values along with reconceptualization values. Although Nicaragua is familiar with the reconceptualization orientation of Latin America, the school has not fully implemented such a curriculum because of the country's past oppressive political environment.

The revision of the curriculum of the School of Social Work at UNAM in Mexico City was greatly influenced by one of the faculty members, who argued against using a social transformation approach exclusively. According to Garcia

Salord (1990), the approach was too narrow. She proposed the construction of a process by which social work is defined, theory and knowledge based developed on a particular point of reference. In the article "Specificity of Social Work," she proposed social work be defined, in terms of social problems, which would becomes the point of reference for developing a knowledge base, theories, and methodologies. This orientation would replace the theory and methods approach that formerly defined the discipline. The social problem becomes the object of the intervention in this orientation.

RANGE AND STRUCTURE OF SOCIAL WORK EDUCATION

Levels of Education

Unlike schools of social work in the United States, not all those in Mexico and Central America are under university auspices. Some are under government departments or institutes, some confer technician titles, others licensure, and a few graduate degrees. When licensure is conferred, the candidate will have met baccalaureate requirements also. Doctoral programs in schools of social work are nonexistent.

Range of Education Needed

Social work is recognized as a profession in most of the Latin American countries; likewise social work functions in the public agencies are recognized. Since many of the first schools were founded under the auspices of a government department (whether social security or social assistance) there has been a perceived need for trained social workers.

The course of study required for the title of *licenciado* is determined by the Board of Regents of the university. The schools of social work which are under university auspices require eight to twelve semesters of study along with baccalaureate course completion to qualify for *licenciatura*. Often a thesis and national examination are also required. Those schools under university auspices who grant a technical degree require six to nine semesters of study.

A country like Nicaragua with few professional social workers trains "auxiliaries of social service" whose preparation is very limited and who receive a salary lower than that of a professional social worker, they are what we would call para-professionals or semi-professionals. The training varies by country and sponsoring institution.

Many agencies use volunteers, and whatever training they receive is initiated by the entity needing their service. For example, the public health service trains volunteers in Juarez, Mexico, called *promotoras* who go into neighborhoods to tell people of services rendered at the clinics and to teach them about health and nutrition.

As mentioned earlier, the only known postgraduate program in Mexico and Central America is found at the Autonomous University of Nuevo Leon in Monterrey, Nuevo Leon, Mexico. In 1962 the United Nations published an article encouraging schools of social work to establish postgraduate programs to (1) educate faculty to increase the number of qualified faculty and to improve the quality of education, (2) to prepare supervisors and counselors, and (3) to prepare social workers for administration (Ander Egg, 1985).

In 1991 Autonomous University of Mexico received approval for postgraduate studies in health care. One of the institutes in Mexico City is offering postgraduate education with concentrations in family therapy, industrial social work, medical social work, and school social work.

Funding Arrangements for Courses for Students

Most of the schools which grant licensure are in academic institutions of higher learning. Some of these institutions are public, but a good number are private Catholic schools. In these private institutions, students are usually responsible for paying their own tuition. While Mexico has private institutions of higher learning, the Catholic church does not own any, as is the case in Central America. By law, all church property belongs to the government. The federal or state governments subsidize higher education in the autonomous universities and institutions (Rangel Guerra, 1978). Mexico has open enrollments. The economy, however, prevents most of the poor from taking advantage of government subsidized education (Guerra, 1978).

In the past, the United Nations helped with funding for the education of future faculty members. A number were educated in the United States, especially in Puerto Rico. Through the years, several of the American schools have established educational collaboratives with Latin American schools. The Catholic University of America (based in Washington, D.C.) has a master's program in social work at the Catholic University of Chile. The School of Social Work at the Autonomous University of Mexico conducted a study of retention and completion rates of the 2063 students enrolled up until 1985. Of the total number of students enrolled, only 15 percent obtained licensure. In studying the reasons for failure to complete the program, the school found that between the completion of course work and the writing of their thesis and their final examination, students lost contact with the school. They may have had family or professional obligations which distanced them. The school realized that the five year curriculum was difficult for students with limited means of support, together with the Department of Continuing Education, it introduced an alternative to the thesis requirement. The course of study would take four months, at the end of which students who made at least a B average would be eligible to take the professional examination and receive the title of *diplomate* upon passing it satisfactorily (Fioriani & Salazar, 1986).

Panama has an evening program which lasts six years, four of these in course work. This structure allows students to be employed. Rodriguez and Tesch (1978) assert that even with this kind of a program there is loss of students. In Mexico and the Central American countries political, social, and economic realities all too often determine retention and completion rates (Fioriani & Salazar, 1986).

"Twinning" projects involving collaborative efforts of NASW chapters or schools of social work with Costa Rica, Guatemala, and Nicaragua to assess social problems, provide training, exchange information, develop training materials, and work on community solutions were initiated in 1990 (Van Soest, 1991).

STATUS AND RELATIONSHIP TO OTHER PROFESSIONALS

The *Conceptualiazcion Del Trabajo Social: Antologia* (1989) published by Pena et al., includes a study conducted by Juan Estruch on the perceived social status of the profession. In this study Estruch asked social workers to rank their status compared to that of other professionals. The two variables considered were utility and prestige. Social workers ranked themselves sixth after physicians and teachers, sociologists, psychologists, and journalists in terms of utility. When asked about prestige social workers placed themselves last. Using utility and prestige as status indicators helps to clarify social workers' own perceptions of their profession. In Central America, the profession came into existence when the need for social workers in the social security or other ministry offices was established. Yet, social workers do not perceive their professional status as high as a consequence of demand or need. In El Salvador professionals receive lower salaries because they do not have university status. In Costa Rica the profession is recognized by law as a discipline along with other professions who have university status. Their status allows them to compete for professional salaries. Most social workers are employed in government institutions, which rank social workers according to their professional education (Rodriguez & Texch, 1978).

Although social work as a profession is recognized by law in Mexico, it is classified as a lower level profession, which means that social workers receive lower wages and are concentrated in nonmanagement positions. Social workers have been nationally visible because the first ladies of the land have been aware of their work and have actively supported and encouraged it. Politically, social workers have aligned themselves with the Institutional Revolutionary Party (PRI), since many of the workers are state employees. Another factor lending visibility and credibility to the profession has been the rapid expansion of schools. Social workers have also organized to enhance their status by working on those problems which contribute to their low status, such as poor wages and level of professional education (Rodriguez & Tesch, 1978).

In Nicaragua, social workers became highly visible during an earthquake when they distributed aid. Unfortunately, they came to be identified as providers of "handouts." Nicaragua is the Central American country in which the profession is least developed. As mentioned earlier sanctions imposed by the United States have limited social service expansion. Nicaraguan social workers take pride in being resourceful in working with refugees in spite of limited resources (Rodriguez & Tesch, 1978; Fernandez, 1985).

QUALIFYING AND POSTQUALIFYING TRAINING

The criteria for admission to schools of social work vary greatly, since standards do not exist across states or countries. While there are over one hundred schools of social work in Mexico under various university and institutional auspices, there are fewer than fifteen in the rest of Central America. Fewer than 15 percent of the schools of social work offer licensure. The majority offer a technical degree and a few offer a course of study which when complete allows an individual to work in a particular government social work program. The following qualifying criteria are applicable to institutions which are under university auspices. A student applying for admission to a school which offers *titulacion* is required to have completed secondary education and to have passed the university admissions examination in most instances. To obtain technical certification, or *titulacion,* the student has to have passed all courses in the plan of studies, have completed six hundred hours in field practice, and be free of any academically related debts.

For admission to the university a prospective student must pass the required entrance examination. A person applying for admission to a school which offers *licenciatura* must have successfully completed the course of study at the baccalaureate level in the area of social science with an average specified by the particular school. Upon completion of the course of study and field practice, the student writes a thesis and takes a professional examination. The student then receives the *licenciatura* (license) (Universidad Nacional Autonoma de Mexico, 1982).

Since social work is registered and legally recognized as a profession, those individuals who are credentialed are hired into social work positions in state and federal institutions in Mexico. In these public institutions, salaries are paid according to a fixed wage scale. Martin-Baro (1985) describes three levels of professional training in El Salvador. The first level, or technical certification, requires two years of training; the second level, professional certification, requires three years of training; and the third level, licensure, requires five years of training. Salaries vary by type of institution employing social workers. The lowest paid social workers are those who work in a state institution, the highest paid are employed in an autonomous institution, and medium wage earners are employed in the private sector (Martin-Baro, 1985). According to Rodriguez & Tesch (1978), the major cause of disparity among social work professionals in Mexico is the diversity in plans of study and certification requirements among institutions.

EVALUATION AND GATEKEEPING FUNCTIONS

While the Central American countries have several organizations established by social workers, none of these serves as a gatekeeper in terms of accreditation. What these organizations have done is to work toward the recognition of social work as a profession, the improvement of wages for social workers, and the incorporation of social work education into academic institutions of higher learning.

One of the major organizations in Latin America is the Association of Latin American Schools of Social Work (ALAETS), which has been the major sponsor of international conferences held in Latin America since 1965. The themes carried throughout the conferences have influenced the curriculum of schools of social work. Initially, this organization was known as the Association of Latin American Schools of Social Service (ALAESS). Through the efforts of the organization the first bulletin for professional exchange was made possible, as was publication of some of the first social work texts in the Spanish language. One of the goals of the organization was to work together to establish a common basic curriculum for all schools of social work (Torres Diaz, 1987; Ander Egg, 1985).

In 1974 the association created the Latin American Center for Social Work (CELATS), among its main functions are social research and dissemination of information of the social reality, of social needs, and of actions to be taken corporately by the Latin American schools. CELATS has been the major source of publications on the state of social work education, materials, and professional literature in Latin America. CELATS has also been responsible for the publication of conference presentations which have influenced both professionals and schools of social work in Latin America (Ander Egg, 1985; Torres Diaz, 1987).

CURRICULA

The social movements of the Catholic church have greatly influenced the conceptualization of social work curricula in most of the Latin American countries. It was the school of social work of the University of Chile which led the way to the establishment of a curriculum that reflects the social action and social reality of Latin America. In some of the schools, students have organized to protest existing curricula and have been instrumental in changes.

Because no formal accreditation body exists, there is great variation among schools in both the course of study and type of certification awarded. The programs under university auspices are required to submit their curricula to the academic committee, which approves content. In 1973, for example, the Autonomous University of Honduras held the First Conference of the University Community in which the faculty defined "social transformation" as their main function. This action facilitated the move made by the students and faculty of the school of social work, which was then under the Ministry of Labor and Social Assistance, to petition for the creation of a professional educational program at the university level. The action of the university to incorporate the school of social work was in keeping with its mission of social transformation. The curriculum presented by the social work faculty reflected the country's social reality and received prompt approval as a result (Donaire et al., 1985).

In a study of the curricula of forty-six schools of social work in Latin America, 39 percent from Mexico and Central America, Alayon (1982) concludes that if there is evidence that there has been a redefining of social work roles, it is not reflected in common objectives and curriculum content. The profile of schools of social work created by the Alayon (1982) study includes the qualification of the social work educators, the courses taught in the schools and program duration. His findings reveal that over 45 percent of the faculty are social workers, almost 9 percent are sociologists, 8 percent are psychologists, 19 percent are from other social sciences, 4.8 percent are physicians, and 14 percent are in other professions. In a subsample of the study which included twenty-three schools, Alayon (1982) identified a total of 889 courses taught among these schools. Thirty-three percent of the courses were in social work, almost 30 percent were in the social sciences, just over 10 percent were in psychology, 3 percent in medical science, 7 percent in law and political science, and 17 percent in other fields. Common objectives or course content was not found, even among schools within the same country. This diversity will continue as long as an accrediting body does not exist.

Although there is a poor fit between U.S. social theory and social work practice in Mexico and Central America, American curriculum is entrenched in most of the programs. In Juarez, because of its proximity to the United States, the curriculum includes many courses modeled after the U.S. model, yet even Juarez integrates the "social transformation " model of South America into its curriculum. In the developing countries, the medical model is out of place as a major curriculum thrust, as the resources to meet basic human needs are scarcely available. The only way these basic needs can be met for the greater percentage of the population is through the transformation of unjust systems.

The social work curriculum is also unjust when its does not prepare its students to work in settings which help change the systems that control resources. The basic concepts for the "social transformation" curriculum were first adopted from Paulo Freire's model found in *Pedagogy of the Oppressed* by the School of Social Work of the Catholic University of Valparaiso, Chile. The objectives established for the model were (1) to integrate the theoretical formation with the practice experience of the student in such a way that the professional formation would constitute a unified social theoretical process; (2) to erase the traditional learning concept of knowledge flowing down to students into one in which the learners take responsibility and become the creators of their own learning process; (3) to join faculty and student in a process in which together they would search for the means to transform systems negatively impacting on the social reality of their community (CELATS, 1989).

Unfortunately, there are as many curricula as there are schools of social work. Most of the schools in Mexico have a mixture of the U.S. traditional practice model and the "social transformation" model. The Central American schools in countries where there is civil strife have tried to integrate a "social transformation" model into their curriculum. Their curricula also have content transported from the United States and from Europe. Conflicts have arisen in updating curriculum because the faculty cohorts who were initially trained in the United States continue to hold on to the model they learned. Until recently, little thought was given to preparing new cohorts to replace the initial faculty as they retire. There are no graduate programs, except in Mexico.

Schools of social work in the United States who want to establish collaborative efforts with the Central American schools have to know the country, the people, and the social structures in order to collaborate. Unfortunately, more harm than good can be done when social work is defined in the U.S. context and then transplanted into the context of a developing country. The Central Americans call the imposition of American values, knowledge base, and structures intellectual colonization, and they deeply resent this intrusion.

ROLE OF RESEARCH

Since the 1970s, CELATS has been the major source of the status of social work practice and education in Latin America. Authors writing about social work complain of the paucity of current information available (Torres Diaz, 1987; Ander Egg, 1985). Mexico, with over one hundred schools of social work, has no central depository of statistics relevant to the status of schools and social work practice. Within the past decade, Mexico has created several research institutes where statistics on the status of the population are gathered. With the changing state of technology, schools of social work are beginning to do more in–depth studies and to find avenues for their publications.

SUMMARY

The schools of social work in Mexico and Central America have consistently strived to upgrade and professionalize the practice of social work in their respective countries. Their curricula are a mixture of U.S. models and those created within the context of their own political reality. The schools in these countries have worked against all odds and have succeeded in spite of civil strife, poor economies, and lack of resources.

In El Salvador and Nicaragua social workers have at times feared for their lives. Faculty members of universities have been assassinated or have disappeared because they spoke against unjust systems.

Schools of social work have improved their curricula, have established collaboratives with other schools, have steadily developed the art of social research and continue to find the means to collect and publish data related to the status of social work education and practice in Central America and Mexico.

The distinguishing features of social work curricula in Mexico and more especially in Central America are a community development focus, rural thrust, family, casework, and social change/action orientation to practice.

In Mexico and Central America social work education has not only contributed to the development of the countries' social systems, but augmented the knowledge base of the profession through each country's unique curriculum. Schools in developed countries have as much to learn from those in Mexico and Central America as they have from the academic colonization by the United States in the past.

REFERENCES

Aguilar Fernandez, G. (1986). Compromiso docente en las escuelas de trabajo social (Faculty compromise in schools of social work). *Revista Trabajo Social, 26,* 19–29.

Aguirre Harris Rivera, Y. (1984). Caracteristicas socioacademicas de las escuelas detrabajo social en la republica Mexicana (Social academic characteristics of schools of social work in the republic of Mexico). Mexico: Universidad Nacional Autonoma de Mexico.

Alayon, N. (1982). *Las Escuelas de Trabajo Social en American Latina* (The schools of socialwork in Latin America). Lima: Editorial CELATS.

Ander Egg, E. (1985). *Apuntes para una Historia del Trabajo Social* (Sketches for a history of social work). Buenos Aires: Editorial Humanitas.

Ander Egg, E. (1989). Ques es el trabajo social (What is social work?). In Arrellano Pena et al., (Eds.). *Conceptualizacion del Trabajo Social:_Anthologia.* Mexico: Universidad Nacional Autonoma de Mexico.

Apodaca Rangel, M., Salazar Hernandez, G.,& Bautista Lopez, E. (1987). La formacion academica del trabajador social en Mexico (The academic formation of the social worker in Mexico). *Revista Trabajo Social, 31,* 1-46.

Arrellano Pena, G., Garcia Salord, S., Lazaro Jimenez, E., Modesto Martinez, S. (1989). *Conceptualizacion Del Trabajo Social: Antologia.* Mexico, D.F.: Escuela Nacional de Trabajo Social, Universidad Nacional Autonoma de Mexico.

Bustamante, M. (1987). La educacion popular en Centro America (popular education in Central America). *Nuevos Cuadernos, 12.* Lima: Editorial CELATS.

CELATS (1989). Curricula de la escuela de trabajo social (Curricula of the school of social work). In Arrellano Pena, G., et al., (Eds.). *Conceptualizacion del Trabajo Social: Anthologia.* Mexico: Universidad Nacional Autonoma de Mexico.

Culturgram for the '90s: Republic of Costa Rica. (1991). Provo, Utah: Brigham Young University, David M. Kennedy Center for International Studies.

Culturgram for the '90s: Republic of El Salvador. (1991). Provo, Utah: Brigham Young University, David M. Kennedy Center for International Studies.

Culturgram for the '90s: Republic of Guatemala. (1991). Provo, Utah: Brigham Young University, David M. Kennedy Center for International Studies.

Culturgram for the '90s: Republic of Honduras. (1991). Provo, Utah: Brigham Young University, David M. Kennedy Center for International Studies.

Culturgram for the '90s: Republic of Mexico. (1991). Provo Utah: Brigham Young University, David M. Kennedy Center for International Studies.

Culturgram for the '90s: Republic of Nicaragua. (1991). Provo, Utah: Brigham Young University, David M. Kennedy Center for International Studies.

Culturgram for the '90s: Republic of Panama. (1991). Provo Utah: Brigham Young University, David M. Kennedy center for International Studies.

Curricúla de la Escuela de Trabajo Social. (1991). (Printout) Juarez: Universidad Autonoma de Ciudad Juarez.

Donaire, A. et al., (1985). El taller rural como modalidad pedagogica en la formacion de trabajadores sociales (The rural setting as a pedagogical model for the formation of social workers). *Nuevos Cuadernos, 8.* Lima: Editorial CELLATS.

Estruch, J. (1989). El status de la profesion y su evolucion futura (The status of the profession and it future evolution). In G. Arellano Pena, G. et al. (Eds). *Conceptualizacion del Trabajo Social: Antolog*(Conceptualization of social work: an anthology). Mexico Universidad Nacional Autonoma De Mexico, pp. 165–166.

Fioriani Martini, A. & Salazar Hernandez, M. (1986). Nuevas opciones actualizacion en trabajo social (New options of actualization in social work). *Revista Trabajo Social, 26,* 1-8.

Garcia Salord, S. (1990). La especificidad del trabajo social (The specificity of social work). In *Antologia de Mujeres Universitarias.* Mexico: Universidad Nacional de Mexico.

Hill, R. (1989). Los objectivos comunes del servicio social. In G. Arellano Pena et al. (Eds.). *Conceptualizacion Del Trabajo Social: Antologia* (Conceptualization of social work: an anthology). Mexico: Universidad Nacional Autonoma de Mexico, pp. 237–256

Kiserman, N. (1989). Etica profesional y servicio social (Professional ethics and social service). In Arellano Pena et al., (Eds). *Conceptualizacion del Trabajo Social: Anthologia.* Mexico: Universidad Nacional Autonoma de Mexico.

Martin-Baro, I. (1985). El trabajo social salvadoreno: situacion y actitudes (Salvadoran social work: situations and attitudes). ECA, (*XL*), 229–240.

Mendez, M., Flores, M., & Amaya, J. (1985). Reflexiones sobre trabajo social hondureno (Reflections of Honduran social work). *Nuevos Cuadernos, 8*. Lima: Editorial CELATS.

Osorio, R.(1986). Costa Rica: los grupos autogestionarios de mujeres como alternativa de empleo y organizacion y participacion popular. In *Anales III Encuentro de Trabajo Social en la Unidad Latinoamericana: Estrategias de Sobrevivencia y Participacion Popular*. Lima: Editorial CELATS.

Palacios, H. (1985). Algunas reflexiones acerca de la practica academica de la carrera de trabajo social (Reflections of the academic practicum of the field of social work). *Nuevos Cuadernos, 8*. Lima: Editorial CELATS.

Rangel Guerra, A. (1978). *Systems of Higher Education: Mexico*. New York: International Council for Educational Development.

Rodriguez, R. & Tesch, W. (1978). *Organizaciones profesionales del trabajo social en America Latina* (Professional organizations of social work in Latin America). Lima: Editorial CELATS.

Torres Diaz, J. (1987). *Historia Del Trabajo Social*. Buenos Aires: Editorial Humanitas.

Torres Torres, F. (1986). La profesionalizacion y el imperismo del trabajo social (The profesionalization and empiricalization of social work). *Revista Trabajo Social, 25*, 37–56.

Van Soest, D. (1991). Twinning projects. *The Child Family Well-Being Development Education Project Biannual Newsletter*, February, p. 18.

Universidad Nacional Autonoma De Mexico (1982). *Escuela Nacional de Trabajo Social*. Mexico: Secretaria de Rectoria, Direccion General de Orientacion Vocacional.

Zellin, A. & Tick, P. (1990). Nicaragua: social problems and community solutions. *The Child Family Well-Being Development Education Project Biannual Newsletter*, February, pp. 12–13.

4

SOUTH AMERICA

Rosa Perla Resnick

INTRODUCTION

The idea of including the Latin American countries in this book is a most welcome development, particularly with reference to social work education systems, where a number of interesting innovations have emerged during the last decades. Some of these have proved to be attractive to American social work educators, an extremely important characteristic in today's world, when interdependence between and among countries is being recognized as a fact of life, and repeated calls for introducing international perspectives into social work education in the United States are made from all quarters (Sanders & Penderson, 1984; NASW/CSWE, 1988-1991).

This chapter deals with social work education in South America, comprising the thirteen countries from the Panama Canal to the Straits of Magellan in the South Atlantic. Mexico and Central America are examined in another chapter. It will not be an attempt to write a study of social work education in all of South America, still less is it intended as yet another summary of social work education therein. These tasks have been well performed already (ALAETS, 1971, 1977; Almeida, 1978; Brant & Faleao, 1979: Freire, 1970, 1973; Gutierrez Merino, 1990; Kendall, 1978; IASSW, 1974, 1975, 1977, 1982, 1984, Molina,. 1992; Resnick, 1976; Resnick, 1980: 123–129; Rodriguez & Telsch 1978; *Selecciones de Servicio Social*, 1975; Stein, 1973; Stickney & Resnick, 1974; United Nations, 1970, 1971; Wolfe 1972). This chapter will instead describe and try to explain as far as possible the changes which have occurred over time as well as current trends in social work education in that part of the world.

In making this attempt we have to draw upon the socioeconomic and political material relevant to present the scenario in which social work education has emerged and developed during the last eight decades. The aim is to paint the main outlines with a broad brush, and to introduce sufficient factual detail to demonstrate the nature, interconnections and significance of the changes described and their impact on social work education.

BACKGROUND

Historical Notes

More consideration will be given to the Southern Cone countries of Latin America—Argentina, Brazil, Chile and Uruguay, where this author has worked and taught for many years. References will also be made to the others on the continent, where she has been involved in research projects and consultation assignments.

It is important to have an understanding of the cultural traditions in Latin America to gain a perspective not only on why social work education is as it is, but on the complex problems of reconstructing both social work education and society. As Alberto Lleras Camargo (1952/1954), the former scholar president of Colombia, has stated:

> Latin America was in the past, and continues to be, the product of the systematic transplantation in the sixteenth century of the cultural and political forms of Spain and Portugal,...including the hardest and most flexible form of government, the most authoritarian bureaucracy. (Leras Camargo, 1952-1954)

Because the cultural foundations of the Latin American republics stem from the culture of the Iberia peninsula at the time of its greatest influence, it is easy to see why Hispanic Iberian was, and largely still is, as monolithic as the autocratic regimes which were replaced by even more autocratic Iberian regimes.

Currently, in C. Wright Mills's use of the phrase, the "power elite" consisting of landowners, industrialists, clericals and the military are not very eager to change a social system which has been and is working directly for their benefit.

Current Socioeconomic and Political Conditions

The last decade has brought democratic regimes to most Latin American countries. However, as was widely reported in the media, an international economic report found two years ago that Latin America was almost falling apart (Wojtinsky, 1989). What was neglected was a massive deterioration of the area's infrastructure in the first half of the 1980s. As indicated in the report, the overall cost was incalculable. Just repairing the roads, for example, may cost $6 billion—more than twice the sum of foreign investment in the region in 1987. Without rapid changes, the economic erosion could spark political upheaval and scare away investors just when they are needed most. Social tensions in several countries have already begun to emerge as a result of debt and mismanagement.

The region's $100 billion collective IOU piles up $100 million in interest charges each day—then, there's capital flight, estimated at $300, billion from several countries. Resolving the debt crisis will not be enough—the region's fledgling republics require massive investment and fiduciary economic reform. More and more, their leaders recognize that they have few choices. Countries in Latin America have already begun to embrace market mechanisms in a way they have not in twenty-five or thirty years. Argentina, Mexico and Venezuela are the leaders along these lines (Brooke, 1993).

Now is the time for a response from the industrialized world. It was the creditor nations that encouraged Latin America to become more market-oriented, holding out the promise of rewards and understanding if they complied. Thus far, the creditors have failed to live up fully to the deal, bringing about much uncertainty and uneasiness in most of South America.

A most recent publication may be one of the most comprehensive single documents concerning the current socioeconomic political situation in the Latin American continent. It states the following:

> In 1985, four out of ten Latin Americans—163 million—were living below the poverty line. For 1990 the UN Project to Overcome Poverty estimates that they will be 204 million, 4.6%, concluding that poverty has become the principal cause of death in Latin America, quoting Peter Townsend as saying: "Poverty kills. This is not a political or social commentary; it is a scientific fact." (Kligsberg, 1989)

Latin Americans want a drastic change in both social and economic conditions. They are confronted with the dilemma of having revolutionary or evolutionary change. The experience of many countries in the area—Allende's Chile and Frondizi's Argentina—has been agonizing and frustrating.

Current trends are toward privatization of industries and services through foreign investment. However, it is apparent that even though some countries fare better than others in pulling out of poverty, the lowest income populations remain as poor as ever. The process has just begun and it is too soon to tell whether its outcome will be successful for all. As recently reported, "In Brazil economic growth projected at about three percent this year is hampered by a lack of trust in the government." (Brooke, 1993a)

Poverty has always been the basic milieu in which social workers in South America and, for that matter, in all of the developing world had to work.

As I have written elsewhere, Latin American is considered part of this underdeveloped world along with the countries of Asia and Africa (Resnick, 1980). However, the three areas cannot be grouped together indiscriminately. As the Brazilian economist Celso Furtado points out, Latin American development is distinguished by two unique factors: (1) it has a "peculiar" dependency on the United States, which has erroneously identified U.S. security with Latin American development; and (2) in contrast to Asians and Africans, fresh from the recent achievement of national political independence, Latin Americans have seen the rise of military dictatorships and have a consciousness, as Furtado (1970: 61–74) sums it up, of "living through a period of decline." This different historical condition, in Furtado's view, has generated a great difference in psychological attitudes. While other Third World peoples express optimism as to their future self-determination, Latin Americans, particularly the younger generation, are rebellious, and, above all, skeptical of developmental promises. It is clear to them that importation of new technology has not guaranteed the concomitant growth of social and political institutions designed to meet the needs and aspirations of the popular classes (Myrdal, 1973).

Another view which emphasizes the historical and political obstacles to development in Latin America is that of Gunnar Myrdal (1973: 73–75). "Before World War II," says Myrdal, "there had been a long colonial era of unawareness and poverty in all the underdeveloped countries of the world, when the big powers dominated and imposed their beliefs and value systems on their colonies." Colonization, in Myrdal's theory, gave rise to indigenous protest. This protest became an essential part of the basic doctrine of the new states formed at the conclusion of World War II. In Latin America, in particular, which had been politically independent long before the war, nationalist sentiment was directed against both foreign economic domination and its accompanying political influence. Moreover, many Latin Americans today support the view that without liberation from foreign control, underdevelopment cannot be overcome, and until it has been overcome the central problem of abolishing mass poverty and achieving justice can never be solved.

In the real world, poverty has always been the setting where social workers in South America and, for that matter, in all of the developing world had to work. The 25th International Congress of Schools of Social Work, held in Lima, Peru, had poverty as its central theme, and most papers dealt with related topics from different national perspectives (Campfens, 1992).

SOCIAL WORK IN LATIN AMERICA

As these views indicate, it is extremely difficult to talk about either social work in the Third World or even "Latin or South American social work." Nevertheless, in spite of the differences among countries, social work in Latin America has historically had a common denominator. Practice and education for the profession were first imported from Europe and later from the United States. For a decade now, countries have also shared in the search for more indigenous approaches to the solution of human and social problems in their areas. This philosophy is reflected in the thinking and writings of many social workers in most of the Latin American countries (Almeida, 1978; Brant & Faleao, 1979; Corney, 1992; Freire, 1978; Gutierrez, 1990; Junqueira, 1980;

Kendall, 1978; IASSW, 1974, 1977, 1982, 1984, Molina, 1992; ALAETS, 1971; Resnick, 1980; Rodriguez & Telsch 1978; *Selecciones de Sericio Social*, 1975; ALAETS 1977; Stein, 1973; Stickney & Resnick, 1974; United Nations, 1970, 1971; Wolfe, 1972). They were disappointed and frustrated that there was little they could contribute to improve social conditions, given the economic and political constraints in their countries. When important and decisive political and social changes took place in that part of the world (e.g., the continuing spread of military regimes, the Cuban revolution, the emergence and failure of the Alliance for Progress, the rise and fall of the Allende government in Chile), social workers began to realize that the prevailing remedial and even preventive approaches they were using were not effective enough to cope with the huge problems they confronted in their everyday work. Therefore, they began to search for new approaches to their developmental needs that would be more responsive to the socio-economic and political problems prevalent in their countries. They were not happy with either development projects established by international organizations or national programs subsidized by foreign capital, because the whole notion of "developmentism" made them feel extremely uncomfortable. As Prebisch has stated:

> While those who mistrust developmentalism do not deny the value of technology as a means of freeing mankind from the age-long burden of heavy labor, the subordination of the human factor to technology causes them extreme concern. Prevalent among them, too, is the idea of genuinely national effort incompatible with old or new forms of dependence, in economic affairs as in intellectual life and cultural patterns. (Prebish, 1970: 18–19)

Therefore, social workers in many countries of Latin American rejected the concept of "developmentalism" because it implied dependency and began using a new idea, "transformation," to explain social change. They saw this change not only in the structure of society and its social institutions, but also, and most importantly, in people's minds.

The renowned Brazilian educator Paulo Friere (1969; 1970) has stressed the need for transformation within individuals if true development is to occur in a given society:

> There is development only when the decision of the transformation that is taking place is found within the subject. And this does not happen in dependent societies, societies that are objects, societies that are alienated. These are simply modernized, since their point of decision—political, economic, and cultural—is outside themselves, in the society upon which they depend economically. (Freire, 1969: 4)

All of these ideas about the real transformation of society—conceived independently of foreign models—have resulted in efforts pursued in many Latin

American countries to develop new approaches, methodologies and strategies in social work. These efforts as a whole have been called the "reconceptualization of social work." The full meaning of this important movement cannot be explored here, given the limited space for this chapter, but more elaboration will be offered in the discussion of current trends.

SOCIAL WORK EDUCATION IN SOUTH AMERICA

Historical Notes

The first South American school of social work was created in Santiago de Chile in 1925 by Alejandro del Rio, an outstanding Chilean medical doctor, with the help of Rene Sand, a Belgian physician who gained worldwide recognition as a pioneer in social work education. Other schools followed soon thereafter in Argentina and Uruguay, but growth was rather slow. By 1937 only those three Latin American countries had schools of social work, but after World War II, more schools were founded throughout the South American continent (Solomon, 1937).

During their first fifteen years, the schools in Chile, Argentina, and Uruguay had a predominantly European influence. 16) However, as early as 1940 the head of the Office of International Relations of the Untied States Children's Bureau, Elizabeth S. Enochs, established contact by visiting different schools of social service in Latin America. Upon her return home, she prepared a report pointing out many positive features of the schools, as well as the need for additional social service training in Latin America. As a result, in 1941 the American Association of Schools of Social Work and the Children's Bureau invited fifteen directors of Latin American schools of social service to visit the United States (Escuela de Servicio Social, 1941).

Soon thereafter, the Inter-American Conference of Social Service was established, and after the First Pan-American Congress of Social Service was held in Chile in 1945, curricula and much of the definition of the social worker's role were shaped by the United States's influence. During the deliberations, groups of delegates from the United States Children's Bureau and faculty members of the National Catholic School of Social Service, who lectured on social group work at several schools, were instrumental in shaping up basic educational frameworks for social work training in the Latin American continent (Escuela de Servicio Social, 1946).

The translation of many social work books and other teaching materials into Spanish and the exchange of faculty and students with schools of social work in the United States resulted in a marked influence on Latin American social work education during the decade of the 1950s. For example, *Estudio de la Communidad* by Caroline Ware (1948) introduced the community as a subject to the schools in Latin America and almost became the Bible for their study of this subject (Ware, 1948). Seminars directly sponsored by American schools and the United States government as well as the United Nations and the Organization of American States influenced and gradually superseded the role once played by European countries.

This trend followed World War II when United Nations experts, many of whom had American background and education, visited various Latin American countries to advise schools of social work in the creation of new programs that would be more conducive to the developmental plans formulated by several national governments. However, although the goals were developmental, the "new" approaches to social work education placed emphasis on what was then current in the U. S. schools—that is, full-time theoretical-practical education at the postsecondary or university level, intensive fieldwork in the three basic methods of social work (casework, group work, and community organization) with some application of the complementary teaching methods (supervision, administration, and consultation), and a thesis for graduation.

The social change and development that Latin America has been experiencing since 1960 have brought about a serious reconsideration of the social work professional role in confronting current social problems and individual needs.

The conceptual and practice framework of social work in Latin America had its origins in the highly industrialized countries, where the profession responded to very different social conditions and relationships. Borrowing these conceptual bases and their associated practice was inevitable when social work was beginning in Latin American. Within a different cultural and social milieu, however, the concepts assumed different meaning, practice produced different effects, and institutions worked in different ways. The transplantation of these concepts and professional practice was further affected by the human, economic, and institutional resources available for their functioning. For them to acquire meaning, concepts and practice had to harmonize with the political aspirations of the people and with the needs toward which those aspirations were directed. The growth of social work in Latin America should have been accompanied by an evaluation in concepts and practices, bringing it closer to regional value premises, to problems and needs as they were understood, and to the existing social institutions and resources.

There has been some progress toward this objective. In the daily task of trying to apply what was learned in school, in foreign experience, and in foreign books, social workers adapted, experimented, and recast.

In the process of experimenting with and adapting foreign methods to the local scene and discovering their underlying universal and scientific basis as well as their translatable and transferable properties, social workers began to recognize the profession's new perspectives (United Nations, 1971). They had known frustration with their first failures; their concern for the future of social work was shared by colleagues of the southern countries in Latin America (Argentina, Chile, Brazil, and Uruguay); and they knew of the dire need to respond to the ongoing economic and social crises that those countries were facing. All this led the most dynamic and ambitious professionals to develop a new concept for the practice of social work. Their purpose was to use social work as a tool for social development, for social change, in a process of conscientization, or raising awareness, so-called conscientizing that would enable individuals, groups, and communities to build a new society in their old countries.

This generation of social workers took a fresh look at social work. In the process they did not dismiss the foreign theoretical-practical model, but considered the local reality and the global framework of underdevelopment in the countries in which they were working. Using an indigenous approach, they began to create and experiment to determine how the social work profession could meet current social challenges and local crises in each country. This was the generation that in the early 1960s capitalized on its feelings of frustration and disappointment by introducing changes in social work education and practice, particularly in field instruction, approaches to learning and teaching, practice concentration, and didactic materials.

Thus, social work experienced the ideological impact of these trends. For years, Latin Americans had been taught that social work should not be related to political ideas. This severely limited social workers' actions even though their work with individuals, groups, and communities made them aware of the factors that clamored for a more substantial form of change within the economic, social, and political structure of society. Social workers were employed by public and private institutions and organizations, and by sectarian welfare agencies (mainly Catholic) that were following the paternalistic patterns of their conservative founders.

A number of important political and social changes took place in Latin American countries—the rise and overthrow of dictators, the Cuban revolution (1953), the Alliance for Progress (1960), and the emergence of the Allende regime in Chile (1970). Slowly social workers who favored the idea of social change, though they were not able to decide whether the change should be through reform or revolution, emerged. A number of young students and social work practitioners seemed much more radical in this respect.

A publication by the United Nations reported the following:

Other reactions to frustration and insecurity, now prominent in the schools of social work and among professionals, should be more instrumental for the formulation and applications of coherent social welfare polices. Social work, and consequently social welfare, must be freed from dependence on imported conceptions and techniques; it must further revolutionary change in social structures and power relationships, rather than limit itself to helping its clienteles to function better with a non-viable social environment. (United Nations, 1971: 271)

All the factors mentioned have produced a tremendous impact on Latin American thinking about social work. During the last decades, many professional groups throughout Latin America have been talking about the reconceptualization, retheorization, and reformulation of social work.

The conflict was recognized in 1965 when a new generation of social workers emerging in Brazil, Uruguay, and Argentina sought new approaches to their developmental needs that would be more in accord with their own socioeconomic and political conditions. They pointed out that although certain universals contribute to shape social work as an international profession, important prevalent differences apply to a culture-oriented field like social work, in which the national society is itself the main variable. The idea of identifying and including in social work the knowledge and understanding of the cultural patterns and value systems of the different countries was widely acknowledged, thus implying that the indigenous component should occupy a significant place in the educational curriculum.

The Reconceptualization of Social Work as an Indigenous Approach in Latin America

After the first Latin American Regional Seminar of Social Work was held in 1965 in Porto Alegre, Brazil, where the revolutionary role of social work was established, others followed throughout South America with the goal of looking for new perspectives for the profession. At the second seminar, held in Montevideo, Uruguay, the following year, the emphasis on the ideological dimensions of social work emerged very strongly in the paper "Ideology and Social Work" by Herman Kruse. By the time of the 1969 seminar in Caracas, Venezuela, the reconceptualization of social work had emerged as a continental movement (Stein, 1973; IASSW, 1975; Resnick, 1976).

Currently there are still about fifty professional groups throughout Latin America who are discussing this issue. Although their views are not always similar, they are linked by a like interest in finding a theory that can provide them with a more appropriate framework for their professional role.

Two basic schools of thought can be identified: the functionalist and the historical-materialist. According to proponents of the former, social workers should be educated to contribute to the development of their countries and to social equilibrium by attempting to eliminate social problems and dysfunctions. Professional action is based on knowledge provided by the social sciences, seeking an integration of theory and practice through the casework, group work, and community organization methods, whether separately or in an integrated fashion.

Proponents of the second approach explain social change by the contradictions in society. The position was also inspired by the ideas of Father Gustavo Gutierrez Merino, a highly respected Peruvian priest, known for his writings on liberation theology, who in his paper delivered at the 25th Congress of the International Association of Schools of Social Work, Lima, Peru, 1990, defined "the role of social work to help the poor overcome their oppressed and marginal condition," because "poverty is not only shortage—the poor not only lack things, but are also capable of doing things—they have a creative capacity" (Gutierrez Merino, 1990). In this philosophy the concept of praxis—the need to establish a theory–practice–theory continuum—has a central place. The method adopted should allow students or practitioners to know and understand a "social reality" and should stimulate the utilization or creation of their own instruments for the desired transformation. Consequently, the method cannot be a rigid one with only general application.

This second school of thought is based on the theory of conscientization, borrowed from the field of adult education, where it was developed by the Brazilian educator Paulo Freire. The establishment and implementation of conscientization within community development projects in Latin American education provided social workers with the inspiration and encouragement to incorporate its principles into their own professional endeavors.

Conscientization implies "an awakening of consciousness," a change of mentality involving an accurate, realistic awareness of one's place in nature and society; the capacity to analyze its causes and consequences critically, comparing them with other situations and possibilities; and a logical action aimed at transformation. Psychologically, it entails an awareness of one's own dignity (Freire, 1970, 1973).

The goal was to help people become aware (conscientized) of underdevelopment and to build new societies in their old countries. Schools of social work were the settings in which this process began to take place. The schools re-examined their objectives, functions, and curricula, searching for a way to implement the basis of the newly reconceptualized social work theory and practice.

The thrust of this new approach was most thoroughly developed in the Chilean schools during the Allende era, but has been spreading to other Latin American countries, depending on the political regime.

Recent Developments

In 1969, when the process of reconceptualization received its first theoretical formulation at the Catholic University in Chile, most of the Latin American schools have been experimenting and gaining experience with these new approaches, with variations on the emphasis and method depending on the individual, social, political, and economic conditions of their countries. All of them were involved in the search for a theoretical framework for social work practice, specifically trying to separate themselves from what they regarded as "the Western model" of social work, which is identified as the U.S. system prevalent in the 1940s through the early 1960s when the civil rights movement also began to influence social work in this country. This model was viewed as being focused too strongly on both the individual and remedial approaches, giving insufficient emphasis to those social problems of a mass nature that are predominant in Latin America and other developing countries around the world.

It is important to note, however, that although Latin Americans have not entirely dismissed some of the imported models using basic principles of the casework relationship, and group dynamics and group work concepts—they are still attempting a meaningful synthesis of their innovative and distinctive approaches after over ten years of investigation and experimentation (Almeida, 1978; *Selecciones de Servicio Social*, 1975).

New forms of social work practice have been experimented with in Argentina, Brazil, Chile, Colombia, Mexico, Peru, Uruguay, and other countries during the last decade. Interesting illustrations came from the Sixth Latin American Seminar of Schools of Social Work held in the Dominican Republic in July 1977, where a school from Bolivia reported on social work intervention at a mining company, with students helping miners to understand the principles of popular education, conscientization, and participation in community work (IASSW, 1977). In Colombia students were doing fieldwork in labor relations and community development projects; in Mexico they were involved in low-income housing projects; and in El Salvador they were placed in labor unions and villagers' organizations. These experiences, in turn, had a great impact on the educational curricula of schools of social work (Stickney & Resnick, 1974). New strategies for working with the poor, the illiterate, the unemployed, the rural populations, and the victims of natural disasters have brought about many innovative approaches to social work education in those countries in relation to curriculum development and content: interdisciplinary collaboration, educational methodologies, and the unique role of the social worker in transforming social structures, sharing in the development of social policies and developing grass-roots people's institutions for popular participation (IASSW, 1977).

The reconceptualization of social work is still a continuing process and no definitive model has yet been established. Countries are following different patterns, placing emphasis on what they call the scientific, methodological, ideological, and political aspects of the model in their respective attempts at finding conceptual innovations. Until recently, it appeared that there has been preference, in most of the Latin American countries, to include ideological-political components at the heart of the reconceptualization process as the organizing principle for the regenerated theory and practice of social work (IASSW, 1974, 1984). Because of this, the profession has tended to become politicized. This tendency has been considered to be the Latin American contribution to international social work. However, in 1980-81 this author, while on a teaching/consultation assignment in schools of social work in Chile, Argentina, Uruguay, and Brazil, found like Wolfe (1972) that there seemed to be some lessening of political emphasis in social work education, and more attention to theory building and the development of new practice.

Current Trends

The *World Guide to Social Work Education* (IASSW, 1974) presents very comprehensive information on seventy-nine schools around the world, nineteen of which are in Latin America. It also presents material on the Latin American Association of Schools of Social Work and the Regional Association of Schools in the area.

A superb analysis of that material was done by Katherine A. Kendall, who analyzed trends in the five continents on a comparative basis. About Latin American schools, Dr. Kendall writes:

> The value of solidarity appears frequently in Latin American materials. Excerpts from the entry for Peru serve as well as an illustration. The point is strongly made that "society is based on human solidarity and cooperation." Emphasis is placed on "what men should be" rather than on what "men should have." This value points to the necessity of changing "all those structures which limit man's self-realization...." It calls for the creation of a true community of people working together in trust and unity. Authenticity has emerged as a significant new value to be achieved through professional education. In Latin America, this seems to embrace a new freedom from imported ideas about social work education and practice. (Kendall, 1978: 161).

With regard to qualification and duration of training we read:

> The most significant change in qualifications and duration of training has occurred in Latin America. Until the mid and late nineteen-fifties, two- or three-year programs leading to diplomas, certificates, or titles were the prevailing pattern. Integration of these programs into universities has led to the extension of social work education from two or three years to four, four and on-half, or five years, with many of the programs leading to the university degree of licenciado." In Latin American and Continental Europe, the concept of different levels of social work education has not yet taken hold to the same degree as in the other regions, although there is now a definite trend in a number of Latin American and European countries to develop postgraduate or advanced training leading to a higher qualification. (Kendall, 1978: 159)

It should be noted that in Latin America the educational system is generally not organized according to the American designation of graduate and undergraduate education. It is offered at the elementary and high school levels and at universities. These programs range from four to seven years of study depending on the degrees granted. A doctoral degree requires completion of a written dissertation and its oral defense before a faculty committee, but no course work.

Currently, doctoral degrees in social work are offered in Argentina and Brazil, and in other countries only as part of sociological studies. At present, a Latin American magister in social work is granted by the Autonomous University of Honduras for professionals from Central America and the Caribbean. An Integrative Seminar in Porto Alegre is currently planned for social work educators of four countries of MERCOSUR (Argentina, Brazil, Uruguay, Paraguay and Chile), which together have more than one hundred schools of social work and over thirty-thousand students. The Mercosur Treaty of Argentina, Brazil, Uruguay and Paraguay is a multilateral trade compact. South American nations have greatly reduced tariffs and other barriers among themselves, leading to a rapid expansion in regional trade. The program will include teaching methodology, production of educational material, research on common problems, continuing education, and systematic and regular exchange of teachers and students.

The following paragraph describes very well the faculty and students of Latin American schools:

Although the data suggest that Latin American schools rely more heavily on part-time faculty than schools in other parts of the world, the conclusions drawn must be tempered by knowledge of work habits and patterns in that region. It is accepted practice for professional people to hold more than one job. Each job would be classified as part-time, but in fact could be practically full-time in terms of work produced. A comparison of teaching hours in Latin American and North American schools of social work might indeed reveal very little difference in the time spent in the classroom by the part-time Latin American and full-time North American faculty member. Students frequently work while attending school and, although both activities are part-time, they are frequently seen and classified as full-time students. (Kendall, 1978: 167)

Dr. Kendall's Analysis reveals that

research is another troublesome area in which there is considerable ambivalence...(which) can be seen in the objectives as well as in the nature of the learning experiences that are provided. Insofar as one can sense any special direction, the present trend seems to be that of preparing students to be consumers of research and not producers. As specific research instruction is reduced, declarations arise that all instruction in social work is or should be research-based, thus providing students with a more meaningful research experience than special courses in statistics or research methods. We shall have to await the outcome. Schools of social work in some parts of the world may actually be the best source of certain kinds of social data which are produced through student projects and thesis. Let us hope those schools, at least, will realize that unless some social welfare research is produced in their countries, there may be little research for students to consume. (Kendall 1978: 166)

A revised edition of the *World Guide* was published in 1984, containing material on seventy-four schools around the world, eleven of them in Latin America (IASSW, 1984).

A cursory comparison of the two editions shows that no major changes were made during the decade that separates them. It is interesting to note, however, that in the most recent edition there appears to be a stronger emphasis on courses dealing with national issues, humanistic values and professional ethics, philosophy and science, and a critical review of teaching and working methodologies.

Data indicate that there is a renewed interest in the "integrated method" for social work practice, where there is a greater emphasis on developmental matters than on remedial approaches. Ideological and political issues continue to be at the core of all the curricula either openly or in a sub rosa fashion. It appears, however, that translating this theoretical knowledge into the fieldwork experience is not an easy process. Schools are still struggling in most countries to do so by programming field instruction both in traditional settings—hospitals, schools, homes for the aged and community centers—and in newer ones such as industries, cooperatives, social promotion and social action centers, community development projects with marginal populations through grass-roots organizations or more formal social welfare agencies responsible for helping rural migrants in their resettlement efforts around urban centers. In this connection the *favelas* in Brazil, the *cantegrills* in Uruguay and the *villas de emergencia* in Argentina have become very dramatic and challenging fieldwork placements in those countries.

The research study as Escuelas de Trabajo Social en America Latina presents an analysis of forty-six schools from thirteen countries in one area, revealing similar findings—there is an interesting conclusion regarding the developmental focus of many schools identified as the newest approach based on ideas for social reform and social action (Alayon, 1982). But there is also the notion that the remedial approach is still prevalent, and that traditional agencies still offer good learning experiences to students. This view relates to the criticism expressed by the author regarding the fact that the schools that were teaching the reconceptualized social work were having serious problems along fieldwork lines. Agencies were unable to provide placement to students coming from those schools. There appeared to emerge a clear mismatch between theory and practice.

Little by little social work educators teaching the new approach realized that no matter how important and interesting it had become, in most cases, it was too idealistic an approach to be applied to the real world and that they had to return to more conservative models (IASSW, 1982, 1984).

Notwithstanding those views, the prevalent current thinking among Latin American social workers strongly supports the notion of change in social, economic and political structures, and in social work practice and education, in order to make a solid contribution to that goal. At the 26th International Congress of Schools of Social Work (Washington, D.C., July 1992), Seno Cornely, who gave the Eileen Younghusband Memorial Lection at that event, indicated in his emotional tribute to Dame Eileen that "she was identified with a humanistic kind of Social Work addressed to meet the real needs of real people." He speculated about which would be Dame Eileen's views had she been alive today, and concluded the "she would conceive social work's mission as justice not charity: as a struggle for workers' rights rather than favors from the State...and should include individual work, community development and political action." These, in Cornely's view, have been the inspiring principles for social workers in Latin America in their struggle to apply them to their professional activities (Cornely, 1992).

At the same Congress, Maria Lorena Molina, the president of the Latin American Association of Schools of Social Work, evoked similar themes in her position paper by first reviewing the dire poverty and concurrent crises in Latin America and blaming the social, economic and political systems for causing and failing to solve them (Molina, 1992).

Molina presented a set of recommendations for social work university faculty, which summarize professional current convictions on the continent. Paraphrasing her Spanish speech, she proposed that university professors commit themselves to

1. develop teaching as an emancipating practice
2. strengthen the schools and universities as democratic institutions
3. recover a community of progressive values by sharing with social movements and institutions
4. speak up against economic, political and social injustice, both within and outside the classroom; create appropriate conditions for students to get adequate knowledge and values in order to commit themselves to the search of human development with equality, without discrimination regarding diversity.

In short "the pedagogical and administrative tasks in our schools should be spaces for teaching–learning on human rights because here is where human hope rests, as well as the upbuilding of what today seems to be a Utopia." She ended her presentation by indicating that "we must persevere in the search to put together a good combination of the transforming spirit and the clarity to preserve whatever safe we now have."

Various trends emerging from the Proceedings of the International Congresses of Social Work Education held in the last decade, including the 27th Congress in Amsterdam (July 1994), present a diversity of ideas:

1. Social work education in Latin America should address the need to consciously study professional problems—both educational and methodological—to contribute to the liberation of humankind as a subject of their own destiny.

2. Latin American social welfare policies on health, housing, education, family, children, working natives in rural areas and Indians should be studied and developed by schools in terms of the "reality" of each country, and with an interdisciplinary approach. Depending on each country's state of social, economic and political development social welfare education systems have varied from a traditional philosophy to a progressive one, bringing about an ample spectrum of practices and programs. Coordination and integration of new forms of teaching and practice with existing forms are advocated.

PROFESSIONAL ORGANIZATIONS

For a few decades there has been throughout the region a strong movement toward professionalization and the definition of professional status by law. In some countries, the professional organization has legal personality and the qualifications, responsibilities, and privileges of the professional are defined. Chile's Colegio do Asistentes Socialies is an example of a highly developed professional organization which is incorporated and provides protection similar to that of a trade union.

The regulation of social work as a profession may be perceived as clannishness, with some justification. However, its valid purpose is to ascertain the competence of the social worker, to establish uniform standards of practice, to provide leadership, and to ensure mobility to the professional within the country.

In recent years, ALAETS has published a report on a research study it conducted, "Professional Organizations of Social Welfare in Latin America," which appears to be the first and only one done so far on this topic (Rodriguez & Tesch, 1978).

There is a striking contrast between the high status of other professions, (i.e., in law and medicine) and the lower status of social work in South American societies. In the author's view various factors account for the difference: social workers have less power and very weak impact on society; have lower income; do not hold higher level social welfare positions in government and are predominantly women. There are professional associations of social workers in most of the South American countries, but it appears that they have no political influence as such and are not actually functioning as unions to protect social workers' rights, except in Brazil, where there are over eleven professional organizations in the most important cities, Rio de Janeiro, Brasilia, Sao Paulo, Porto Alegre and Belo Horizonte.

Very few countries have a law for professional practice. Argentina, after many years of struggle and debate, passed National Law 23.377 in 1988 "to protect professional social workers and to ensure them with the maximum guarantees and freedom for professional practice as well as to protect the community from professional malpractice." The law also creates the "Professional Association of Graduates in Social Service and Social Work, whose responsibility shall be to govern professional credentials and practice and which will be incorporated as a professional corporation." All professional social workers in the country are mandated to become affiliated to the association in order to practice professional social work; "otherwise they would be subjected to disciplinary actions." This law is applicable to all of Argentina, Antarctica and isles of the South Atlantic, which are considered to be part of Argentinean territory by its national government.

In spite of this apparent progress, a word of caution is in order as political changes in South American countries often bring about correlative changes in the educational and professional systems. Social work education and the practice have always been among their most important targets because of the nature of the profession's mission and its impact on society.

It is important to note that the Latin American Association of Schools of Social Work is the only body affiliating schools of social work in Latin America. It was established in 1965 as an outgrowth of the II Pan American Congress of the Conference of Social Work. An example of what may occur under changing political conditions is found in the Chilean experience. After the September 1973 coup d'état all universities and graduate departments (particularly in the social sciences) were closed while the authorities sifted out supposed left–wing extremists and Marxist courses. Schools of social work were especially hard hit in this purge: many of their faculty were ousted, and others resigned voluntarily. The few who were allowed to stay were requested to formulate a totally revised social work curriculum along traditional lines of study. For a full account of these developments see the "Editorial" and "Parte del Documento Basico de la Restructuracion de la Escuela de Trabajo Social de la UC" (Part of the Basic Document to Restructure the School of Social Work). *Trabajo Social*, is published by the School of Social Work, Catholic University of Chile, Sasilla 114D, Santiago, Chile.

ALAETS has the following objectives:

1. Encouragement of relationships and coordination of programs among the schools of social work in Latin America, with the goal of establishing consistency in the basic theoretical and practical components of social work education

2. Promotion and coordination of relationships among the schools and the associa-
    tions of schools of social work and with existing associations of social workers in
    each country
3. Promotion of a greater understanding of social work as a profession
4. Encouragement of the creation of associations of schools of social work in Latin
    America
5. Support and defense of schools and associations of schools of social work, when
    necessary

Membership

Schools of social work and national associations of schools of social work in
Latin America can be members of ALAETS. To become affiliated to ALAETS,
schools must (1) have a recognized university level and (2) grant a recognized
university degree. At present ALAETS has 141 member schools of a total of
235 existing on the continent. It has six national associations representing
twenty countries.

CONCLUSION

1. On the basis of the preceding discussion, it appears that in Latin America there
    has not yet emerged a clear-cut and unique profile either of social work as a pro-
    fession or of social work education. Presumably, this is due to the frequent
    changes and diversity in the circumstances of the various countries in the region.
    This influences the professional philosophy, methodology, and actions as well as
    the educational objectives and teaching/learning modalities undertaken by the
    schools to fulfill their mission.
2. The theme of poverty and the need to free people from oppression are recurrent
    issues for teaching and learning in schools of social work to this date.
3. There is a demand for the development of new theoretical frameworks for social
    work practice and for social work policy formulation to respond adequately to the
    constant emergence of new problems in South American societies and, for that
    matter, in all Latin American countries, as well as the increasing expectations of
    their populations.
4. There is a call to accept existing forms of social organization (health, education,
    family, children, the aging) but also to create new ones leading to more active
    participation, novel methodologies, and, above all, professional intervention in
    new sectors committed to reviewing their social responsibilities and translating
    them into social action.
5. Future changes in social work education in South American (Latin America),
    where most countries are currently enjoying elected albeit weak democracies,
    cannot be predicted because political ideologies are generally the final determi-
    nants of the nature of social work education in that part of the world.

This is the challenge for social work education in Latin America in the coming decades. Time will tell!

REFERENCES

ALAETS. (1971). *Report of the "Third Seminar" of the Latin American Association of Schools of Social Work.* Quito, Ecuador.

ALAETS. (1977). *Papers from the Sixth Seminar of Latin American Schools of Social Work,* Santo Domingo.

Alayon, N. (1982). *Las Escuelas de Trabajo Social en la Argentina.* Buenos Aires: Editorial Humanities.de Almeida, Anna Augusta. (1978). *Possibilidades e Limites da Teoria do Servico Social.* Rio de Janeiro: Livraria Francisco Alves Editora S. A.

Brant, Maria do Carmo. & de Carvalho, Faleao. (1979). *Servico Social: Uma Nova Visao Teorica.* Sao Paulo, Brazil: Cortez e Moraes.

Brooke, J. (1993). Inflation saps Brazilians' faith in democracy. *The New York Times,* July 25.

Campfens, H. (Ed.). (1992). Poverty and interventions: special issue. *International Social Work, 35* (2).

Carrasco Reyes, E. (1987-1989). *La Formacion de los Trabajadores Sociales en America Latina,* Nuevos Cuadernos. Lima: CELATS.

Cornely, J. S. (1992). En la Busqueda de Caminos Para el Manana (Conferencia en Memoria de Eileen Younghusband). XXXVIth Congress of the IASSW, Washington, D.C., July.

Escuela de Servicio Social del Museo Social Argentino. (1941). Viaje representative de ex-alummas. *Boletin del Museo Social Argentino, 79.*

Escuela de Servicio del Museo Social Argentino. (1946). Curso sobre servicio social de grupo, *Revista de la Escuela de Servicio Social de Santa Fe,* August–October.

Freire, P. (1969). (Mimeo). *Cultural Liberty in Latin America.* CICOP Conference.

Freire, P. (1970). *Pedagogy of the Oppressed.* New York: Herder and Herder.

Freire, P. (1973). *Education for Critical Consciousness.* New York: Seabury Press.

Furtado, C. (1970). U.S. Hegemony and the Future of Latin American. In Horowitz, I.L., De Castro, J., & Gereassi, J. (Eds.). *Latin American Radicalism.* New York: Vintage Books, pp. 61-74.

Gurdian Fernandez, A., et al. (1992). *Planificacion y Evaluacion Curricular en Trabajo Social.* Lima: ALAETS/CELATS.

Gutierrez Merino, G. (1990). Poverty from a liberation perspective. *Accion Critica, 28.*

Helena Iracy Junqueira. (1980). Quase duas Decadas de Reconceituacao de Servico Social: Abordagem Critica. *Servico Social e Sociedade, 4.*

IASSW. (1974, 1984). *World Guide to Social Work Education.* New York.

IASSW. (1975). Indigenous approaches to social work education, Report from Discussion Group F, *Education for Social Change: Human Development and National Progress.* Proceedings of the XVII International Congress, of Social Work, Nairobi, Kenya, July 1974. New York: IASSW.

IASSW. (1977). De Mateo Alonso, L. R., Professional education for social work: the universal and the particular. In *Social Realities and the Social Work Response: The*

Role of Schools of Social Work. Proceedings of the XVIII the International Congress of Schools of Social Work, San Juan, Puerto Rico, July 1976. New York: IASSW.

IASSW. (1982). Proceedings of the International Congress of Schools of Social Work. Brighton (1982); Montreal (1984); Tokyo (1986); Vienna (1988); selected papers from the XXVth International Congress of Schools of Social Work, Lima (1991). Published in *Accion Critica,* 1990, *28.*

Kendall, K.A. (1978). *Reflections on Social Work Education, 1950-1978.* Vienna: International Association of Schools of Social Work.

Kligsberg, B. (Compilador). (1989). *Como Enfrentar la Pobreza? Estrategias y Experiencias Organizacionales Innovadoras.* Centro Latino Americano de Administracion para el Desarrollo (CLAD) y Programa de las Naciones Unidas para el Desarrollo (PNUD). Buenos Aires: Grupo Editor Latino Americano.

Leras Camargo, A. (1952-1954). The to Americans. *The Lamp,* March 1952-November 1954.

Mardones de Martinez, L. (1957). *Estudio de Tres Escuelas de Servicio Social en America Latina.* Washington, D.C.: Pan American Union, Department de Asuntos Economicos y Sociales.

Molina, M.M.L. (1992). La Asociacion Latino-Americana de Escuelas de Trabajo Social en el Panel Interregional Congreso Mundial de Escuelas de Trabajo Social. XXVth International Congress of the IASSW, Washington, D.C., July.

Myrdal, G. (1973). *Against the Stream.* New York: Random House, pp. 73–75.

National Association of Social Workers/CSWE. (1988-1991). Child and Family Well Being Development Educational Project. Washington, D.C.: p. 30.

Prebish, R. (1970). *Change and Development: Latin America's Great Task.* Washington, D.C.: Inter-American Development Bank, pp. 18-19.

Resnick, R.F.P. (1976). Indigenization of social work: conscientization and social work in Chile. Doctoral dissertation, Yeshiva University, New York.

Resnick, R.P. (1980). Social work education and social development: the Latin American experience. In *Discovery and Development in Social Work Education.* Proceedings of the XIX International Congress of Schools of Social Work, Jerusalem, August 14-18, 1980. Vienna: International Association of School of Social Work.

Rodriguez, R. & Telsch, W. (1978). *Organizaciones Profesionales del Trabajo Social en America Latina.* Lima: Ediciones CELATS.

Sanders, D.S. & Pedersen, P. (Eds.). (1984). *Education for International Social Welfare.* Manoa: Hawaii School of Social Work and the CSWE.

Selecciones de Servicio Social. (1975). *8* (26).

Solomon, A. (1937). *Education for Social Work: A Sociological Interpretation.* Zurich: Verlag fur Rochfund Gesellschaft, A.G. Leipzig.

Stein, H.D. (1973). Cross-national themes in social work education: a commentary on the sixteenth IASSW Congress. *New Themes in Social Work Education.* Proceedings of the XVth International Congress of Schools of Social Work, The Hague, The Netherlands, August 1972. New York: IASSW.

Stickney, P.J. & R.P. Resnick. (1974). (Comps.). *World Guide to Social Work Education.* New York: International Association of Schools of Social Work.

United Nations. (1970). *Social Change and Social Development Policy in Latin America.* New York: United Nations, p. 271.

United Nations. (1971). Training for social welfare: fifth international survey. In *New Approaches in Meeting Manpower Needs.* New York: United Nations, p. 48.

Ware, C. (1948). *Estudio de la Comunidad.* Washington, D.C.: Pan American Union.

Wojtinsky, W.S. (1958). *The US and Latin American Economy.* New York: Tannimet Institute and Library, p. 12.

Wojtinsky, W.S. (1989). Reward pragmatism in Latin America, Down and Out in Latin America, *Business Week,* July.

Wolfe, V.A. (1972). The dilemma of Latin American social work. In *Les Carnets de l'Enfance.* Bellinzona, Switzerland: UNICEF, pp. 29-42.

5

ARGENTINA

Irene Queiro-Tajalli

HISTORY OF SOCIAL WORK EDUCATION

The roots of social work education in Argentina are closely tied to universities and institutes of higher education, unlike the early educational developments of social work education in the United States of America, where the first schools were part of private social services (Trattner, 1989). One predecessor of the first professional school in Argentina was the two year program of social hygiene visitors begun in the School of Medicine at the University of Buenos Aires in 1924. The graduates of that program not only were concerned with hygiene issues of the poor, but were also to be the link between physicians and patients and between social problems and health problems. This educational program was similar to those in other countries of Europe and the Americas. In 1940, the program was changed to a three year program, and currently it is a four year program that grants a degree in social services and health.

In 1927, the Ministry of Justice and Public Instruction sent a number of its representatives to Europe to study the educational programs and institutions of social services. As a result, a project to create the first National School of Social Service was submitted in 1928. The objectives of this school were to provide technical and administrative education to young people who wanted to work in human service organizations and further educate nurses, hygiene visitors and those already working in social services. Unfortunately, this project was not approved by the legislators.

Paralleling these government efforts, some educators were interested in the creation of a social services program in the Argentine Social Museum, founded in 1911, which was based on the Social Museum of Paris. In 1928, the executive committee of the museum approved a proposal to create the School of Social Service, and in 1930 it was added to that institution's educational programs. This program offered the first professional social work curriculum. It was a two year program and the admission requirements included being eighteen years of age or older, having two references who would address the personal qualities of the candidate, and having completed at least primary education or being an employee of a social service organization. In 1938, the educational plan was revised and the program became a three year program. The courses offered by the school included psychology and abnormal psychology, social medicine and social hygiene, economics, law, social services and practicum.

When the museum became a private university in 1956, the School of Social Service began to offer a four year degree and a five year doctorate in social services, the first in Latin America. Graduates of a three year social work program were eligible to apply to the doctoral program and complete two additional years of social work education. The curriculum was composed of thirteen courses, of which only three were social work-specific. This degree is no longer offered. Currently, the four year curriculum includes thirty-five courses, of which fourteen are in social work. It is interesting to note that students must complete four practicum courses in the following sequence: working with individuals, working with groups, working with communities, and, concurrently with the community work practicum, taking another practicum course in research methodology. Also, students complete a monograph on a social service–related area. They can also complete a fifth year and receive a degree similar to a master's of social work.

The School of Social Work at the University of Buenos Aires was initially related to the Patronage of Imprisoned and Formerly Incarcerated Women, which was created in 1933 to defend and provide social assistance to indicted women. In 1941, the Argentine School of Assistants for Minors and Penal Assistants was created; later it was named the Argentine School of Social Assistants. At the time of its creation, the school offered a two year program, and admission required a high school diploma. The curriculum included three courses in law-related areas, one in psychology, one in pedagogy, and one in psychopathology.

In 1946 the school was placed under the umbrella of the School of Law and Social Sciences, University of Buenos Aires. The curriculum was revised and new courses were added without changing the length of the degree. In the years that followed, the educational program was changed from a two year program, to a three year program, to a four year degree. Because of its place within the university structure, the School of Social Assistants was for many years influenced by the School of Law, both in its curriculum as well as in its administration. As a result, the school did not have the desired autonomy to realize its objectives until 1985, when it became an independent unit reporting directly to the university. A new reorganization took place at the university level, and, since 1988, the school functions as an independent unit within the College of Social Sciences of the University of Buenos Aires and offers a five year degree. In 1989, the number of students in the school was approximately eleven hundred, and it was the third largest within the College of Social Science after Sociology and Communication Science (Toto, 1989). The current director is a social work educator, highly committed to a social work education that prepares professionals to face the role demands generated by the sociopolitical and economic realities of the country.

Even though it is no longer in existence, it is worth noting the historical developments of another school of social work under the auspices of the National Ministry of Social Assistance and Public Health. In 1957, the government asked the United Nations to provide guidance in social work education. That same year Valentina Maidagan de Ugarte, a Chilean social work expert, was sent to Argentina to study, reorganize and coordinate the educational programs of the schools of social work in Argentina. The findings of her investigation indicated that the educational programs had considerable variations, that some of them offered few social science courses, and that, in general, most were greatly influenced by other disciplines. The latter is not surprising, considering that the beginnings of social work education were spearheaded by medical doctors, lawyers and other professionals. Alayon (1980) indicates that Maidagan de Ugarte made significant recommendations such as encouraging the development of a strong social work faculty who would take responsibility for the educational curriculum as well as of an extensive group of field instructors to provide field education. She advised that social work education take place at the university level only, and that human service organizations be engaged in the educational process as field sites. Apart from her consultant role, she taught courses for social work graduates and met with social work educators to discuss curriculum issues. Since few changes had taken place in the curricula of different institutions of social work education, the government asked Maidagan de Ugarte in 1959 to plan a school of social work that would follow the recommendations of her report. She presented a project for the creation of a school of social work, the Institute of Social Service, that was approved in mid-1959 and started functioning that same year under the leadership of a psychiatrist. Obviously, the administration of social work education was still under the influence of other professions. The institute was the first program that granted the title of social worker rather than that of social assistant to its graduates. The curriculum had a heavy emphasis on social work even though students were required to take courses in social, medical, legal, and pedagogical sciences. Students were required to complete 1440 clock hours of practica in a three year period. The practicum courses covered individual, group and community practice as well as an investigation of a social issue to serve as a basis for a final thesis. The mission from the United Nations was completed in 1960. As a result of political and institutional changes in Argentina, the institute came to an end in 1969 (Alayon, 1980).

From the early 1920s to the present the number of schools of social work has increased to sixty-two. Of these, seventeen are in public universities, five in private universities, and forty under the auspices of provincial ministries of health, education, and social action, as well as private organizations such as foundations or religious institutions (Federacion Argentina de Unidades Academicas de Trabajo Social, 1990).

CULTURES, VALUES, RELIGION AND POSSIBLE VALUE CONFLICTS

Argentina, a country of diverse native groups and immigrants, has a rich culture based on God, family, homeland and freedom. Matera and Serrano (1986) describe these four elements by saying that love for God is closely related to the Christian religion, which was brought to the land by the Spanish conquistadors and the missionaries. The family, as currently conceptualized, was developed by the Spanish and Italian groups as well as other immigrants who made Argentina their homeland. Furthermore, the concept of homeland is based on the identification process with the community where socialization takes place. The concept of freedom is closely related to the spirit of the gaucho, the cowboy of the pampas, who struggled to maintain his cultural identity and his spiritual connection to nature and who was nearly exterminated while trying to resist the foreign domination of those living in the cities. These four elements, in varying degrees of intensity, influence social work education and practice.

Social work practice was originated by charity groups, religious groups and mutual aid societies. Social welfare policies emphasize the importance of the family and try to protect its unity. At various historical points of social work practice and education, the profession has tried to delineate national approaches according to the country's social realities. Finally, freedom from oppression has been one of the goals of social work practice during certain periods of Argentine history. Needless to say, these concepts are relative and in need of reconceptualization within the profession. For example, is there a value conflict between the concept of the family as recognized by the law and studied in the social work curricula, and the various family configurations developing in society? Social work educators talk about the roots of social work being in the Judeo-Christian tradition; is there a conflict in terms of training graduates in this traditional perspective when many will be helping new immigrants with different religious or philosophical orientations? How is the concept of homeland interwoven in social work education and social work practice, when it may be experienced differently by the "haves" and the "have-nots?" Finally, the concept of freedom has been the most dramatic and challenging issue for social work educators and practitioners since the country has experienced great doses of domination by oppressive governments. Some educators question the whole concept of freedom as it relates to social work practice when the country is so immersed in its international debt, $62 billion U.S., and ruled by the economic restrictions imposed by the foreign lenders.

RANGE, STRUCTURE AND FUNDING OF SOCIAL WORK EDUCATION

Social work education takes place at two levels. One is at the university level and provides a degree in social work or social assistance that is similar (but not equivalent) to a master's degree in social work in the United States. The educational programs require a minimum of five years of study. The other level of social work education is provided by religious and private institutions and governmental organizations. Their graduates receive a social assistant degree after the completion of four years of study. Admission to these schools requires a minimum of a high school diploma. Currently, some of the schools at the university level offer specializations in postgraduate education, including family and children, social policies, mental health, and social sciences. Some of these specializations are taught on an interdisciplinary basis. All of the educational programs require a combination of theoretical and practicum courses. Variations may exist in the emphasis given to classroom teaching and field experience. Also, schools may have different ways of designing their practicum - component. For example, the School of Social Work, University of Buenos Aires, requires students to be in an agency four hours per week for two full calendar years, starting in the third year of studies. They also have a three hour weekly seminar at the school to discuss field practice with a faculty member. The School of Social Service at the University of Argentina Social Museum requires four practicum courses, one on research methodology. Research is an integral part of the educational process. The educational objectives of the research sequence include the development of skills for a systematic practice, the development of a spirit of inquiry, and development of skills to generate new knowledge to improve practice. Most social work programs require students to take a minimum of one course in research methodology; while others require several research oriented courses.

Social work education is geared to prepare the graduates to intervene at different system levels in a variety of fields of practice. Social workers have a wide spectrum of job possibilities in areas such as health, mental health, education, housing, child and family welfare, legal systems, gerontology, industrial social work and rural social work. The largest employer for social workers is the government: almost 90 percent of the professionals work in governmental institutions, approximately 5 percent are employed by private industries, and the rest work in not-for-profit organizations and labor unions (Toto, 1989). The role of the government as an employer of social workers is not surprising since it is deeply involved in the provision of social services. However, this situation may change as Argentina undergoes severe privatization of its human services.

A brief review of the social welfare system indicates that care of those in need has been the responsibility of the private and public sectors. During the colonial times, the church and other private institutions played an important role in providing social assistance to the needy. In 1823, a women's society called the Charity Society was authorized by the government to administer children's institutions, the women's hospitals and other welfare institutions serving children, women and the aged. This institution was by far the most powerful charity organization in the nineteenth century (Grassi, 1989). In 1948 the functioning of the Charity Society came to an end, and its assets became part of the National Department of Social Assistance. Apart from this charity organization there were other groups concerned with the welfare of the people, mainly the government, ethnic and religious organizations, private institutions and labor organizations. Even though the goal of these institutions was to assist those in need, they held different orientations as to whom they were to serve. These orientations ranged from that of the Charity Society of helping the "deserving poor," to that of the government of favoring universal services, to that of ethnic organizations helping immigrants from their home countries to adjust to a new environment, to religious groups developing services for the poor and other vulnerable groups in society, and to labor organizations providing social services to upgrade the quality of life of workers and their families. Throughout the years, the main service providers within this wide range of sectors have been lay volunteers, physicians, members of religious denominations, social hygiene visitors and trained social workers. Social work graduates in Argentina, as in many other countries, have to struggle to protect the domain of the profession and prevent other professionals such as psychologists or sociologists from taking the paid positions in fields of practice traditionally claimed by the social work profession. In most settings, social workers are partners of other professionals, as in community services, income maintenance programs, group and youth services, child welfare and aging. In other settings, such as medical and corrections, social workers provide supportive services as a secondary discipline.

Funding of Education

Argentina has a long tradition of free public education at the preschool, elementary, secondary and university levels. Expenditure on education by the central and provincial governments totaled 3081m australes in 1986 (1 austral = 0.94 U.S. dollar). In the 1993 national budget, 1243m pesos (1 peso = $1.00 U.S.) were devoted to finance national universities. This budget has left administrators, professors and students highly dissatisfied since it barely meets the urgent financial needs of higher education. Social work education, like other curricula, is free in the national universities and those sponsored by government units at the provincial level. Traditionally, the national universities have had the reputation of providing high quality education. However, because of the economic crisis of the government for a number of years, the resources allocated to higher education have diminished considerably with the inevitable result of damaging the quality of education. At the same time, many private universities are providing solid education and attracting a large number of students who are concerned about the national universities, being destabilized by economic forces and political ideologies. Currently, the discussion about funding for higher education centers around whether or not college education should be free. This discussion raises a number of significant questions yet to be answered by educators, policymakers, students and others. They must carefully analyze the ramifications of supporting the current system of free education at higher levels of funding or encouraging the development of a more extensive private system of higher education, philosophical conceptualization of higher education, the degree of accessibility of education to all economic classes, the quality of education, the kind of professionals the country wants to have, and the affordability of either system are just a few of the areas in need of careful scrutiny.

STATUS OF SOCIAL WORKERS

In general, social workers are well respected by other professionals, but the status of the profession has not achieved that of other professions such as medicine. The profession's roots in charity work, its primary mission of helping the poor and the oppressed, and its dependence on other disciplines do not help to improve the public image of social work. Furthermore, the conceptualization of social work as a "women's profession" allows society to pay lower salaries than those of other professionals and request from social workers "sacrifices, abnegation, and altruism without any demands" (Alayón & Grassi, 1986: 62).

DESCRIPTION AND EVALUATION OF ARRANGEMENTS FOR GATEKEEPING TO THE PROFESSION

In order to apply for admission to a social work program, candidates are required to have a minimum of a high school diploma. Other requirements depend on the specific educational institution. The profile of those who choose social work include such variables as young persons, mainly women, from the middle and working classes, who are not always clear about the purpose of the profession or convinced that it is the right career choice. Other students are motivated to enter social work because of their political or philanthropic orien-

tations or their religious affiliations (Federacion Argentina de Unidades Academicas de Trabajo Social, 1990).

Social work education does not have its own accrediting body like the
Council on Social Work Education (CSWE) in the United States of America,
rather, the creation of a school is subject to governmental approval. The process
of supervision of programs within universities is the responsibility of that
institution. Private schools are supervised by the National Institute of Private
Education.

However, a number of professional organizations have as their mission the
support and enhancement of the profession. In 1948 the first Federation of Social Assistants was created by the Italian social assistant Carmen Bellavita
(Alayon, 1980). Among the objectives of this organization were the promotion
and improvement of social work education. The membership of this organization was composed of individuals rather than organizations. In 1967, a number
of social work leaders began to plan for another federation, that was officially
incorporated in 1969. This federation consisted of social work associations,
rather than individual social workers. This federation ceased to exist in 1972
with the withdrawal of one of its main organizations. During its existence, the
federation promoted the creation of social work associations in various parts of
the country and dealt with labor-related issues faced by social work practitioners. Currently, there exists a strong federation of social work organizations
which provides leadership and guidance in the field of social work.

The profession is regulated by certification in most provinces of the country.
The general purpose of this regulation is to protect the social work title. Only
those trained in social work can call themselves social workers/social assistants.
National law 23.377 (Consejo Professional de Graduados en Servicio Social o
Trabajo Social, 1989) regulates social workers in the nation's capital, the national territory of Tierra del Fuego, Antarctica and the islands of the South Atlantic and those working in federal institutions. It recognizes social work
practice as that professional activity of education, promotion, prevention and
assistance geared to addressing situations of impoverishment, social disintegra-
tion or disorganization experienced by individuals, groups and communities as
well as those activities that only require advice or motivation to utilize potential
resources to a maximum. Supervision, consultation, research, planning and
programming are also considered components of social work practice. Finally,
social workers can be engaged in institutional practice as well as private or non-
agency-based practice. According to National Law 23.377, certification is
granted by the Consejo Profesional de Graduados en Servicio Social y Trabajo
Social, one of whose objectives is to provide consultation to social work programs regarding their educational training. Another important function of this
organization is administering disciplinary action to those social workers who are
found to be unethical or incompetent to practice social work. The disciplinary
actions range from alerting the professional about unsatisfactory practice

activities, to fines, to suspension of certification, to withdrawal of certification. Overall, certification recognizes the practice of social work at the micro, mezzo and macro levels, as well as agency-based and non-agency-based practice. The latter is quite significant since historically social work has been closely related to agency-based practice. This type of legislation favorably impacts the education and practice of social work by raising the status of the profession to that of other professions.

RELATIONSHIP BETWEEN GOVERNMENT ORIENTATIONS AND EDUCATIONAL PLANS

Social work education has been impacted by the ideologies of those persons in control of the country during different historical periods. Furthermore, social work education and social work practice have evolved according to the socioeconomic realities existing in society. As previously mentioned, the first school of social work was created in 1930 under a conservative government and the thrust of professional education was to teach students to intervene at the individual level, with an emphasis on helping the person to adapt to the environment. Social work education was greatly influenced by the medical profession, which was in need of assistance regarding the social conditions of poor patients and the lack of health education in many communities. Charity organizations, functioning with the help of female volunteers, were an important source of assistance to the needy, and therefore an early conception emerged from this, that social work was a women's profession. This conception was also supported by the traditional view of social workers as trained female volunteers, as suggested by the fact that the first graduates of the School of Hygiene Visitors in the School of Medicine at the University of Buenos Aires in the 1920s were integrated into the labor force as volunteers (Alayón, 1980). In the 1940s, the curricula of many schools of social work continued to be influenced by medical and legal education institutions, since many of the schools were under the auspices of those disciplines and a significant number of the graduates were mainly employed in the health and legal arenas. The schools maintained their curricula primarily focused on the individual. In the late 1940s and 1950s, the programs were influenced by the North American models of individual, group and community approaches. Argentina, like many other Latin American countries, experienced the formation of two parallel societies, a modern, urban, consumer-oriented society, and another one suffering from anomie, lack of development, supposedly resistant to change. The members of this disadvantaged group were excluded from mainstream society. They were the farmers, indigenous people and those dwelling in slum areas: in sum, the poor people of the social system (Alayón, 1989). In order to integrate these people into the modern, industrialized and capitalist sector, the government began to use community development projects without challenging the presence of oppressive elements in the fabric of the society. Obviously, this approach was palliative and fell short of positive results for those living in poverty. By the mid-1960s, the climate in Argentina, as in many other Latin American countries, was rapidly changing in a quest to eradicate oppressive social conditions. The ideologies promoting these changes were many. Among them were the messages from the Vatican Council (1962–1965) II, liberation theology and Paulo Freire's method for teaching literacy through consciousness-raising. Briefly, Vatican Council II (1962–1965), called by Pope John XXIII, had far reaching ramifications in the church and the work of thousands of Roman Catholic nuns, priests and lay activists. As Berryman (1987) says, "Far more important than any of its particular decisions was the fact that the council led Latin American Catholics to take a much more critical look at their own church and their own society. Not only did they seek to adopt the council to Latin America, they began to ask Latin American questions" (p. 17). Latin American liberation theology developed in the 1960s, partly as a response to the political, cultural, economic and religious crisis in that part of the Americas (Ellis, 1988). Berryman (1987) defines liberation theology as "an interpretation of Christian faith out of the experience of the poor. It is an attempt to read the Bible and key Christian doctrines with the eyes of the poor" (p. 4). Furthermore, "it is at the same time an attempt to help the poor interpret their own faith in a new way" (p. 5). The Brazilian educator Paulo Freire, in the late 1950s and early 1960s, developed a method of teaching literacy to the peasants through consciousness-raising. His model, based on Christian concepts, includes the recognition of the unification process of knowing and praxis, a denunciation of a society divided between oppressor and oppressed, and *conscientizacao* as a technique of intervention. By the late 1960s the universities became highly politicized and an incredible amount of power was given to students. Students requested greater participation in the development of curricula and in the administration of institutes of higher education. They were interested in open universities, and in curricula that would identify with the national characteristics and realities of the country rather than with the forces of "foreign colonization." It is within this sociocultural political context that during the mid-1960s and early 1970s the social work profession was reconceptualized to denounce the forces of institutional oppression unequivocally and to seek new approaches to intervene in society according to its socioeconomic realities. The process of reconceptualization emerged in Brazil, Argentina, Chile, Colombia, Peru and Uruguay and extended to other Latin American countries (Palma, 1977).

It seems appropriate here to present briefly some of the conceptual work developed by social work educators during that period. Natalio Kisnerman (1975) wrote, on the basis of his work with Argentine rural workers, that given the socialization process experienced by members of the working class by the ruling class, they were not prepared to question the inhuman societal conditions to which they were subjected. As they became conscious that their oppressive reality was the result of a class phenomenon, they would take action to change their situation. Kisnerman added that the focus was not merely to become aware of one's reality, but also to assume the responsibility of working toward social change. Women, a key group in the process of liberation, were to be integrated into workers' organizations, since they were closely related to the production market while working side by side with men in the fields. Kisnerman conceptualized social work as an educational process of developing a critical and objective posture about the causes and effects of oppression, and the available solutions to produce structural modifications. This educational practice was to target the relationship of the oppressed to the socioeconomic, cultural and political systems. In sum, social work practice was to strengthen those organizations of the working class which struggle against the colonization of the capitalist class.

Another well-known Argentine educator, Sela Sierra (1984), reviewing social work practice and education between the mid-1960s and mid-1970s, indicated that during the reconceptualization period, Latin America stopped searching for answers from Europe and the United States of America and engaged itself in the discovery of its own authentic potential to become a free continent. It is within this sociopolitical context that social work left its traditional and conservative ways of helping people to adjust to the environment to become autonomous in its orientation and in its interventive modalities to liberate the oppressed. In one of Sierra's presentations in 1976 (Sierra, 1987), she summarized her conceptualization of social work as a change process seeking the humanization of social conditions and a progressive social liberation. Social work practice was to emerge from a thorough understanding of the social reality through the critical analysis of that reality. This humanizing process was to develop from a sincere dialogue between the professionals and the disadvantaged, where both entities were equal partners in the change process. Furthermore, the process required social equality where people would participate in the efforts to create a just society, as well as in the benefits of those efforts and in the distribution of resources, including power. Thus, social work was seen as a professional commitment that transcended the importance of life itself. Sierra (1987) indicates that the reconceptualization period was influenced by Paulo Freire's idea of the person as being capable of reflection, criticism, dialogue, creativity, solidarity and both social and political commitment. Many authors throughout Latin America used Freire's conceptualization to define social work. Palma (1977), indicates that in the results of documentary research done by the Instituto de Solidaridad Internacional based on papers presented in a number of conferences held by that institute between 1969 and 1973, of the 122 documents reviewed, 30 (24.6 %) showed the clear influence of Paulo Freire's work. Furthermore, other documents were clearly based on his work regarding anthropological philosophy.

The work of these writers and others was well known to social work educators, and the impact of their ideas was felt in the restructuring of educational plans. Many schools changed their educational programs to reflect the nationalist-populist movements based on liberation theology, social action and conscientization of the oppressed. However, the reconceptualization of social work did not always develop under the auspices of democratic governments. As an example, in June 1966, the president of Argentina was ousted, the military took office immediately, intervened in the national universities and police were instructed to use force to remove from the university property those students and professors who allegedly were spreading the seeds of communism (Rock, 1989). The intervention of the universities brought about the abolition of student unions. As Rock (1985) describes the situation, "For three years students could but silently nurse their grievances in isolation. The longer their grievances accumulated, the more likely it became that a relatively trivial issue could trigger a violent response" (p. 350). By 1970, armed confrontation between guerrilla groups and the official forces of social control was a reality and the country was set for a long, horrifying journey of terrorism, counter-terrorism, riots, abductions and tortures. Within this societal unrest, student organizations became extremely active again and had strong influence in the administration of all aspects of the university life.

In 1973, the country returned to democracy to be governed by Juan Manuel Peron once more. (Peron had been president of Argentina from 1946 to 1955.) However his presidency had a short existence because he died in July 1974. Isabel Peron, who was his wife and the vice-president, became president. Civil unrest, kept under control during Peron's government, was experienced once more all over the country, and a strong wave of guerrilla attacks covered the country between 1974 and 1979. In March 1976, a new military government began to rule the country. The next years had the cruel marks of repression and violations of human rights. Between 1976 and 1979 more than twelve thousand citizens were abducted, tortured and then killed. The war against subversion was an attempt to silence the people by torturing and killing the young and the old from all socioeconomic levels. Some of the violations of human rights by the military have been captured in the novel *Imagining Argentina* by Lawrence Thornton (1988). The report from the National Commission on the Disappeared published in Spanish in 1984 indicates that very few of those who disappeared or were subsequently released from detention centers were connected with left-wing terrorist groups, whose activities were used as an excuse by the military government to destroy any political opposition. Many were blue-collar workers (30.2 %), students (21.0 %), white-collar workers (17.9 %), professionals (10.7 %) and teachers (5.7 %). Another 14.5 % comprised the self-employed, housewives, military conscripts, members of the security forces, journalists, actors, nuns and priests (Argentine National Commission on the Disappeared, 1986). As expected, there was no tolerance for the previous conceptualization of social work within the new social order. Many social work educators, as well as practitioners, were dismissed from their educational positions, persecuted, jailed, or killed, while others moved to other parts of the world. The paralyzing of the democratic institutions in society gave the opportunity for the flourishing of the most conservative perspectives within the profession. Many schools were closed, while those which remained open experienced a weakening of the educational programs. The discussion of the reconceptualization process which had taken place in the previous decade was absent from the curricula (Alayon, 1988). As mentioned by Sierra (1987), during this period the readings were highly censored and field instruction was designed far from the realities of the communities to prevent students from becoming involved in community action activities. Social work graduates were prepared to work in institutions with no training to challenge oppressive societal conditions. Like many repressive regimes that in Argentina could silence the true voices of the people temporarily, but they could not exterminate them completely nor destroy the people's ideas. In 1977, under the auspices of the national universities, all of the schools of social work but one began to meet again to reorganize the curricula. In order to not upset the mechanisms of oppression, this was done in a very careful manner. For example, students were not invited to these meetings, since they were banned from all forms of participation in the educational leadership of the universities. The work of this group was supported by international organizations such as the Council on Social Work Education from the United States of America, the Latin American Association of Schools of Social Service and the International Association of Schools of Social Work. Documento de Tandil (Sierra, 1987) was developed in 1978 to present a conceptualization of social work education based on a national educational policy with a clear vision of social work that was in accordance with Argentine values, with a deep Latin American identification and broad understanding of universal solidarity. This document had underlying themes from the reconceptualization period, but the writers were very careful in the way they expressed their ideas not to raise alarm among and opposition from the higher ranks of university authorities and the government. This document also presented a guideline for a curriculum divided into the following two areas: supported area requirements and social work courses. In the first group, the requirements covered such content as philosophy, psychology, social psychology, educational psychology, sociology, anthropology, public health, political science, social history, economics and law. The social work component included courses in social work practice such as planning and administration, fields of practice, practicum, supervision, social work ethics, professional organization and research. This document also called for a five-year educational plan. A rather courageous recommendation, considering the political situation of the country, promoted the creation of community councils which would provide an educational perspective according to the realities of the specific communities and the country. Furthermore, the

document called for the termination of the artificial dichotomy between university and community. Because of the characteristics of this document and as a way of avoiding charges against any one of the schools, its publication was the responsibility of the newly created Argentine Council on Social Service Education. This council, created in 1978 as another important outcome of those meetings, had as a main function the unification of the various schools of social work in the country. Unfortunately, the Council on Social Service Education was not seen favorably by those in power and, as a result, the members decided to stop its activities for a while. This organization initiated activities again in 1984, and in 1987, it developed into the Argentine Federation of Academic Units of Social Work. Even though the guerrillas had been exterminated by 1980, the days of the military regime were limited. A number of factors such as a weak economy, bankruptcies, an alarming increase in the foreign debt, defeat in the Islas Malvinas (Falkland Islands) in 1982 and strong pressure from human rights groups seeking justice in the name of the *desaparecidos* brought the military regime to an end. A new democratic government was elected in October 1983.

The period from 1983 to the present has been one of reorganization of social work education after so many years of military repression and governmental control of the educational plans and practice of the profession. Educators are trying to integrate the best of the reconceptualization period with the socioeconomic realities of the country. For example, Argentina has experienced quadruple-digit annual inflation and negative economic growth rates for many years with a devastating impact on the population. Currently, the government is implementing economic reforms, including privatization of state-owned companies, geared to develop economic stability, as well as to create a budget surplus to pay more than $66.3 billion in foreign debt. It is within this reality of great austerity and hardship for those most at risk that educators are delineating curricula both to prepare students to intervene at the micro level to address the concrete needs of the disadvantaged and to impact the creation of humanistic policies which take into consideration the needs and wants of those vulnerable sectors of society. There is a return to the concept of integration of theory and practice in the curriculum which was somewhat lost during the military regime for fear of promoting radical interventions by students.

EDUCATIONAL PLANS

According to the Federacion Argentina de Unidades Academicas de Trabajo Social (1990), the educational plans are divided into two distinctive groups. The first group includes those programs that have a well-conceptualized curriculum based on a broad liberal arts perspective integrated with a social work component which includes classroom teaching and field practice. Field practicum has a special place in the curriculum and students perform their practica in communities and diverse institutions. Students are expected to become involved in research activities in areas such as employment, health, education, and nutrition. The leadership for the curriculum is provided by a team of seasoned educators. The second group includes those plans that are fragmented and have no clearly articulated educational outcomes. Nonsocial work requirements are not well integrated with social work courses. In these programs there exists a division of social work practice into the traditional case, group and community approaches without a frame of reference that provides for integration. The educational thrust of some of these programs is highly influenced by disciplines outside social work. Most of the teaching takes place in the classroom and there is a very weak practicum component. Finally, in some of these programs the presence of social work faculty is very limited.

From the preceding discussion, it is clear that there is not a widely accepted curriculum policy statement that provides for the standardization of educational plans throughout the entire country.

1. This diversity within educational programs is due to the fact that social work education is offered by universities as well as educational institutions under the auspices of provincial ministries and private organizations.
2. It is the result of politics at the provincial level where the government, under the pressure of powerful groups, authorizes the opening and continuation of social work schools.
3. The situation is aggravated by the fact that the universities' budgets have been reduced as a result of the economic crises in the country.

As previously stated, one of the current debates in higher education is the place and future of public education in the restructuring of the government role in areas such as socialized education, welfare, and health.

In summary, social work education has a tradition of combining liberal arts, social work theoretical courses and field practicum. The curriculum emphasis on micro and macro interventions has depended most often on whether the generalists had conservative or more liberal orientations. Currently, educators leading social work education emphasize the importance of integrating theory and practice, the need to work at the micro and macro levels, and the necessity of interventions that respond to the socioeconomic and political realities of those being served. Once again, students are actively involved in the governing bodies of institutes for higher education, and associations within the schools, and they have created a national student federation. Undoubtedly, this involvement will enrich the efforts of the faculty in the development of meaningful social work training.

In closing, Argentine social work education has a well-qualified cadre of faculty and field instructors committed to high quality education as well as a diversified student body eager to learn and participates actively in the reconstruction of the country.

REFERENCES

Alayón, N. (1980). *Hacia la Historia del Trabajo Social en la Argentina*. Lima: Celats Ediciones.
Alayón, N. (1988). *Perspectivas del Trabajo Social,* 2nd ed. Buenos Aires: Editorial HUMANITAS.
Alayón, N. (1989). *Asistencia y Asistencialismo: Pobres Controlados o Erradicacion de la Pobreza*? Buenos Aires:Editorial HUMANITAS.
Alayón, N., & Grassi, E. (1986). *El Trabajo Social de Hoy y el Mito de la Asistente Social*. Buenos Aires: Editorial HUMANITAS.
Argentine National Commission on the Disappeared. (1986). *Nunca Mas: The Report of the Argentine National Commission on the Disappeared*. New York: Index on Censorship.
Berryman, P. (1987). *Liberation Theology*. New York: Pantheon Books.
Consejo Profesional de Graduados en Servicio Social o Trabajo Social. (1989). *Ley Nacional No 23.377 y Decreto Reglamentario 1568/88 Ejercicio de la Profesion del Servicio Social o Trabajo Social*. Buenos Aires:
Ellis, M. H. (1988). Liberation theory and the crisis of western society. In Rubenstein. R. & Roth, John K. (Eds.). (1988). *The Politics of Latin American Liberation Theology*. Washington, D.C.: The Washington Institute Press.
Federacion Argentina de Unidades Academicas de Trabajo Social. (1990). *Aproximaciones a un diagnostico de las UnidadesAcademicas de Trabajo Social*. Argentina.
Grassi, E. (1989). *La Mujer y la Profesión de Asistente Social-El Control de la Vida Cotidana*. Buenos Aires: Editorial HUMANITAS, pp. 2-3.
Kisnerman, N. (1975). *Practica Social en el Medio Rural*. Buenos Aires: Editorial HUMANITAS.
Matera, R. & Serrano, M. (1986). *Cual es el Futuro del Pais de los Argentinos?* Buenos Aires: Plus Ultra.
Palma, D. (1977). *La Reconceptualizacion, una Busqueda en America Latina*. Buenos Aires: ECRO S.R.L.
Rock, D. (1985). *Argentina 1516-1982 from Spanish Colonization to the Falklands War*. Berkeley, California: University of California Press.
Rock, D. (1989). *Argentina 1516-1987, Desde la Colonizacion Espanola Hasta Raul Alfonsin*. Buenos Aires: Buenos Aires S.A.
Sierra, S. (1984). *De Colega a Colega, Testimonio de una Asistente Social*. Buenos Aires: Editorial HUMANITAS.
Sierra, S. (1987). *Formando al Nuevo Trabajador Social*. Buenos Aires: Editorial HUMANITAS.
Thornton, L. (1988). *Imagining Argentina*. New York: Bantam Books.
Toto, O. (1989). *Boletin de Informaciones*, No. 3, Universidad de Buenos Aires, Facultad de Ciencias Sociales.
Trattner, W. (1989). *From Poor Law to Welfare State: A History of Social Welfare in America* 4th ed. New York: The Free Press.

II

EUROPE

6

EUROPE

David Kramer and Hans-Jochen Brauns

SOCIAL POLICY IN THE EUROPEAN COMMUNITY AND THE SCOPE OF THIS SURVEY

A survey of social work education in Western Europe must be viewed in relation to the development of social policy within the European Community. This may at first glance appear paradoxical, since social policy is still a relatively underdeveloped area among the concerns of the European community and also because a number of Western European states are not even members of the Community at the present time. Thus some explanatory comments are called for.

From the signing of the Rome Treaty establishing the European Economic Community (EEC) on March 25, 1957, the focus of the community has been overwhelmingly economic and political. Social questions have consistently been subsumed under these broader categories or relegated to the margins of public attention. Article 123 of the Rome Treaty established the European Social Fund (ESF) as an instrument "to improve employment opportunities for workers in the common market and to contribute thereby to raising the standard of living. ...It shall have the task of rendering the employment of workers easier and of increasing their geographical and occupational mobility within the community" (Leonard, 1988: 113). In other words, this instrument, which has been described as being "at the center of the EEC's social policy" (Leonard, 1988: 113), is directed primarily at the labor market and regional development.

The White Paper of 1985, in which the EC Commission proposed an agenda of measures aimed, as its title indicated, at "Completing the Internal Market," also had little to add on the subject of social policy beyond the admonition that "the interests of all sections [of the economy] ... should be incorporated in the policy of the health and safety of workers" (Calingaert, 1988: 46). The Single European Act, which came into force on July 1, 1987, replaced the principle of unanimity in decision making with the more flexible doctrine of qualified majority in a number of areas, but excluded social policy from the less-stringent procedure (PROGNOS, 1991: 11).

In recent years a number of papers, meetings and working groups have pushed for action on a "social agenda." In 1989, these efforts culminated in the "Charter on the Fundamental Social Rights of Workers," which was adopted by eleven members (excluding Great Britain) not as a binding law, but merely as a political declaration. Aside from a rather vague statement that those who are excluded from the labor market should be provided with maintenance support consistent with their personal circumstances, this document was also directed primarily toward the social rights of the employed.

Thus we have the peculiar situation that at this time of rapid progress toward a single European market and growing political unity among member states, the rudimentary development of social policy at the European Community level contrasts sharply with the advanced level of social policy in a number of member states. Since, however, social work in the various national contexts often has more to do with those persons excluded for whatever reason from the labor market than those participating in it, it is not surprising that social work practice and social work education reflect national laws and guidelines more strongly than the still inchoate shadows of European Community social policy.

Nevertheless, the economic success of the EC, together with the progress toward a single European market and the collapse of Soviet hegemony in Eastern and Central Europe, have led to an unprecedented attraction the community among its nonmember neighbors. Even convinced "neutral" states such as Austria, Sweden and Switzerland either have petitioned for admission or are seriously considering the idea. The centrifugal pull of the EC on all states which are geographically or politically part of Western Europe (and even beyond) simply can no longer be ignored.

For the purposes of this survey of social work education in Europe, we have decided to include the twelve members of the EC (Belgium, Germany, Denmark, Spain, France, Great Britain, Greece, Italy, Ireland, Luxembourg, the Netherlands and Portugal) together with the following nonmember states: Austria, Switzerland, Iceland, Norway, Sweden, Finland and Turkey. We recognize that the arguments for leaving Finland and Turkey out of such a survey are perhaps nearly as compelling as those which can be made for inclusion, but we decided to include them anyhow. With the exception of the former German Democratic Republic, which, of course, is now incorporated in an expanded Federal Republic of Germany, we have excluded the former Communist states of East and Central Europe; we have also decided to exclude the former Yugoslavia, both on the grounds of its former communist orientation and because it is no longer a single state.

In 1986, the present authors edited a comprehensive description of social work education in Europe (Brauns & Kramer, 1986), which included chapters on each of the nineteen countries in the present survey, plus Israel and Yugoslavia. Persons seeking greater detail on specific cases are referred to this volume. A disclaimer is in order: while we have made some effort to update the information in the present survey, it was not possible to reconfirm all the information from our previous work.

SOCIAL WORK EDUCATION WITHIN THE NATIONAL SYSTEMS OF EDUCATION

In all countries under consideration, the education of social workers takes place within the tertiary system of education and mostly at the undergraduate level. Ireland and Great Britain offer the possibility of a (first) qualification in social work also for graduates and nongraduates. Belgium, France, and the Netherlands offer highly specialized courses of study (Luxembourg, too, which has no schools of social work of its own, has licensing regulations which favor the highly specialized courses offered by most of its neighbors). In all the other countries, students receive a generic qualification which formally qualifies them for the wide range of social work practice. However, this is the result of a long and controversial process which has led from specialization to greater generalization (see Table 6-1). Germany, Ireland and Great Britain adopted the generic approach rather recently, and the issue is still quite controversial.

Table 6-1
Specialization and Central Regulation of Training*

		Generic	Central Regulation	
			Type	Body
A	(Austria)	yes	Regulation	Education
B	(Belgium)	no	Regulation	Education
CH	(Switzerland)	yes	no	no
D	(FR Germany)	yes	no	no
DK	(Denmark)	yes	Regulation	Legislation
E	(Spain)	yes	Regulation	Legislation
F	(France)	no	Regulation	Legislation
GB	(Great Britain)	yes	Accreditation	CCETSW
GR	(Greece)	yes	Regulation	Education
I	(Italy)	yes	no	no
IRL	(Ireland)	yes	Accreditation	CCETSW
IS	(Iceland)	yes	no	no
L	(Luxembourg)	no	Regulation	Health
N	(Norway)	yes	Examination	RSU
NL	(Netherlands)	no	Regulation	Government
P	(Portugal)	yes	Regulation	Education
S	(Sweden)	yes	Regulation	Education
SF	(Finland)	yes	Regulation	Legislation
TR	(Turkey)	yes	Regulation	YÖK

    *   For the sake of convenience, our tables use the abbreviations of international automobile registrations.

Four countries do entirely without centralized supervision of social work education (Germany, Iceland, Italy and Switzerland). Rather centralized forms of oversight exist in Ireland and Great Britain; in these countries the Central Council for Education and Training in Social Work (CCETSW) closely monitors requirements and content of courses as well as degrees and certification. Some other countries regulate social work education in varying measure through legislation (e.g., Denmark, Finland, France and Spain), while still others (Austria, Belgium, Greece, Luxembourg, the Netherlands, Portugal, Sweden) delegate authority for oversight to the Ministry of Education or of Health or to some other special body (Norway, Turkey). Such arrangements guarantee the comparability of courses through more or less detailed curricular regulations (e.g., France and Spain), through appointment of external examiners (e.g., Norway), or—as especially in Ireland and Great Britain—through prerequisites and criteria for courses of study and examinations, validation and recognition of degrees and professional licensing. A certain tension seems to exist nearly everywhere between centralized regulation and institutional autonomy, although the balance between the two appears to be drawn somewhat differently in every country.

INSTITUTIONS OF SOCIAL WORK EDUCATION

There are a total of at least 428 institutions offering social work education in the countries included in this survey. This figure, which should be regarded as an order of magnitude rather than a hard fact, comprises only distinct institutions, not various faculties, divisions, departments, and so on, within a single institution: that is, it ignores the fact that in Germany and Great Britain, for example, social workers are sometimes educated in more than one department of the same institution. (It also ignores the fact that higher education is in a period of reorganization in the former GDR, and it is not yet possible to say how many schools and/or departments of social work will eventually be established there.) Also not included are institutions in France and Belgium which educate for professions other than that of *assistant(e) social(e)*. Thus we are aware of at least 160 educational institutions in France which offer various specializations within the social professions, but only 52 of these are included in our compilation (see Table 6-2).

Table 6-2

Schools of Social Work-Demographics

	Total	Number: University	Extra	Private	Character: Public	First School
A	8	—	8	2	6	1912
B	23	—	23	4	19	1920
CH	11	2	9	9	2	1908
D	49	5	44	19	33	1899
DK	6	1	5	—	6	1937
E	28	28	—	24	4	1932
F	52	2	50	41	11	1907
GB	86	33	53	—	86	1896
GR	3	—	3	—	3	1945
I	98	7	91	86	12	1928/45
IRL	3	3	—	—	3	1934
IS	1	1	—	—	1	1981
L	—	—	—	—	—	—
N	6	1	5	1	5	1920
NL	36	—	36	36	—	1896
P	3	—	3	2	1	1935
S	7	6	1	1	6	1910
SF	7	7	—	—	7	1918
TR	1	1	—	—	1	1961
Total	428	97	331	222	206	—

Social work education is offered exclusively by publicly financed institutions in Denmark, Finland, Greece, Iceland, Ireland, Turkey and Great Britain. Dutch schools of social work are private institutions. All other countries are characterized by a mixture of private and public institutions. In some countries, private status and religious orientation are closely related. In Portugal and Spain there is a numerical preponderance of educational institutions with some affiliation to the Roman Catholic Church (in Italy the situation is in a complex state of transition, but the strong historical influence of the Roman Catholic Church is still observed). In the remaining countries, public institutions are more numerous.

The trend toward integration of social work education into the tertiary system of education—and the increased qualitative, quantitative and, particularly, financial challenges which this implies—has exacerbated the inherent difficulties of organization and funding social work education under private auspices. In some countries (e.g., Germany), private institutions benefit from considerable public subsidies. In general, however, the relative weight of private institutions has declined with the "academization" of social work education. This process is well under way in Greece; similar developments seem likely in Italy and Spain.

Social workers are educated exclusively at universities in some countries (Finland, Ireland, Iceland, Spain, Turkey). In others they are educated both at universities and in other types of institutions (Denmark, France, Germany, Italy, Sweden, Switzerland, Great Britain). But only in Sweden and Great Britain are university and extra university education accorded a status which is ostensibly equal. In a number of countries social work education takes place exclusively in extra university institutions of higher education (Austria, Belgium, Greece, the Netherlands, Portugal).

In several countries, the situation can be described as an incomplete transition to "academization"—a transition, however, whose outcome is still not entirely certain. Most common is the type of independent institution offering only courses in social professions (Austria, Belgium, Denmark, France, Italy, the Netherlands, Norway, Portugal, Switzerland). Otherwise, social work education is offered as one option among several in a university or extra university setting.

Relatively small institutions with one hundred to two hundred or even fewer students are widely typical of social work education (Austria, Belgium, Denmark, Finland, France, Ireland, Italy, Norway, Spain, Switzerland, Great Britain). In Greece, Portugal, Sweden and Turkey, the institutions have approximately double this number of students. Germany and the Netherlands are unusual in that some of their institutions (or faculties) of social work education encompass more than five hundred—and sometimes as many as one thousand or more—students.

Not all institutions of social work education enjoy rights of autonomy and self–government with respect to decisions on personnel, academic questions and finances. Autonomy appears to be greatest where the courses are offered at universities. In countries where they are offered in institutions more or less resembling the secondary school system, there often seems to be a lack of the characteristics of academic freedom (Austria, Belgium, Denmark, France). The possibilities for research also vary greatly according to national settings. The trend toward academization here also appears to be dominant. In most countries, research is now included in the legal mandate of social work education (Finland, Germany, Greece, Ireland, Iceland, Portugal, Norway, Sweden, Great Britain). However, social work research is still in its infancy,or, at least,it often falls far short of meeting qualitative expectations.

It remains the exception that postgraduate and doctoral courses are offered by institutions of social work education (as distinct from neighboring disciplines such as "educational science," sociology or psychology).

Table 6-3

Characteristics of Schools of Social Work

	Student Body	Academic Autonomy	Independent Department	Research	Task MSW	DSW
A	100	no	I	no	no	no
B	200	no	I	no	yes	no
CH	60–200	yes	both	no	no	no
D	150–1200	yes	both	yes	no	no
DK	100–300	yes/no	I	no/yes*	no	no
E	100–500	yes	D	no	no	no
F	100–200	yes/no	both	no/yes*	no	no
GB	40–150	yes	D	yes	yes	yes
GR	300-600	yes	D	yes	no	no
I	20-240	yes	both	no/yes*	no	no
IRL	50-100	yes	D	yes	yes	yes
IS	60	yes	D	yes	no	no
L	—	—	—	—	—	—
N	150	yes	I	yes	yes	no
NL	300-1600	yes	I	no	no	no
P	260-400	yes	I	yes	no	no
S	400-600	yes	D	yes	no	yes
SF	60-450	yes	D	yes	yes	yes
TR	640	no	D	no	yes	yes

*"yes" restricted to university institutions

THE NATURE OF SOCIAL WORK EDUCATION

Despite being anchored in divergent national legal and social systems, social work education in all countries under review evinces certain similar structures, which often produce quite similar problems (see Table 6-3). The basics of the social sciences and of the national legal and administrative system are taught everywhere. Likewise, the organization, professional fields of activities and methods of social work are on every national training agenda. Finally, complementary disciplines such as statistics, empirical social research and foreign languages have their place in most national curricula. Characteristic of social work education is a considerable amount of variation in the length, organization, timing and supervision of the placements. However, the rule seems to be that at least one-third of the training for social work should be in placement; only Denmark and Austria require somewhat less. The basic training of social workers lasts for three or four years. However, Great Britain and Ireland also offer one and two year courses for postgraduates and a two year diploma course for nongraduates with appropriate job experience.

In some countries, the education of social workers rests upon a rather long tradition. The first courses were instituted prior to World War I in Austria, France, Germany, the Netherlands, Sweden, Switzerland and Great Britain. Formal training began between the world wars in Belgium, Denmark, Finland, Ireland, Italy, Norway, Portugal and Spain. Greece and Turkey, where courses were first organized after World War II (see Table 6-2), were latecomers. Everywhere the scope of social work education was greatly widened after World War II in keeping with the expansion of the welfare state.

Many of the courses have been substantially reformed since 1970. Various reasons are given for the recent reforms. The need to respond to changes in professional practice seems to have been the dominant motive in Italy and Great Britain. In other countries, the reform of social work education appears to have been rather incidental to a comprehensive reform of the educational system. Often, the reforms seem to have started at the organizational or institutional level without really penetrating to questions of content; this seems to be the case in Germany, Greece and the Netherlands.

Table 6-4

Characteristics of Social Work Qualifying Courses in Europe

	Duration years	Field work %	Fees*	Qualification
A	3	25	free	Diplom-Sozialarbeiter
B	3	30	5,000	Diplôme d'État
CH	3	33–50	0–6,000	Diplom-Sozialarbeiter
D	3/4	33–50	free	Diplom-Sozialarbeiter
				Diplom-Sozialpädagoge
DK	3/3.5	20	free	Socionon/Socialraadgiver
E	3	40	60,000	Diploma
F	3	50	500	Diplôme d'État
GB	4	50	free	BSW
GR	3.5	45	free	Ptychion
I	3	30	free	Diploma
IRL	3/4	50	850	Bach. Soc. Science
IS	4	30	free	Felagsradgjafi
L	4	30	—	Diplôme d'État
N	3	30	free	Socionom
NL	4	30	1,000	Diploma
P	4	40	35–60,000	Diploma
S	3.5	30	free	Socionom
SF	4	20	free	Socionom
TR	4	30	20,000	Sosyal Çalismaci

*Per year in the respective national currency unless otherwise noted.

Postgraduate Courses

The varying organization and structure of social work education within the European Community make it difficult to generalize about postgraduate qualifications (see Table 6-4 and 6-5). The following remarks are restricted to postgraduate degrees in social work, not in various related disciplines.

Postgraduate degrees are available in Ireland, some Scandinavian countries, Great Britain, Belgium, France and Turkey. An undergraduate qualification in social work or social science is a standard prerequisite for such courses. Ireland and Great Britain also require personal interviews and at least one year of professional experience for admission. In these two countries, it is possible also for graduates of other undergraduate courses to enroll in a two year course in social work; however, the professional qualification thus achieved corresponds to the standard undergraduate degree in social work. The only advanced degree in social work available in Sweden is the doctorate. Finland, Switzerland,

Ireland, Great Britain and Turkey offer the doctoral degree in addition to other postgraduate degrees.

Table 6-5

Higher Degrees and Doctoral Programs in Social Work: Admission Requirements, Degrees, Duration

	Admission Requirements	Duration	Degree	Doctor
A	—	—	no	no
B	Diplôme d'État	2 years	License	no
CH	Diplôme, License	2 years	Certificate	yes
D	—	—	no	no
DK	Diploma, 5 years	1 year	no	no
E	—	—	no	no
F	Diplôme d'État	600 hrs*	Diplôme	no
	Diplôme Universitaire	2 years	supérieur	no
	Licence	1 year	Licence	no
			Mâitrise	
GB	BSS, 1 year, interview	1 year	Master	yes
	any B, 1 year, interview	2 years	Master	yes
GR	—	—	no	no
I	—	—	no	no
IRL	BSS, 1 year, interview	1-2 years	Master	yes
IS	—	—	no	no
L	—	—	no	no
N	Diploma, 1 year	2.5 years	Master	no
NL	—	—	—	no
P	—	—	no	no
S	—	—	no	yes
SF	Y. kandidaatti	3 years	Lisensiaatti	yes
TR	Diploma	2 years	Magister	yes

*In-service training over a period of two years.

Degrees

With the successful conclusion of an undergraduate or postgraduate course of studies, the student receives certification of an academic qualification from the institution at which the course was undertaken (see Table 6-6). In some countries, where courses of differing length are offered, graduates may receive different types of certification (Belgium, Finland, France, Ireland, the Netherlands, Great Britain). In general, academic certification is equivalent to a license of professional qualification. Only a few countries require professional licensing in addition to the academic certification. As a rule, this license is granted by a government ministry (Germany, Greece, Luxembourg) or a special licensing body (Ireland and Great Britain).

Table 6-6:

Professional Qualifications in Social Work—Europe

A	Diplom-Sozialarbeiter
B	Assistant Social (because of specialization there are also other qualifications)
CH	Diplom-Sozialarbeiter, Travailleur Social
D	Diplom-Sozialarbeiter and/or Socialpädagoge (Staatliche Anerkennung)
DK	Socialraadgiver, Socionom, Socialformidler
E	Diplomado en Trabaj Social
F	Assistant en service social (because of specializations there are also other qualifications)
GB	Bachelor or Master of Social Work (Certificate of Qualification in Social Work - CQSW)
GR	Ptychion in Social Work (License)
I	Diploma d'assistente sociale, Diploma universitario di servizio sociale
IRL	Bachelor/Master of Social Science, Diploma in Social Work (CSQW)
IS	Felagsradjafi
L	Assistant d'hygiène sociale or assistant social
N	Sosionom
NL	Diploma Hoger Beroepsopleiding in the various areas
P	Diplomado em Serviço Social (Assistente social)
S	Socionom
SF	Yhteiskuntatieteiden kandidaatti (sosiaalihuoltaja sosionom)
TR	Sosyal Hizmet Usmani/Sosyal Çalismaci

The Student Body

Yearly admissions to social work courses in the countries under observation total approximately twenty-nine thousand (including an estimated intake of two thousand for Italy). The majority of beginning students are female. In most countries, the proportion of women in the student body is about two-thirds. The schools in the Netherlands and Turkey constitute an exception in that approximately an equal number of men and women are present in the student body. On the other hand, in Finland, France, Greece, Iceland, Italy, Portugal and Spain very few men study social work; here the percentage of female students is often around 90 percent or greater.

Even when all due allowance is made for imprecisions in compilation, wide variations in the national ratio of students of social work to overall population are apparent (see Table 6-7). Small countries, like the Netherlands and

Belgium, have the highest ratio of social work students to overall population. Interestingly, Germany is the only large country among those having one social work student per less than ten thousand population (this statement only applies to the preunification Federal Republic). Most European countries have one student of social work for between fifteen thousand to thirty thousand population.

Table 6-7

Student Populations in European Social Work Programs

	Intake	Women %	Student Population	Graduates	Total Population (Mill.)	Intake/ Population (1:10,000)
A	330	75	650	300	7.51	22,750
B	1800	75	5400	1500	9.87	5,480
CH	300	66	1000	140	6.34	21,130
D	8000	66	37000	7000	61.34	7,660
DK	340	80	970	345	5.16	15,170
E	1300	90	3900	?	37.18	28,600
F	2000	95	6000	2000	53.48	26,740
GB	3500*	67	6450*	3440*	55.82	15,940
GR	370	89	1000	169	9.36	25,290
I	no data**	90	6000 (est).	no data**	56.91	—
IRL	150*	80	550	40	3.36	22,400
IS	30	90	100	15	0.23	7,640
L	10	—	—	5	0.36	36,000
N	260	70	780	—	4.07	15,650
NL	7200	56	26400	5900	14.03	1,940
P	330	90	950	210	9.87	29,090
S	1100	75	4000	1000	8.30	7,540
SF	230	90	1000	210	4.76	20,690
TR	160	50	640	150	44.00	275,000

* Including undergraduate, graduate, and nongraduate.
**   No exact data available.

Few figures are available on the social structure of the student bodies. In Germany, the percentage of students from working class families in social work education is approximately twice as high as that of students in general. The indications are that social work education is not a typical academic field in the sense that the overwhelming majority of its students come directly from the secondary schools. Rather, it is characteristic of this course of study that many students have already gathered work experience and are often older than standard student cohorts. In some countries, this tendency is encouraged by mechanisms such as an obligatory minimum age of admission or required job experience.

All countries regard the national secondary school–leaving certificate which qualifies for university studies as the standard of admission. In addition, many countries require further proof of personal suitability. Applicants are often obliged to submit to interviews, psychometric tests or special admission examinations. In some countries it is possible for people without the standard secondary school–leaving certificate but with appropriate job experience to gain admission to courses in social work.

Faculty

The composition of faculty reflects the diverse, interdisciplinary focus of social work education. Integration of considerable placement elements is secured by the use of practitioners as advisers or supervisors. The weight of these and other groups in the faculty varies from country to country, depending on national circumstances.

Teaching staff generally includes academic social workers, social scientists and active social work professionals. Almost all countries distinguish to some degree among these groups. This is symptomatic of the fact that in nearly all countries social work does not yet enjoy (or has not long enjoyed) full academic recognition. Thus the curious situation arises in many countries that social workers as teachers in courses on social work are relegated to a lower status than representatives of other academic disciplines. In some countries, this seems to be a transitional problem which the formal academic recognition of social work training will, in time, allow to be solved (e.g., in Finland, Ireland, Sweden and Great Britain). However, in a number of countries the partial academization of social work education first caused the problem to appear and the present immobility in this process admits of no easy solution (Germany, Greece, Italy, the Netherlands, Spain). It seems to us self-evident that the equal participation of trained social workers as faculty is desirable.

Status and remuneration of staff depend on many factors. Some staff are employed on a full-time, others on a part-time basis. As a rule, all schools have a "core" of permanent, full-time faculty members. Spain is a problematic exception in that schools there usually have only one or two permanent faculty members, while the rest of the teaching staff are only engaged on the basis of honoraria. As a permanent arrangement, this situation is probably incompatible with high-quality education. Some countries report that staff are encouraged to participate in social work practice and all make use to a large degree of the teaching services of social work professionals on a part-time basis.

Social work appears to have a relatively large proportion of women among teaching staff. However, academization has had effects here as well. The proportion of men is higher among faculty from disciplines other than social work. The experience in Germany may be illustrative. The integration of social work education into the tertiary educational system with its traditional academic standards of employment led to the hiring of many more men than women since 1971. Presently there is much pressure to redress this imbalance.

SOCIAL WORK, SOCIAL MOVEMENTS, SOCIAL REFORM

The early history of social work shows a clear connection between social work as a profession and social movements of the time. In those countries in which modern social work began to take shape prior to World War I, it derived its main impulses from the women's movement. The "founding mothers" of social work regarded the embryonic profession not only as a lever for social reform but also as an instrument of emancipation for women. This was no longer so clearly the case in countries in which social work developed between the wars or after World War II.

From the very beginning the churches have played a significant role in the development of social work. Throughout Europe, Roman Catholic and Protestant organizations were active in the founding of institutions for social work education. In many cases, the churches have maintained a considerable engagement to the present.

During the early years of social work practice, there was often a close connection between the organized workers' movement and social work in many parts of Europe. More research will be needed to clarify why the connection between social work and social movements such as the women's movement or the workers' movement has become quite tenuous, while the connection to the churches—though diminishing—has proved more durable.

There is historically a strong connection between social work education and the process of social reform. Legally mandated social services seem to have a particularly strong impact on both social work practice and education. But in a more general sense, an interdependence of social work education and social policy trends can be postulated. The "crisis of the welfare state" which is perceived in many advanced industrial countries has already had far-reaching qualitative and quantitative effects on social work education. In this situation, social work often seems to be on the defensive: criticism of social work mounts while the problems with which it is confronted fester. Resignation and embitterment among social service professionals are often the result. However, there appear to be certain exceptions which deserve careful examination. In Greece, Spain and Turkey, social work is still a "growth industry." It is an open question whether social work will eventually run up against its own specific "limits to growth" in these countries as well.

"EUROPEANIZATION" OF SOCIAL WORK

As we have seen, the origins of social work education in Western Europe are rooted deeply in the national history of the various countries. The women's movement, the churches and the worker's movement all played a role. However, the search for international cooperation was also a factor which should not be forgotten. The founding of the International Association of Schools of Social Work in Paris in 1928–29, under the leadership of extraordinary personalities like Alice Salomon, was an important milestone. International cooperation in the field of social work suffered setbacks under the influence of ultranationalism, fascism and national socialism between the wars and especially as a result of World War II and the subsequent division of Europe into antagonistic blocs. After World War II, American experts and ideas played a key role in the (re)construction of social work and social work education and practice in much of Europe. This development probably reflected not only the strength of the United States at the time but also the relatively developed state of the U.S. social work profession.

The first postwar generation of teachers of social work in Europe was educated to a remarkable extent in the United States, but in recent years certain trends seem to point in the direction of a "europeanization" of social work methods. Roughly parallel developments can be observed in many European countries. The search for a "holistic" or unified approach to social problems seems to be replacing reliance on "imported" American methods. The focus in Europe seems to be shifting toward a new, more comprehensive type of "community social work" which incorporates elements of all the "classical" methods while rejecting what is felt to be their individualistic orientation.

PROFESSIONALIZATION THROUGH ACADEMIZATION

The status of social work education in the various national systems of education seems to be an indicator of the degree of professionalization which has been achieved. Social work education is involved in a secular process of transition from the secondary to the tertiary level of education. In most countries, it is situated in a curious position within the tertiary system, but outside the universities. However, even in countries where it has received full university recognition, the status of social work education is sometimes still overlaid with ambiguity (e.g., in Great Britain, social work education still coexists in university and extra-university institutions). Other countries are considering the integration of social work with the established academic disciplines on the one hand and with the social work profession on the other (e.g., Germany, Greece, the Netherlands, Spain).   Nevertheless, the process of professionalization through academization of training appears to us to be inevitable and—in the final analysis—desirable.

The process of professionalization through academization seems to be related to "secularization" of social work education. The trend throughout Europe seems to be overwhelmingly in the direction of increasing state responsibility for previously private or church-related institutions. This process can be clearly observed in France, Germany, Greece, Italy, Spain and the Scandinavian countries.   It appears that the financial demands of modern social work education increasingly exceed the resources which nongovernmental organizations can—or are willing to—devote to it.

In general, professionalization of social work seems to parallel increasing male participation. The percentage of male social workers and social work students is quite large in some but not all countries in which social work is most strongly professionalized (Germany, the Netherlands, Norway, Switzerland, Great Britain).   However, there are so many anomalies on the international scene that one should not jump to early conclusions; the high percentage of male social workers and social work students in Turkey certainly is culturally determined and does not necessarily reflect an advanced state of professionalism.

A notable feature of recent years in highly developed European countries is a blurring of the boundaries between professional social work and other forms of intervention. The renaissance of self-help initiatives and other types of voluntary work is certainly related to the financial crisis of the "welfare state," but it also seems to imply a criticism of the bureaucracy which professionalism often entails.   In many countries, public criticism of professional social work has become widespread. However, even within the profession there seems to be a growing sense that self-help and voluntary efforts need to have a greater role in social work practice.

One indication of the uncertainty of professionalization within an increasingly academized social work education is the unequal status of faculty members with social work degrees in many countries (Belgium, Germany, Greece, Spain). Perhaps this, too, is a transitional problem, which will disappear in the future as social work teachers take advantage of doctoral level degrees offered within their own discipline. In any case, it is not surprising that many countries with highly professionalized social work establishments either have already created possibilities for doctoral degrees in social work or are debating the issue seriously.

The tenuousness of social work professionalization can also be observed on the job market, where social work graduates compete with an array of others, including sociologists, psychologists, teachers and even those with legal training. Social workers not only are experiencing increased competition from better established academic disciplines for entry-level jobs, but are often at a distinct disadvantage for leadership positions. In some countries, competition also exists with other qualifications for social services, such as the *educatore specializzato* in Italy and "administrative civil servants" (*Verwaltungsbeamten*) in Germany and Denmark.

SOCIAL WORK BETWEEN THEORY AND PRACTICE

European social work is torn between its striving for academic status and the demands of daily practice. This tension, which is deeply rooted in the history of the profession, finds expression in an uneasy coexistence between an eclectic social–scientific discipline on the one hand and a specific form of vocational training on the other. No Western European country seems to have found an entirely satisfactory solution to the quandary. Even Great Britain, with its long and venerable tradition of university education for social workers, still appears to be struggling with this problem. The balance between the academic discipline and vocational orientation is struck in widely varying ways in the different countries.

All countries show a degree of reverence for the vocational side of social work education by requiring practical placements and by incorporating practicing social workers in the teaching staff. By the same token, most countries make gestures in the direction of subsuming the social-scientific disciplines under a problem-orientation ostensibly derived from practical necessity. Some efforts seem quite promising in this regard. Denmark and Germany are experimenting with projects as the integrative centers within courses. Other countries, such as France, Ireland, Great Britain and Denmark, encourage full-time teaching staff to renew their personal experience in the field.

However, the difficulties of integrating theory and practice are not merely a result of "overacademization." Social work education can also be "underacademic," that is, lacking in scientific foundation. This tends to be the case in countries in which teaching is done primarily on a part-time basis by active social work professionals and/or other itinerant academics who have neither time nor opportunity to reflect on their practice and teaching in the light of current research.

This situation is exacerbated by a general dearth of specific, reliable research in the field of social work; thus it is, among other things, a concern for the quality of education (not merely practice) which leads to complaints from all parts of Europe about insufficient support for social work research. In fact, dissatisfaction with the state of research in the field seems to be one of the uniting links in social work education in Europe.

The institutions for mediating the tension between theory and practice are as varied as the countries in Europe. Centralized regulation and local autonomy are the two poles between which a spectrum of possibilities unfolds. Great Britain has created a centralized, nongovernmental certifying agency which promulgates minimum standards of education and monitors their observance. Germany, on the other extreme, has an exquisitely decentralized system of institutional autonomy (in which, however, the various provincial governments constantly meddle in inscrutable ways). In Austria, France, Spain and Denmark standards of social work education are prescribed by statute at the national level, while Belgium entrusts a government ministry with the task of supervising the issuing of separate guidelines for Flemish-, and French-speaking schools.

Each of these approaches has its advantages and disadvantages. The British solution gives employing agencies a degree of influence which many Europeans would view as untoward; however, it also makes possible a great deal of professional flexibility. Countries relying strongly on legislation are necessarily much less flexible, unless (as seems to be the case in some Mediterranean countries) room is left for "paralegal" fudging with the letter of the law.

Despite the differences in approach, the majority of countries appear to have some mechanism for enforcing a semblance of national standards with respect to educational structure and content. It would be very useful to have more research on the varieties of approach and the differential rates of success or failure. However, measured by the criticism of social work education which is uttered by employers in Great Britain on the one hand and Germany on the other, it appears that the actual results of diverse organizational schemes may not be all that different from each other.

TRAINING, EDUCATION, FURTHER EDUCATION

Many European countries obviously believe that effective social work requires personal qualities which are not necessarily reflected in academic transcripts. In Ireland, Spain, Great Britain and some other countries prospective students undergo interviews and other forms of subjective evaluation. Low teacher/student ratios discourage anonymity and ensure a personal relationship between faculty and students. But whereas most European "schools of social work" have around two hundred students, it is not rare for West German and Dutch "schools" to be three to five times as large. Moreover, in Germany, at least, selection procedures are based on the assumption that personal traits should be bracketed out of the admission process. The anonymity and impersonality of this process have generated much dissatisfaction.

Three general directions are discernible among countries which presently offer instruction beyond the undergraduate level:

- Academic postgraduate courses (leading often to an MA or PhD degree)
- Thematic specializations (particular fields of work, client groups or methods)
- Intensified qualifications for leadership and administrative responsibility

This is an area which certainly calls for increased international cooperation. The great challenges with which social work is confronted already transcend national boundaries, and this process can be expected to intensify in the future. Long-term unemployment, labor migration from the countryside to the city and from less developed to more developed areas, nationalism and ethnic strife—particularly in parts of Eastern Europe—and demographic shifts and changes in values are issues which confront all the countries of Europe. Postgraduate education would therefore seem to be an ideal area for European social work education to cultivate elements of a transnational professional identity equal to the changes taking place at the political and economic levels.

TRENDS

Some of the most significant trends in European social work education have already been described:

- Academization
- Secularization
- An increasingly "generic" approach
- "Europeanization"

It is certain that "Europeanization" will continue and perhaps even intensify; but the content of this phenomenon may change profoundly. Political transformation in Eastern Europe and European integration open completely new dimensions and perspectives. The gap between local and/or regional developments and the European backdrop must be bridged in social work and social work education. Social workers and social work educators must recognize the new challenges and opportunities offered by these events. They should strive to play an important role in the social integration of Eastern and Western Europe. They need precise analyses of the processes involved and their possible role in them; but they will also need the courage to grasp opportunities as they arise.

Widespread public skepticism toward social work has become apparent in many Western European countries in recent years. While this is often attributed exclusively to the financial "crisis" of the welfare state, we see it as also inextricably bound up with an "identity crisis" of social work itself. Competition from voluntary and self-help initiatives on the one hand and from other professions on the other is forcing professional social work in many countries to specify its unique contribution and to justify its cost.

REFERENCES

Brauns, H. J. & Kramer, D. (1986). *Social Work Education in Europe: A Comprehensive Description of Social Work Education in 21 European Countries.* Frankfurt a. M.: Eigenverlag des Deutschen Vereins für öffentliche und private Fürsorge.

Calingaert, M. (1988). *The 1992 Challenge from Europe: Development of the European Community's Internal Market.* Washington, D.C.: The National Planning Association.

Leonard, D. (1988). *Pocket Guide to the European Community.* Oxford and London: Basil Blackwell and the Economist Publications.

PROGNOS A .G. (1981). *Freie Wohlfahrtspflege im zukünftigen Europa. Herausforderungen und Chancen im Europäischen Binnenmarkt.* Köln/Berlin: Studie der Prognos AB im Auftrag der Bank für Sozialwirtschaft GMBH.

7

UNITED KINGDOM

Doreen Elliott and Ronald G. Walton

INTRODUCTION

The development of social work education through the twentieth century in the
United Kingdom is characterized by a number of key issues. The increasing
trend throughout this period for social workers to become government employees implementing social legislation is evident and an inexorable increase in the
role and influence of government in training, both of central government and of
local government employers, as a result of increased social legislation. The increased influence of employers led to a decrease in the influence of academics
as social work educators. The debate over generic or specialized training continues throughout the period. The policy of promoting various routes to a
qualification in social work at different academic levels has many advantages
for recruitment to the profession but sets up problems in terms of the lack of a
clear statement on educational level. In-service training, or the apprenticeship
model, versus an academic education have been competing models throughout
the century. The appropriateness of part-time training has also been debated.
Finally, professional training for social work has taken much criticism in recent
years for the poor public image suffered by the profession.

In the following review of social work education in the United Kingdom,
these themes will emerge and reemerge in Gestalt fashion as ground and figure
through the different phases of development. These phases of development are
roughly divided as follows: the beginnings till 1945; the development and consolidation of the welfare state 1945–1971; a radical change in the organization
of service delivery in the post Seebohm period 1971–1979; and period of radical
change in the structure of social work education 1980–present.

The importance of training was recognized from the very beginnings of the
social work profession. The Charity Organization Society (COS) at first trained
its visitors in assessment through practical training based on an apprenticeship
model to distinguish the "deserving" poor from the "undeserving" poor.
However, the society also began to espouse a more "scientific" approach and
published papers, and books and established its own journal. It formed a special

committee on social education in 1902 which led to the establishment of the School of Sociology in London in 1903, independent of the COS. The philosophy of the COS, which emphasized individual responsibility for poverty, was challenged by the Fabian Society and the settlement movement, who founded a School of Economics, emphasizing economic and political issues relating to poverty. In 1913, these two educational ventures merged to become the Department of Social Administration at the London School of Economics. (Walton, 1975; Jones, 1979).

In Liverpool, the School of Social Science was established in 1904 and incorporated into the university in 1918. However the University of Birmingham became the first university in Britain in 1908 to set up a course which accepted internal students. Other universities later followed suit: Bristol, Leeds, Manchester, Edinburgh and Glasgow.

During the 1920s and 1930s, social work training developed in the health service sector with training for hospital based medical social work through the Institute of Almoners, and training for psychiatric social work in hospital and child guidance settings was established in university settings such as the London School of Economics. The probation service was another setting for which training was developed. Thus a clear pattern of specialized training for various settings had been established and child welfare services and family casework were still carried out mainly by unqualified workers.

In the postwar period the National Health Service Act (1946), the National Insurance Act (1946) and the Children Act (1948) heralded significant changes by dismantling the Poor Law and developing the welfare state and social welfare services. The postwar period to 1971 saw developments in training for these specialist fields. Social work training was under the auspices of three public bodies: the Central Training Council in Child Care (CTC) formed in 1947, the Council for Training in Social Work (CTSW) formed in 1962, and the Probation and Advisory and Training Board (PATB) formed in 1936. The Institute of Almoners became the Institute of Medical Social Workers (IMSW) in 1963 and played a major part in the training of medical social workers. The Association of Psychiatric Social Workers was also influential in determining the content and pattern of social work training (Younghusband, 1978b).

The 1948 Children Act created local government departments headed by a children's officer and staffed by boarding out visitors, later to become known as child care officers. The Curtis Committee recommended that university training rather than apprenticeship on the job training was the appropriate preparation for these new positions.

The 1950s saw an expansion in child care services and the demand for trained workers exceeded supply (Younghusband, 1978a). The CTC initiated discussions with a number of universities to set up courses for graduates with "nonrelevant," that is, nonsocial science, degrees. Training expanded to include part-time qualifying training on an in-service basis and establishment of emergency training courses. Separate training courses were set up for residential child care workers. Thus this period highlighted issues which are reflected in social work education and training in the United Kingdom today: the different routes to qualification, the establishment of postgraduate training with non-relevant degrees, and the separate system for training residential social workers, which was to be continued later with a Certificate in Social Service (CSS) and the present National Vocational Qualification (NVQ).

The Institute of Almoners was the largest professional body involved in social work training in Britain during the 1950s. However, during this period following a 1949 working party recommendation, it lobbied for the one year post–social science degree training to be transferred to the universities, although it was not until 1970 that the training course was terminated. In 1963 the Institute of Almoners had become the Institute of Medical Social Workers. Thus the trend to academic university based training was reinforced in the health services as well as in the child care services. Training for psychiatric social work was offered at the London School of Economics and at the Universities of Edinburgh, Leeds and Manchester. Thus fewer places were available and the Association of Psychiatric Social Workers exercised a strong gate-keeping function. Along with the psychoanalytic orientation of the casework model used, these factors combined so that psychiatric social workers were an elite group within the social work profession.

In contrast to psychiatric social workers, many social workers in the health and welfare departments of local authorities were untrained. The Council for Training in Social Work was established in 1962 to address the problem and the new qualification, the Certificate in Social Work (CSW), was introduced. It was located in colleges of further education and illustrates the different levels of educational routes to social work qualification.

Probation training represented yet another aspect of social work training in the period 1945–1970 and also reflected a two-level approach. Candidates under thirty were required to complete nine months' specialized probation training at Rainer House, operated by the Home Office, after completing a university social science course. Older candidates were required to complete twelve months of Rainer House training only. It was this latter route which trained the majority of probation officers, and by 1970 the Probation Service had 74.2 percent of trained service officers. This was higher than for other social work settings (Younghusband 1978 a). Thus Social work training was a kaleidoscope of specialist and generic training, different levels of education, in-service and university based, and financed from a number of sources.

In 1970, the Local Social Services Act, marked a very significant change in the structure of social services and consequently in education and training for the profession for staff. The 1970 act, on the recommendation of the Seebohm Committee, created unified departments of social services under the director of

Social Services, to carry out the functions of the former Health and Welfare Departments and Children's Departments.

These new Social Services Departments were to become the major employers of social workers in England and Wales. In Scotland, similar departments were established by the Social Work (Scotland) Act, 1968, and in Northern Ireland, personal social services were the responsibility of joint health and social services boards. The trend of the state's becoming the main employer of social workers, which began with the children's department in 1948, was reinforced, even though voluntary organizations such as Barnado's, the National Children's Home, the Children's Society and the National Society for the Prevention of Cruelty to Children remained significant lesser employers of social workers. During the 1970s and 1980s there was a continuing expansion of personal social services and of the number of social workers. Although social workers were less than 10 percent of total employees of these departments, they were a critical part of the department's welfare with important assessment and decision-making functions as in the fields of child abuse and neglect and mental health.

At the same time as the establishment of social services departments, the Central Council for Education and Training in Social Work (CCETSW) was established. Despite the variations in service provision and legislation in the different parts of the United Kingdom, the new council had full responsibility for training across the United Kingdom (Cooper, 1983).

The second trend has several strands and relates to changing demographic and social patterns in the United Kingdom which have influenced service delivery in the welfare services. This is most sharply illustrated by the increase in the number and proportion of elderly people in the United Kingdom and by the number of single parent households, combined with high rates of divorce and separation. Other social changes such as increasing levels of recorded crime, the social impact of economic change, the decline in manufacturing industries (particularly coal, steel and engineering industries) and the growing numbers of racial minorities were all associated with increased levels of social need. Despite legislation to outlaw race and sex discrimination, the United Kingdom still provides ample evidence of race and gender discrimination in employment, housing, education and social services.

A third trend relates to social policy in the United Kingdom. For a quarter of a century, governments have advocated a greater emphasis on community care than institutional care. However, progress was very gradual until a new impetus was given during the 1980s as a result of attempts to cope with increasing demands on personal social services and the high cost of all forms of residential provision. Major legislation in the 1980s increased the community care focus: the Mental Health Act (1983), the Disability Act (1986), the Children Act (1989), the Health and Community Care Act (1990). Each piece of legislation placed new responsibilities on local government social services departments. The combined effect of broader roles for social workers, new statutory responsibilities for social services departments, the effects of demographic and social change, as well as lack of adequate service resources have meant that services are stretched to the limit and often social workers are placed in the role of "rationers" and "gatekeepers."

Before going on to outline major trends in social work education and training since 1971, it is useful to identify key issues implied by the trends just outlined. Increases in demand for services and enlarged statutory responsibilities would always tend to put pressure on the education and training system to produce sufficient new staff to meet replacement and development needs. How well did the United Kingdom system cope with this? It is not only the numbers of trained workers which is important, but also how well they are equipped to work in the services. The changes in the role of social workers and the extended range of skills required of them were generated by the new unified social services departments and by the increased emphasis on community care. The Barclay Report (1982) epitomized the debates of the period about the emphasis to be given to traditional counseling roles, case coordination and management, supervision of support staff and volunteers and community work oriented roles.

A final issue is who controls and influences the education and training system? Is it the teachers in universities, polytechnics, and other colleges; the powerful group of social services department employers together with the probation service managers, or the central government?

CCETSW POLICY AND DEVELOPMENT 1971–1979

When the new council was formed in 1971 it inherited two main types of social work programs: postgraduate and one year courses, the majority of whose students had previously studied social administration or other social sciences, the two year courses for nongraduates or graduates with nonrelated degrees. There were also a small number of four year degree courses. Previous qualifications such as certificates in child care, psychiatric social work or medical social work, were all replaced by a new certification of qualification in social work (CQSW). Two year nongraduate courses had expanded rapidly in the 1960s (following the Younghusband Report of 1959) as a result of the inability of the universities to expand to meet the need for qualified social work staff. Thus even at this time there was already major ambiguity about the level of social work qualifications when graduates and nongraduates received the same qualification.

The other main programs inherited were one year residential child care courses, two one year advanced residential courses and a number of in-service and preliminary certificate courses for residential staff. Thus at the inception, CCETSW had to face major problems—to produce sufficient new qualified social workers with a balance between graduates and nongraduates; to address the problem of training for residential and day care staff; and to review the needs of social workers who were already qualified.

Starting from a low base, output of courses increased rapidly from 2078 in 1971 to 3023 in 1975 and 3390 in 1977. In the late 1970s the pattern was already established of approximately half the annual output being from nongraduate courses. There was a fast expansion of two year postgraduate courses for students lacking social science study in their first degree (intake increased from 381 in 1974 to 593 in 1977). Undergraduate courses increased their intake from 151 to 235 from 1974 to 1977. The largest number of graduates still took one year postgraduate courses in 1977 (1070). The total intake to all CQSW courses was just 4000 in 1977 (CCETSW, 1973 a, 1978).

There was still considerable concern about the adequacy of output with fast expanding services, but particularly about the availability of training opportunities for residential and day care staff. This problem had been pinpointed earlier by the Williams Committee in 1967, but CCETSW established a working group to try to resolve this policy, which, at that point, had been to encourage CQSW courses to provide for staff from the residential sector. The group's report *Residential Work Is a Part of Social Work* (CCETSW, 1973), showed considerable diversity of views about whether there should be separate training to CQSW or whether a new intermediate tier of qualification should be introduced. CCETSW eventually decided to introduce a new training and qualification: the certificate in social service, directed to residential and day care staff, coupled with the encouragement of CQSW courses to establish options for residential staff. The new certificate in social service was introduced in 1975/76 and was modular in pattern. It was different from the CQSW in that students remained in employment throughout the courses and employers bore the main costs of training.

By 1976, a number of issues relating to education and training were identified in a government report (Birch Report, 1976). This report made projections for a large expansion of training, envisaging that CSS courses should ultimately produce three times as many qualified staff as CQSW courses. The projections of the Birch Report were never to be realized; by 1979 only 205 awards of the CSS were made and it had increased to only 1131 awards by 1987. In the latter year there were, 3093 awards of the CQSW. The reasons for this failure to meet the needs of residential and day care staff can be largely ascribed to the complexity of the scheme, the high dropout rate and the costs of the scheme. From the mid-1970s social services departments experienced severe financial difficulties and transferred financial support from secondments for CQSW to support for CSS students. Neither the resources nor the commitment to enlarging the CSS schemes to a scale sufficient to make a major impact on staffing in residential and day care services never became available. But the CSS and the management structure reflecting a major involvement of employers showed that agencies wanted to be involved and have influence on the education and training system, and to some extent, signified their distrust and suspicion of programs of universities as being too academically oriented. Employers complained frequently about the quality of university-trained social workers but failed to produce evidence of any general lack of quality or standards of practice.

The other major preoccupation in the early years of the council was to accredit and promote postqualifying training. By 1977, there were twenty-four postqualifying programs with a total intake of 153 students. These courses ranged from shorter programs of three to six months to master's level courses usually of one year's duration. Entry requirements were a minimum of two years' experience since qualification and the particular admission prerequisites for each course. The areas of study involved a wide range of social work practice, management studies, social work education, community work and research. Some of the programs were clearly at an advanced level, while others were an extension or further development of practice with particular client groups or methods of working. Expansion was so slow mainly because of the problems of funding. CCETSW provided some support with fees and maintenance, but employers gave very limited support even in allowing time to study when students were prepared to pay their own fees.

During the early and mid-1970s, the elements of an overall strategy of social work education and training were already in place. But only for qualifying training (CQSW) did the output of trained staff meet the needs of the services. For residential and day care staff and for qualified social workers, provision was minuscule in relation to the number of staff requiring training. Despite the efforts of CCETSW, a number of strategic problems were already evident. There was the question of the quality of the social workers who were qualifying. In the post–Seebohm years when social services departments were themselves coping with adaptation in larger organizational systems, courses aimed to prepare their students for all branches of social work in contrast to the specialized courses before 1971. This was largely in response to the generic structure of social work teams in social services departments. It was inevitable that newly qualified workers would be less likely to be fully conversant with specialized practice in different client fields. Since the provision of qualifying training was negligible and agency developmental programs were limited, there was frustration that newly qualified workers could not manage complex child care or mental health cases. There is a certain irony that agencies were complaining about the products of courses when courses had changed their structure and content to respond to changes in service patterns within agencies.

Quality was also related to the intake to courses and educational level of courses. The many routes into the profession of social work might be seen as an advantage in terms of the broad range of staff recruited, including mature students from all walks of life. But the variety of levels of students and of courses in the United Kingdom system was confusing to agencies, the public and the educational institutions themselves as there was no niche in the educational system where the level and standard of social work were clearly and unambiguously located. Universities saw their social work courses as mainly vocational with limited academic status and could never quite understand how the same qualification and standards were applied to a CQSW course in a college of further education recruiting nongraduates and in a postgraduate course in a university department. Most social work courses and universities were a part of social science departments (usually in social administration but occasionally in sociology departments) and academic research and publication were usually far less than in other disciplines. CCETSW's signal failure to establish clearly the academic level of social work training in the United Kingdom was to have repercussions through the 1980s. One of these was the embarrassing position of United Kingdom–trained social workers, who had difficulties in meeting the requirements of professional associations in the United States of America, Australia and New Zealand, when they sought to work in those countries.

CCETSW attempted to influence the quality of social work education programs by initiating papers on curriculum and other aspects of social work as applied to social work education: for example on values in social work (CCETSW, 1973); community work (CCETSW 1975a); day services (CCETSW 1975b); social work with children and families (CCETSW, 1978); and assessment of students (CCETSW, 1979). The council also gave increasing attention to the quality of fieldwork practice as in its paper on student training units in social work education (CCETSW, 1975c). The active formation of working parties and publication of papers on all aspects of social work education and training were very positive contributions which continue to the present day. One could observe that in other countries these activities have been the preserve of professional associations. This feature of U.K. education and training, a quasi-governmental organization known as a "quango" to oversee and be responsible for social work education, has its positive features but also has its downside. Sorting out policy and strategy among government departments, social service agencies and educational institutions has always had to be conducted with an additional central player in the form of CCETSW. Since CCETSW was financed directly by the Department of Health and Social Security (later the Department of Health) there was always the possibility that it would follow a policy line which reflected the Civil Service as well as the government of the day. Initially CCETSW was governed by a large council of fifty-nine members nominated by a wide variety of constituent bodies, an arrangement which gave a degree of independence. Council membership was made up of eleven ministerial appointments, twelve educational institutions representatives, twelve professional associations representatives and eleven employer representatives. The diversity of the council meant that important issues were debated keenly and it was impossible for one group, whether employers or educational bodies, to dominate policy or to disregard the interests of other parts of the education and training system. In the 1980s this was to change quite dramatically. CCETSW in the first decade of its existence, whatever the shortcomings, had some major achievements to its credit. It had established the framework for a comprehensive structure of training at prequalifying, qualifying and postqualifying levels. A major expansion of qualifying training (the introduction of the CQSW) had been introduced as well as a new model of training (the CSS), directed to the needs of residential/day care staff. All parties in the education and training system were brought into a continuing dialogue within the council and CCETSW commenced a regular program of publishing papers to promote improved quality in education and training in the United Kingdom. CCETSW was seen as a powerful body and universities had concerns about its influence on academic matters and its growing bureaucracy. Nevertheless, despite their reservations, universities found it possible to work with the council and even draw on the its support in pressing for resources from the DHS.

CCETSW POLICY AND TRAINING 1979–1991

In 1979 a conservative government was elected and the next decade in the United Kingdom bore the heavy imprint of Margaret Thatcher's policies in both economic and social ideology. At a stroke, the welfare consensus which had existed for a third of a century was broken. There was a new emphasis on individualism and on citizens' responsibility for their own welfare. From the perspective of social work a number of conflicting forces were at work. A substantial section of conservative ideology was antagonistic toward and dismissive of social workers, as reflected in the controversial debate "Can Social Work Survive?" (Brewer & Lait, 1980), which attacked the radicalism of the 1960s and 1970s. Yet the macro economic and welfare policies ensured that under Thatcherism social workers were necessary to paper over the cracks of a beleaguered welfare state.

The demands and pressures for services continued to grow partly as a direct outcome of policy changes. The deep recession and unemployment in 1980–1981 resulted in greater poverty and social malaise. Over a decade later we are experiencing a similar recession, sharpened, if not wholly caused, by conservative economic policy. Social security benefits were made more restrictive, for example, in the freezing of child benefits, tougher criteria for receiving unemployment benefits, reduced eligibility to young people sixteen to nineteen, and a considerable reduction of discretionary grants to those receiving supplementary "assistance benefits." The main housing policy, of selling council houses but preventing local councils from using the receipts to build low cost rental accommodations, led to significant increases in homelessness with many young people on the streets and an increasing number of families living in expensive bed and breakfast accommodation of low quality.

The decade witnessed several major pieces of legislation: the Mental Health Act, 1983; the Disability Act, 1986; the Children Act, 1989 (implemented in 1991); Health and Community Care Act, 1990 (to be implemented in 1993).

Each of these acts had large–scale resource requirements for social services departments, but local authorities were themselves in financial difficulties as a result of the Poll Tax (Community Charge) which replaced local rates in the second half of the decade and of the general policy limiting local authority expenditure by tight central government controls. There was an inherent problem in conservative ideology whose policies promoted poverty and social distress. No conflict was seen in implementing new legislation which increased the responsibilities of social services departments while restricting the financial resources to make the services effective. Each person's or family's problem was seen as an individual phenomenon unrelated to the structural features of unemployment, homelessness and poverty.

It was no accident that Mrs. Thatcher's praise of Victorian values should be mirrored in a view of social work not unlike that of Victorian charity coupled with encouragement of voluntary societies and private agencies as providers of service. One other general feature of policy influencing agencies and educational institutions was the emphasis on efficiency and standards. Beneath the rhetoric of the policies of community care and children and family services was a hard-nosed concern about costs. Residential provision was costly whether in the form of hospital care or establishments run by the personal social services. Community care was cheaper, although not as cheap as right-wing ideologues would have liked. Residential care of children had been markedly reduced by the mid-1980s, but perhaps the clearest exposition of the new drive for efficiency was in the care of elderly. Two major reports by the Audit Commission (1985, 1986) analyzed in detail the structure of services for the elderly and the relative costs of residential and community services: they were followed by the Griffiths Report (1988) and 'Care in the Community' (1989) a White Paper (government discussion document) which presented the intended structure for the new era of community care (Department of Health, 1989). As in the health services and education, integral to this philosophy was the development of indicators and measures of quality as well as quality of service. The educational institutions which hosted social work courses were themselves subject to the twin pressures of rising student numbers and constrained budgeting. For example during the 1980s there were great difficulties in ensuring that social work courses were placed in subject categories which took account of the professional and practice elements in training; the ultimate achievement of this was largely dependent upon CCETSW support and to some extent coordination, of the efforts of social work teachers in universities and polytechnics.

Against such a backcloth it is understandable (in retrospect) that social work training should have been under the microscope throughout the 1980s. A series of child abuse tragedies in the 1970s and 1980s had often shown that the social workers involved either had limited experience of child protective work or had made basic errors in their practice. Agencies moved to a more specialized organization of their work, but social work education was still generically focused. Shifts toward a redefined community care policy threw into question the traditional roles of social workers. What social workers should do and, by implication, how should they be trained was a burning question and the confusion and tension in U.K. social work was best illustrated by the Barclay Report (1982), which examined the roles and tasks of social workers. The majority report crudely categorized social work roles into counseling and care coordination/management, but the most interesting element was the two minority reports, one advocating a broad community work approach and the other a full blooded, highly professionalized casework approach. This conflict epitomized the debates of the 1960s and 1970s between the traditionalists and the radicals.

During the 1980s the progress of social work education was heavily influenced by shifts in political, economic and social policies. Central government developed a much greater direct influence on CCETSW, social services departments and higher education institutions. When the Conservatives came to power, one of their early initiatives was to replace the more independent systems of nominating or selecting the members of a wide range of quangos (quasi–governmental organizations) with direct appointments by the relevant minister. Thus the CCETSW council was reduced to twenty–six in number with only about one-fifth directly involved with teaching and researching in social work. Within the council the effects were twofold: agency influences were much stronger in developing policy and the small size of the council made it possible for CCETSW's permanent staff to exert stronger influence in directing the shape of policy. Externally, the council, which had always received its financial report from the Department of Health, developed much closer links with the departmental civil servants. To obtain government financing, education and training objectives had to be closely tied to central government policy. This is clearly illustrated by targeted funding for approved social worker training (Mental Health Act, 1983) and child protection training (the outcome of political concern over child abuse tragedies). A broader implication was that the view of social work gradually emerging within training policies was much closer to a traditional professional/technocratic model of training and practice than a radical model encompassing social reform. During the 1980s all the parties to social work education—courses; agencies, government and CCETSW—were faced with resolving the legacy of the problems of the 1970s. The basic structural scaffolding had been erected in the form of prequalifying and postqualifying levels, but the output from prequalifying and postqualifying courses was limited and the research study awards were not linked to any rec-

ognized national structures of training. The changing patterns of service provision had not yet been fully reflected in the CQSW training pattern.

QUALIFYING TRAINING

A prolonged national debate in the early 1980s culminated in agreement
within CCETSW that to include relevant social services, generic elements and
also specialized content, a new diploma with a standard three years should be
introduced. The full details of CCETSW's proposals for three year training were
set out in the paper *Care for Tomorrow* (CCETSW, 1987). In addition to the
length of training, closer collaboration between agencies and educational
institutions and preservation of a variety of patterns leading to a new qualification were proposed. After much effort and many consultations, it was a blow to
CCETSW when its proposals were rejected by the government as too costly.
There were commentators who believed that CCETSW's staff had been naive in
thinking that a Conservative government, needing to do something about social
work training in response to the series of child abuse inquiries criticizing
training but also committed to restraining public expenditure and suspicious of
the professional aspirations of social workers, would contemplate extending the
length of training. The decision rocked the council and there were even suggestions that the government would dismantle CCETSW. The council staff had
to devise a new strategy and regain government confidence. This it did by accepting the constraint of two year training and introducing a number of significant changes as the basis for a mark II diploma in social work to replace the
existing CQSW and CSS programs. Essentially, the modified strategy incorporated key features of *Care for Tomorrow*, such as closer collaboration between
agencies and colleges, and funding was obtained for establishing interim planning committees to establish a framework of collaborative structures on a geographic basis.

CCETSW was faced with a credibility problem. Having strongly advocated
three year training how could it reasonably present revised proposals for two
year training and make a case for its being improved training? The direction
followed was to propose a more specialist approach to the structure of courses
with a substantial part of a final year to be spent practicing and studying a recognized area of concentration. Combined with this was a strengthening of assessment and monitoring student performance. Such a focus on outcomes rather
than content was compatible with the trends in service delivery and agencies and
the managerial/efficiency orientation of the conservative government.
Competence was to be the master concept. Accordingly, practice supervision
had to be strengthened through an expanded program of training for practice
teachers with both practice teachers and agencies subject to accreditation.

The new proposals were accepted by the Department of Health and set the scene for the release of new funds for the diploma. One other major issue had been resolved in 1988. The certificate of social service (CSS) had been recognized by CCETSW as a form of qualifying training to social work (i.e., equivalent in standing to the CQSW), resolving ambiguities about its academic and professional status. Thus the new diploma in social work would replace both the CQSW and the CSS and incorporate features of both patterns, thus retaining an in-service training route to professional qualification. Regulations for the new diploma were published in September 1989 and the timetable set for all programs to switch to the new pattern by 1995 (CCETSW, 1989 a). Phasing programs in gradually was important as government funds had to be increased significantly to permit one year postgraduate courses to be increased to two years.

From its own perspective, CCETSW had staged a remarkable recovery from the trough when its 1987 proposals were rejected. But there were some serious criticisms which could be mounted against the revised diploma in social work. A fundamental problem remained about the level of social work training within educational institutions. Although CCETSW maintained that the diploma in social work (DSW) would be at degree level, it could be awarded to students enrolled in colleges of further education, polytechnics and universities and to those remaining employed. The same professional award would be offered to nongraduates, undergraduates and postgraduates. The failure to identify social work courses as degree level clearly leaves a large area of ambiguity about the educational level of some programs and did nothing to enhance the status of social work courses in the universities or in the public eye. The two year minimum length of program also led to complications in relation to Europe. The European Economic Community had determined that three years was the recognized length of social work training, enabling social workers from EEC countries to be employed outside their own country. CCETSW's insularity with regard to international social work was coming home to roost, resulting in the strong possibility that U.K. social workers would be considered to have a lower level of training than most of their EEC counterparts.

A further deficit was the inadequacy of resources for training and accrediting practice teachers. A core part of the proposals was the assessment of competence. Yet the system relied for its practice teachers on social workers/practitioners, the majority of whom might change from year to year. A full accreditation training would be available to a minority of practice teachers while the majority would, in effect, be blanketed in with a short orientation program.

A more global consequence of a decade of turmoil in social work education was the distraction of large amounts of time from developing excellence in research and teaching. United Kingdom social work has historically derived most of its theory from the United States of America, initially from the transfusion of psychological (mainly Freudian) theory brought back in 1927 by the group of social workers funded by the commonwealth institute. Later in the 1960s the psychosocial theories of Helen Perlman and Florence Hollis held sway, to be followed by unitary methods and system theories in the 1970s. These influences were succeeded by the later task centered theories and behavioral approaches. The failure to produce homegrown social work theory in the last decade is partly due to the absorption of social work teachers in perpetual machinations to defend their programs within their educational institutions and against the ever increasing demands of CCETSW. The content of courses has gradually become dictated more by government policy and legislation than by independent critical thought. Whereas social policy as an academic discipline in the United Kingdom has generated a sizable output of research and publication, social work as an academic discipline has not extended the boundaries of knowledge through emphasis on research and theory building. Direct practice in social work in the United Kingdom has relied almost entirely on reworking of U.S. theory.

One feature of CCETSW's work which has had a positive influence on curriculum content in social work programs: its papers on teaching welfare rights (CCETSW, 1989 b); teaching law related to social work (CCETSW, 1991 a); teaching antiracism (CCETSW, 1991 b); teaching issues related to disability (CCETSW, 1991 c), gender and antisexism (CCETSW, 1992 a), acquired immunodeficiency syndrome (AIDS) (CCETSW, 1992 b), and substance abuse (CCETSW, 1992 c). Two studies were particularly substantive, Study V focusing on the structure and content of social work programs and Study VI focusing on research and practice (CCETSW, 1982, 1983). The pattern of such studies is to collate information on what is taught and produce recommendations on what should be. These guidelines are useful, but such an erratic approach to curriculum content and structure inevitably leads to proposals for accumulating more content without a sense of the whole. The overcrowded curriculum has been a consistent feature of U.K. social work courses for the last two decades. The new diploma with its partial return to a more specialist approach may alleviate the problem, yet not sufficiently to avoid the high risks of thinning out basic teaching in the social sciences so that many students are left with superficial knowledge and insufficiently developed capacity for critical and independent thought. By far the most interesting debates on social work education are to be found in CCETSW's publications and in the journal *Issues in Social Work Education* sponsored by the Association of Teachers in Social Work Education and published at the start of the 1980s. In spite of this, it remains a stark fact that the preoccupation with the structure of training and resources issues have led to an almost total neglect of the applications of educational theory and practice to social work education. There have been only two centers in the United Kingdom (the National Institute for Social Work and the University of Wales, College of Cardiff) where it has been possible to study educational theory and practice for social work educators. This has not been a field which has attracted significant research study. There have been a number of works (e.g. Pettes 1979; Butler & Elliott 1985; Danbury 1986) dealing, for example, with supervision practice. However, Gardener's 1989 work on supervision is one of the few based on empirical research. It is ironic that major upheavals in the education and training system have such a weak and insecure foundation, indicating the way in which the agenda for change has been set by political and policy pressures rather than evidence the new pattern will produce better quality social workers.

COMPLEMENTARY STRATEGIES: NATIONAL VOCATIONAL QUALIFICATION AND POSTQUALIFYING STUDIES

In the publication *Care for Tomorrow* (1987) CCETSW was already moving in a new direction for training social care staff in the personal social services (predominately residential and daycare staff). A major national review of vocational qualifications was initiated by the government and a report published (Manpower Services Commission and Department of Education and Science, 1986). The aim was to overcome the problems associated with a wide and disparate range of technical training schemes and qualifications by developing a national structure with uniform standards and opportunities for progression from simple levels of competence to complex skills and competencies associated with professional work. Key elements for the new approach would be assessment in the workplace and credit accumulation.

Anticipating that the certificate in social service would be later fully incorporated into a redesigned professional level, it was logical for CCETSW to link as quickly as possible with the emerging national vocational qualification (NVQ) pattern which had been fully endorsed as government policy . Existing schemes such as the preliminary certificate in social care and the in-service social care program had no general educational standing and the possibility of channeling those resources into a new pattern of progressive qualification provided an attractive rationalization of preprofessional awards. These training schemes had been valuable as the only opportunity for a staff person unable to enroll in the CSS and CQSW courses but had the limitation that they had not provided recognized qualifications which would assist their entry to high level courses.

CCETSW's speedy response to NVQ proposals meant that it was able to play a key role in the development of NVQs in social care. By 1990 requirements for the approval of assessment centers and awards issuing guidelines on assessment arrangements were established (CCETSW, 1990 a; CCETSW, 1990 b). Also, work on categorizing competency and training assessors was undertaken. To give an idea of the educational level of the NVQ it is useful to note that the overall scheme has five levels with levels four and five linking with professional training. The first two NVQs in social care are titled Residential Domicillary and Daycare: NCVQ level two and three. Many educators and agency staff who had strong commitment to residential care were strongly critical since an expectation would develop that the vast majority of residential and day care staff would be normally trained at NVQ levels two and three, with few progressing to levels four or five or to a diploma in social work courses. It is paradoxical that it is quite acceptable that services for individuals who are the most vulnerable in society and frequently have high levels of dependence and complex needs should be provided mainly by workers with low or intermediate levels of competence. Since the development of the scheme is heavily dependent on agency resources only time will tell whether this will restrict the number of staff able to have access to NVQ training and able to progress to high levels. The numbers involved are substantial; it has been estimated that there are almost 350,000 staff in the personal social services related to competency levels two and three and further 84,000 related to competency levels four and five (CCETSW, 1987).

Postqualifying training is the third sector in the United Kingdom's three pronged approach to social work education which consists of professional education and training, national vocational qualifications, and postqualifying training. During the 1980s the existing pattern was continued with limited change. Some new courses dealing with management, child care and mental health were established and there were efforts to establish joint training with nursing in work with people with learning difficulties. But there was no large increase in numbers of students, who often had great difficulty in obtaining financial support or secondary from agencies. There was significant development of part-time and modular patterns which began forward to a major shift in direction of partnership with agencies and credit accumulation. It was noted in discussing the new diploma in social work that its greater specialist orientation had major implications for postqualifying courses. The proposed new structure outlined in CCETSW Paper 31 (1990c) was similar to the diploma of social work (i.e., partnership with agencies and stress on competency and assessment). From the developing NVQ policy the influence of a credit accumulation pattern was also evident. The main features of the new system were to be the following:

1. Provision through regional consortia (agencies/colleges) approved by CCETSW
2. Differentiation of postqualifying (four year degree equivalent) and advanced levels (equivalent to master's)
3. Assessment through a variety of methods including portfolios relating to academic and practice competence
4. CCETSW postqualifying and advanced awards based on accumulation of appropriate credits

At present only approximately 0.5 percent of social workers attend postqualifying programs. CCETSW established a group of pilot programs in 1990–91 and with the goal of having its structure in place by 1993–95. The crucial issue is whether sufficient funding will be available to expand the total program. One of the reasons for the low provision at present is the low priority given by agencies. The new pattern would require a major reorganization of agency resources and staff development programs to meet the requirements. Subsidiary issues of the overall programs focus on advanced practice, education and training, management, research and the problems of catering for smaller fields of practice such as sensory impairment, employment services and educational services.

SOCIAL WORK AND EDUCATIONAL TRAINING: THE SERVANT OF THE STATE

Social work and training can not isolate themselves from the complex changes in society or from the network of social institutions involved in the discourse in social problems, a discourse which embraces conflicting views on the causes of the problems inside responses to them. Yet if education and training institutions are not able to retain some degree of autonomy and independence this zaps the capacity for critical and creative thinking. It has been one of the major strengths of social work education in the United Kingdom since the Second World War that major developments have been sensitive and responsive to need in the community and linked closely with social policy initiatives; most legislation affecting social work has been enacted with support from all major political parties. This should not have prevented us from posing the question, Have education and training become too closely reflective of state policy and philosophy?

Much of the evidence touched on in this review would indicate that this question should be answered affirmatively. The pattern of government nomination to CCETSW, very close financial and policy links between CCETSW and the Department of Health, the targeting of training funds mainly to preparing agencies and staff for implementation of the Children Act 1989 and the Health and Community Act 1990 and to introducing the diploma in social work, NVQ system and postqualifying strategy, all point to an extended state influence on the structure and content of social work educational programs. It can also be observed that whereas personal social services, including social work, were viewed in the 1960s and the 1970s as predominantly public services which were client oriented, they are now approached with significant elements of a commercial/industrial ideology; for example, the NVCQ care consortium is simply one of a number of industrial led bodies. Increasingly the type of service clients receive and the priority given to different clients are contingent on government priorities transmitted by financial leverage to agencies. Gradually the cost of different services is a stronger factor in decisions than their effectiveness. The extent to which social work education and training have been hijacked from the state aptly signaled *Personal Social Service Training: A Resource Strategy for 1991–1992 to 1993–1994* (Department of Health 1991). This report gives details on additional funding, rising from £5,000,000 in 1991–1992 to over £12,000,000 in 1993–1994. In her foreword the government minister, Virginia Bottomly, refers to CCETSW as a "Key partner in taking forward the strategy," but it is abundantly clear who the paymaster is and that the price is obedience to government policy.

To illustrate what this means, the field of social work practice in child abuse provides a useful example. Child abuse has been a political issue in the United Kingdom since the mid 1970s of a series of inquiries into cases where children were abused and ultimately died and inquires into social service departments in Cleveland, Rochdale, and the Orkneys, where children were removed from their families in highly contentious circumstances. These inquiries have almost invariably identified faults in social work practice, inadequate training and poor agency management administration as well as poor interagency coordination and communication as important factors. Also, the contributions of poverty and environmental stress to abusive situations receive little attention compared with the individual pathology approach to abusing parents and other adults. During the last decade, which has seen a large increase in recorded child abuse, the government has saved many hundreds of millions of pounds by reducing financial support for poor families and failing to address problems of squalor and homelessness effectively. Thus the additional resources for social work education and training, while significant compared with existing levels of funding, are small compared to the savings the government has made in supporting families, for example by freezing the level of child benefit through most of the 1980s. The education and training system for social work has been insufficiently critical of government policy in recent years and thus reinforces an ideological view of child abuse as almost entirely the result of parental abnormality, directing attention away from the social and environmental factors which increase the risk of abuse.

In one key area CCETSW has developed a powerful structure independently of government. This is in the field of antidiscrimination policies and equal opportunity. CCETSW established a powerful Black Perspective committee in the late 1980s which led to the formulation of a clear antiracist policy and the inclusion of requirements about antiracist practice and equal opportunities with the new diploma in social work and infused the whole of the council's work. Faced initially by a lukewarm reaction from the Department of Health, CCETSW has incorporated this theme in a central thrust, by recognizing that it will take years to implement it fully. Through an initiative with the National Institute for Social Work a series of publications and curriculum materials are being developed which will support a major enhancement of quality of teaching in this field. A less prominent but no less important focus for CCETSW attention in the 1980s was in fostering initiatives in interprofessional training for those working with people with learning difficulties. While small scale this initiative was progressive and creative, building bridges between the nursing and social work occupations.

Is the ever tightening control of the state over social work education in the United Kingdom inevitable or could the future unfold in a different direction? In the United Kingdom there is no independent professional council regulating admission to social work. The British Association of Social Workers is the main professional association for social workers but does not regulate entry to the profession or have a strong professional discipline function. In the last ten years there has been renewed interest in the concept of a general council for social work, which, if it were to gain widespread support, would exercise a disciplinary role but also provide a much stronger professional forum influencing the structure and standards of social work education. In part the evolution of social work in the United Kingdom over the last two decades has exhibited many of the characteristics of a semiprofession with bureau–professional roles and functions for social workers. This first drift away from professionally autonomous roles can be linked to the absence of strong professional institutions which could have acted as a counterweight to political and civil service control mediated through a large government quango in the form of CCETSW.

There may be further shifts with the growth of the single European market which will provide impetuous for change to the end of the decade. As an example, United Kingdom social work has had to address a failure to meet the European standard of three years as the standard length of social work courses. Nonetheless, the immediate future for social work education, in spite of CCETSW's achievements in establishing a coherent strategy, is likely to be troubled. There is no guarantee that the NVQ and postqualifying arms of the strategy will be adequately funded. CCETSW has failed to establish social work education as an unambiguously degree level field of study when half of the intake is studying on courses equivalent to the second year of a three year degree program. The research remains weak and pressures in higher education are likely to continue to restrict the scale and quality of social work research. But the outlook is not wholly bleak. During the mid–1980s there were fears that social work education would largely disappear as a subject for university study. But the resilience of social work teachers and some powerful defenders in related disciplines, coupled with strenuous efforts by CCETSW to maintain university courses, have ensured that social work has survived with a secure base in the university and in the polytechnic. The granting of university status to polytechnics has reinforced the role of social work training at university level. Once this period of major change and reorganization in social work education is worked through the stage could be set for a more creative and productive period during the latter part of the decade.

REFERENCES

Audit Commission. (1985). *Managing Social Services for the Elderly More Effectively*. London: Her Majesty's Stationery OfficeAudit Commission. (1986). *Making a Reality of Community Care*. London: Her Majesty's Stationery Office.

Barclay Report. (1982). *Social Workers: Their Role and Tacks*. London: National Institute for Social Work, Bedford Square Press & National Council for Voluntary Organisations.

Birch Report. (1976). *Manpower and Training for the Social Services*. London: Her Majesty's Stationery Office.

Brewer, C. & Lait, J. (1980). *Can Social Work Survive?* Aldershot, Hants, England: Temple Smith (Gower).

Butler, B. & Elliott, D. (1985). *Teaching and Learning for Practice*. Aldershot, Hants, England: Gower.

Central Council for Education and Training in Social Work (CCETSW) (1973a). *Report 1*. London.

CCETSW. (1973b). *Residential Work is a Part of Social Work*. London.

CCETSW. (1975a). *Social Work Curriculum Study: The Teaching of Community Work*. Paper 8. London.

CCETSW. (1975b). *Day Services: An Action Plan for Training*. Paper 12. London.

CCETSW. (1975c). *Student Units in Social Work Education: A Research Report by Kathleen Curnock*. London.

CCETSW. (1978). *Report 3*. London.

CCETSW. (1982) *Social Work Courses: Their Structure and Content (Study V)*. London.

CCETSW. (1987). *Care for Tomorrow*. London.

CCETSW. (1989a). *Dip. SW: Rules and Requirements for the Diploma in Social Work*. London.

CCETSW. (1989b). *Welfare Rights in Social Work Education: Report by a Curriculum Development Group*. London.

CCETSW. (1990a). *National Vocational Qualifications (NVQs) in Social Care: Requirements for Approval of Assessment Centers and Award of Qualifications by CCETSW (Paper 29)*. London.

CCETSW. (1990b). *National Vocational Qualifications in Care: Guidance on Approval of Assessment Arrangements (Paper 29.1)*. London.

CCETSW. (1990c). *The Requirements for Post-Qualifying Education and Training in the Personal Social Services: A Framework for Continuing Professional Development (Paper 31)*. London.

CCETSW. (1991a). *Teaching, Learning and Assessing Social Work Law (Paper 7)*. Improving Social Work Education Training Series. London.

CCETSW. (1991b). *One Small Step Towards Racial Justice: The Teaching of Anti-Racism in Diploma in Social Work Programs (Paper 8)*. Improving Social Work Education Training Series. London.

CCETSW. (1991c). *Disability Issues: Developing Anti-Discriminatory Practice (Paper9)*. Improving Social Work Education Training Series. London.

CCETSW. (1992a) *Practicing Equality: Women, Men and Social Work (Paper 10)*. Improving Social Work Education Training Series. London.

CCETSW.. (1992b). *Substance Misuse: Guidance Notes for the Diploma in Social Work (Paper 14)*. Improving Social Work Education Training Series. London.

Cooper, J. (1983). *The Creation of the British Personal Social Service, 1962-1974*. London: Heinemann.

Danbury, H. (1979). *Teaching Practical Social Work*. London: Bedford Square Press/National Council of Social Services.

Department of Health. (1989). *Caring for People: Community Care in the Next Decade and Beyond*. London: Her Majesty's Stationery Office.

Department of Health. (1991). *Personal Social Service Training: A Resource Strategy for 1991-1992 to 1993-1994*. London: Her Majesty's Stationery Office.

Gardener, D. (1989) The Impact of Conceptions of Learning on the Quality of Teaching and Learning in Social Work Education. *Issues in Social Work Education, 9* (1/2), 74–92.

Griffiths Report. (1988). *Community Care: Agenda for Action*. London: Her Majesty's Stationery Office.

Jones, C. (1979). *Social Work Education in 1900-1977*. In Parry, N., Rustin, M., & Satyamurti, C. (Eds.). *Social Work Welfare and the State*. London: Edward Arnold.

Manpower Services Commission; Department of Educational Science (1986). *Review of Vocational Qualifications in England and Wales* (Chairman: H. G. Deville). London: Her Majesty's Stationery Office.

Pettes, D.E. (1979). *Staff and Student Supervision: A Task-Centered Approach*. National Institute Social Services, Library No. 34. London: George Allen & Unwin.

Seebohm Report. (1968). *Report of the Committee on Local Authority and Allied Personal Social Services*. Cmud 3703. London: Her Majesty's Stationery Office.

Walton, R. G. (1975). *Women in Social Work*. London: Routledge & Kegan Paul.

Williams Committee Report. (1967). *Caring for People: Staffing Residential Homes*. London: George Allen & Unwin.

Younghusband, E. (1978b). *Social Work in Britain: 1950-1975*, vol. II. London: George Allen & Unwin.

Younghusband Report. (1959). *Report of a Working Party of Social Workers in the Local Authority Health and Welfare Services*. London: Her Majesty's Stationery Office.

8

SWEDEN

Willy F. Frick

HISTORICAL AND SOCIOCULTURAL CONTEXT

Development of the Swedish Welfare State

Education for social work in Sweden is characterized by historical traditions and cultural values of the Swedish society. Therefore, I would like to start by giving a short outline of some typical organizational and cultural features in the development of the Swedish welfare state. Sweden has always been a very sparsely populated nation. This has brought forth a form of social organization characterized by considerable decentralization of power, where local self-government under the influence of laypersons has been more prominent than in perhaps any other country (Sundlin, 1982). The most important local unit up to the middle of the nineteenth century was the parish. The inhabitants of the parish made their decisions at the parish meetings, where the priest served as chairperson. As time passed, the parish made more and more decisions in matters other than clerical functions. Some of these would later become classified as social work, involving care of poor, sick, and old people; measures against alcoholism; problems in the bringing up of children; conflicts within families and between neighbors.

After the Reformation during the sixteenth century, the organization of Swedish society became legitimized by principles based on Martin Luther´s Protestantism. According to this ideology, every individual was obliged to accept his/her role in society. At the same time, everybody was considered to be equal before God. The role of the priests was to function as masters in their parishes, but most of all as the people´s teachers. The king was considered the master of the whole nation. According to Swedish law, every citizen who did not work in an approved free trade had to belong to a domestic establishment. By doing so, he or she was also obliged to obey his or her master. On the other side, the masters were obliged to take care of their servants. And in some estates and factories they developed services such as family allowance, medical care, and pension insurance for their workers and their families (Hellspong &

Löfgren, 1977). Most people were not this lucky. But for most Swedes, for hundreds of years, a good society was a society where the masters at different levels were just and took good care of their subordinates.

In the middle of the nineteenth century, a new local government system was established. The new municipal system was based upon the old parish system, but now there was a separation between ecclesiastical and civil matters. From then onward, the municipalities have been responsible for the social welfare services. As time went on, the municipalities' responsibilities in these matters became quite regulated in different laws.

When the Swedish social democratic labor movement became a dominant political power during the 1930s, the metaphor of a good family as a model for a good society was revitalized. But now the ideal was no longer a good guardian. The new society should, like a good modern family, be characterized by democracy, social solidarity, equality and brotherhood. Individuals' rights as citizens were stressed together with the belief in collective solutions to social problems and a preparedness to use the state as an instrument for such solutions. There was some inspiration from traditional European utopian ideas, and a firm belief in the possibilities of rational social engineering prevailed (Hirdman, 1989). In social policy, this meant systematic efforts to create security for the citizens by universal reforms. The aim of these reforms was to create a safety net that would eliminate the need for what was considered humiliating means tested forms of assistance (Forsberg, 1984).

The socioeconomic development and the social reforms during the twentieth century brought about more duties and technically more complicated tasks for the municipalities. To make it possible for the municipalities to handle these tasks, a new organization of municipalities into larger units took place during the 1950s and 1960s. The number of communes was reduced from about 2500 to about 280. These new, larger municipalities needed to employ officials with professional competence in different areas, among them social workers (Frick, 1982). These officials' main tasks were, and still are, to prepare decisions made by boards of laypersons.

Structural Changes and Consequences for Social Work

After World War II, the demand for educated social workers increased rapidly. But that was not the only consequence. The conditions for practical social work also went through considerable changes. The following were some of the reasons.

Rationalizations within trade and industry created adjustment problems among workers. The number of people with adjustment problems became larger. At the same time it became more and more difficult to rehabilitate these people back to the labor market. This situation became quite frustrating to many social workers (Frick, 1982).

Structural changes within the economy have also created problems in the organization of different communities. In some places, people had to move out in order to get jobs, while other places grew much faster. These trends have created a situation where preventive social work and participation in community development have become more important tasks for social workers.

Since the 1960s, the immigration of refugees to Sweden from all over the world has increased rapidly. To social workers, this was a new form of stress. They were used to dealing with people from a very homogenous cultural background. Now they had to adjust to dealing with people with very different backgrounds. An ethnologist formulates the problem in the following way:

> The newcomers bring with them styles of life from the south of Europe or from the Middle East which are very foreign to the traditional Swedish mentality. The mentality of these Catholic, Orthodox or Muslim people, often with close ties to the traditional countryside, is far remote from that of the Swedish civil-servants who are in charge of their introduction into the host country. The latter are usually middle-class urban people whose lives are permeated with Lutheran and social-democratic traditions. (Sjögren, 1990: 63)

At the same time, there was an ongoing process of deinstitutionalization in Sweden. More and more old, mentally ill and handicapped people were living in their own homes, and they needed special services and care.

This situation required a new kind of legislation which provided a general framework for activities but set no detailed rules (Ministry for Social Affairs, 1974). In 1982 a new law, the Social Services Act, was implemented. This law did not regulate social work in its details. The municipalities themselves were left to apply rules to suit local circumstances and individual cases. The overall aims of the social services are presented in Section 1 of the law:

> Public social services are to be established on the basis of democracy and solidarity, with a view to promoting economic and social security equality of living conditions and active participation in the life of the community,
>
> With due consideration for the responsibility of the individual for his own social situation and that of others, social services are to be aimed at liberating and developing the innate resources of individuals and groups.
>
> Social service activities are to be based on respect for the self-determination and privacy of the individual. (Social Services Act, 1981: 5)

The Social Services Act also states that the municipality bears the ultimate responsibility for the people within its jurisdiction. It gives the boards of lay-persons and the social workers more freedom for social planning, organization of social programs and social work. But it is also more demanding. There is a need for a lot of knowledge, imagination and will power to be able to realize such aims as "equality" and "active participation" among the poor and maladjusted people in a society. Therefore, the commission that was proposing the new law was also a strong advocate of more extensive social research (Ministry for Social Affairs, 1974).

History of Social Work Education

Before World War II, most of the municipalities in Sweden were quite small. In these small municipalities social work was performed by laypersons. The first officials who were employed were usually accountants, who sometimes also had to perform different tasks within the social welfare services (Berglind & Pettersson, 1980).

Because the municipalities assumed responsibility for social services, there was little need for charitable organizations. One exception was the Central Association for Social Work (CSA), which from its establishment in 1903 was an important advocate for social policy and education in social work. This association offered courses in practical social work from 1910.

In 1921 the Institute for Social, Political and Municipal Education and Research was founded by CSA and the municipality of Stockholm (Elmer, 1991). This became Sweden's first school for the training of social workers. Similar schools were founded in Göteborg 1944, Lund 1947 and Umeå 1962. In the beginning the education was a general program for training of municipal officials. Some of the students chose to concentrate on law and social policy as their specialization. Courses in methods in social work were not so important in the beginning. Social casework as a special method in social work was not recognized until the 1950s.

Since the 1960s, the education of social workers has gone through two major changes. In 1964, the autonomous schools were turned into state-owned colleges, and 1977 they were integrated into the universities. At the same time, there was a huge expansion in the training during the 1960s and 1970s. By 1978, a total of more than twelve hundred new social work students were admitted each year (Lindholm, 1988: 118).

At the present, complete undergraduate programs in social work are offered in four universities and three colleges in Sweden. The number of undergraduate students in each program varies from about four hundred to about seven hundred. All schools are owned by the state, except one college, which is a foundation within the Swedish church. Postgraduate programs up to the doctoral degree are offered at the universities in Stockholm, Göteborg, Lund and Umeå.

Besides these programs there also exist shorter educational programs in social work at about twenty different local colleges in Sweden. These programs are mainly concentrated with working with mentally retarded, the elderly and the disabled people. These study programs last 2 to 2.5 years and do not lead to the degree of bachelor of science in social work. In my later discussion I do not include these shorter programs.

The Organization of Social Work Education

Universities in Sweden are organized in departments. A department is responsible for courses and research within a subject such as social work, psychology, sociology, law, and political science. Each department has one or more full professors in charge of research and postgraduate studies. But the administrative head of the entire department–budget, staff, students and so forth–is a chairperson, *prefekt*, who is appointed for three years at a time. Working with the chairperson is a director of studies who is responsible for the coordination of courses within a program and the teaching within the department. More than one department is usually involved in different programs. The major decisions concerning matters of the departments or the study programs are made by the boards of the departments or the program committees. These and other committees at different levels in the universities comprise teachers, researchers, students and administrators.

To become a university teacher, a doctoral degree is usually required. But once a teacher has a position at a university he or she usually can expect to stay at that position as long as he or she wants. There is no difference between teachers in social work and those in other disciplines in this respect. Many teachers in social work have their background in other disciplines, such as psychology, sociology, economy, law and political science, partly because it has only recently become possible to complete a doctoral degree in social work. These teachers have a degree that entitles them to hold academic positions and to do research. But their background also makes them part of a culture that is more or less removed from the world of practical social work. As a rule the theory teachers lack experience of professional social work.

For other teachers, practical experience is a requirement as they have to lecture in social work methods. They have the responsibility of interpreting social work from a theoretical perspective. Their background is usually a doctoral degree in social work.

Another category of teachers have as their main responsibility supervising the placements of students in practical social work and finding new fieldwork placements. They also train the student supervisors in the fieldwork agencies. This separation between teachers in theoretical and practical social work has, according to Lindholm (1988), created some problems.

The Field work training is in Sweden handled by practitioners who do not themselves have any class room teaching, and not by the social work methods teachers. This makes it difficult for the methods teachers to keep an ongoing contact with developments in the field, as they on the other hand, have too many teaching hours in school. There seems to be a lack of initiative or fear on both sides, theory and practice, regarding contacting one another. (Lindholm, 1988: 120).

Besides the teachers at the universities, the students have supervisors during their fieldwork. In addition to their salaries as social workers, the student supervisors in the fieldwork agencies receive remuneration for their work from the universities. But they are employed by the municipality, county or state.

Students

Students can apply for enrollment in a program in social work twice a year. A high school diploma with pass grades in Swedish, English, civics and mathematics is required for acceptance. However, students can also be accepted without a high school diploma. But in these cases, they have to be at least twenty-five years old, have been working at least four years and have a certificate of an acceptable level of knowledge in Swedish, English, civics and mathematics. Otherwise there is no minimum age and there is no admission interview.

About one thousand students, or about one–third of the applicants, are accepted in undergraduate programs in social work every year. Most of the students (more than 80 percent) are females. Close to 90 percent of the students who enroll in the program complete their degree (Sydow, 1988: 16). Universities and colleges are financed by the state and consequently the students do not pay any fees for the courses. However, they have to buy their books and pay for their subsistence during their time of study. Because the programs are organized as full–time studies it is not possible to work during the study period. Students who manage to keep up with their studies are entitled to loans and grants from the state. During 1991, the total sum for these loans and grants was 57,960 krona (Skr) for one year, of which 40,804 was a loan.

For almost three hundred years, students at Swedish universities have been required by law to belong to a student union and to pay a membership fee. These unions advocate the students' interests in such issues such as the quality of education, study grants and counseling. They offer a number of services to students such as book stores, health care, access to sport facilities, social welfare advice and lodging services.

The Study Program

The length of the program is 3–5 years of studies. Every year is divided into two terms–from January to the beginning of June and from the end of August to the beginning of January. At Swedish universities and colleges, courses and programs are measured according to a point system. One point corresponds to one week of full–time study. The social work program consists of 140 points according to this system.

During a term all students study full–time, one course at a time. The study results are assessed and recorded according to two or three levels–based on a pass or fail system. If a student fails a test he or she will get at least two more opportunities. Even if close to 90 percent of the students manage to complete their degree, some of them will have had to write a few tests more than once.

The organization of courses is quite similar among the universities. The broad framework and the aims of the program are centrally devised and ratified by the government, while the universities take care of the details. Teachers, students and professionals take part in the planning process at both the state and the university level.

According to the latest central study program from 1990, the aims of professional education are to provide the students with a general knowledge of individual, society, social work and social research (National Board of Universities and Colleges [UHÄ] 1990). This includes knowledge in the following areas:

- The history of social work and the development of the Swedish welfare state from a comparative international perspective
- The economic and social structure of the Swedish society, its formal organization and the way it is governed
- The living conditions for people during different stages of life and the way society effects their social problems
- The social institutions, organizations and groups for social work,
- The theories and methods of psychosocial work with individuals, families and groups
- The theories and methods of structural social work such as social planning and development of organizations and communities
- The theories and methods of social research and documentation of experiences from development projects.

The plan stresses that the education shall provide special knowledge about conditions which create social problems and the prospects of different kinds of measures against these problems. This includes such areas such as labor market and unemployment, environmental problems in workplaces and rehabilitation, family relations, obstacles to and conditions for healthy growth among children, processes of segregation, minority conflicts and immigration, and uses and abuses of drugs and alcohol.

During their education, the students are also supposed to develop their ability to communicate, to analyze and evaluate information and to present facts and assessments orally and in writing.

The preceding is the content of the program according to the central plan. In practice the different universities are free to provide this knowledge in their own ways. This leads to courses which can vary in order and content between the universities. So can the theoretical perspectives that are used in the different courses. Therefore, one can hardly say that there is one single dominant theoretical orientation in the education of social workers in Sweden. But there has been one common attitude among social workers and teachers in social work, and that is to stress the client´s rights and normality rather than the client´s obligations and abnormality. Most teachers and social workers would agree that it is better to regard the client, at least by way of introduction, as a normal person in abnormal circumstances rather than an abnormal person. But there has also been an increasing awareness of the necessity to stress the differences between men's and women's situations and experiences in society. On the other side, there are no special courses in feminist social work at the undergraduate level.

When it comes to theoretical perspectives there are a lot of variations. However, a few general tendencies can be pointed out. In working with individuals and families, different theories on crisis intervention are important. The psychoanalytic tradition, especially in the form of object relation theory, advocated by scholars such as Fairbairn, Guntrip, Klein, Mahler, and Winnicot, has a strong position. But lately, cognitive and existentialist theories have been given more and more attention. Learning theory has not been popular in social work in Sweden. In working with deviants, groups and social planning, the sociological theories of symbolic interaction and the Chicago School have given a lot of inspiration. As a consequence of the preferred theoretical perspectives, research in social work and education in research in social work are more influenced by hermeneutic than positivistic scientific philosophy and method.

Because of the central plan, the curriculum adheres quite closely to the following model independently of the university or college in which the studies are undertaken.

Terms one and two (forty points) consist of a base course in social science, including communication and perspectives from different subjects such as psychology, sociology, economy, law, political science and methods in social work.

During *term three* (twenty points), the student, besides theoretical courses, performs a fieldwork placement of at least ten points. This fieldwork is performed in cooperation with students, teachers at the university and professional social workers.

Term four and five (forty points) consist of theoretical studies on issues presented in the central study plan.

Term six (twenty points) is a period of supervised practicum in social work. It is performed in a social work setting and with a supervisor approved by the university.

During *term seven* (twenty points) the student can choose among different courses in order to get a deeper knowledge in the chosen area. In this course, he or she also writes an essay corresponding to at least ten points.

Finally, students who have passed all courses receive a diploma and a bachelor of science degree in social work.

Postgraduate Education in Practical Social Work

Besides undergraduate education, universities and colleges offer a variety of postgraduate courses in social work. Some of these courses aim at practical social work. Here there are some variations among the universities because there are no central study plans. However, two courses are offered at most of the universities and colleges with social work education: social work with a concentration on psychosocial treatment and supervision in social work.

The course in social work with a concentration on psychosocial treatment is offered to social workers who have been working a few years at work tasks entailing long-term contact with clients. The course consists of forty points and extends over two years because the students are expected to continue their work along with their studies. The course has both theoretical and practical aspects. Among the theoretical aspects are psychological and social theories relevant to social work, ethical issues, and evaluation of social work. The practical aspects of the course are mainly supervised by qualified social workers while the students are working with their clients.

The course for supervisors in psychosocial treatment aims to train supervisors for the course just discussed. It is offered to social workers who have at least five years of practical experience in psychosocial treatment and have passed the postgraduate course in psychosocial treatment. The course is both theoretical and practical and consists of thirty points.

Besides these courses, other courses are continuously under development depending upon needs expressed by social workers. The motives behind these courses are not only to contribute to the knowledge in practical social work, but to train social workers to be useful in future educational programs.

Since fall 1993 it has been possible for students in Sweden to combine different postgraduate courses for a master's degree program. The rules for acceptance and the number of points needed to reach a masters degree are the same for all disciplines and universities.

To be accepted the students need at least three years of work within a relevant field after examination from their undergraduate programs. The studies consist of a total of forty points. This includes twenty points from a mandatory basic course in philosophy of science and methods in research in social work–or any other field with a master's degree program. In this course the student has to write a thesis corresponding to ten points. Besides this course, the student can choose two courses from those offered within the master's program. In this way a student in social work can specialize in social administration or social treatment. After forty points he or she reaches the master of social work degree.

The regulations concerning master programs also mean that a student who has forty points from the course in social work with a concentration on psychosocial treatment has to complement that course with the mandatory course in social research in order to receive a master's degree.

Postgraduate Education in Research in Social Work

Since the end of the 1970s, education up to the doctoral degree in social work has been possible in Sweden. The aim of these programs is to provide the postgraduate student with the knowledge and skills necessary for independent scientific work within this field of study. This includes a deeper knowledge of sociopsychological theory, epistemology and empirical research methods.

The courses in social work follow a pattern similar to those in other disciplines. To be accepted in these courses the applicant must have completed undergraduate study of at least 120 points, of which 60 points should be in a subject relevant to the postgraduate education. The social science faculty boards have usually limited the number of students admitted to doctoral studies. In social work, this means that there are many applicants who cannot be admitted. Professional experience in social work is a considerable advantage in the admission process. Further grounds for selection are indicators of the applicant´s capability to complete doctoral studies in social work, such as results from earlier studies in social work, research skills as evidenced by reports, and project work references. At the beginning of the 1990s, there were about two hundred students in doctoral programs in social work in Sweden. Most of them are part–time students because they have to work during their studies. Some of the students have long experience in practical social work.

The courses in social work research normally requires four years of full–time study. These studies comprise a total of 160 points–theoretical courses of 60 to 80 points and a dissertation of 80 to 100 points. The courses can be taken in stages, so that the student first takes a MSc degree and then completes his or her studies for the doctoral degree in a second stage. Master of Science studies normally requires two years of full–time studies–courses of 50 points and a thesis of 30 points.

The dissertation is considered to be the most important part of the doctorate studies. It should be based on independent scientific work within the field of social work. The dissertation may be written as one complete entity or as one compilation of several reports or articles within a certain field. Dissertations and theses are defended at a public presentation seminar for which an examiner is nominated by the faculty committee. They are graded either pass or fail.

Because most of the students are working as social workers along with their studies, usually more than four years is required to complete a doctoral degree. However, at the beginning of the 1990s about thirty students had completed the doctoral degree and about twenty students had completed the master's degree.

Labor Market and the Status of Social Workers

In Sweden, organized social work is almost totally the concern of the public sector. Only about 3 percent of the social workers are employed in private companies and organizations. According to labor market statistics, about twenty-three thousand active social workers in Sweden , in the middle of the 1980s, were working in the sectors presented in Table 8–1. This table gives only a rough picture. Although most of the educated social workers are employed in the social welfare services, people with a degree in social work can be found at all levels and in many sectors of the public sector. Many have reached high posts in the administration The social work courses have given a general social science base, which has been useful in other careers (Ricknell, 1986). On the other side some people in social work positions do not have a degree in social work. One reason for this is that the labor market for social workers after World War II was expanding faster than the educational system could produce social workers Another reason is that in Sweden it is not the degree in itself that determines whether or not one can get a job in the public sector. At present, social workers are among these groups of professionals who do not have a legitimation that give them an exclusive right to certain positions.

Table 8-1

Employment Structure of Social Workers (Percentage)
(Sydow, 1988: 12-13)

Municipal social work in social agencies and schools, etc.	66%
County social work at hospitals and institutions.	17%
State social work in criminal care, employment agencies, etc.	14%
Private social work in companies and organizations.	3%+

There have always been enough jobs for educated social workers in Sweden. But the social workers who have graduated since the middle of the 1970s have had some difficulties in finding permanent positions immediately after their graduation. On the other side, it has been fairly easy to get a job as a temporary replacement, which often leads to permanent employment (Ricknell, 1986).

Social work is not a well–paid job in Sweden. In the municipal social services they receive salaries at the same level as that of elementary school teachers. Their salary (11,000–15,000 Skr) is paid monthly, and they are entitled to five weeks of paid vacation per year.

For social workers with a master's or doctoral degree the situation is a little different. Because this is a new kind of social worker there is no traditional labor market for them. Some of the new doctors in social work stay at the universities as teachers or researchers after they have completed their studies. But there is also an increasing need for applied research and developmental work in the social services. Centers for this kind of work have been established in several municipalities and counties in Sweden during the last decade. At least for some time, they will need more social workers with the knowledge and skills necessary for independent social research.

Some Trends in Social Work and Social Work Education

Structural changes in Sweden since World War II have altered the conditions for social work and consequently for social work education extensively. The Social Services Act of 1982 gave the municipalities and their social workers more freedom to organize social services according to professional rather than legal standards. Many social workers' first reaction to this was not only satisfaction but confusion. What they needed was not only knowledge but the confidence to act independently. They needed to analyze their own experiences, to perform experiments and to analyze the results. In this situation, the establishment of social work research and postgraduate education was important to boost self–confidence among social workers. Social workers now have the opportunity and have willingly assumed the responsibility for developing knowledge in their own profession. However, this does not mean that increased knowledge will solve all problems.

Social statistics is another important source of information that traditionally has been quite extensive in Sweden. As the social services have become more and more extensive, the costs for these services have also become more pronounced. According to a report from the National Social Welfare Board (1993), the need for development of empirical information in this area will be important in the future in order to make evaluation of social services and social planning as effective as possible.

Also, today laypersons in different boards and committees are formally responsible for the social services. How to control the quality of the social services in Sweden is therefore at least formally a question of political control. In practical life the situation is a little different. It is the social worker who meets the client in his or her daily work. And today social workers also have more freedom to make their own decisions within certain limits. As representatives of the state, social workers have the responsibility of securing reasonable living conditions for individuals in need. They work with people who find themselves outside the general safety net of the welfare system.

On the other side, individuals in society have their own responsibilities. It can be very frustrating to try to maintain an atmosphere of equality, democracy and freedom when the social worker has to deal with parents who abuse their children or with people who are pushing drugs. In these situations the social worker is not only a helper but also, as a representative of the state, a potential threat to the client. The new legislation with its lack of detailed rules also means that the social worker finds himself/herself with the problem of weighing the individuals' responsibilities and interests against that of society without having access to clear guiding norms and precedents. Perhaps as a consequence of this situation, there has been a growing interest in ethical issues among social workers during the last decade (Ronnby, 1988). As a response to expressed needs by social workers, guiding principles in ethical matters were developed and presented in 1985 and 1986 by the two unions which have social workers as members. However, there is no system of sanctions for social workers who deviate from these principles. In my opinion, the social workers dilemma cannot be solved in educational programs because it is a structural, and perhaps universal and unavoidable problem in social work. But it is possible to make the students more capable to handle this dilemma in a constructive way. This was also one of the major concerns of teachers in social work in Sweden during the 1980s.

Other ongoing general political and economic processes will have consequences for social work as well as social work education. One of these processes is related to globalization or international integration processes. Especially since World War II, interdependence among nations and regions in the world has been increasing in many areas such as economy, trade, culture, communication and education. One example is the development of the European Economic Community (EEC). For the present, negotiations are ongoing with regards to a Swedish membership in EEC. There have been many discussions in Sweden about the consequences of membership for the Swedish welfare system and for social work (Nygren, 1992a). For the moment nobody really knows. But one thing is clear: It will have consequences for education in social work by speeding up an already ongoing internationalization process. To participate as an equal partner in a future exchange of teachers and students among universities in Europe, Swedish universities will have to offer internationally attractive courses. Therefore, there is an ongoing process of developing courses in important languages such as English at Swedish universities. In the future, more and more courses in social work will also be given in English. This process has already started.

Another political and economic development which will affect social work is what Mishra (1984) has called "the welfare state in crisis." The fact that social work in Sweden was almost exclusively work in the public sector was rarely called in to question until the end of the 1980's. Both social planning and education in social work were based on the idea that social services were provided by people employed in the public sector. This situation started to change at the end of the 1980s and the beginning of the 1990s. Citing conservative ideas and liberal economic theories the New Right claimed that the public sector was too extensive for a well–functioning economy. These arguments gained some support from such economic circumstances as a rapidly increasing state budget deficit from the beginning of the 1990s.

Although the difference is not always clear, the arguments were both economic and ideological in nature (Nygren, 1992b). The economic arguments were mainly that the public bureaucracy was too inflexible, was ineffective and was spending money that was needed in the private sector. The ideological arguments claimed that people should have more freedom to choose among different kinds of services, including social services. They also claimed that a generous social policy obstructed people's will to work and to take responsibility for their own lives. The solutions to these problems were to privatize as much as possible of the public sector, to increase fees for public services and to reduce social benefits such as unemployment benefits, sickness benefits, and pensions.

So far, the privatization of social services has mainly affected social services such as day care for children, homes for the elderly, domestic services, some health care institutions and some institutions for rehabilitation of alcoholics and drug addicts. Within these areas there are relatively few professional social workers. Most of the staff have other kinds of education. At the same time, those who are working in the private institutions are doing about the same work as they did in the public sector. Therefore, these changes can hardly be expected to lead to any drastic changes in the labor market for social workers or in social work education. But, of course, teachers in social work will have to observe developments in the labor market and adjust the content of courses accordingly.

Reduced benefits from the social insurance system may have other consequences for social work and social work education. Because of reduced benefits from the state, more people will probably become dependent on the municipal social services. Squeezed between the municipalities' struggle to save money and the demands from an increasing number of clients, social work may become a more and more tough and frustrating job. If this happens, there is also a risk of a change in the relation between social workers and their clients. Already today, many social workers feel like targets for the conservative propaganda. According to this propaganda, too indulgent social workers are depriving their clients of their power of initiative and are making them incapable of taking responsibility for their own life. In this literature (Riviere, 1993), social services, social workers and their clients are often described in extremely disparaging ways. At the bottom, there is a general expression of contempt for human weakness which is quite unfamiliar to traditional Swedish culture. In this situation it is (in my opinion, and, I daresay, in that of most social workers and teachers in social work) important to defend those "feminine values" which, according to Hofstede (1980, 1991), are deeply rooted in the Swedish culture and which constitute the basis of the Swedish welfare state. Ideally this task will characterize social work education in Sweden during the coming years.

REFERENCES

Berglind, H. & Pettersson, U. (1980). *Omsorg som yrke eller omsorg om yrket* (Care as profession or care of the profession). (Report from the Secretariat of Future Studies). Stockholm: Liber.

Elmér, Å. (1991). Socionomutbildningen i Sverige (The education of social workers in Sweden). *Nordisk socialt arbete, 11,* 31–40.

Frick, W. (1982). *Strukturomvandling och social utslagning* (Structural change and social elimination), Doctoral dissertation, Research reports from the department of Sociology, 67, University of Umeå.

Forsberg, M. (1984). *The Evolution of Social Welfare Policy in Sweden*, Lund: The Swedish Institute.

Hellspong, M. & Löfgren, O. (1977). *Land och stad* (Countryside and city). Lund: Natur och Kultur.

Hirdman, Y. (1989). *Att lägga livet tillrätta* (To put life in order). Stockholm: Carlssons.

Hofstede, G. (1980). *Culture's Consequences.* London: Sage Publications.

Hofstede, G. (1991). *Organisationer och kulturer* (Organizations and cultures). Lund: Studentlitteratur.

Larsson, S. (1991). Forskning i socialt arbete - svenska erfarenheter (Research in social work - Swedish experiences). *Nordisk socialt arbete, 11,* 103–111.

Lindholm, K. (1988). *Den sociala utbildningens identitet* (Identity of social work education). (Report in social work, 43). Stockholm: University of Stockholm, Department of Social Work.

Ministry for Social Affairs. (1974). *Socialvården Mål och medel* (Social services - Goals and means). (Report from the Swedish Commission on Social Services, SOU 1974:39). Stockholm: Göteborgs Offsettryckeri.

Mishra, R. (1984). *The Welfare State in Crisis.* Brighton, England: Wheatsheaf.

National Board of Universities and Colleges (UHÄ). (1990). *Central studieplan för sociala linjen med föreskrifter av universitets- och högskoleämbetet (UHÄ)* (Central study plan for social work education with directions from the national board of universities and colleges (UHÄ)). (Regnr D 23–1307–90). Stockholm.

National Social Welfare Board. (1993). *Statistik för uppföljning och utvärdering av socialtjänsten* (Statistics for follow-up and evaluation of social services). (Report SoS - 1993:1). Stockholm: Norstedts.

Nygren, L. (1992a). *Sverige och EG - Anpassing till vad?* (Sweden and EEC - Adjustment to what?). University of Umeå, Department of Social Welfare. Unpublished manuscript.

Nygren, L. (1992b). *Trygghet under omprövning* (Security under reconsideration). Stockholm: Publica.

Ricknell, L. (1986). Social work education in Sweden. In Brauns, H. J. & Kramer, D. (Eds.). *Social work education in Europe.* Frankfurt: Deutscher Verein Fur Offentliche und Private Fursorge.

Riviere, H. (1993). *Meningen var ju att hjälpa människorna, inte att ta ifrån dem ansvaret* (The meaning was to help people, not to take away their responsibility). Stockholm: City University Press.

Ronnby, A. (Ed.). (1988).*Etik och idehistoria i socialt arbete* (Ethics and humanities referring to the history of social work). Umeå: Socionomen.

Sjögren, A. (1990). Intregity and honor. In *The Organization of Diversity in Sweden.* Botkyrka: The Swedish Immigration Institute and Museum.

Social Services Act and Care of Young Persons (Special Provisions) Act /LVU. (1981). Stockholm: Ministry of Health and Social Affairs International Secretariat.

Sundin, J. (1988). *Kontroll - straff och försoning* (Control - punishment and reconciliation). (Forskningsrapporter från historiska institutionen, 1). Umeå: University of Umeå, Department of History.

Sydow, B. (1988). *Utbildning för socialt arbete* (Social work education). (UHÄ - report, 1988: 1). Stockholm: National Board of Universities and Colleges.

9

FRANCE

Paul V. Taylor

HISTORY OF SOCIAL WORK EDUCATION

Social work arises out of, exists because of, the relationship between a society and those who are deemed to be "in need." This is a simplified rationale of diverse and complex processes of aid, care and protection to which must be added the key feature of contemporary European social work: that is, the pivotal role of the state as the broker of this relationship. Consequently, the history of social work education has to be seen against the backdrop of the intricate and frequently changing interplay of these three variables: the state, the individual and the society.

In France, social work has not generally been considered an academic discipline, nor a profession. While the practice of social work has a coherent fieldwork identity, the training and education for such work are largely undertheorized and sectorized. The reasons for this are both ideological and historical.

The term *travail social* (social work), which came into vogue in the early 1970s, was a direct translation of the Anglo-American expression, although the French term has a wider connotation than the English and would include, for example, some teachers, doctors, court officials and even civil servants within the Department of Social Security.

The *work* element of *travail social* covers four main areas: the provision of aid (*aide sociale*) for those in financial need; social security (*sécurité sociale*) based on based on welfare allowances and benefits, particularly for those in work, and financed by an individual's/employer's contribution system; social action (*action sociale*), the widest and least defined domain of social work, which concentrates on social groups rather than on individuals and covers such issues as immigration, urban rehabilitation, antidrug campaigns, the transition from school to work for the young, rural deprivation and provision for the elderly; prevention (*prévention sociale*), mostly founded on a medicopathological model of society which targets anticipated or actual problems (e.g., delinquency, unemployment, lack of social adaptation, and rehabilitation and reeducation of the mentally or physically handicapped).

The *personnel* of this wide range of social work comprises three main "professions" (*carrières sociales*): social assistants (*assistantes de service social*) who offer psychosocial or material help to families or individuals in difficulty; special needs educators (*educateurs spécialisés*), who work, mostly outside the formal education system, with the mentally and physically handicapped or those with severe behavioral problems; community and youth workers (*animateurs socio–culturels*), who are engaged more in social or community development with particular groups or in specific institutions (Ion & Tricart, 1984).

French *travail social* therefore represents not a single profession but a range of activity (*une mode d'intervention*) in the social sector which is undertaken by a very disparate group of workers who by qualification are recognized by the Ministry for Social Services (*Ministère Chargé des Affaires Sociales*) and who "see themselves having social, educational, psychological or medico-social responsibilities to work with people in difficulty" (Thévenet & Désigaux, 1985).

The social assistant is the most established and perhaps the most widely recognized social worker. The first nationally accredited diploma in social work (*diplôme d'etat*) was created in 1932. The French title *assistante* indicates that this was and remains a female profession. Many of the first workers were nurses, and certainly the main thrust of the work has been directed toward medicosocial aims. From the turn of the century, but especially in the interwar years (Verdès-Leroux, 1978), there was a major concern for public health, and the assistants targeted families, particularly with children, for example through antituberculosis campaigns. The dominant motivation was the protection of children in the context of improved public health.

This therefore also gave the social worker a social control or normalizing role reflected, for example, in campaigns against alcoholism or through preventative education initiatives on personal hygiene, infant care, nutrition and proper housekeeping. According to a later ministerial decree,[1] the role of the assistant was "to identify the things which threaten the physical, psychological, economic or moral stability of an individual, family or group, and to take all necessary remedial action" (Decree, 1959).

This basic role of the assistant was supplemented in 1949 by the first training and certification of family workers (*travailleuses familiales*), whose main role was to help with the family and with housework, either "working with the mother in the home, or working with the elderly, the sick or the disabled." A further aim of the family worker was to contribute to the "maintenance or reestablishment of a stability in the family with whom she works" (Decree, 1974).

While considering this aspect of social work, which is concerned primarily with the family, children or the elderly, we can note also the home helps (*aides ménagères*). Their training is organized by their employers, either a private association or the Bureau d'Aide Sociale, and has been formally recognized since 1962. They work with families but mostly with the elderly, helping them with housework, cooking, cleaning and looking after their personal needs.[2]

Since 1960, there has also been a specific training for economic counselors (*conseillers en economie sociale et familiale*). They usually work in Social Security offices, hospitals or large social centers, and their role is to "offer information and advice or training to adults to help them resolve problems in their daily life" (Order, 1973). With the advent of the economic crisis of the early 1970s, and the recidivism of poverty in the 1980s, the function of the economic counselor as a key actor in social work provision was reinforced.

The importance of economic development as the central factor of social development has critically influenced both social policy and social work practice in the last twenty-five years. The traditional social work approach concentrating on children and the family was seen to be making only a cosmetic difference to problems of unemployment, immigration, urban deprivation, failure at school (*échec scolaire*) and profound alienation of young people (Dubet, 1991; Ion: 1990, Rupp, 1986).

There was a return to "global politics" that sought to move away from blaming the victims to confront the complex and interlocking problems of social disadvantage. Within our review of the history of social work training, four points need to be noted.

First, the central government, faced with the often conflicting issues of, for example, urban agglomeration and housing need, immigration and racism, unemployment and national minimum wage, guaranteed apprenticeship for young people and the crises of confidence in the education system, has frequently resorted to processes of consultation and decision making based on interministerial advisory councils and committees. The Council of Social Work (*Conseil Supérieur de Travail Social*) and the National Commission for the Training of Youth and Community Workers (*Commission Nationale pour la Formation à l'Animation*) typify such multidisciplinary, multiagency policy planning and administration. The process may indeed bring a wider perspective to bear on critical social issues, but one other effect has been the reinforcement, at this governmental level, of the priority of generic social work.

Second, through such processes, social work training and certainly the qualifying entrance exams and criteria for selection are subject to central government control and monitoring. While most diplomas or certificates in social work are nominally delivered in the name of the minister of education, the organization of the course and the exams is frequently done conjointly by "the Minister of Justice, the Minister of Education, the Minister of Health, and the Secretary of State responsible for Youth, Sports and Leisure" (Decree, 1970). Again, while this collective view aids the politics of consensus, it does not necessarily mean that those involved have a detailed knowledge or appreciation of social work practice. The advantage may lie in the standardization or uniformity of training, parallel in many ways to the models of the *National Curriculum* which are prepared for all subjects and disciplines within the education system (*education nationale*). The disadvantage is that such models of professional training reflect the urban focus of central government concerns and do not sufficiently take into account the needs and interests of the large population who live in the often deprived rural areas of the country.

This centralization of education and training for social work, which applies to all levels of courses whether they are offered by universities, colleges or private associations, is in contrast to the decentralization of social work practice whereby central government has devolved to the *départements* responsibility for service delivery across the board (Thévenet, 1989).

The key dates of a two-stage reform that resulted in the creation of the Regional Councils of Social Services (*Direction Régionale des Affaires Sanitaires et Sociales: DRASS*) which brought together the administration of social security, social services, and public health are 1964 and 1975. Each region comprised a number of divisions (*circonscriptions*) which were further localized into sectors (*secteurs*). It was intended as a structure which would support "global social action" and which would give a coherence to social work intervention of all the workers in a given area, "social workers, para-medics, social administrators, inspectors, doctors, teachers, magistrates and other representatives of local groups" (Decree, 1975).

One important outcome of these organizational changes has been a growing recognition of the core content of social work. Despite the differences in training, job titles and employers, many social workers are doing the same or very similar work with families, individuals and communities. There is, therefore, an important contemporary debate about the specificity of training and the identification of core training pertinent to all social workers and about the validity of discrete courses and qualification for those who are in effect generic social workers.

This potential return to generic social work contrasts with the emphasis on specialist training in the 1960s and 1970s which accompanied a movement to respond to social deprivation not by treating families or individuals but by educating for prevention and by promoting social and cultural action.

The role of the special needs educators (*educateurs spécialisés*) has its origins not in the construction of the industrial base from which the social assistants came (Kaluszynski, 1986) but in the social reconstruction which started in Vichy France during the war where many sections of the population, particularly children, were for many reasons "maladjusted" (Chauvière, 1980). The educators worked predominantly in the private sector, and the first actual state control was brought about through regulating entry into the profession through a formal diploma in 1967. Their main role was and is in working either in institutions or in the community with adolescents and children who are maladjusted or who are mentally or physically disabled. Their emphasis is on medi-cosocial curative intervention, and on psychoeducational therapy and guidance.

The post of educational monitor (*moniteurs educateur*) was created three years later, 1970, as a supplementary post to assist the special needs educators. Although both educators worked to the same salary scale and with the same clients, the role of educational monitor was deemed to be of lower status, requiring only two year training leading to a certificate rather than a diploma.

In the political and economic atmosphere where to be out of work was to be out of society, and where to have a job was seen as a key test of integration and social adaptation,[3] a high proportion of the educators' work was in getting their clients into work, protected workshops or apprenticeships. The post of special needs technical educator (*educateurs techniques spécialisé*) was created in 1976, with entry through three year certified training (Order, 1976). The technical educator is primarily responsible for providing or organizing training and apprenticeships for groups of handicapped people to enable them to get jobs and be fully active members of society.[4]

This theme of active social and personal development, which finds its origins in the long taproot of community education (*éducation populaire*), went wider than the sphere of directed learning (Prost, 1986). In the post 1968 years, great emphasis was placed on cultural and recreational development as a means of creating social stability. This resulted in the accreditation and training of a third group of social workers, the youth and community workers (*animateurs sociaux et socio-culturels*).

The youth and community workers, qualified by a university diploma (*diplôme universitaire de technologie*) from 1970 or by a state diploma (*diplôme d'etat relatif aux fonctions d'animation*) delivered since 1979 through accredited colleges or Associations, are at once social assistants, educators and community organizers. They work in community centers, hostels for young people or the elderly, holiday centers, and sports and recreational facilities, as much in urban rehabilitation projects as in rural development (Poujol, 1989).

THE CULTURAL CONTEXT OF SOCIAL WORK

The threefold division of social work reveals the fundamental value system which underpins such work and which seeks to define the norms on which social integration is based in terms of the family, education and culture.

More liberal attitudes in recent years to marriage, sexuality, homosexuality, the role of women and the place of children in society have undoubtedly influenced reactions to contraception and abortion, single parent families, divorce, parental responsibilities, and the role of elderly parents and grandparents in the family (INSEE, 1990). However, despite important demographic changes in population (for example, a birth rate of only 1.8, which suggests the demise of the traditionally French *famille nombreuse)*, the "family" is still seen as the standard bearer of established values (INED, 1990).

The traditional view that the family is the cornerstone of the society remains true for many today. In a country impregnated with the values of the Catholic church (less than 7 percent of the population have not been baptized), most social welfare provision is directed toward the family, and particularly toward the mother and child, and toward children in danger, be that physical, financial, moral or cultural.[5] The church's charitable commitment to aid the deserving poor and deprived was incorporated into the laicized welfare state (*etat providence*), which equally strives to come to the aid of all its citizens while maintaining a degree of social order by so doing.

The model of the child in need epitomizes the "typical" social work client as someone who needs to be educated, socialized, adapted to or integrated into the society. Those who are not integrated into society or who do not conform to the norms and to accepted social controls are commonly seen as deviants, marginalized, maladjusted, delinquents, or ill (*déviants, marginaux, inadaptés, délinquants, malades*) and are, therefore, proper targets of educational initiatives. By extension, other nonconforming individuals or groups (e.g., the elderly, the unemployed, the handicapped, the poor, and especially immigrants), must also be educated to find their proper place in society (Lesaulnier, 1991).

Therefore, while the social assistant may speak of social equilibrium, integration or mainstreaming, the special needs educator will emphasize rehabilitation, reintegration and reeducation (Valls-Lacroix, 1989).

The explicit rationale of social work is, therefore, that there is some normative society to which the deprived or marginalized can be helped to adjust. The social worker, who frequently acts as intermediary between the two groups, is thereby placed in a dual role as an agent of change and development *and* an agent of control and conformity.

The contradiction in a professional practice which seeks to censure deviancy and encourage movement toward a social norm is most particularly evident in the ambivalence of values associated with cultural identity.

The growing influence in France in recent years of the extreme Right has revived charges of anti-Semitism, racism and the politics of exclusion. The question of immigration, cultural invasion and cultural protectionism arises in almost any contemporary debate about employment, education, housing or youth–all fundamental social issues whose practical consequences (in terms of discrimination, marginalization, poverty and alienation) confront social workers every day (Taguief, 1991).

On the one hand, liberals assert the value of cultural diversity, the right of the individual, and tolerance of any group's wish for self-determination (Commission Nationale, 1991). On the other hand, there are many countermovements, which are by no means all from the extreme Right and which lie between an ill-informed cultural protectionism and an informed and thoroughly justified desire not to dilute or lose a personal and collective sense of cultural and national identity (Hurstel, 1988). In response to this social and professional tension, generally the training programs do not include the examination of, or experience of, social work theories and practices from other countries: they are markedly monocultural, supporting a practice which aims more at cultural integration than at pluricultural diversity.

The benchmarks of cultural integration and adaptation which underpin the objectives of social work are normally set at the level of speaking and writing French (*school*), living a family life based on Christian values (*church*), and being gainfully employed (*economic state*). It is therefore straightforward for social workers who work *for* the state to identify their clients among the unqualified, the young unemployed and those of "ethnic origin," or among the poor, the elderly and the handicapped. What is not clear is how social workers who want to work *with* their clients to confront the structural inequalities contributing to alienation and marginalization can construct objectives and strategies of professional practice which are not in conflict with the values of their employers and the dominant society (Rupp, 1986).

The fact is that they are not prepared for that conflict. In no social work diploma or certificate course is there any formal consideration of personal racism/sexism awareness training, nor any in-depth analysis of cultural hegemony. On the contrary, the dilemmas which confront the social worker as broker or intermediary between the state and the individual are assuaged by the repeated assertion that the social worker is professionally neutral.

In pursuing this goal of professionalism, which echoes the new schools of modern management and administration, social workers find themselves lacking the committed clarity which their forbears had about social, charitable militancy. They occupy the hinterland between the state and society and those who are disadvantaged and excluded. However, they tend, by personality and by training, to identify with both parties (Secretary of State, 1988). Thus, in a very real sense the current tensions and conflict of values within French social work both are caused by and in turn reproduce the problems and conflicts in society which it is meant to treat (Valls-Lacroix, 1989).

THE RANGE AND STRUCTURE OF SOCIAL WORK EDUCATION

As we have seen, the term *social work* does not connote a single profession but rather a disparate group of professionals and semiprofessionals who work in the area of social deprivation and marginalization and who are involved in social action in a way that is, essentially, either *reactive* or *proactive* (Alfandari, 1989).

This obviously means that there is an equally wide range of social work education and training. Thévenet and Désigaux (1985) identify a hierarchy which is widely recognized and which is based on levels of recruitment and educational attainment.

- Level 1: Training approved or organized by the Ministry of Social Affairs through accredited colleges or Associations which does not require a School Leaving Certificate (*Baccalauréat*) (e.g., home helps, family workers)
- Level 2: Training which may require only a preliminary certificate of schooling (*brevet*), but which may require several years of relevant experience (e.g., monitors–educators, marriage guidance counselors)
- Level 3: Training of two or three years which requires the *baccalauréat* or an equivalent qualification (e.g., social assistants, special needs educators, community and youth workers)
- Level 4: Training for managers (e.g., regional or area directors), which is undertaken by an approved National Center of Training (*Ecole Nationale*) or the higher diploma in social work (*diplôme supérieur de travail social* [DSTS]).

While most professions within social work offer initial, in-service and postqualification training, the diversity of training is such that there is no one "professional route," although training at Level 3 is perhaps numerically the most significant. What is more significant in the field is that although workers may be involved in the same or similar tasks, their individual levels of salary are related more to their level of training and qualification than to their years of service or experience.

To illustrate how access to the profession is controlled, how the courses of training are constructed within a particular rationale and ideology of social work, and how that relates to the kinds of social work interventions which we have outlined earlier, we can look at selected programs of basic education and training (for Level 1: family workers; for Level 3: special needs educators and community and youth workers) before considering the higher diploma in social work.

The Training of Family Workers: *Travailleuses Familiales*

The training for family workers (Order, 1974), which lasts eight months, starts with an introductory field placement of four weeks. After that, there is a course of fourteen weeks, which covers home economics, hygiene, child care and family life and society. A part-time placement of four weeks in a *creche*, kindergarten, play group, or other setting is followed by a final six weeks of paid placement working with a family.

At the time of the final examinations, the student must be at least twenty-one years old. No previous academic qualification is required, but a medical certificate attesting that the student has adequate physical and mental health to be a family worker is demanded.

The Training of Special Needs Educators: *Educateurs Spécialisés*[6]

The training for special needs educators (Decree, 1990: 574) parallels that of social assistants: a three year initial training, followed by the possibility of in-service training and finally progression to a higher diploma (DSTS). The courses can only take place in those colleges or training agencies which have been formally accredited, and therefore financed, in part or in whole, by the ministers of education, youth and sports, justice, and health.

Candidates for entry must have passed the *baccalauréat* or the special entrance exam (*examen de niveau*). This latter comprises three written exams which test essential literacy skills and knowledge of current affairs. The initial training is made up of 1450 hours of course work, plus fifteen months of field placements. The course focuses on the educator "together with all others who are involved in educational, therapeutic or social action," who have "responsibilities for looking after children, adolescents or adults who are psychologically or physically deficient, or who have behavioral or social problems" (Order, 1990). Hence the rationale for the eight modules of the course:

1. General psychology: human relations, 180 hours
2. Communication skills: 160 hours
3. Handicap: disability and special education, 240 hours
4. Group work: 160 hours
5. Economics and society: 160 hours
6. Introduction to law: 180 hours.
7. The professional context of education: 160 hours
8. In-depth study of a selected topic: 160 hours

For each of these modules, the main outlines are given by the ministers as are the means for examining and assessing each module. The latter include written essays, bibliographic reviews, individual or group projects, detailed observation notes, and a dissertation.

The fieldwork placements, of which there are four, begin with a seven month placement. Two further field practices, each of two months' duration, must cover different aspects of special needs education. The final practice of at least one month is not institution based but must be related to education. The ministers require that students be assessed on their personal and professional competence, their ability to relate professionally with clients, and their capacity to work in a team with other educators as well as on their written fieldwork reports and on an *autocritique* of their practice.

To obtain the diploma (*diplôme d'etat d'educateur spécialisé*), students must present a written dissertation which is also subject to an oral examination by a jury comprising tutors and fieldwork specialists. In addition, they must present four pieces of course work and their fieldwork record book. Finally, there is a written examination of four hours on selected course modules. Within the overall framework of assessment, the successful student must achieve at least 50 percent of the available marks.

Training of Youth and Community Workers: *Animateurs Socio-Culturels.*

There are two professional diplomas in *animation socio-culturelle,* the DUT and the DEFA. For entrance into the latter, the *baccalauréat* is not required but usually candidates must have at least three years of professional experience.

The course comprises a taught element, practical experience and a probationary period of professional work. The course taught is based on five modules, each of 160 hours minimum, covering interpersonal relations, management and administration, techniques of community/youth work (an introductory and an advanced module) and the social context of community/youth work. A system of continuous assessment applies throughout the modules.

The field practice lasts a minimum of four months, within which there must be at least two hundred hours of direct contact with the public. After satisfactorily completing these two parts of the initial training, the student must undertake a supervised probationary period of nine months before the diploma is awarded.

The DEFA normally lies within the domain of the associations and accredited training agencies,[7] while the DUT is offered within the initial cycle (the first two years) of a university, for which, normally, the *baccalauréat* is required. This does mean, in the latter case, that the average age of students is nineteen to twenty years.

Typically, such training follows the pattern of multidisciplinary teaching (psychology, sociology, history, law, management) alongside practical workshops on technical competencies (video, sound, dance, theater, photography) and communication skills. The course is structured around three field placements.

The academic course is based on five modules, each of which lasts between two and five months:

1. Social work and community/youth work
2. The family and society
3. Communication and language
4. Culture, youth and society
5. Education, therapy and social work

This represents some thirty hours of class work or workshops per week throughout the university year of thirty weeks. To this is added the three placement periods: one month introductory placement in the first weeks of the course, a second month in a different center or agency in the first year, and a final placement of two months during the second year. By the end of the course, each student must have worked in two of the three main areas of *animation*: sociocultural, prevention and medicosocial.

The Higher Diploma in Social Work: *Diplôme Supérieure en Travail Social*

Certain social workers (assistants, educators or animators) can continue to postgraduate training. They will have an initial qualification and will have been in post for at least five years. During this time they will have undertaken between five hundred and six hundred hours of in-service training. Effectively they will be senior practitioners who are in a position that entails some managerial responsibility (Order, 1978).

The course is under the aegis of the minister of health. It is based on a maximum of 670 hours of education and training and is in two parts.

- **Part 1** (350 to 420 hours) is obligatory for all students. Its seven modules cover social policy, management and administration, the organization of social services, social action initiatives, introduction to research skills, education and teamwork.
- **Part 2** (180 to 250 hours) offers three options, of which the student must choose one:

  1. The structure and management of social work
  2. Training the trainers: course development and managerial supervision
  3. Research and Social Work: statistics and research techniques and implementation

The diploma is awarded primarily on the basis of a research thesis relating to a subject within the option chosen. For the written thesis and for the subsequent oral examination, the successful student must achieve at least 50 percent of the marks available.

COMMENTARY

As a generalization, it is probably true to say that social workers have a sense of powerlessness, faced as they are with individual social and individual problems of enormous complexity (Rupp, 1986: 140). They feel themselves simply functionaries, the service delivery arm of state policy.

This view is understandable when one sees the central role of the state at all levels of social work from planning and training to policy and delivery. Ceccaldi (1984) notes how the state has taken over the traditional charitable task of caring for families, protecting children and looking after public health. In fact, the decrees and orders relating to social work training and provision have increased, certainly since the war, in exactly the same degree as the state has become more and more interventionist in the domain of social welfare (Fouquet & Clavel, 1978).

The state plans, controls and finances social work education and training. Some students are thereby eligible for certain grants and bursaries; others receive allowances during their training. Of particular importance is the training within employment (*formation en cours d'emploi*), for which employers are currently obliged to contribute 1.4 percent of their total salary costs (Order, 1991: it was intended that this percentage should rise to 2.1 percent in 1993).

As we have seen, historically social work has extended from assistance to education and more recently to community work. This range is reflected in the widening of the periodic "national plans" since the war. The three plans between 1947 and 1958 were concerned with modernization and reconstruction. The dominant theme of the next five plans, from 1962 until 1980, was economic and social development. Since 1984, the plan has been targeted on social and cultural development (Rupp, 1986).

This broadening of the field of social work has brought into relief the debate about generic versus specialist workers. One the one hand, there is a clear overlap in the work of assistants, community/youth workers and educators and certainly in the subprofessions in those three areas. The reforms concerning the training of special needs educators and monitor-educators clearly note the complementary nature of their work. However, this has not yet led to the creation of core courses or common foundation courses except at the level of the higher diploma.

At the lower end of professional training, the tendency is toward further specialization and role demarcation. The more the "social field" has become the common denominator of numerous professions, including those which previously were more clearly "health professions" (child welfare workers [*puéricultrices*] and midwives [*sages-femmes*]), the more has there been a movement to distinguish the contribution of each profession, either through independent management processes or, most often, through separate professional training and qualification (Blanc et al., 1986).

The devolution of service delivery to the *départements* implies therefore the coordination of disparate workers within differing agencies rather than the management of a single Polytechnic service.

This also means that the control and monitoring of the service lie at national rather than at departmental level. One the one hand, there is no union or association which can impose or sanction a professional code of practice. Complainants alleging malpractice must take their case to the civil or criminal courts. It is assumed that the filtering mechanisms for entry into the profession have taken place through selection processes prior to training. On the other hand, research and assessment of social needs and interests and thereby the evaluation of the efficacy of social work remain the responsibility of the state and not of field practitioners.

Research methodology and action research feature little in the training programs and then mostly at the level of postinitial qualification, for example, within the higher diploma in social work (Duchamp et al., 1989). Nonetheless, the current Directory of Research relating to social work and social sciences (Cahiers, 1989) lists some ninety-seven research groups or institutions from both the public and private sectors,[8] but only thirteen universities, notably Paris, Nantes, and Lyon, which offer studies in related disciplines (sociology, psychology, economics, science of education) through to doctoral level.

The role of research in social work essentially serves the political and administrative arm of the state in that it provides a quantifiable, scientific measure of both governmental policies and social needs provision. The majority of research projects in this field are in fact commissioned by government ministries. For practitioners, on the other hand, research provides a framework of ideas, a professionalizing or "scientifizing" of their work rather than a means of adapting or perfecting the content of their involvement with those in need (Martin, 1986).

Social work, from its initial training to its implementation, is thus clearly anchored within the social policy and welfare ideology of the state. It can be said that the provision of social work is franchised as much to the *départements* of local government as to the many associations and charities in the voluntary sector which are now indispensable to the provision of state welfare.

While in other countries, this might provoke a debate about the responsiveness to local need versus funding from central government, or bring into question the value of supposed distinctions between statutory/voluntary, professionalizing/deprofessionalizing of social work, this is not currently the case in France. What concerns the providers and the users of social work is not a holistic analysis of social need based on the right of the individual to state-provided welfare, but rather the principles of egalitarianism which seek to standardize such provision at the point of individual need. There is thus a panoply of complex administration, regulations and controls which govern all aspects of social welfare, little of which, however, is taught in formal social work training. The social worker is seen by clients and by administrators primarily as an agent, an implementer of state welfare, a functionary (*fonctionnaire*) or civil servant for whom the state necessarily provides an adequate education and training. It is in this light that social work has come to be seen as a profession rather than as a vocation.

NOTES

1. References are given in this chapter to Decrees (*décrets*) and ministerial orders (*arrêtés*) which are identified in the text by date and in the References by date and by serial number or page of the full text which can be found in the *Journal Officiel de la République Française*.

2. Not included here are other groups of workers who would be considered social workers: family or marriage guidance counselors (*conseillers conjugaux et familiaux*), and social work auxiliaries (*auxiliaires de vie*). While they have an important role in the delivery of social services, they are not a priority in terms of social work training and education.

3. The Schwartz Report (1980), on which was based the *Missions Locales* and a major program to encourage youth training and employment, reflects these fundamental values.

4. Not included here are other groups of workers who would be considered educators: Medical assistants (*aides médico-psychologiques*) who were recognized as a social work profession in 1972, and kindergarten/play group assistants (*educateurs de jeunes enfants*), for whom a two year training course was initiated in 1973 (Decree, 1973). Most notably not included are the probation service educators (*educators de l'education surveillée*), who work within the Ministry of Justice. Since the Decree of 1990 (166), the term *education surveillée* has been replaced by "the judicial protection of young people" (*la protection judiciaire de la jeunesse*).

5. A detailed historical account of the "discovery of childhood" and the emergence of the child-centered family is to be found in Ariès (1986).

6. The selection here is made on the basis of a recent survey of social workers which suggested that special needs educators spearheaded social work provision. In 1990–91, there were some 35,500 educators (more than double the number in 1974) and some 33,000 social assistants. See "Les éducateurs spécialisés: le vécu en chiffres" (1991, September 19) in *Le Lien Social*, pp. 11–14.

7. Among the many could be noted Centre National de Formation à l'Animation (CNFA), Comité Protestant des Centres de Vacances (CPCV), Institut National Leo Lagrange (INLL), Institut de Formation aux Carrières Sociales (IFCS), Mouvement Rural de la Jeunesse Chrétienne (MRJC), and les Scouts de France (SDF).

8. Of particular importance might be Institut National de la Statistique et des Etudes Economique (INSEE), Institut National d'Etudes Démographiques (INED), Centre National de la Recherche Scientifique (CNRS), Centre de Recherche sur le Travail Social (CRTS), Mission Interministerielle Recherche Expérimentation (MIRE), and Centre de Recherche Interdisciplinaire de Vaucresson (CRIVE).

REFERENCES

Alfandari, E. (1989). *Action et Aide Sociales.* Paris: Dalloz.

Ariés, P. (1986). *Centuries of Childhood.* Harmondsworth: Peregrine.

Blanc, B. et al. (1986). *Actions Collectives et Travail Social.* Vol.1. *Contextes et Réalisations*, Paris: Editions E.S.F.

Ceccaldi, D. (1984). *Les Institutions Sanitaires et Sociales.* Vol.1. *Cadre Général et Grandes Structures.* Paris: Foucher.

Chauvière, M. (1980). *Enfance Inadaptée: l'Héritage de Vichy.* Paris: Les Editions Ouvrières.

Commission National Consultative des Droits de l'Homme. (1991). *La Lutte contre le racisme et la Xénophobie*, Paris: La Documentation Française.

Cahiers de la Recherche sur le Travail Social (CRTS). (1989). *Annuaire de la Recherche sur le Social*, CRTS, Université de Caen.

Decree (1959) *Le Journal Officiel*, 19 October, p.10003. (1970) *Le Journal Officiel*, 9 March, No. 70/240. (1973) *Le journal Officiel*, 11 January, No. 73/73. (1974) *Le Journal Officiel*, 15 February, p.2217. (1975) *Le Journal Officiel*, 15 October, p.10640. (1990) *Le Journal Officiel*, 21 February, No.90/166. (1990) *Le Journal Officiel*, 8 July, No. 90/574.

Dubet, F. (1991). *Les Lycéens.* Paris: Seuil.

Duchamp, M., Bouquet, B., & Drouard, H. (1989). *La Recherche en Travail Social*, Paris. Centurion.

Fouquet, M. & Clavel, J. (1978). *L'Educateur et Ses Responsabilités.* Paris: Editions E.S.F.

Hurstel, J. (1988). *Chroniques Culturelles Barbares.* Paris: Syros/Alternatives.

Institut Nationel d'Etudes Démographiques (INED). (1989) *Population et Sociétés*, INED, Mars, No.233.

Institut National de la Statistique et des Etudes Economiques (INSEE). (1990). *Données Sociales*, INSEE, Paris.

Ion, J. (1990). *Le Travail Social à lEpreuve du Térritoire.* Toulouse: Privat.

Ion, J. & Tricart, J-P. (1984). *Les Travailleurs Sociaux.* Paris: La Découverte.

Kaluszynski, M. (1986). "L'Emergence de la Notion de Prévention en France à la Fin du XIXème Siècle." *Annales de Vaucresson*, 1 (24), 129–143.

Lesaulnier, C. (1991). *Le metier du secteur Social: Educateur, Assistant Social, et Animateur.* Paris: Bayard.

Martin, C. (1986). *Les Recherches Actions Sociales: Mirroir aux Alouettes ou Stratègie de Qualification.* Paris: M.I.R.E., La Documentation Française.

Order (1973) *Le Journal Officiel*, 13 May, p. 5304. (1974) *Le journal Officiel*, 28 August, No.74/146. (1976) *Le Journal Officiel*, 6 February, p. 1171. (1978) *Le Journal Officiel*, 14 November. (1990) *Le Journal Officiel*, 6 July, p. 8091. (1991) *Le Journal Officiel*, 10 June.

Petonnet, C. (1985). *On est Tous dans le Brouillard*, Paris: Galilée.

Poujol, G. (1989). *Profession Animateur.* Toulouse: Privat.

Prost, A. (1986). *L'enseignement s'est-il démocratisé ?.* Paris: Presses Universitaires Françaises.

Rupp, M-A. (1986). *Quarante Années d'Action Sociale en France.* Toulouse: Privat.

Secretary of State for Youth and Sports. (1988). *Les Professionnels de l'Animation.* Tome 2. *Les Qualifications Individuelles et Itinéraires Professionnels.* Paris: La Documentation Française.

Taguief, P-A. (1991). *Face au Racisme.* Vol.1. *Les Moyens d'Agir.* Paris: La Découverte.

Thévenet, A. (1989). *L'Aide Social Aujourd'hui après La Décentralisation.* Paris: Editions E.S.F.

Thévenet, A. & Désigaux, J. (1985). *Les Travailleurs Sociaux.*   Paris: Presses
      Universitaires de France.
Valls-Lacroix, M-N. (1989). *Praticiens du secteur sanitaire et social- qui êtes-vous?*
      Paris: Editions Ouvrières.
Verdès-Leroux, J. (1978). *Le Travail Social.* Paris: Editions de Minuit.

10

GERMANY

Hans-Jochen Brauns and David Kramer

INTRODUCTION

The former German Democratic Republic (GDR) joined the Federal Republic of Germany (FRG) on October 3, 1990. Politically, constitutionally and legally Germany today is unified. The former GDR has adopted the educational system of the former FRG and is developing its system of social services according to (West) German legal and administrative guidelines. Consequently, there is no point in discussing purely East German contributions to social work education, except in a historical context.

Since social work and social work education in the West German sense were unknown and unfamiliar to the GDR, the five (or, more accurately, including unified Berlin, six) new states are adopting a completely different and unknown system of social services and social work education along with West German standards and structures. The former GDR is facing an enormous task of adjustment in this and other areas.

It is difficult to compare the two German systems: they were based on two fundamentally opposed ideologies systems. Social problems, social work and social work professionals in East Germany for a long time were considered to be typical consequences of capitalism and to have only transitional importance for a country on its way to socialism. But, in fact, the GDR had social services and social work professionals: different structures and designations were used. Much "social work" in the GDR was organized by sociopolitical organizations such as the communist trade unions, the communist Free German Youth and the Young Pioneers; by the National Front (uniting all political parties and other important organizations); by the Kombinate (production trusts). Public, government-run services were very common in the areas of education and youth work, but less common in other areas such as care for handicapped or elderly people. Private nonprofit organizations were almost unknown, except the social services of the Protestant and Catholic churches and a few, but important organizations like the Volkssolidarität (nonresidential care for the elderly) or associations for the blind and the deaf.

Social work education was a nongeneric, and in some areas, highly special-ized training of professionals. At the secondary level, the GDR trained Sozialfürsorger (the profession closest to a social worker), Gesundheitsfürsorger (health worker) and youth workers. At the university level, professionals for work with handicapped persons were trained (Rehabilitationspädagogen); training of professionals for generic social work tasks (Diplompädagogen) played only a marginal role and should not be confused with the training of Diplompädagogen at West German universities. Many medical doctors and nurses worked in essentially social work positions–public social services, for example, for the elderly, were part of public health administration and domi-nated by medical professions.

We indicate only some major differences without intending systematically to compare the systems at work in the (former) two Germanys. In the following we describe German social work education: For western Germany we describe a tradition and a reality; for eastern Germany we describe the future and a chal-lenge, since the former training of social work professionals has been abolished and the new educational system is only now becoming fully functional.

SOCIOECONOMIC CONTEXT

Social problems at the end of World War II were overwhelming in both East and West Germany: broken families, orphans, widows, refugees from Eastern Europe and veterans presented cities and voluntary organizations with a heavy burden transcending the normal problems. The German economy was largely crippled and the country was under occupation. Although the social problems were similar in all areas of the former German Reich, the western zones of oc-cupation were particularly challenged by the mass emigration from the east. Nearly 10 million more people lived in the western parts of Germany after the war than had lived there before.

West Germany was able to cope with these problems because of the rapid and unprecedented economic recovery after 1948. The foundations for the mod-ern West German welfare state were laid by conservative political coalitions during the 1950s and 1960s. Social Democrats entered the federal government in the late 1960s and greatly expanded government services and expenditures. The expansion faced increasing financial difficulties after the so-called second oil shock of 1979, while the federal German government was still under Social Democratic leadership. From the early 1980s, West Germany was once again governed at the federal level by a conservative coalition with strong tendencies toward at least controlling the growth of social expenditures, if not cutting them back. In contrast to that of earlier years, there is now much public criticism of welfare state programs and institutions, and financial difficulties have increased notably since reunification.

East Germany considered social problems to be transitional difficulties on the road to socialism. Ideologically and economically, this part of Germany did not pay much attention–and especially did not offer social services–to the traditional clientele of social work. This changed in some policy areas during the 1970s (e.g., the Communist government now set aside significant funds for pensions and services for elderly people), whereas youth activities had always enjoyed a high level of support for political reasons.

SOCIAL WORK AND SOCIAL ADMINISTRATION

The political and legal framework for social policy and welfare programs is set at the federal level in West Germany (e.g., by legislation on social security, on welfare benefits or on youth work), while the states (Länder), local authorities and private organizations administer and run different programs and institutions of social work. Main areas of social work have developed over the years:

- Work with families and youth
- Work in health services
- Work in social affairs
- Work with delinquents
- Work in schools and other educational institutions

There have been efforts to reorganize social services in order to offer generic social work at the local level. The attempts to decentralize and debureaucratize have not yet resulted in sufficient, efficient services at the local level. A large number of welfare programs are administered by private organizations. During recent years in conjunction with criticism of bureaucratic administrative social work, much grass-roots activity has sprung up. Self-help groups and volunteer work have clearly gained in importance. They have received support from various political movements for different reasons: from the ecological movement because of its criticism of large bureaucratic social work organizations, and from conservative parties for financial reasons and because of their criticism of inefficient professional social work.

With unification, West German structures and norms of social work and social administration were introduced into East Germany, but since the East Germans have neither the money, the experience, nor the personnel to develop these structures fully, there are many conflicts and contradictions at the present. Almost nothing of the minimal, sparse services existing in the former GDR has survived.

DEVELOPMENT OF SOCIAL WORK EDUCATION

The beginnings of education in the social professions in Germany go back as far as the first courses of the Girls' and Women's Groups for Social Assistance-Work founded in Berlin in 1893 by Jeanette Schwerin and the German Society for Ethical Culture. In 1899, a one year program was first established under the direction of Alice Salomon. In 1905, the Protestant church in Hannover founded the first real Women's School for Social Welfare. In 1908, Alice Salomon opened the first women's social school with a two year program in Berlin–a program which was soon to be emulated all over Germany.

The first schools of social work developed in conjunction with institutions of social welfare on the example of the settlement movement in England and America. However, the traditional institutions of social work, especially the Protestant and the Roman Catholic churches with their welfare organizations (the Inner Mission/Diaconical Work and the Caritas), struggled to expand their influence. When social work became a profession during and after World War I, the majority of schools and programs of social work were church-related. Alongside these, there continued to exist a large number of secular schools (e.g., Alice Salomon's school in Berlin) as well as some training programs run by the Social Democratic workers' welfare organizations. In the early 1970s, the ties of the schools with the various types of welfare organizations became ever weaker; this development was largely due to the "academization" of social work education and its integration into the system of higher education.

The former GDR started the training of social professionals rather belatedly. There was only one state school in the entire GDR for the training of Sozialfür-sorger (an antiquated title in Germany for social workers); this school also offered training to persons throughout the former GDR by means of correspondence courses. Training took place at the secondary level of education. This school, which previously had approximately 150 graduates per year, was dissolved in 1991.

THE INSTITUTIONS

That professionals in social services in Germany are trained at various types of institutions is a result of both historical developments and the structure of the civil service. Personnel for kindergartens, residences for youth, youth centers, and residential care of senior citizens–Erzieher and Altenpfleger–are trained at the secondary level in vocational schools (Fachschulen). Social workers and social pedagogues are trained at Fachhochschulen, institutions which are part of the system of higher education. Some courses for social workers and social pedagogues are offered by the newly founded Gesamthochschulen (comprehensive universities). Universities and teachers' training institutions began to establish study programs in Erziehungswissenschaft ("science of education") parallel to practice-oriented teachers' training courses. The educational hierarchy corresponds to the structure of civil service entry requirements (and pay schedules).

The curriculum for university-based courses in the science of education includes a concentration on social pedagogy as well as on pre-school education, adult education, education of the handicapped, and school pedagogy. Qualified graduates of this program can continue to a doctoral degree in their field. Because of their academic orientation and their less practical training, graduates of the universities are often not accepted by the employing agencies and have always had great difficulties finding jobs. The state of Baden-Württemberg has created another type of social work training at so-called professional academies (Berufsakademien): the students are employed by welfare organizations and during a three year training period follow a sequence of three month study periods and three months of work. Graduates receive the same degree as graduates of Fachhochschulen in Baden-Württemberg, but these institutions are limited geographically to one German state and produce relatively few graduates. The rest of this report will concentrate mainly on social work education at Fachhochschulen, to which we shall also refer as schools of social work.

Schools of social work and science of education department are being established at a number of locations throughout the new states in the former GDR; since this process has not been completed, the following figures refer to the states of former West Germany. Programs in social work are offered at seventy departments of fifty Fachhochschulen and Gesamthochschulen; twenty-eight universities and teachers' training institutions offer science of education programs with a concentration in social pedagogy. Universities and Fachhochschulen in West Germany are generally public, government-funded institutions; social work education is an exception, because sixteen Fachhochschulen are sponsored by the Lutheran (nine) or the Roman Catholic (seven) church. Higher education is almost entirely financed by state government (Länder)-it is not a federal responsibility. Nonstate institutions of higher education such as the church-related Fachhochschulen receive important subsidies from the states and are required to conform to the general directives of legislation.

The size of the departments of social work at the Fachhochschulen varies considerably. In some departments there are scarcely more than one hundred students; others have more than one thousand. The majority has an average of four hundred to five hundred students. The standing faculty varies between ten and fifty full-time professors, and in 1980 there were approximately one thousand professors teaching at schools of social work (Baron et al., 1986: 179–187).

Universities and Fachhochschulen in Germany enjoy a high degree of constitutionally guaranteed autonomy. Within the legal framework they operate independently in all academic affairs: study programs, examinations, curricula, and admissions. They put forward names of professors, who are then hired by government, and they decide on hiring part-time teaching staff. Therefore, each department is autonomous in developing study programs in social work as well as in other fields and programs and curricula vary greatly from school to school. There is no external control, coordination, or accreditation on a national level.

Universities and Fachhochschulen are corporations of public law where faculty governance is practiced. All members-faculty, students, administrators are represented in all important decision-making bodies of these institutions. The structure and composition of the bodies are regulated by federal and state law. As a rule in all important matters the tenured faculty have the majority of votes, but students are rather influential as well. Deans, chairpersons, and presidents are elected from the tenured faculty.

Higher education is free in Germany. The state ministries of science and universities oversee the institutions of higher education within the legal framework. They are guided by legislation in dealing with academic affairs. Government has considerable influence in financial matters and in the appointment of tenured professors. Professors are civil servants and are appointed for life.

Fachhochschulen are comparable in many ways to the polytechnics in Great Britain, which give more priority to academic professional training than German universities do. The teaching load of the faculty at Fachhochschulen is higher than at universities and professors have less opportunity to do research. The curricula are more structured and the faculty work more directly and more intensively with the students. The faculties of the schools of social work integrate all relevant social sciences, law, medicine, and economics. The required length of study (excluding the required placements) is three years, and the actual length of enrollment is generally more than two years less than at the universities.

A university degree is required for the highest level in civil service. The next lower level is accessible with a degree of a Fachhochschule. Because of the rigid structures of the German civil service, possibilities of promotion are limited, but since there are few jobs at the highest level of the civil service in the field of social work, this has little real significance for social workers.

STAFF

Qualifications, status, and salary of the faculty are set by federal legislation. There is little room for the states-not to mention the schools-to decide on working conditions of the faculty. Professors are required by federal law to have a doctorate and a postdoctorate degree (Habilitation) or an outstanding professional career of at least five years outside higher education. As a rule, most university faculty members in social sciences in fact have no professional experience outside the educational system. Fachhochschulen generally require a doctorate and professional experience for appointment to the faculty.

The academic staff at the Fachhochschulen includes full-time professors and part-time instructors hired for a term. The hiring of social work practitioners is a particular problem: Since social workers until the early 1970s did not receive academic training and later were trained at the Fachhochschulen, they were not able to acquire the doctorate necessary for appointment to a professorship. Therefore, it has proved almost impossible to hire social work practitioners as professors. At many schools they can only be employed with a lower status and a lower salary for specific teaching tasks. The appointment of professionally experienced academics very often also proves to be difficult because of better career patterns, opportunities, and salaries outside higher education: This is especially true for medical doctors and law-trained faculty.

Each professor is expected to teach, to do research, to participate in examinations, in continuing education and in administration. The teaching load of professors at a Fachhochschule is fixed by law at eighteen hours per week for seven to eight months per year. Generally, professors are eligible for a sabbatical every four years; however, funds are insufficient to grant sabbaticals to all eligible professors. Some Fachhochschulen have been very active in the field of continuing education, while universities generally pay very little attention to it presently.

Within the schools of social work, part-time term-appointed instructors from the field play an important role. Their proportion to the total faculty varies; as a rule they teach approximately 20 percent of the courses. Over twenty percent of time spent teaching by field personnel at some schools has a negative impact on the quality of the training because of the break in instructor continuity, a lower percentage can have negative effects by placing over emphasis on academic content and less stress on the integration of professional experience into the social work programs.

STUDENT BODY

The Abitur-granted by secondary schools after thirteen years of education-qualifies for admission to both universities and Fachhochschulen; students with the Fachhochschulreife-granted by specialized secondary schools after twelve years of education-can be admitted only to the Fachhochschule. In the past, most students of social work did not come directly from school; they began their studies only after several years of work. Today the average student enters immediately after secondary school.

In comparison with universities, the Fachhochschulen have nearly twice as many students from the lower-middle and the lower classes (27 percent as against 14 percent - Baron, et al., 1986: 184). Students with rather atypical educational backgrounds and students with work experience are more prevalent at Fachhochschulen as well. Two–thirds of the student body in social work education at the Fachhochschulen and at the universities is female.

Many students of social work were until the late 1970s politically very active; often they participated actively in the students' movement, worked in model-projects of social work, and engaged in the peace and ecology movements. In the past several years, there appears to have been a general decrease in political interest and engagement, but students of social work are nonetheless still more often involved in social and political activities than their counterparts in most other departments.

The number of social work students has literally exploded since the early 1970s, partly because of a politically motivated interest in social work, partly because of good job opportunities, and partly because of the improved system of scholarships and grants. Because of limited capacity, institutions of higher education had to restrict the number of admissions. For legal reasons state schools of social work have no influence on the admission criteria and the selection of their students. The primary criterion as established by nationwide law is the average of the secondary school grades. Not the faculty but the administration of the school selects the students according to strict legal guidelines. Church-related schools are not bound to these legal selection procedures and criteria; interview applicants before admitting them.

At present, there are approximately thirty-two thousand students of social work at the Fachhochschulen and approximately fifteen thousand more with a concentration on "social pedagogy" at the universities. The schools admit approximately eight thousand and graduate approximately seven thousand students each year. Precise data from the universities are not available, but the number of graduates in social pedagogy is, according to conservative estimates, in the range of one thousand to two thousand each year (Baron et al., 1986: 185-186). The demand for social workers decreased sharply in West Germany during the 1980s; this could change with the unification and the demand for professionals in the eastern part of the country.

Because of the orientation of the study programs to the national system of social work, the number of students from foreign countries at schools of social work is very low. Some schools have made considerable efforts to raise the number of foreign students, especially from countries whose nationals provide immigrant labor like Turkey, Spain, Italy, Yugoslavia, and Greece. Many schools have been very active in establishing contacts with schools in other countries and developing exchange programs for faculty and students.

STUDY PROGRAM

Content and structure of courses of study vary greatly from school to school because of their autonomy. Since 1971, the individual schools have been free to reform their guidelines for courses and examinations as they see fit; these must only be confirmed by the respective state ministries of science and universities. Previously, the procedures of official recognition of the social work qualification by state governments set minimal demands on the courses of study, and there was a certain uniformity among the different programs. Currently, there are only a few, relatively weak tendencies toward uniformity in Germany. A national commission for the reform of study programs in social work, social pedagogy and science of education was set up at the federal level in 1980 and made recommendations for reform in the spring of 1984. The national commission, however, has no power to implement its recommendations; it is up to each school to heed them or not.

At schools three different types of study programs are offered: (1) social work, which is oriented toward traditional administrative tasks in agencies; (2) social pedagogy, which is directed to areas like youth and community work and other educational tasks outside schools; (3) Sozialwesen, a study program integrating elements of both social work and social pedagogy. In Bavaria, Bremen, Hamburg, Schleswig-Holstein, Berlin, the Saarland and Lower Saxony, only integrated courses of Sozialwesen are offered by the schools. Schools of the other states (Northrhein-Westphalia, Rheinland-Pfalz, Hessen and Baden-Württemberg) offer courses in both social work and social pedagogy. Because of increasing lack of clarity over the exact difference between social work and social pedagogy and growing difficulties of professional mobility within the entire social work field, there seems to be a tendency away from the distinction between social work and social pedagogy.

The common elements of the different study programs can easily be described. With varying foci and different ways of integrating fieldwork, the following areas of knowledge are covered:

- Social work and social pedagogy: history, theories, organization and institutions, methods
- Social sciences: sociology, social policy, political science, economics, statistics, empirical social research
- Psychology/pedagogy: developmental psychology, therapeutic methods, theory and practice of education, theories of socialization
- Health: health care delivery, institutional and legal framework, medicalsurvey
- Law and Public Administration: legislation concerning family, youth, social welfare, social insurance, labor and administration
- Music, drama, sports, arts, film, video, work with media

Many study programs include courses in English, Spanish, and French. Schools with a focus on work with immigrants often offer courses in the main immigrant languages. At church-affiliated schools, social ethics and social philosophy are included in the curricula.

Courses traditionally have been rather structured and sometimes very rigid. They include the important academic disciplines and generally are structured according to these disciplines, not according to professional areas of work or problems. This system has created problems of integrating knowledge and skills of different academic disciplines. Many schools have reformed their study programs, giving up the discipline-oriented, rigid structures in favor of prob-lem-, client- or area-oriented curricula offering different foci and choices to students.

Training during the early terms generally concentrates on teaching basic knowledge in various social sciences and on introducing the student to theories and practice of social work. At many schools, the student has to pass an interim examination before he or she can continue the training. The second part of the study programs at most schools allows the students to choose from among different concentrations according to client groups, areas of social work and/or methods. Various types of fieldwork placements are integrated into this part of study, although many schools already require fieldwork during the early terms as well.

A comment concerning instruction in the methods of social work is in order: the classical American methods of casework, group work and community work played a large role in the reconstruction of German social work after World War II. During the 1960s and 1970s these methods were subject to increasing criticism from the student movement in Germany. For a time it seemed that the social sciences might replace the "American" imports (nobody seemed to mind that the "social sciences" were also largely American imports); but with the waning of the student movement this no longer seems certain. Confidence in the efficacy of social science seems to be giving way to a "boom" in indi-vidually oriented psychological approaches. At present, the teaching of meth-ods is dominated by a voluntarism in which widespread confusion as to the purpose of instruction and the professional identity of social workers is evident.

The forms of instruction differ from school to school, but the norm seems to be seminars with twenty to thirty participants–faculty-led courses in which stu-dents present papers for discussion. Only a few schools offer lectures.

Professional placements play an important role in social work education. The length of academic training at schools is three years. The length of pro-fessional placements is at least one year. The placements are organized accord-ing to two models: a one-phase and a two-phase model. The one-phase model integrates two six-month terms of fieldwork into the academic study program; students pass their final examinations at the schools after four years of training and receive state certification at graduation. This type of training is offered by the schools in Bavaria, Baden-Württemberg, the Saarland and two schools in Hessen (Wiesbaden and Kassel). The two-phase model offered by all the other schools requires a one year, paid fieldwork placement after graduation from three years of academic training at the schools. Under this model, students receive state certification only after successfully completing field work.

In addition to the one year fieldwork at the end of the two-phase model, most of the study programs of this type require fieldwork of their students before graduation. The length of fieldwork generally varies between three and six months. At some schools, students work four or five days per week in an agency during their placement. Other schools prefer part-time placements of one or two days per week for a longer period. Mostly schools prepare, observe and evaluate placements, but sometimes fieldwork and academic training are barely integrated.

During their placement students generally work in an agency and are supervised by a social worker. The supervisors are not paid, and their workload is not reduced. Because of the rapid growth in student numbers, placements have become an increasingly heavy burden for social workers in the field. It is presently difficult to provide all students with qualitatively good placements.

DEGREES AND CERTIFICATES

Upon graduation from a study program in social work or social pedagogy, students are awarded the academic degree of social worker or social pedagogue (Diplom-Sozialarbeiter, Diplom-Sozialpädagoge). Upon completion of their fieldwork-in one-phase models at graduation, in two-phase models after graduation-students receive state certification as social worker or social pedagogue (Staatliche Anerkennung). This is a prerequisite for entry into the civil service; it is a protected title. In states with only one generic study program (Bavaria, Lower Saxony, Schleswig-Holstein, Bremen, Hamburg, Berlin, Saarland) students generally receive the degree of social pedagogue and corresponding state certification. Graduates from university study programs of educational science receive the degree of pedagogue (Diplom-Pädagoge). University graduates are not eligible for state certification.

FUTURE TRENDS AND DEVELOPMENTS

Until quite recently, social workers and social pedagogues were a "commodity in demand." The number of professionals in social work has increased rapidly in the last thirty years. Exact data are not available; the Federal Office of Labor estimates that the number grew from 40,000 in 1950 to 182,000 in 1982. Next to local authorities, the five largest employers are the private welfare organizations (the Diaconical Work of the Lutheran Church, Caritas of the Roman Catholic church; the Arbeiterwohlfahrt, an organization close to the Social Democratic party and the trade unions; the Parity Welfare Group, an umbrella organization for agencies of different size and background, and the German Red Cross).

With the economic crunch and a political swing to conservatism during the 1980s in West Germany, the welfare state has been subject to increasing criticism. Planned reforms have been stopped and the social budget has been cut back substantially in certain areas. Reductions of social programs and budgets as well as the steady increase in the number of graduates led to a sharp rise in unemployment among social workers and social pedagogues during the 1980s. This problem is likely to increase as more than seven thousand graduates enter the job market each year.

Within the process of unification, social questions play a major role and may be decisive for the future social, cultural, political and economic union of Germany. This situation offers an opportunity and a challenge to social work and social work professionals.

Social work education is currently caught in a tension between raised expectations on the one side and reduced resources on the other. Attempts are being made to develop flexible responses in social work education to demographic changes, to a likely structural unemployment at a rather high level, to the social impact of economic and technological changes, to the needs of ethnic and cultural minorities, to the demands of the growing percentage of the elderly and to the demands and challenges of uniting the two culturally and socially completely different parts of Germany. Rising expectations of professional social work cannot be met only by improving initial training, but also require an intensification of continuing education. Recently, courses of further education and postgraduate studies have been established to prepare for work with mentally ill, handicapped, and elderly people; immigrants, and drug addicts. New areas of work and changes of professional qualifications need intensive study and discussion in order to cope with the future challenges of the profession. There is much evidence that schools will be forced to reconsider the goals and the role of professional social work intensively and earnestly in the face of manifold alternatives: self-help activities, calls for more voluntary social work, and shifts in favor of less qualified personnel.

REFERENCES

Baron, R., Brauns, H-J., & Kramer, D. (1986). Education of social workers and social pedagogues in the Federal Republic of Germany. In Brauns, H-J. & Kramer, D. (Eds.). *Social Work Education in Europe: A Comprehensive Description of Social*

Work Education in 21 European Countries Frankfurt/M: Eigenverlag des Deutschen Vereins für Öffentliche und Private Fürsorge, pp. 169–208.

Der Bundesminister für Bildung und Wissenschaft. (1989). *Grund und Strukturdaten 1989/90*. Bonn: BMBW.

11

CENTRAL AND EASTERN EUROPE

Charles Guzzetta

INTRODUCTION

Just sixty years ago, the philosopher-historian Carl Becker warned us of the difficulty in describing, let alone explaining historical changes. If you try to describe a place in time, the events lose their dynamism and velocity; but to ascertain its velocity, we lose the ability to describe a determinable position.

Becker could have been referring to the developments in Central and Eastern Europe over the past decade. The changes have been so extraordinary and so rapid that simple description beggars comprehension and any attempt to fix the events in time guarantees that they, like the reflections that follow this statement, will be dated before they can be printed.

No one, inside or outside the sphere of Marxism-Leninism, predicted with any semblance of accuracy the incredible speed with which that political-economic system would be discarded and replaced by a headlong plunge toward Western-style economies and political systems. In some respects, the people most startled were not those within the reach of Stalinist totalitarianism. Many of them had risked their lives and personal safety for years in the struggle for a more open society and were confident of their ultimate success. Among those truly surprised when they achieved it were some social workers in Western countries, who had been able to provide explanations and excuses for every excess of Stalinism and who never tired of predicting the coming glories of the workers' paradise, once the Soviet miracle exported its blessings to North Atlantic industrial countries, as it had to Nicaragua, Ethiopia, Albania, Cuba, and others in the nonindustrialized world.

Within the satellite countries (or "client states"), there had long been an underground of discontent, known in the Soviet Union as "counterrevolutionaries" or "hooligans" and by other descriptors and known in the West either as "dissidents" or as "lackies of imperialism," depending on the perspective of the person doing the describing. The most noted of these dissidents were "hard" scientists, whose notoriety was a function of their celebrity and former high positions in Soviet governmental scientific circles. But there were many others, less celebrated, but no less ardent in their determination to open some doors and let in the winds of change. A solid core of these activists were social scientists.

In the West, social problems tended to be seen as situations requiring social policies and social programs of correction or relief. Official state policy in most Warsaw Pact countries did not recognize the existence of such conditions, or else defined them as political and economic problems requiring political and economic solutions. After the Soviet army crushed the Hungarian attempt to liberalize its form of socialism in 1956, the disciplines of sociology and psychology were struck from the university curricula as bourgeois artifacts counterproductive to central planning and, of course, contradictory to official explanations of politically embarrassing circumstances. The social sciences were treated similarly in other countries which had long traditions of liberal arts scholarship; or else, those disciplines were converted into puppet status, allowed only to endorse the accuracy of the current line issued in Moscow. Free and open social science research was quashed in Czechoslovakia after Prague Spring; it was suppressed in Poland; and it was never allowed to get started in most other places.

Internal Developments in Central and Eastern Europe

Social work education programs in Central and Eastern Europe had not existed since the war, except in Poland and Yugoslavia. Hence, neither social work education nor the academic disciplines from which it drew the substance of its theory were preparing practitioners to address the social problems in these societies. By 1965, an initial thaw began in Hungary, where the Kadar regime, put in place and supported by Moscow, started to look for explanations outside official Party policy. That position had not been moving the country forward in an acceptable way. Sociology and psychology began to make their way back into the university.

In due course, a team of sociologists was assigned to study conditions in the country, to identify problems, and to propose possible ways of addressing those problems. The five-year research revealed officially what had long been known unofficially: Hungary faced a number of social problems not unlike those known in the West. Among the recommendations, appearing after the mid-1980s, was a proposal for a social work–like program of education.

At the same time, a group of socially concerned professionals, living mainly in Budapest, took advantage of the liberalizing atmosphere to create an alternative to the state social welfare agencies. Their conception was of a general service agency which could address common personal and family problems on an individual level. The agency, called LARES after a Greek word for "caring," was founded "on a shoestring," and initially was staffed entirely by volunteers whose training covered the range of professions—law, medicine, nursing, engineering, and so on—as well as those trained in the related disciplines of sociology, psychology, political science, et cetera.

According to Ewa Les (1991), parallel developments were taking place in Poland. After "Polish October" in 1956, social work, which had been suppressed by the Stalinist regime, was again recognized by the state as necessary to deal with social problems which "did not disappear in socialism." Postsecondary programs specifically to train social service workers were reestablished beginning in 1966, and by 1969, service agencies were starting to appear.

With the move toward democracy in the late 1980s, the state monopoly on social welfare was set aside in favor of a mixed state-voluntary arrangement with central and local government and not-for-profit joint involvement. Legislation accompanying this transformation required formal education for all social agency staff members by 1995. However, as Les (1991) points out, most Polish social service agency personnel at present still are without social work training.

As social work began to reappear in the 1980s, the position of the Roman Catholic church in social services again received legitimation. What will be the long–term relationship between the church's tradition of centrally planned charitable work and the emerging state decentralization of services has yet to be finally determined. State legislation now recognizes the church as an agent of social services, and there has been a strong initiative by the church to fill the social policy vacuum.

The 1990 Social Welfare Act decreed programs creating a need for fifteen thousand social workers in a short time. This legislation emphasized the urgency of the need for social work education and prompted development of such programs. By 1991, about three thousand students attended thirty-six social work schools in the country, many on a part-time basis. All these programs were on a postsecondary level. Four universities offered social work education: Warsaw, Krakow, Poznan, and Bydoszcz. Plans to expand higher education in social work were well under way. As recently as early 1992, only the venerable Jagiellonian University in Krakow offered the degree master of social work in a program of advanced social work education for students who had completed undergraduate degrees in that field. But it was then already clear that this monopoly would not long stand.

Poland and Hungary took the lead in establishing social work education in Eastern Europe when the grip of Stalinist control began to ease. Czechoslovakia's attempted political revolt had come later and had been suppressed more brutally. Military domination there tended to be stronger and to last longer.

Programs to train social policy personnel and staff persons for government social agencies existed all along. The central program was in Prague, with branch programs in six locations throughout the country. The loosening of control that Poland and Hungary enjoyed as early as 1965 did not come to Czechoslovakia until nearly a decade later. It was 1983 before restructuring of the political-economic system permitted review of social problems in a systematic way, and from a perspective that was not exclusively politicoeconomic.

The long tradition of social work education in Czechoslovakia, extending back to the year of the country's creation in 1919, had lost its independent character in 1954, with the initiation of a program closely tied to central government policies and priorities.   For example, admission to the one free-standing program, in Prague, was tied directly to the state's five year projection of need for personnel in state employment. All graduates were guaranteed employment in the state social welfare system. Curriculum content clearly reflected this bond.

By 1989, the current of change was being seen in Czechoslovakian social work education. The beginning identification of social work as a legitimate university study led to the introduction of a few courses in Prague's prestigious Charles University.

As the democratic movement led to intensified regionalism in the country, university programs in social work education were created in 1991 at both Brno and Bratislava, with all programs beginning to compete for students.   By 1992, the development of university-based, professionalized social work education was well under way in Czechoslovakia, but without any workable common agreement respecting the content of study.

It was evident that the university programs in the Slovak and the Czech sectors had settled into a kind of academic rivalry not entirely unlike that often seen in the West. For example, study at Charles University was based upon the traditional European model of theoretical and largely independent study, while the Bratislava program took great pride in its base in practical research and social planning, including its concern for the development of policies and programs for employed women, child care, young people released from prisons, and similar vulnerable populations.

In Czechoslovakia it became clear early that the success of the democratic movement and its freedom from outside domination carried the extra baggage of regional competition and the emergence anew of ancient ethnic and cultural struggles. Since the division of the country, the rivalry has continued. In education, as in most other respects, it is an uneven contest. The social work education programs in Slovakia continue to be starved for such basic resources as books for their libraries. Some Western organizations have helped, but the Czech Republic and especially Prague, with its great university, seems to receive a disproportionate amount of attention and support from these outside groups.

What in Czechoslovakia is still "competition," has become in Yugoslavia deadly forced battle. The ethnic, religious, and cultural rivalries in that country have never been resolved, and only the force of a totalitarian central government prevented them for forty years from returning to centuries-old warfare. However, even under the centralized government, social work education in Yugoslavia always has had more of a regional identification than in other East European countries.

Social work education never disappeared under communism in Yugoslavia as it did elsewhere, probably because Tito was so successful in keeping the country's sovereignty intact and free of domination by directives from Moscow. Nevertheless, the programs of social work education displayed a pattern of regional uniqueness, making them readily distinguishable.

In some ways, the premier program—or at least the one with the closest ties to the West— has been the undergraduate social policy studies at the University of Zagreb, situated in the Faculty of Law. Founded as a free-standing two year program in 1952, it became a full four year course of study about thirty years later. In 1984, the study was reorganized into a university subunit with two functions: social work education and social research.

The program of social work education in Slovenia also was started as a two year study in 1957, now affiliated with the University of Ljubljana. This program was upgraded to three year study in 1985, as a step toward full four year status.

A four year course of study for Bosnia-Hersegovina is located in Sarajevo, affiliated with the Faculty of Political Science since 1980; at the University of Skopje in Macedonia, the social work program became the Institute for Social Work and Social Policy, affiliated with the Faculty of Philosophy in 1987. Both were started as two year programs, the first in 1957, and the second in 1960.

In Serbia, two programs have been offered in Belgrade: a postsecondary program of two years, begun the same year as the Ljubljana and Sarajevo programs, and a four year course in the Faculty of Political Science. In 1974, the latter program became the Department of Social Work and Social Policy.

A center for postgraduate studies and training was located in Dubrovnik, but its future remains uncertain in the upheavals that have shaken the country. Of these programs, only one has provided study for both the master's and the doctor's degrees in social work—that at Sarajevo.

By 1991, a certain measure of consistency had been achieved among the many programs, the result of two years of effort, led by the Yugoslav Association of Social Work Studies. The number of compulsory subjects, made more congruent, ranged from eighteen in Belgrade, Sarajevo and Skopje to twenty-six in Ljubljana.

At the beginning of 1992, the stability and future development of social work education could not be determined with any degree of reliability. The faculties of the several programs remained in contact and continued to seek collaborative development of social work education, but the economic and political situations were so volatile that attention had to be given to matters of simple survival.

According to Milan Martinovic (1991) of Zagreb, there remain many "peculiarities" among the programs. He described the programs at Belgrade,

Skopje and Sarajevo as being based on "theoretic eclecticism and pragmatism," with Zagreb more of a scientific study of social work itself, since most of the study is organized around social work theory, methodology, and fields of practice. A new program in Ljubljana, begun in 1992, is the first faculty-level social work program in Slovenia, designed to combine certain features of American social work education with aspects of the German Fachhochschulen. (It should be noted that the Fachhochschulen, meanwhile, have been moving to polytechnic and university status in Germany.)

Presently, the situation in the former Yugoslavia is still in a state of flux, although the social work faculty of the various institutions continue to collaborate to the extent that they are able, and to maintain their contacts with colleagues outside the country. Since the early, rather steady transformations of social work education in Hungary and Poland, the pace seems to have quickened, with developments most hectic in the countries most recently involved in social work education development or reform.

As reforms were being slowly introduced to the east and north, Romania moved in 1969 to abolish what fragments of social work education then existed in that country, and to curtail sharply the number of workers who had provided state services similar to social services.

After 1965, faculties of psychology and sociology existed in the universities at Bucharest, Iasi and Cluj. By 1978, a modified kind of social work education was tried in these locations, but it was not until 1990 that courses of study specifically identified as "social work," based on a short-term model of training, were authorized there. The 1990 government decree authorizing social work study set in motion a round of curricular planning by the faculties, in cooperation with the Ministries of Education and Science, and Labor and Social Protection.

The problems in Romania relate to more than formal curriculum, as identified in the West. According to Silvia Pasti (1991), problems involve "a certain bureaucratic mentality" and ignorance respecting the educational needs of social workers. Having been so long isolated from world developments, Romanian social work education progress has had to rely on limited contact with international organizations.

By 1991, the government had adopted an "open policy" with respect to outside contacts with social work educators from other countries, introducing a different sort of problem, to be addressed later. It is understood by Romanian policymakers that their efforts will not produce a sufficient number of social workers for several years.

The most recent (not counting Bulgaria and Albania, which in 1992 were only at the beginning stages of examining their social work education needs), and in many respects most frantic developments have taken place in the former Soviet Union.

Social work education had been provided in the USSR in the 1920s, but during the 1930s, it was condemned as a bourgeois artifact and eliminated.

In the hurricane of changes under perestroika, the Moscow Academy of Pedagogical Sciences developed a framework for the initiation of social work education, restoring the field of social work to its official list in 1991. One preferred title for the practitioner was *social pedagogue*, familiar from the German model. The National Association of Social Pedagogues was organized and took responsibility for developing a social service network, as well as for a program of education to train social pedagogues. The preferred term of study selected was three years in postsecondary education, followed by a specialization year.

A program at the university level optimally would provide five years of study combining theoretical and practical work, the latter alternating between the concurrent and block models of field practicum.

With the continued fragmentation of the former Soviet Union, the development of social work education programs has shown considerable lack of cohesion. Initiatives seemed to emanate from many directions, with the result that by the end of 1991, there were more than thirty programs in various stages of development. Among the problems faced in understanding the direction of the training in these programs is the necessity to differentiate between social pedagogues of the German model and an emerging concept of social worker on the American model.

Major support for early development was provided by the Moscow Pedagogical University and the Centre for Social Pedagogy, but the final political breakup of the Union of Soviet Socialist Republics in December 1991 left open the question of how social work education development would proceed in the Commonwealth of Independent States. The continuing leadership of Russia seemed the most likely course, although it was by no means assured.

Among the last of the former Iron Curtain countries to move to develop social work education programs were Latvia, Estonia and Lithuania. Of these, Estonia and Lithuania seem to have taken the lead, with vigorous activity commencing in 1991 in Lithuania. Work may be progressing at a somewhat slower pace in Latvia, although two programs were reported to be under way by the middle of 1991.

Part of the reason for the delays in such traditionally progressive societies may relate to the lack of basic economic means after the break from the Soviet Union. Shortages of the most basic goods, complicated by almost unchecked inflation, represented problems of such urgency that little attention could be directed elsewhere, even to the social crises that the economic crisis precipitated. The collapse of the ruble left many in those countries with life savings worthless, jobs and job security gone, and no clear sense of when things would get better. The other side of that situation, of course, was the recognition that the social, political and economic changes produced social problems calling for the intervention of trained social workers. The very desperation of the populace may have been the catalyst that set off a leap into social work education. At present, no one can be sure exactly where that leap will land.

At the beginning of 1992, tentative feelers to the West from Bulgaria and even Albania and Armenia indicated that those countries wished at least to explore the possibilities of social work education to prepare personnel capable of dealing with social problems there. Possibly, they wished to avoid being left behind in the march of progress of their neighbors, but it seems equally likely that they were discovering social problems which the old regime had not been able to solve and for which the West seemed to have the answers.

Hungary, the country which in many respects set off the whole movement for the development of social work education in countries in Central and Eastern Europe, provides an interesting case study of the current status of that movement.

A group based in the Hungarian Academy of Sciences had been formed in 1985 to plan a three year course of study; four years later, some of the group formed the core of the Social Policy Department of Eotvos Lorand University in Budapest. In 1990, the university began to offer the first full-time degree in social work and social policy, while retaining the earlier course of study that it had been offering.

The present program of social work education comprises a two tier model which provides a four-year course of study leading to a social work diploma; a five year course of study leading to a social work degree; and a five year course of study leading to a social policy degree. For all three options, the first two years represent a "unified theoretical introduction"; the third year concentrates on field instruction; commitment to one of the degrees is made at the beginning of the fourth year.

The present plan for development of social work education is to prepare future teachers as well as practitioners in the five year university program and to open four year programs in institutions of higher education throughout the country to prepare practitioners, but not theoreticians or faculty.

UNANTICIPATED PROBLEMS

Until the mid-1980s, access to Eastern Europe was complicated for Western social work educators. Yet, contacts between social work–oriented scholars and activists in Eastern and Central Europe and the West seemed more frequent and open than among the eastern socialist countries themselves. Curiously enough, it was not uncommon for scholars from the East to struggle for permission to attend Western conferences, as much to find out what was happening in neighboring Moscow Pact countries as to learn what was happening outside their region.

Selected personnel always were able to get out to conferences, on a limited basis, and with heavy restrictions on travel, contacts with foreigners, and duration of absence. Typically, other family members were required to stay behind.

In a session at the UN Centre in Vienna during the early 1980s, the then–secretary-general of the International Association of Schools of Social Work (IASSW), Marguerite Mathieu, met a prominent sociologist from Budapest who was leading the Hungarian study of social problems. Seizing the opportunity to open discussion with potential Hungarian colleagues in a part of the world totally unrepresented in the IASSW, Mathieu went to Budapest and established a relationship upon which future visits could be built.

Mathieu's strategy to assist the Hungarians in developing social work education was to try to make it possible for some of them to attend the biennial congresses of the IASSW, which are held at various locations around the world. In 1984, Mathieu arranged for an American, who was serving as a volunteer at the Secretariat in Vienna, to go to Budapest as a representative of IASSW, for the purpose of consulting on the development of social work education programs and to meet with government officials to try to obtain permission for selected participants in social problem/social work study to attend the 1984 IASSW Congress in Montréal.

This visit was the first of a series in which representatives from a variety of Western countries provided ongoing consultation as the Hungarian scholar-activists moved forward with their plans to introduce the profession of social work to the country to deal with the newly acknowledged social problems there.

Shortly after the Budapest visit, the IASSW Secretariat arranged for the same representative to go to Prague, to meet with the faculty of the Prague School and to petition government officials for an official delegation to the Montréal Congress. Although both governments were noncommittal at the times of these visits, delegations from Hungary and Czechoslovakia attended the Congress. To provide a hospitable welcome, as well as an orientation to Western social work education, another program was created. Using resources related to her position as the Moses Visiting Professor at the Hunter College School of Social Work in New York City, Katherine Kendall, honorary president of the IASSW, set up a special seminar for Third World and Eastern European social work educators, intended to provide an opportunity for them to mingle with each other, to meet with IASSW board members and other colleagues from the West, and jointly to examine problems common to all, in a congenial atmosphere. The seminar, which included formal papers from the participants, lasted for the entire week before the Montréal Congress. Interaction was intense and vigorous, and formed the basis for an ever-expanding network of contacts from which the newcomers continued to draw consultants and later to receive a steady supply of materials, books and other forms of aid.

By the time the Budapest program officially started, Hungary had an association of social work educators; by 1990 it had obtained membership status in
the IASSW.

The door was ajar by 1984; after Gorbachev assumed leadership of the Soviet Union, the door was virtually thrown open wide, at least in those nations
which bordered the West. The new openness entailed certain complications,
generally unanticipated by the East Europeans, and, in their enthusiasm, they
did not immediately recognize the problems even after they appeared.

One was their passion for things Western, especially things American.
Overlooked in the eagerness to Westernize was the fact that the West had yet to
solve its own most grave social problems. If the heavy hand of Stalinism
stripped the people in Central and Eastern Europe of their political liberties, it
also had provided certain basic necessities of living. In the eager study of North
Atlantic politicoeconomic systems, the freedom to get rich was recognized; the
risk of impoverishment was not seen so clearly.

With the movement to the free market, changes in status came with terrible
speed. Among the first to feel the pain were pensioners, who found inflation
wiping out their incomes and what little savings they may have had. Many professionals, artisans, and skilled laborers quickly capitalized on the chance to
make extra money. Severe dislocations of social standings followed. People
who had special skills, services, or products to market, whether carpentry or
medical care or a taxicab, found that they could earn as much money on a
weekend as the state paid them in a month. People on fixed incomes, such as
civil servants and academics, found that their incomes had dropped in relative
terms to poverty levels. Dissatisfaction led to increases in crime and different
kinds of crime; stress was felt in workplaces and in homes; tensions increased
between the generations.

For vacationers and "consultants" from the West, the Central and Eastern
European countries were a dream come true. Prices were unbelievably low and
outsiders were treated as honored guests, every utterance receiving attention and
belief totally beyond the experience of academics in their home institutions.
Once the borders were opened and the word was out, the stampede was on.

While the initiatives in the countries which made the earlier transitions
tended to be in the hands of scholar-activists, the collapse of the economic-po-
litical structure in the most Stalinist countries (which also were the last countries
freed of Stalinism) brought a change in this power alignment and, with it, a
different kind of problem.

In some of those countries which came late to the movement, the political
debacle had been anticipated by old power figures. Those socialist countries had
elaborate government systems for the distribution of goods and services provided by the state. The state functionaries who operated these systems enjoyed
positions of favor and influence. Indeed, the life–styles which they enjoyed
may have helped to hasten overthrow of the system, as ordinary people saw the

children of the government workers attending the best educational institutions, enjoying access to travel and holidays, and generally living a life which was being denounced as decadent and bourgeois when identified with the West.

As it became clear that the political changes would sweep away the offices and with them, the privileges, the more astute among the government apparatchiks accurately assessed the developments in the other Eastern countries as harbingers of the future in their own. Having formerly resisted the incursion of Eastern-style social work, some of them now embraced it with the fervor of the convert. Rather than being dragged into the change, or being shunted aside, as happened elsewhere, they took up positions as leaders of the changes.

As a consequence, some of the key personnel in the development of social work education in certain places in Central and Eastern Europe were often the same bureaucrats who had been the official dispensers of welfare and favors in the discredited regimes. The social service agency networks being developed were sometimes dominated by these ex-bureaucrats, and there was evidence that they were moving into programs of social work education, as well. The development has not been without opposition. Students have loudly complained that some professors who had taught them Marxist-Leninist ideology one year were their ethics professors the next; some who made careers of denouncing capitalism switched easily to teaching about the virtues of the free market economy. In fact, evidence has been growing that many of these converts may see social work education programs primarily as conduits for attracting western financing from which they expect to benefit.

Most disturbing to students and many new social workers has been that where these old party operatives have taken over the social services and social work education, they block further reform, and close younger scholars and newly trained practitioners out of jobs. In a sense, the old party has gone underground, disguised in some places as new social agencies and social work educators.

This problem is made worse by the naiveté of many Westerners, who since 1990 have been flooding into the formerly communist countries. There are reports that many of these innocents have been charmed and simply co-opted by the old apparatchiks who, after all, would not have survived the old regime if they had lacked skill in manipulating the system and the people in it.

Rather than take some responsibility for preventing or exposing the old nepotism, cronyism, and favoritism, it would appear that some Western consultants have been simply unaware of what was happening; or too timid to criticize, not wanting to be seen as insensitive or inappropriate in their appreciation of "indigenous" movements; or guilty of "exporting" Western social work, a change which would open them to the risk of being called "cultural imperialists." It is too early to determine the full damage to real professional education that may result from this combination of political maneuvering by old bureaucratic survivors and the polite silence of Western consultants. But there are few historical precedents to suggest that professions or their potential clients are well served by this kind of tolerant collusion.

Other problems, just as serious as those outlined, have emerged or, more properly, have emerged from their presumed graves with the ageless persistence of Draculas. They are the timeless prejudices that many East European shared against certain groups, but most particularly against Jews and Gypsies. Open acts of aggression against these minorities were checked by the central socialist governments. Semiofficial discrimination existed, but the fall of the central governments has permitted a blatant, fierce oppression unmatched since the end of the Second World War.

Work and on behalf of such populations represents social work in its most noble form, but assures hostility from many in the general populace, as well as scorn and outrage from a significant portion of academe. Western consultants do not appear altogether clear on how to confront this growing problem.

Up to the present, there has been no clear coordination of the efforts of consultants and researchers from the West. Every major meeting of people in international work includes stories of social work colleagues who meet each other in some ministry, each unaware that the other was even in the country. At one meeting in Budapest in late 1991, a consultant who was working with the faculty of a major university in Romania met representatives from the two ministries responsible for higher education in that country; neither was aware of what the other was doing. Within three months of that meeting, three other initiatives were under way, all working in entrepreneurial fashion, still without any kind of organized planning or coordination.

In some places, it is worse than in others. For example, Russian educators have reported that welcome and ready acceptance await anyone from the West who is willing to "teach" for a month or longer, provided no payment is expected. American professors have been known to spend ten days or two weeks of summer recess in one of the East European countries and return ready to present papers on their new-found "expertise." The problem is familiar to academic and government officials all over Eastern Europe, where enthusiasm and traditional courtesy are abundant, but resources are more and more limited.

Apart from the political problems, and the burden of random outside assistance, the new programs have been facing internal educational difficulties as well. One has been the proper status of social work as a field.

It has been a widespread belief throughout Europe that social work is not a proper university study. It has tended to be paid poorly and to suffer from low status. Education for social work typically has taken place in two and three year schools without university affiliation. Programs have filled a place in higher education above secondary schools, but below the university, since the content and study have been considered technical rather than theoretical. Accordingly, social work programs have been considered technical schools, not research institutions; with educational curricula based on experience rather than on theory.

For a number of years, the social work programs in Western Europe have moved toward university affiliation. (The institutes, in some cases, have been elevated to the status of colleges/universities similar to the British polytechnics. In other cases, the study has been offered in major universities such as Jagiellonian in Krakow, Tubingen in Germany, etc.). As early as 1974, a program was initiated at the University of Trondheim in Norway leading to the degree of master of social work. At first welcomed by the *sosialskolen*—the free–standing postsecondary social work education programs located throughout the country—the program came to be seen as a threat to their autonomy. However, the university program survived and the trend grew.

Recently, the elevation of social work education to university status or directly into universities has accelerated in the Common Market countries. Within just the past few years, Italian schools have been required to affiliate with universities or to close. In Germany, Fachhochschulen are in the process of being transformed into the equivalent of university study, not unlike the British polytechnics, and authorized to award advanced degrees. Similar changes can be seen in Belgium and Holland, and virtually everywhere throughout Europe.

The locating of social work education programs in Central and Eastern Europe at the university level was an important decision and seems to have met with significant success. However, location and acceptance are not the same. The resistance of old-line faculty in the disciplines is far from over. Even within the social sciences, there is considerable skepticism about the professional nature of social work, which is widely seen as neither a true profession nor a legitimate discipline. Some of the social scientists who led the development of the social work education programs face a kind of ostracism from the more traditional faculty.

Attempts to create professional programs encounter resistance in specific parts of their design. Typically, traditional academics can see no justification for considering field instruction as "study." Where it is called "field research," it may receive a somewhat warmer reception, but the warmth is likely to cool if academic credit for the experience is sought. To many European scholars, field instruction in social work simply is not serious study. Perhaps they feel that it is trying to masquerade as "fieldwork" in other disciplines, such as anthropology, where the objective is not practice skill, but discovery of new knowledge. It is a topic worthy of further examination.

Related to this reluctance of traditional academics to accept admission of social work education into universities is another situation which creates a puzzling and troubling dilemma. The very openness that made the open market a possibility in Central and Eastern Europe introduced market thinking to universities, as well as national economies. As a result, just as social work programs are entering universities, the governments that sponsored or permitted them are requiring the universities to operate at least partly by market rules. As in the United States, departments which are "cost–effective," which is to say

those that bring in revenue or patents, are the ones being supported and expanded, while those that represent net debits are being starved for funds.

In this atmosphere, social work faces the situation of having been developed
to address the old problems of the socialist system and the new problems of the
open market system, only to find itself losing any support from the old socialist
system while being closed out of the market in the new system. In some of the
old Warsaw Pact countries, social work education has reached the universities
just in time to fight for its survival in competition with the entrenched disciplines.

Aside from the political and economic difficulties faced by the emerging
programs of social work education are practical pedagogical issues, as well as
issues of culture and tradition, and the absence of supports taken for granted in
the West.

One of the most critical is the lack of teaching materials. Most published
social work literature is written in English. The Euro-American model of social
work by far dominates the world scene, and the literature is based on it. Most
educated Europeans speak, read, and write English but cannot be expected to
learn social work appropriate for their countries from reading texts written by
and for a Euro-Anglo-American audience.

This creates a painful dilemma. Organizations in Western countries have
been generous in collecting social work texts for use by the new programs,
which have had none of their own. However, as welcome as these contributions
have been, they are of limited use because of differences in assumptions in almost every area.

Even the most basic terms present difficulties. The title *social worker*, for
example, has a fairly common meaning in the West, even though some countries
have selected other names. (Scandinavians may refer to *socionoms*, Germans
distinguish between *social work* and social pedagogy, etc.). In Eastern Europe,
words such as *social* and *work* have potent meanings which often are negative.
They may imply exactly opposite meaning in the formerly socialist countries
and the Western countries.

Another example of such a word is *volunteer*. At a time when volunteerism
is increasing rapidly in popularity throughout the West, Central and Eastern
European social work educators must deal with a different historical experience.
In some places, the Soviet Army was accustomed to conscripting civilians to
perform difficult, dangerous, and unpaid labor, calling them "volunteers." The
notion of trying to create a cadre of volunteers or to generate enthusiasm for
volunteerism must deal with the obstacles presented by such precedents.

In fact, many, if not most, of the programs presently identified as "social
work education" in Central and Eastern Europe would not be recognized in the
United States as such. Perhaps the most common form is the program in "social
policy," whose graduates typically are expected to take positions as government
functionaries. A major effort of many of today's pioneers in social work

education is to achieve recognition and acceptance of a more Western model, with emphasis on professional practice informed by a profession-created system of ethical behavior, not slavish application of government rules and regulations.

The determination of what represents "research" in the new programs is different from that of American schools, being much closer to the European model. The devotion to empirical, statistical studies which represents the elite of present-day American social work research does relatively little to help teach research in Central and Eastern Europe, where social research tends to be much more practical, more concerned with identification of human problems than with mathematical purity. In some ways, research in Europe, and especially in Central and Eastern Europe, is much closer to research done by American social workers in the 1930s and 1940s, but for which most texts are now long since dated, are out of print or have completely disappeared.

An interesting historical irony is that American social work research as practiced and taught today may resemble the traditional social science discipline of European universities, while the hands-on social research which built American social work and is essential to sustain it represents the model which Central and Eastern Europeans are trying to have accepted by their universities.

A final example of these problems of meaning is in the selection of terminology for the intended beneficiaries of social work activity. The title *social worker* has been shown to lend itself to misunderstanding; equally important is the lack of a satisfactory term for the other actors. The American term *client* and the British terms *consumer* and *user* do not capture the same intended meanings in the East. With a history of social welfare as a service of the state, distributed as a reward for ideological loyalty, social work educators in the East are sometimes at a loss for a clear term, or even a neutral term, with which to describe the persons served. In some respects, even more difficult is the attempt to describe in social work terms the practice of collaborative work to a common end.

Aside from the difficulties in introducing field instruction to the curriculum; developing acceptable research courses; trying to balance theoretical with practical instruction where tradition holds that all instruction must be theoretical; trying to emulate a Euro-Anglo-American model while adapting it to local conditions, but without native–language texts or case studies; and in the other matters already discussed, several other challenges face social work educators in Central and Eastern Europe.

Since social agencies as known in the West have not existed in Eastern Europe, they have had to be created. But the personnel to staff them have not been social workers in the professional sense. Consequently, just as the university programs have had to begin with faculty who were not trained and experienced in professional social work, the agencies have had to try to create social work programs without trained and experienced social workers. What this has meant in the politics of educational programs is that while university social work educators are defending field instruction as a legitimate and essential part of professional education, they have not had adequate social agencies for student placements, nor a cohort of trained, experienced social work practitioners to serve as field instructors. It has been estimated that the time from creation of the program to the development of adequate placements and field supervisors is about five years. That is a long time to fight a rear-guard action.

It would be reasonable to conclude that all these hurdles should discourage social work educators in Central and Eastern Europe from trying to complete the job of creating a profession where none existed before, at least for two or more generations. To be sure, these leaders report periods of discouragement bordering on depression. However, they have been working steadily to create networks of mutual support within their region, rather than automatically or exclusively looking to the West for help. This has been difficult in the past, partly because of Moscow's purposeful policy of preventing its client states from getting together and posing a possible threat to Soviet domination. But it would have been difficult to form coalitions in any case, since the Central and Eastern European countries have traditions and cultures which are very different from each other.

Before the communist take-over, Russia had been a totalitarian tsarist state; Hungary was a monarchy until the Nazi invasion; Czechoslovakia was a democracy before being sold out by Britain and France in 1938; Albania was a backwater of the old Ottoman Empire; Yugoslavia had been the Kingdom of the Serbs, Croats, and Slovenes until 1929, and an independent communist state after World War II—it is difficult to imagine greater differences among nations within so confined a geographic area. The fact that these countries are beginning to join in a common cause is even more astounding than the creation of the European Community and the Parliament of Europe. But it is happening.

Despite such formidable obstacles in the areas of understanding, resources, and politics and culture, impressive progress can be seen. Strong ties have been developing between West European programs and Central and Eastern European initiatives. A number of German Fochhochschulen have collaborative arrangements with schools in the East, including exchange of faculties: the Fachhochschule fur Sozialarbeit und Sozialpadagogik in Berlin is moving its entire campus into what was East Berlin.

Programs under the aegis of the Nordic Council have been especially active in building bridges between Eastern Europe and Scandinavia, with exchanges, joint programs, and technical assistance.

The European Community has included social work in its TEMPUS scheme, aimed at cooperation and mobility between its members and Central and Eastern Europe higher education programs. As just one example of the possibilities of this opportunity, during the academic year 1992–1993, a special TEMPUS program linked social work schools all over Western Europe with programs in Poland, Slovenia, Macedonia, Czech Republic, and Hungary as "partners."

U.S. initiatives have taken various forms and have met with assorted degrees of success. One impressive example is a program devised and supervised by Robert Constable. This program provides qualified American social work educators with transportation, housing, and a modest stipend in exchange for teaching a minimum of one semester in Lithuania. In another case, two American educators, Richard Steinman and Margaret Yeakel (1993), spent two years in Hungary helping to develop viable field instruction in an atmosphere dominated by what they delicately described as "discordant values." A major project to develop volunteerism and community–based programs involves the Alliance of Universities for Democracy, a confederation of more than one hundred U.S. and Central and Eastern European schools and universities (Granger, 1993).

CONCLUSION

Only the very inexperienced or exceedingly bold would predict what will happen in the development of social work education during the next few years in Central and Eastern Europe.

No one's wildest dreams could have imagined the speed or thoroughgoing nature of the changes which have taken place in less than a decade. While it is true that the roots of change were well set by the 1960s, the pace of change was agonizingly slow, carried forward by a dedicated but very small band of courageous reformers.

It would seem that there will be no turning back. Although social work and social work education over the next few years are certain to change in Central and Eastern Europe, it is too early to predict the forms they will take.

After a period of experimentation with Euro-Anglo-American models, it is reasonable to expect Central and Eastern European programs to develop their own particular styles, based on their own traditions and cultures. Certain influences are likely to be pervasive in these developments.

One such influence is religion. In Poland, the Roman Catholic church continues as an important presence and is closely associated with the changes which made social work there again possible. Its weight has been felt already in major social policy decisions enacted into law. Hungary, on the other hand, has a long history of religious pluralism and toleration; a strong effort by any single faith would have to deal with many other religions and beliefs. In the former Soviet Union, the role of religion in the lives of the people is again taking on significant meaning, particularly the role of the traditional Russian Catholic church. Fundamentalist Protestantism seems to be increasing its presence. The influence of Islam is quite certain to help mold social work in those countries such as Albania where that religion is dominant, in line with deep–seated

Moslem beliefs about the importance of charity, or *zakah*, one of the Five Pillars of the faith.

The potential for dissolution and disruption from religious and cultural conflict already has been seen in Yugoslavia; there is no way to tell where the fracturing of that ancient and tortured area may end or what it will mean for social work.

Different paths being taken in the two states which formerly were Czecho-slovakia should be monitored, with emphasis by outside colleagues on collaboration rather than competition. The continued fragmenting of the former Union of Soviet Socialist Republics virtually guarantees difficulties for real professional unity, particularly for a profession as new to the experience of its people as is social work.

The problems faced by social workers and social work educators in Central and Eastern Europe should make social workers in the West blush to use the word *problem* in describing difficulties they face. Yet, despite what all reason might predict, the movement toward sound new professional programs of social work education in those countries has been steady, for the most part cautious, and rapidly maturing. Just as new models of social work have been given to the world community by some Latin American constituencies; as a different model even now is coming out of the experience of Asian social workers; and as black Africa is struggling to create its own unique system of social work, it is not unreasonable to assume that the Central and Eastern Europeans will learn what they can, create what they need, adapt what they want, and end with a social work practice and education model which is both similar to and different from the models so familiar in the world today.

REFERENCES

Bocharova, V. (1991). *Social work in the U.S.S.R.* Moscow: Center for Social Work Education and Social Work. Unpublished.

Bochenska-Seweryn & Krzysztof Frysztacki. (Eds.). (1990). *The Emerging Independent Nonprofit Sector in Poland.* Cracow: Second Annual Johns Hopkins International Fellows in Philanthropy Conference.

Brauns, Hans-Jochen & Kramer, David. (1986). *Social work education in Europe.* Frankfurt: Deutscher Verein fur Offentliche und Private Fursorge.

Buncic, Ksenija & Maglailic, Dada. (1988). *An Experiential Programme in Yugoslavia as a Model for Social Work Education.* Unpublished. Eotovs Lorand University. Degree in Social Work/Social Policy.

Granger, Ben. (1993). Eastern Europe and democracy: Enhancing common needs and values while maintaining diversity. In Proceedings of the Third International Conference, Alliance of Universities for Democracy, Krakow.

Hegyesi, Gabor. (1991). *The Context of Welfare Practice.* Summary of a presentation, privately circulated, Budapest.

Kopecky, Jiri et al. (1988). *The Education of Social Workers in Czechoslovakia.* Unpublished.

Les, Ewa. (1991). *Social Work in Poland.* Unpublished, privately circulated.

Martinovic, Milan. (1991). Characteristics of Social Work Study in Yugoslav Countries. Presented at the Conference on Social Work Education in Central/East Europe, Budapest.

Pasti, Silvia. (1991). *The Current State of Social Work Education in Romania.* Unpublished.

Report on social policy and social education in the Czechoslovak Socialist Republic. (1989). Unpublished.

Steinman, Richard & Yeakel, Margaret. (1993). *Preparing Field Instructors in Eastern Europe.* Unpublished

Talyigas, Katalin, & Hegyesi, Gabor. (1991). *Social Work Education in Hungary as Part of a Social Policy Reform.* Unpublished, privately circulated.

12

RUSSIA AND THE REPUBLICS

Otto H. Driedger

HISTORY OF SOCIAL WORK EDUCATION

The history of social work education in the Republics of the Commonwealth of Independent States (CIS) is very short. There has been no social work profession, and no social work education, but there are beginning initiatives and developments. The primary human service professions that have developed are psychiatry, psychology and nursing, in addition to medicine, law and education. Semiprofessionals have been trained in areas such as child care (day care). Professional education is provided through institutes that focus on education for each specific profession. Decades ago, in North America, teachers were trained in "normal schools" and nurses in nursing schools, attached to hospitals. These would be the closest approximations to professional education facilities in the republics.

The major locus for the work of human service professions is in institutions where the focus has primarily been on working with the individual. Social issues were dealt with on a societal, structural level. For example, the policy of full employment in the former USSR was designed to prevent problems of unemployment and poverty. If a person had difficulty on the job or was in poverty, it was seen as a problem of that individual.

The institutional focus on responding to human needs did not provide a climate for the development of social work. In contrast, the development of social work in Western societies has been a community based history whether in community development, casework or group work.

Initiatives established confidential telephone counseling services in many cities across the former USSR. The very first such development occurred in 1953 when two pastors published their telephone numbers so people could call them for help (Mokhovikov, 1991: 1). This movement gave rise to identifying a range of needs and problems which prompted the early development of community-based services. Further development of community-based services had to wait for the Gorbachev era to gain the flexibility to allow such services to develop. In addition to Confidential Telephone Counseling services identifying needs, psychiatrists and psychologists, teachers, priests and pastors identified special needs of children, youth, seniors, and disabled and other disadvantaged groups. Once flexibility of response was tolerated under Gorbachev's leadership, supplementary services began to be developed. People who were part of a religious group, who were sensitive to the needs of people in the community, and who had the freedom to volunteer their services, began to respond to the needs of people in the community. Such developments have generally begun since 1987 or later.

The cataclysmic changes in the former USSR as a result of perestroika (restructuring) and glasnost (openness) have meant the development of unemployment, with no structures to deal with it. The disbanding of Komsomol (the Communist Youth League) means that the vehicle for youth services is no longer in place, and new policies, programs and services must be developed. The approaches used by Komsomol, the tool used to inculcate communist ideology into youth, did not adequately deal with the needs of those youth. The approach used was very structured, with strong emphasis on communist values, rigid implementation of accepted patterns of dealing with youth and little focus on interpersonal relationships. A hypothetical parallel example in the United States or Canada would be if youth who wished to be involved in activities had to attend the activities and camps of one faith group. The emphasis and focus would be on the youth accepting that specific faith and designing their life according to specific dictates. With the discrediting of the Communist party, Komsomol, the vehicle for indoctrination, also is discredited. Therefore, not only is there a vacuum due to the disbanding of Komsomol but large gaps in needed service now exist. These are a few examples of changing patterns that demand new approaches to responding to human needs.

The combination of circumstances such as the prohibition to respond to emerging or existing needs under the former system and the requirement to respond to new issues and problems necessitated by basic restructuring has produced great demands on those who presently work in the human services field. This includes psychiatrists, psychologists, nurses, and government staff who had responsibility for programs such as those for youth.

Many in the human service fields are acknowledging limitations in their society for responding to human service needs and recognizing the lack of professionals or professional education for community based human service. This is the context in which there is great interest in development of social work education in some of the Republics of the Commonwealth of Independent States.

CULTURE/VALUES/RELIGION

The history, culture and religion, in fact the whole context of the republics of the former USSR are rich, varied, diverse and complex. As a result, it is important to recognize that developments vary greatly from republic to republic. In addition, there is great variation in the Russian Federation, particularly because there are many semiautonomous regions within that federation.

One of the great experiments of the Soviet Union since 1917 was to respond to human needs by structuring a society that would fulfill the basic needs of the individual, the family and the community.

The move in 1917 was from a preindustrial, semifeudal, imperial empire to a Marxist, Leninist, and then a Stalinist communist/socialist state. The historic religions in the Union were severely restricted and controlled. This included the largest groups (particularly in Russia and Ukraine: Orthodox Christianity, which had been the state religion prior to 1917, and Islam, which was predominant in some of the republics such as Khazakstan, Turkmenistan, Kirgizia (now Kirgizstan), and Azerbaijan.

Not only religions were controlled by the state: every aspect of life was. This was very forcefully stated by Alexander N. Mokhovikov in his presentation to a conference in September 1991 in Odessa:

> The human being is deprived of personality, he is a screw in a gigantic hierarchic structure of such a state. He has a function—to be part of the monstrous machine, deprived of individuality. But he has no rights: he cannot live on his own free will, he has no right to die. He can either be destroyed or be given the possibility to exist. Therefore, a person in a crisis situation is dangerous. A willful act, independent of the authorities, even if it is suicide, indicates that in the country there exists some undergoverned life, the existence of uncontrolled individuals. (Mokhovikov, 1991: 2)

Mokhovikov also addressed the issue of moral principles and religion in his characterization of the values context in the USSR in the past seven decades: "The religion of totalitarianism (in the U.S.S.R.) is atheism. Therefore, the real 'opium for the people' (Karl Marx) becomes class consciousness. It imminently presupposes the existence of 'enemies' and insists on the relativity of morals and ethics" (Mokhovikov, 1991: 3).

A third point he made that is particularly relevant here is the idea that "for the post-totalitarian society a characteristic feature is the slow lumpenization of society" (Mokhovikov, 1991: 8). By this he means that instead of everyone in a classless society being raised to a common humanity and respect, everyone is reduced to powerlessness, control, fear and suspicion, which puts everyone into the lowest class. The German word *lumpen* literally translated is "rags." The idea then is that this term refers to the underclass, the proletariat in rags.

Bottomore (1983) refers to Karl Marx's 18th Brumaire, pt. V, in describing the meaning of *lumpenproletariat*.

> Marx describes the lumpenproletariat as the "refuse of all classes," "a disintegrated mass," comprising "ruined and adventurous offshoots of the bourgeoisie, vagabonds, discharged soldiers, discharged jailbirds...pickpockets, brothel keepers, rag-pickers, beggars" etc., . . . The main significance of the term lumpenproletariat is not so much its reference to any clearly defined social group which has a major socio-political role, as in drawing attention to the fact that in extreme conditions of crisis and social disintegration in a capitalist society large numbers of people may become separated from their class and come to form a "free floating" mass which is particularly vulnerable to reactionary ideologies and movements. (Bottomore, 1983: 292)

The irony Mokhovikov identifies is that Marx's criticism of capitalism has actually become the situation for the majority of people in former Soviet society.

Writers, artists and musicians have played an important part in setting the societal context for dialogue in the former USSR. Values, social issues, societal analysis and criticism were unacceptable under the tsar and under the Soviet regime. In spite of threats and repression, writers such as Tolstoy, Dostoyevsky, Chekov, and, since 1917, Solzhenitzyn and Evtushenko, have examined social issues and provided social commentary.

When Gorbachev set the door ajar by proclaiming openness and restructuring, albeit in the Communist context, the pressures that had built for such a long time could not be contained, and the flood gates were forced open.

In political terms, Gorbachev had a model available that could be used to initiate change. This was the democratic model that could be transformed to respond to the needs in the republics. The flood soon made it apparent that events could not be controlled and change happened very quickly.

Economically, Gorbachev continued with the socialist model, but the successors used the market economy model. Many people were eager to abandon the model of central control because they had endured the shortages and limits to individuality that the model brought with it. Resistance to changes in the existing model was extensive, and a new set of problems emerged, including unemployment, inflation and disruption of productivity.

In the area of social well-being, social systems, services and developments, there was no model. Western countries have generally formulated their social programs and services on socialist principles or a combination of religious principles and socialist principles. Acknowledgment of some or substantial societal responsibility, for the well being of its citizens has moved from the concept of charity in religious terms, to social responsibility which is a blend of religious philanthropy, social conscience and socialist philosophy. In some countries, especially in Europe, there is a greater reliance on socialist philosophy, whereas in the United States there is more emphasis on social conscience and religious philanthropy. Canada finds itself somewhere between the two.

The republics of the CIS have rejected the socialist model. As a result, there is a vacuum in social policy perspective and planning. Some of the developing responses to social need appear to use terminology reminiscent of a religious, charity-based orientation. There is also some indication of a humanistic basis in some of the developments.

The vacuum appears not to be based exclusively on the rejection of socialist values and assumptions. Totalitarian states are generally not enthusiastic about an analysis of their patterns of control and therefore allow a very limited development of the social sciences. As a result, research and examination of social issues as well as discussion of development of policies, programs and services to respond to changing conditions have not occurred. Analysis and development have not been possible in universities, nor have organizations or opportunities developed outside the university.

One can, therefore, see that the situation in the republics of the CIS is substantially different, even from that in other Eastern European countries, where social work education has developed.

AGENDA FOR SOCIAL WORK EDUCATION

My most extensive discussions about social work education have occurred in Odessa, Ukraine. I will draw primarily upon my experience in Odessa, supplemented by discussions in Kiev and St. Petersburg, and with persons from most republics at several conferences.

Dr. Boris Khersonsky, a psychiatrist, journalist, Odessa City counselor (alderperson), and educator, who was involved in establishing the Odessa Open University in 1991, has important insights into human service and social work educational needs. His perspective is that the social sciences, especially sociology, must be developed extensively at the universities and that social work education, as well as education in other social professions, must be developed in a way that reflects the needs in the society. The approach being used to develop educational opportunities, therefore, is based on the exchange of information and materials, as well as opportunities for dialogue and discussions among educators and practitioners from the republics and the West. In this way, the training and educational patterns that will meet the needs of the society can develop.

Such an approach has the most potential to provide effective professional services. I have had the opportunity to visit numerous social work programs in other countries, both Western and developing countries. There is often a tendency to parachute programs from one society into another. The social work educational programs and those for other social professions that have been most effective, however, are the ones that have been developed in their own societal context.

The objective in Odessa is to have education for the social professions, including social work, at the Open University. This is in contrast to a European model for professional education which is generally carried out in specialized institutes for professional education, separate from the university context. This is changing in Europe also. The new model being developed is seen as the preferred model, in that social work needs a strong base in the social sciences and should be developed in such a way that such an interrelationship can readily be established.

The training demand for volunteers and support services is also in its infancy. Conferences and workshops are being organized for the development of specific skills. Experts from other countries are invited to assist in training and education, to provide consultation in development of services, and to create links with international organizations.

Links with international agencies provide expertise and build in basic principles and standards. The connection between the University of Regina, Regina, Saskatchewan, Canada, and the Open University in Odessa is supplemented by linkages with the International Association of Schools of Social Work, Vienna, and with a range of research and policy institutes. including the European Centre for Social Welfare Policy and Research in Vienna, the Swedish Institute, and the Canadian Council on Social Development.

I would expect that eventually there will be direct linkages with IASSW, and other international organizations. I can see a BSW-MSW continuum being developed sometime in the future, but the nature of the professional content should reflect the context and reality of the republics. Because the range of social professions in North America and Europe is not developed in the CIS republics, it may be that a broader human service professional will emerge, or that social work will become a more inclusive interprofessional and interdisciplinary profession. Many of us would think that a broad base does exist for social work, and it could respond to the broad needs for human service professionals. On the other hand, there are some in the profession who move it toward a clinical or therapeutic concentration, and in such circumstances social work would be too narrow. One of social work's strong orientations is "helping and caring." Social work also has a strong focus on justice, fairness and rights, whereas the principle of justice is a stronger focus in the human justice professions. It will be interesting to see how human service professions develop. From my perspective, it will play a key role in developing the professional educational base for the many human and social services that will emerge in the coming decades.

So much in Ukraine and other republics is presently in a state of flux that it is difficult to see how social work as a profession will ultimately develop, and how social work education and training will be established. There is great interest in the development of skills in work with people. Some, particularly those with program and policy responsibility, also have a concern for the development of competence in social analysis, policy and program development, and creation of agencies and organizations for service.

CURRICULUM

In the discussion of curriculum development in the CIS, the Open University of Odessa will be used as a case example. At present, there is no generalized approach to curriculum development in social work in the CIS.

The Open University was established in fall 1991 through the collaboration of Odessa University, the City of Odessa and community-based interest groups. Universities tend to be very formal and restrictive in admissions policy and in capacity to develop educational programs that are not part of a mainstream academic discipline. Odessa University was willing to cooperate because it supported the objectives of providing greater access to university education and increasing the flexibility of what could be offered at a university setting.

Social work and education for other social professions will be developed in the context of the Open University. A unit or department has been established in which forty students began studies in fall 1991. The first two years are general university studies, after which twenty students focus on psychological counseling and the other twenty on social work.

The model of education parallels the Canadian university programs of clinical psychology and social work. Although it is not clear exactly what the curriculum for the psychological counseling stream will be in the third and fourth years, it is anticipated that it will be similar to that of clinical psychology as we know it. Psychology is a long-standing profession in the former USSR, and this course of study would make counseling more accessible in the community. It should be remembered that both programs are being designed and developed by persons who have a background in psychiatry and psychology and are exploring the potential contributions of social work. In practical terms it is difficult to see exactly what the differences between the two fields might be. They may be heading toward the same dynamic operative in North America between social work and psychology. The motivation in developing social work appears to be the identified necessity to develop a profession that can respond to more than the psychological needs of people by developing systems of support and organizational infrastructure, social policies and programs.

It is expected that the graduate in social work will have a "middle" level of professional education and competence. By this is meant that it will not be a technical training program, nor a postgraduate program. The first professional degree would be comparable to the Canadian or American BSW.

The Canadian model has been adapted and modified to respond to the needs, structures, laws and developments in Ukrainian society. The program in Odessa will incorporate courses in national social law, social institutions and services, as well as develop practice competence. Courses in the social work aspect of the program started in 1993. Some persons from Odessa have already visited Canada and will do so again in the near future. Some Canadian professors also have been in Odessa for consultation and will follow up with further contacts. There has also been an exchange of information, materials, and some books. It is expected that there will be much more exchange of information.

The intention is to have English as an important aspect of study for students in social professions because books, journals and other literature are more accessible in English than in any other language. Exchanges of professors and students, dialogue with professionals, and so on, have greatest potential when one has some proficiency in English. At present, there is an intense interest in learning English for many reasons. It is a required course, beginning in the fourth grade.

Another element that is seen as important is a study of the social sciences. The objective of incorporating this element into the curriculum is not as obvious as it may seem. For reasons identified earlier, some of the social sciences have not been well developed. The development of the social sciences, therefore, is high on the agenda at the Open University and will be prominent in the social work curriculum. Sociology appears to be least developed. Psychology and economics have been in the curriculum at universities but have been focused on approaches consistent with the political philosophy, so new approaches and ideas are being encouraged.

Social philosophy and social theory are seen as important components that will require considerable development. Designing new programs and services in response to the basic restructuring of society requires an important policy and program development component as well as a focus on the development of skills in working with people individually, in groups or in communities.

Social action, advocacy, empowerment and principles of self-help have not been clearly identified as areas of priority as yet. There are indications that as developments continue, such principles will be seen as important elements.

There are beginnings in developing an information center for the development of human services in Ukraine. The Ministry of Sport and Youth and the Ministry of Labor have asked the Odessa group to develop a nation-wide information center and establish a journal. The economic uncertainties have delayed funding for these activities, but it is expected that as the situation stabilizes, these plans will be implemented.

The linkages that are being made with Western European and Canadian universities and research centers are seen as important in developing the capacity to provide education, research and written materials.

One of the observations made to me in November 1991 by Boris Khersonsky is that "there are so many initiatives we must take simultaneously that it often appears that we are all over the map, but with the rapid change, there is no alternative."

The Ukrainian Research Institute for Youth in Kiev has a national mandate to initiate research, develop policy for services to youth, and facilitate education and training for people who will work with youth. There is developing collaboration among the Open University in Odessa, the Federation of Social Services and Programs and the Research Institute in Kiev.

The close linkages among persons such as Dr. Khersonsky, who is designing the social work curriculum; the Federation of Social Services and Programs in Odessa; and the Research Institute in Kiev assist in developing a curriculum that is sensitive to the needs in Ukraine.

The relationship and exchanges with the University of Regina, Faculty of Social Work, Regina, Saskatchewan, Canada; with the International Association of Schools of Social Work; and with centers such as the European Centre for Social Welfare Policy and Research in Vienna facilitate the building of a curriculum that is internationally recognized as well as locally relevant.

ISSUES AND OBSERVATIONS

Ukraine and the Russian Federation have a wealth of culture, a long history, a diverse population, and a very high level of literacy and education. The creativity and dynamism could very well explode into another golden age. On the other hand, if political stability, economic equilibrium and social well-being are not achieved, there could be a dark age on the horizon.

To date, the primary Canadian and U.S. responses to the republics have focused on democratization and the market economy. The third element, social well-being, is an equally urgent area in need of attention. In the words of the Canadian ambassador in Kiev, Nestor Gayworski, "If one does not address social issues and the well-being of people, one cannot even begin to address issues of democratization."

Unemployment resulting from a market economy, without a safety net such as unemployment insurance, inflation without an incomes policy; youth on the streets without programs for youth; a lack of an agency for social development to parallel economic change and democratization, will doom the country to failure.

The approach being formulated by the European Centre for Social Welfare Policy and Research, Vienna, shows some promise as a theoretical model that could be used. The concept of the welfare mix (Evers & Wintersberger, 1990) suggests there are four major elements that enhance the well-being of people. The market economy is the basis for productivity and economic activity that provides the financial base for the general public. The state provides a safety net and structure for human services that ensure basic quality of life. The household (the word *family* is not used because of the wide range of patterns of the basic unit of society) is the fundamental unit that provides a wealth of support and well-being to people. The community and its systems of support are the fourth element.

In the last half century, there has been a polarized approach to social analysis and planning. The polarization has been between the "socialist" and the "capitalist" views of the world. The European Centre suggests that approach is no longer useful, and generally has never been very helpful. The four elements referred to have historically played an important role in most societies, and the debate should focus on the nature of the mix. Some societies that are more capitalist focus more strongly on the market economy. Others have a heavier reliance on the role of the state in assuring the well-being of citizens. The roles of the household and the community vary in relation to the other two but also depend on the culture and values of the society.

In conclusion, my observation is that there is great potential for development in the republics. The opportunity for cooperation, collaboration and exchange is unlimited. The need for development of social services, programs and systems is urgent. Attention must be given in the republics to formulation of a social philosophy that can provide a solid base for social policy and programs. Education and training in human professions, and especially in social work, are a high priority and offer many opportunities for joint work. Finance is and will continue to be a major problem for at least a decade. Funds for collaboration and development will be needed from international sources, but there is a very strong desire to provide as much financial support as possible from within the republics.

There are an energy and creativity emerging which should be supported and encouraged internationally. The challenge will be there for all international agencies, and the opportunities to learn and be enriched will flow in both directions.

REFERENCES

Blake, Patricia & Hayward, Max. (Ed.). (1964). *Dissonant Voices in Soviet Literature*. New York: Harper Colophon Books, Harper & Row.

Bottomore, Tom. (Ed.). (1983). *A Dictionary of Marxist Thought*. Cambridge, Mass.: Harvard University Press.

Canadian-Soviet Studies. (1990). *The Changing Societal Structure in the Soviet Union: Implications for Canada and the World*. Ottawa: Carleton University.

Driedger, Otto & Driedger, Florence. (1992). A time of drama and change. Report to Health and Welfare Canada on Social Development in the Republics of the Commonwealth of Independent States, (1989). March.

Driedger, Otto. (1989).   Mental Health Services in the U.S.S.R: Focus on V.M. Bekhterev Research Institute, Leningrad.   Report to Mennonite Central Committee, Akron, Pa., December.

Driedger, Otto. August 19, 1991 - the day the clock stopped in the U.S.S.R.: experiences shared at Odessa. Unpublished article.

Evers, A. & Wintersberger, H. (Eds.). (1990). *Shifts in the Welfare Mix: Their Impact on Work, Social Services and Welfare Policies*. European Centre for Social Welfare Policy and Research. Campus Verlag, Frankfurt am Main. Boulder, Co.: Westview Press.

Landy, Joanne. (1991).   Politics and the economy: what's to come in the USSR? *Social Policy* Fall *17*.

Mennonite Central Committee Canada, Council of USSR Ministries.   (1992). Newsletter, January. Winnipeg, Canada.

Mokhovikov, Alexander T. (1991). The youth confidence telephone services and the psychological processes in the post-totalitarian society: problems and perspectives (eleven theses).   Paper presented at Odessa Conference on Confidence Telephone Service personnel from all Republics of C.I.S. September.

Solzhenitsyn, Alexander. (1972). *For the Good of the Cause*. London: Sphere Books Limited.

Tretyakov, Vitali. (1989) *Philanthropy in Soviet Society*. Moscow: Novosti Press Agency Publishing House.

USSR Academy of Sciences. (1989). *People's Well-Being in the USSR: Trends and Prospects*. The Soviet Economic Science Series 9. Moscow: Nauka Publishers.

III

AFRICA

13

AFRICA

Yvonne W. Asamoah

INTRODUCTION

Social work education in Africa has both profited and suffered from its many legacies. These legacies are rich and varied and contribute in special ways to the uniqueness of social work education and practice in developing and developed countries in Africa. They are also responsible for the variance in definitions of social work and account for the differences between social work in many countries in Africa and the Western model. African countries, prior to independence, during the independence struggles and after, honed out their own forms of social work practice and developed institutions where this knowledge could be transmitted to others. What has emerged is a fascinating mosaic of programs at various levels designed to meet the needs of citizens on the most diverse of all continents. Many dedicated social work educators and practitioners deserve credit for working tirelessly over the years, against many odds, to shape social work education in Africa.

HISTORICAL CONTEXT

Social work education in Africa, as in many other parts of the world, has both formal and informal elements. While the beginning of formal training in recognized institutions can be traced to a specific date, performance of social work–like tasks (such as community work, mediation, advocacy, helping others) has always been a part of African tradition. Just as Western social work is rooted in certain values and specific philosophical perspectives from many parts of the world, African social work has historical roots which are value based, indigenous and imported. Indeed, the goodness of fit between indigenous and imported elements of social work practice and education has formed the basis of healthy and heated debate for the past several decades (Association for Social Work Education in Africa [ASWEA], 1982; Drake, 1962; Hammoud, 1988;

Khinduka, 1971; Midgley, 1983; Patel, 1987; Shawky, 1972; UN, 1968, 1971; Walton & Abo El Nasr, 1988.

Africa has the largest collection of recently independent countries of any continent, with the majority gaining independence as late as the early 1970s. Most attained independence in rapid succession during the 1960s. Although there are many regional differences with regard to social problems, economic growth, social development and political arrangements, Estes (1987) correctly noted that newly independent African countries south of the Sahara had inadequate political and social infrastructures to support rapid social change and industrial development. They still struggle to find positive solutions for meeting human need in the face of rapid population growth and declining resources. This history, coupled with the current social and economic realities, has left a definite mark on social work education.

Part of the colonial legacy for both anglophone and francophone countries was a formal welfare system that reflected the ideology and basic structures of the former colonial power. The development of social welfare systems, social work practice and social work education must be understood within the historical context of each country's precolonial and postcolonial experience. The basic institutions (political, legal, social, economic, educational) of all African countries both influenced and were influenced by the formal response to the meeting of human need. Hill (1962) observed that, within the African context, historical and contemporary political systems and the institutions determining human welfare are often in conflict. Elements of this conflict are reflected in the way needs are translated into policy and policies are translated into social and educational programs.

Francophone and anglophone countries in Africa inherited different legacies. According to Hill (1962), this reflected differences in social and political structure, and intellectual values and concepts of the colonial powers. Colonial legacies directly influenced the development and nature of social legislation, the nature of social security systems, and the role and training of professional personnel including social workers (Hardiman & Midgley, 1982; Her Majesty's Stationery Office [HMSO], 1960; International Labour Office [ILO], 1983; Wicker, 1958).

Britain exported a remedial model which was based on the principles underlying remedial social services in the United Kingdom. Therefore, services in former British colonies focused on rehabilitation and, not surprisingly, selected as the unit of attention vulnerable individuals including women, migrants, homeless children, the disabled, juvenile delinquents, the unemployed, and the physically and mentally ill. Comprehensive social security and social insurance schemes were viewed as a luxury which could not be undertaken for such a limited number of wage earners (HMSO, 1960). Social policies and systems in former French colonies and territories reflected the more comprehensive approach embodied in the French Overseas Labor Code. Neither the British nor the French approach placed much emphasis on prevention. Prevailing social problems were targeted for cure, and a developmental focus was virtually non-existent. Perhaps even more important, many of the approaches and practices labeled social work were not compatible with the cultural traditions of the countries in which they were carried out. Nevertheless, they continued for many years.

There was one bright note, however. Many countries, particularly in West Africa, but also to some extent in East and Southern Africa, benefited from the colonial administrations' recognition of the need to develop rural areas. While infrastructures were created for the convenience of the administrators, the net effect was to make rural areas accessible to health and other personnel. The welfare systems of countries affected reflect this dual perspective-attention to social problems and rural development. Ghana (then the Gold Coast) is an excellent example. In countries where rural development was taken seriously, community development, both as a movement and as a process, flourished and in some countries became an integral part of social work education (Brokensha & Hodge, 1969; DuSautoy, 1958). In others, it remained outside the realm of what was considered social work and social work education, but nevertheless played an important role in the postcolonial development process.

Perhaps the most significant event in the 1960s for both social work practice and social work education in Africa was the first Conference of Ministers Responsible for Social Welfare held in 1968. During the early part of that decade, the newly emerging African nations were preoccupied with nation building and both economic and social development. According to the Association for Social Work Education in Africa, the social welfare policies, approaches and programs inherited from the West were not adequate and appropriate to stimulate nation building. Nation building demanded indigenous trained personnel with a new perception in socioeconomic development (ASWEA, 1982: 9).

The 1968 Conference of Ministers recommended that priority in developing countries be given to social welfare and that social welfare training prepare workers for carrying out developmental roles. This conference challenged the international social work community to pursue a dynamic agenda that would put social work out front on issues of development and make it, as a profession, more relevant to current realities.

A New Era Dawned

Leading social work educators in Africa (Shawky, 1972, Tesfaye, 1974) took up the challenge and, with assistance from many quarters, helped move social work in a new direction. The link between social work education and national development goals became the theme for many regional, national and local conferences in the 1970s (Anders, 1974; International Association of Schools of

Social Work [IASSW], 1973, 1974, 1977; UN, 1970; Yiman, 1976). Several schools restructured their programs and redesigned curricular offerings; others upgraded their programs by instituting higher level diplomas and bachelor's degrees. This reflected a perceived need to develop a cadre of professionals who could function on many levels-as future ministers of social welfare, as administrators of social programs, as direct practitioners, as workers at the grass roots level, as community organizers, and as educators.

To facilitate this new thrust, the third Expert Group Meeting of Social Work Educators and Administrators in Addis Ababa in 1971 resolved that an Association of Social Work Education (ASWEA) be established. ASWEA came into existence in March 1971 (ASWEA, 1982) and in cooperation with the International Association of Schools of Social Work and other national and international organizations (Economic Commission for Africa, Organization of African Unity, Center for Social Science Research and Documentation in Africa South of the Sahara [CERDAS], Center for African Family Studies [CAFS]) has taken a strong leadership role in this area. Since its inception, ASWEA has promoted indigenous social development education; balancing curricula with regard to social science, theoretical and practice content; refocusing on rural development, women in development, child survival and development, family planning and family welfare; and training of trainers. These themes were stressed through various collaborative workshops during the 1970s and 1980s.

While the 1970s witnessed needed changes in the structures and curricula of schools of social work in Africa, progress was slow, economic problems escalated, social conditions continued to deteriorate, and political leadership was often unstable. At times, leaders appeared to be so overwhelmed by the degree of human suffering and lack of resources that they were too paralyzed to take meaningful action.

The second Conference of African Ministers of Social Affairs, held in 1977, and the third, held in 1980, continued to press the issue of reorienting social welfare services to a developmental model and training key personnel accordingly. Out of this renewed effort came the establishment of the African Center for Applied Research and Training in Social Development (ACARTSOD), under the auspices of the Economic Commission for Africa (ECA) and the Organization of African Unity (OAU) and designed as a center for research studies and the training of higher level personnel in the social development field. Direct support by African governments for ASWEA and ACARTSOD was encouraged. This was especially critical because schools of social work and social work training institutions that wished to change their focus to a more developmental one lacked the resources to help faculty and training staff take advantage of the new opportunities for learning spearheaded by these two organizations. (Many schools could not even afford the modest membership fee).

The cooperation between ASWEA and other organizations stimulated exchange of ideas through publications and expert working papers, encouraged collaboration between training and major research institutions, contributed to the development of indigenous teaching materials, and encouraged public debate on key developmental issues. For example, one of ACARTSOD's most significant publications in the 1980s was *Social Implications of the Lagos Plan of Action* (ACARTSOD, 1983). This document attempted to operationalize the principles contained in the Plan of Action prepared jointly by the United Nations Economic Commission for Africa and the Organization of African Unity, draw attention to implications and possible pitfalls, carve out a role for the public and private sectors, and prioritize services to specific populations. This was helpful to social work educators as they struggled to keep training programs relevant to the ,economic and social goals delineated by African governments themselves. Recommendations included (1) formulation and implementation of population and family policies, (2) strengthening national health systems including primary health care, (3) eradication of adult literacy, (4) improvement of the status of women, (5) tackling youth unemployment, (6) dealing with the problems of refugees and displaced persons, (7) focusing on agricultural development, and (8) redefining industrial priorities (ACARTSOD, 1983).

The developmental approach, to which ACARTSOD alluded, required that social work focus on larger population groups and revitalize self-help grass roots initiatives and community based programs to supplement public programs. Social workers were again called upon to redefine their priorities and channel their efforts into those pursuits that would have the greatest impact on raising standards of living. This new challenge reinforced the professional self-examination that had already started in the 1970s (Asamoah, 1977; IASSW, 1973, 1974, 1977).

Following on the heels of the charge of the Conference of Ministers Responsible for Social Welfare in 1968, the United Nations issued *Training for Social Welfare: Fifth International Survey* (UN, 1971). This report, as would many others shortly thereafter, drew attention to the unintended consequences of development and the critical role that social welfare personnel must play in ensuring that the social objectives of national development are kept in focus. The report noted that social welfare personnel would be called upon to plan and implement programs and formulate social policies in relation to the rapidly emerging social problems at the time-unemployment, underemployment, unplanned migration, lack of housing, rising and unfulfilled expectations of a rapidly growing youth population.

Moving social welfare into an expanded role in which programs would be integral parts of overall development strategies was not seen as an easy task. Although not relinquishing remedial or residual functions, emphasis on preventive and developmental functions took social welfare beyond the narrow fields of activity with which it had been traditionally associated. This included ensuring that human and material resources were deployed to deal successfully with the social requirements of change and contribute to nation building. Unfortunately, the needed changes in education and training to implement the new roles would be slow because of the lack of acceptance of social work as a profession and the lack of resources to launch social welfare training efforts (UN, 1971). Although there has been some improvement over the past decade, lack of acceptance and lack of resources continue to plague social work in many African countries.

RANGE AND STRUCTURE OF SOCIAL WORK EDUCATION IN AFRICA

The range and structure of social work education in Africa varies from country to country and region to region. However, there are sufficient similarities to enable one to make some generalizations. The shared experiences of colonialism and the need to respond to common problems associated with rapid industrialization, urbanization and their social consequences partially account for the similarity, as do attempts to operationalize, within the African context, the challenge given by the Ministers Responsible for Social Welfare in 1968 (UN, 1969). ASWEA's compilation of curricula for social work education and training (1982) and Rao and Kendall's (1984) world guide are the sources for much of the information in this section.

Levels of Education and Training

In the ASWEA document, data were reported for thirty-five countries (excluding South Africa), and seventy-eight training/education programs were identified. The majority of the institutions were founded in the 1960s and 1970s (thirty-six and fourteen respectively). Approximately ten countries developed training programs in the 1940s and 1950s. Egypt and South Africa were the first two countries to offer social work training at higher institutions (Egypt in the 1930s and South Africa in the ,1920s).

The majority of training programs, whether in institutions of higher learning (university) or intermediate or middle-level institutions, are preservice. That is, the training prepares students to undertake certain kinds of jobs in the welfare field. Applicants for such programs may or may not be currently employed in social work or social work–related jobs. Admissions criteria are set by academic boards (in universities), certified training boards or ministries in which social development training takes place. If applicants to these programs are employed, there is often an arrangement for released time to pursue formal education in social work, but the standard for the award is not set by the employing body.

In-service training programs in Africa are widespread and often involve instruction for social and community development workers. This training is at the discretion of the employer (often in consultation with an institution of higher learning) but may not prepare personnel for further study at an institution of higher learning unless they also possess the requisite academic credentials. Many certificates are offered at this level and may be a requirement for employer sponsorship for training at the next highest (often diploma) level.

Levels of training include certificate, diploma, bachelor's, master's, postgraduate diploma, DPhil and PhD. While the bachelor's and master's degrees generally have the same or similar entry requirements and approximately the same length of study, certificate and diploma requirements vary widely among countries. In recent years, there have been attempts to increase uniformity among countries in the classification of awards in terms of the nature of the course, entry requirements, and duration of training.

Countries have different patterns and combinations of programs, which include (1) one level of training at one institution, (2) several levels of training at one or two institutions, (3) several levels of training at several different institutions. Egypt has the greatest range (from diploma to PhD). The PhD programs, offered at two different universities, date back to the early 1970s. Ghana, the Sudan, South Africa and Zambia are the few countries that offer a postgraduate diploma, a qualification that requires a bachelor's degree, but may be of shorter duration and/or more practically focused than a master's degree. In Sudan, this degree is intended for senior level administrators with experience in social welfare who need further grounding in social work knowledge and practice. In Ghana, this degree provides a grounding in social work theory and practice to those with a solid social science background (BA level) who wish to take up careers in social welfare or who have worked in social welfare agencies after obtaining the BA. In Ghana and Sudan, the courses were initiated in the 1970s, and at that time, neither country offered social work at the bachelor's level. In South Africa, the course concentrates on preparation for supervision. In Zimbabwe, the diploma is a three year course for nongraduates and a two year course for graduates.

A qualification at this level may be very appealing for countries with strong BA programs in the social sciences (especially economics and sociology) that have no BA or master's programs in social work or social development. Bachelor's degree level graduates will automatically gravitate to the higher levels in the civil service structure. Additional training in social work and social welfare might assist in bringing the necessary social perspective to development planning whether it is in housing, social welfare, education, health, local government, or agriculture.

Training at the intermediate level generally results in either a certificate or a diploma in both English-speaking and some Arabic-speaking countries and takes place in institutes. These institutes may be semiprivate with some government funding, but the usual pattern is a fully government funded institute overseen by either the Ministry of Education or the Ministry of Social Welfare/Social Development/Community Development. Some training takes place in polytechnics (e.g., in Nigeria).

There has been a gradual trend of raising social work training to higher levels (at least ten countries now offer BA programs). However, there is still a great need for intermediate level training which bridges the gap between those working in administrative positions (with or without a degree) and those working at the community or grass roots level. Clearly the bulk of the resources go into grass roots and intermediate level training, but the gradual emergence of more training at institutions of higher learning suggests a recognition that there is a need for social workers to function at a number of different levels. It should also be noted that training is not necessarily expected to be progressive. That is, a certificate or diploma may be a career end point for some workers. Also, a social work qualification is not always a prerequisite for entry into a university program in social work or social development except at the highest levels.

South Africa is the only country offering more training in social work at the university level than at intermediate levels. All of South Africa's twenty universities offer professionally recognized programs in social work through four year bachelor's degrees. Only two nonuniversity institutions offer nondegree programs in social work. However, the awards received from these institutions are recognized as professional qualifications (Mazibuko, et al., 1992). Some South African universities also offer several levels of degrees beyond the bachelor's including a BA (honors), MA, advanced diploma, DPhil, and PhD. For all of these, there is a prerequisite in social work training at a lower level (Rao & Kendall, 1984).

The duration of the various programs depends upon the level of the final award. The PhD programs may take three or four years, reflecting the amount of course work required and the time needed to complete the research and dissertation. The prescribed minimum for the D.Phil in South Africa is two years, and the majority of the higher level diplomas offered in universities require one to three years of study. Bachelor's programs are all of either three years' or four years' duration, and this generally depends upon the country's basic educational structure. Training at the certificate level ranges from several months (e.g., six in Lesotho, Liberia, and Sierra Leoné, seven in Kenyå, nine in Botswana) to two years (ASWEA, 1982). Some of the training at this level is in-service. The preservice training is generally designed to give entry level workers basic skills in generic social work practice, community development, rural development, adult education or literacy, and health. The duration of training for the diploma has the widest range-from nine months to four years. Diplomas are awarded by both intermediate institutions and universities.

Entry Requirements

Entry requirements vary according to the level of qualification sought and the educational system in the specific country. Generally, in universities, admission requirements are set by academic boards, and in intermediate institutions by whichever body is responsible for that level of training-usually a ministry of education or social welfare/social development. Even private or semiprivate training institutions (e.g., those run by missionary societies or voluntary agencies) are under some state jurisdiction and regulation.

Admission requirements differ between the anglophone and francophone countries, and the differences reflect those in the formal educational system. The francophone countries follow the French system of training and education, and the anglophone countries follow either the British or American system (this difference largely accounts for the differences among countries in duration of training for the BA degree).

The most common admission requirement to francophone schools of social work awarding diplome d' aid sociale is ten years of formal education. For the diplome d'etat d'assistant sociale, the admission requirements range from ten to thirteen years, and the duration of the course also varies from two to four years. The baccalaureate is a common requirement as well as an entrance examination.

In anglophone countries, entry requirements at certificate level require as a minimum successful completion of formal education at school certificate level and often some prior experience in social or community work. Some countries require a certain number of passes at the general certificate of education (GCE) level (Ghana, for example). Many countries require a GCE O level certificate or, in West Africa, the West African school certificate (WASC) or teacher's certificate (which represents postelementary training of several years).

Entry for diplomas in higher institutions often requires GCE passes at A level, thus conforming to normal university entry requirements. Entry for postgraduate diplomas requires a bachelor's degree and usually several years of experience. At the intermediate level, formal educational requirements may be waived if candidates have several years of successful experience in social work or community work.

At the bachelor's level, some countries recognize a diploma in social work as a sufficient entry requirement, but most require a good GCE A level certificate or, as in the case of South Africa, the senior high school certificate. Countries offering master's degrees in social work (Egypt and South Africa) require a bachelor's degree in social work; those offering BA (honors) degrees beyond the bachelor's (South Africa, Zimbabwe) require a social work qualification at the bachelor's level; and those offering the PhDs or DPhil require previous social work training (Egypt and South Africa).

Although entry requirements for all levels of training are spelled out, it can be assumed that some flexibility and discretion exist where entrance examinations are also required. This is a method of assessment which can be used to waive the formal requirements or minimize their importance if the applicant does not have a strong certificate or diploma. Such discretion is less often possible at the first degree and higher levels because the formal requirements apply to all disciplines within the university, not just social work, and are regulated by academic boards and/or councils of higher education.

South Africa represents, perhaps, the most unique case of social work education and training that does not reflect the composition of the potential pool from which to select for training and the nature of potential clientele, according to Mazibuko, McKendrick and Patel (1992). Although an increasingly large number of African, Asian, and colored persons have been drawn into the profession over the past two decades, whites still predominate. Of South Africa's 7,767 registered social workers, 66 percent are whites, 16 percent are Africans, 12 percent are colored persons and 6 percent Asian. While in theory, undergraduate education is open to people of all racial groups at all universities, with the exception of English-language urban universities, many universities have uniracial faculties and student bodies (Mazibuko et al., (1992).

Curricula and Course Content

In a comparative analysis of social work education in Africa, the first point that strikes one is the variety of institutions in which social work training is offered and of programs. Although social work training in Africa is often compared to and contrasted with the Western model, it must be noted that that model encompasses elements from American, British and European social work, and these may be very different. For example, the United States and South Africa probably have the smallest range of programs that produce graduates eligible for the designation *social worker* and the course requirements are standardized by a regulatory council. Some countries make a distinction between community development worker and social worker. In some, a person receives a qualification in social administration but is perceived to be doing social work. Training for grass roots community work is different from that for work in hospitals, work in the juvenile justice system, and work with the disabled.

This dichotomy between community work and other types of social work is reflected not only in educational programs, but at ministerial level. Social workers in some countries are employed by ministries of health; in others by departments of social welfare; and in others by departments of community development/social development and/or education. Perhaps the most significant difference between training programs is whether they are designed to provide a comprehensive background in the social sciences as well as social work skills, or whether they are designed primarily to give rudimentary skills in an area for immediate practical application.

Courses at the postgraduate, BA and master's levels have heavy concentrations of social science subjects including economics, sociology, social psychology, social administration, anthropology, general psychology, research, political science, personnel management, and demography. Social and general psychology are often required in addition to courses in human growth and development at the BA and higher diploma levels. A few countries have courses which are intended to orient students to the prevailing political philosophy of the country. Many courses contain subjects that are culturally specific, such as introduction to Islamic law, Islamic civilization and Arab thought: African traditional religion; and French culture. In some cases, specific subjects within a broader discipline are offered such as criminology, family studies, the legal system, role theory, rural sociology, urban sociology, sociology of deviant behavior, and population studies. A local language and/or courses in the official language are requirements in some training institutions, but not generally at degree or higher degree level.

Professional social work courses at higher diploma, BA and graduate levels include both generic and method-specific courses. A multimethods focus is common, with the designations the same as used in Western schools for casework and groupwork. One important difference is that community development and not community organization is a core component of most training programs-referred to as community work in some countries. Courses under the rubric *social administration* using the British nomenclature include training in working with individuals, groups, communities and should not be construed to mean a specialization in administration. Casework, group work and community development are also important components of certificate and diploma level courses, but courses at this level also have more practical subjects, and specific topics from social science disciplines are covered rather than the entire disciplines themselves. Research and statistics are requirements at degree and higher levels, but some programs require competency in research at diploma levels.

It would appear that graduates with BA degrees have an excellent grounding in social science as well as social work as a profession, making this degree a very functional one in a developing country. The breadth of the curriculum is extremely impressive. However, there is still some concern that the social work content is not sufficiently indigenous.

Intermediate diploma courses in community development include both practical subjects and those associated with traditional social work education. The practical subjects include adult education, general agriculture, cottage industries, poultry raising, nutrition and health literacy. The objective of many of these courses is to help students understand and develop an awareness of the needs of the community and to be able to intervene in specific practical ways (ASWEA, 1982), including skill development.

In the francophone African countries, intermediate level training is tied very closely to health related activities, and social workers play an active role in maternal and child health and prevention programs. Courses at this level, in addition to background subjects in the social sciences, cover many subjects related to health.

Field education is considered a fundamental part of social work training at all levels. According to ASWEA (1982), about one-third of the total program is devoted to this in social work training institutions in Africa. Patterns include both block and concurrent, and many schools have a combination. Field education in university programs is under the supervision of faculty. The field requirement often includes a mini research project. Field practicum is designed to relate theory to practice.

Some schools require students to have placements in both rural and urban areas during the course of their training. Others require only that they have a placement in an area that is different from their usual experience (if they are employed). This means that students working in juvenile settings might have a field placement in a hospital setting. Unfortunately, some programs may allow students to graduate with no practical experience in rural areas or community work.

Finance

One of the most important constraints on social work education in Africa is finance. Almost all training is heavily subsidized if not totally funded by the state. Some schools are fortunate to obtain assistance from outside sources, but these are often project-specific and therefore of short duration. Schools often benefit from large-scale research efforts coordinated by national research institutes and funded by international organizations like the United Nations or the World Bank. Private donors such as the Freidrich Ebert Foundation in Germany have also provided assistance. The International Association of Schools of Social Work has played a key role in providing funds for social work educators to take advantage of training opportunities and conferences in other countries. Missionary societies and other charitable groups may fund grass roots level training in activities limited to their specific mission.

Many schools are fortunate to have special collaborative arrangements with overseas schools of social work or social work organizations which provide either direct funding, or more commonly, resources in the form of personnel, literature, exchange opportunities, and equipment.

The International Activities Committee of the National Association of Social Workers in the United States has spearheaded a twinning program which links NASW chapters in the United States with ongoing projects and/or agencies in developing countries. So far, a few African countries are involved in this effort and several others have expressed interest. This program, and others like it, could provide indirect benefits to African social work educational institutions. International collaboration can be very beneficial. However, it must be undertaken with great care and concern, and with the assurance that all parties involved are clear about the expected outcomes and the means for achieving them. For example, one erroneous assumption is that because African social work training institutions lack financial resources, they also lack technical expertise and thus require the services of an outside expert. In many cases, financial assistance is all that is needed to enable well-trained indigenous experts to perform their roles effectively (for example, to enable a field supervisor with a BA or MA degree to travel to the hinterland to supervise students in field placement or engage in a research project). Imported experts can be as much a hindrance as an asset to social work education programs (Asamoah & Beverly, 1988).

CURRENT PROBLEMS AND FUTURE DIRECTIONS

Despite the recognition by African schools of social work in the 1970s that their structures were too Western in orientation and that more of a developmental focus was needed, articles written by social work educators since the mid-1980s continue to echo the same theme (see, e.g. Asamoah & Beverly, 1988; Hammoud, 1988, Kendall, 1986; Mazibuko et al., 1992; McKendrick, 1990; Patel, 1987; Walton & Abo El Nasr, 1988). There is progress, however, even if it is extremely slow. In many countries, budgets for remedial services have been curtailed, making these services more dependent upon voluntary efforts and thus freeing up trained social workers to undertake more developmental tasks.

Africa's severe economic problems in the 1970s, made worse by the global recession of the 1980s and the implementation of structural adjustment programs in some countries in the mid-1980s, posed new challenges for social work education. The focus on development has never been more compelling, but now the emphasis is on human development and preservation within the context of economic development (IL0, 1983; UN, 1986; 1990; UNICEF, 1993). The events of the 1980s have forced social work training institutions to adopt more developmental approaches-approaches that are effective in bringing about change and not just dealing with its consequences (Kendall, 1986). The debt crisis has been the driving force for economic initiatives and responses in Africa in the 1980s and l990s. The need for structural adjustment of economies out of balance has placed a heavy burden on the poorest segments of the population and has forced policymakers to choose among services (Sawyer, 1990). It is not a choice between adjustment or no adjustment, but between adjustment aimed solely at balancing budget and trade deficits and adjustment that also seeks to protect the poorest and the most vulnerable while enhancing their productivity. Countries which are not a part of formal structural adjustment and debt repayment programs are still struggling with problems of meeting basic human needs in the face of shrinking prices for their primary commodities. The challenge to social work is perhaps even greater given the current constraints on institutional changes and the requirements for institutional change imposed by the economic recovery programs adopted to comply with structural adjustment directives.

Current approaches will require more community based grass roots work and implementation of global and local programs by organizations and agencies to mitigate the costs of structural adjustment (e.g., Government of Ghana, 1987). The training of front-line personnel remains a critical component of social work education (UN, 1980). Increasingly, however, with the current focus on the social consequences of economic development, social workers with a strong background in the social sciences, particularly economics, have an important role to play at levels where policy decisions are made. It appears that economic growth and development of infrastructures are beginning to be regarded as means to the fulfillment of basic needs and not as ends in themselves.

In many countries, social work programs are hindered by lack of qualified personnel, particularly full-time faculty with work qualifications and experience in social development who can both teach and provide field supervision. Reliance on part-time faculty may have some cost benefits, but it also has disadvantages in terms of continuity.

In South Africa, social work educators are rethinking social work education for the post-Apartheid era. In a South Africa beyond Apartheid, the accent will not be on an unfortunate minority, but on a disadvantaged majority within a developing country (McKendrick, 1990: 245). Such an accent will require much needed changes in the educational structures and course content. Perhaps more emphasis will also be placed on training workers at intermediate levels for work at grass roots level, with a deemphasis on the clinical, individualistic approach inherited from abroad. The possibilities for a new approach to social work in post-Apartheid South Africa are among the most exciting challenges facing social work education on the continent.

In many countries, males outnumber females in social work training institutions at higher levels. To a large extent, this may reflect the differential access to education at primary and secondary levels of education of females. It may also reflect the fact that teaching and nursing have traditionally been the careers of choice of many women. Social work as a profession is not as well known or understood as nursing and teaching. Training institutions at certificate and diploma levels with emphasis on women's work might, of course, reflect a different pattern.

Because the civil service and other public institutions have traditionally been the primary employers of personnel with social work training, pay differentials of males and females for similar jobs may not be very apparent. However, at the higher administrative levels, men are likely to outnumber women. As more countries pay attention to gender equality in both access to education and promotion, this pattern is likely to become less prevalent.

Research must be given priority if social work is to develop a perspective pertinent to the solution of its unique problems. Agouba's (1977) description of social work's needed response to Africa's problems remains relevant. Research efforts should focus on practice, program evaluation, and specific population groups. Given the nature of the problems and the range of possible solutions, it is clear that African social work education will need to remain interdisciplinary and provide its graduates with a wide range of intervention skills applicable in multiple settings with a variety of clientele and constituencies.

REFERENCES

African Centre for Applied Research and Training in Social Development (ACARTSOD). (1983). *Social Implications of the Lagos Plan of Action.* Tripoli.

Agouba, M. I. (1977). Africa. In *Social Realities and the Social Work Response: The Role of Schools of Social work.* New York: International Association of Schools of Social Work, pp. 37–55

Anders, J. R. (1974). Social work training as a means of achieving national development goals. In *Relationship Between Social Work Education and National Development Planning.* Addis Ababa: Association for Social Work Education in Africa, pp. 58–59.

Asamoah, Y. (1977). Training for the integrated approach. In *Family Welfare in Africa: Educational Strategies.* New York: International Association of Schools of Social Work, pp. 77–91.

Asamoah, Y. & Beverly, C. (1988). Collaboration between Western and African schools of social work: problems and possibilities. *International Social Work, 31,* 177–193.

Association for Social Work Education in Africa (ASWEA). (1982). *Survey of Curricula of Development Training Institutions in Africa.* Addis Ababa.

Brokensha, D. & Hodge, P. (1969). *Community Development in Ghana.* San Francisco: Chandler.

Drake, St. C. (1962). Social Problems in West Africa. In Drake, St. C. & Omari P. T., (Eds.). *Social Work in West Africa.* Accra, Ghana: Ghana Publishing Corporation.

DuSautoy, P. (1958). *Community Development in Ghana.* London: Oxford University Press.

Estes, R. J. (1988). *Trends in World Social Development: The Social Progress of Nations, 1970-1987.* New York: Praeger.

Government of Ghana. (1987). *Republic of Ghana, Programme of Actions to Mitigate the Social Costs of Adjustment.* Accra, Ghana.

Hammoud, H. R. (1988). Social work education in developing countries. *International Social Work, 31,* 195–210.

Hardiman, M. & Midgley, J. (1982). *The Social Dimensions of Development: Social Policy and Planning in the Third World.* New York: Wiley.

Her Majesty's Stationery Office (HMSO). (1960). *Social Work in the U.K. Dependencies.* London.

Hill, A. C. (1962). The administrative structure for social welfare in West Africa. In Drake, St. C. & Omari, P.T. (Eds.). *Social Work in West Africa.* Accra, Ghana: Ghana Publishing Corporation, pp. 41–56.

International Association of Schools of Social Work (IASSW). (1973). *New Themes in Social Work Education.* New York.

International Association of Schools of Social Work (IASSW). (1974). *A Developmental Outlook for Social Work Education.* New York.

International Association of Schools of Social Work (IASSW). (1977). *Social Realities and the Social Work Response.* New York.

International Labour Office. (1969). Social change and social progress in Africa. Report of the Director-General Third African Regional Conference, Accra, Geneva.

International Labour Office (ILO). (1983). Social aspects of development in Africa: the role of social institutions. Report of the Director-General, Sixth African Regional Conference, Tunis. Geneva.

Kendall, K. (1986). Social work education in the 1980's: accent on change. *International Social Work, 29,* 15–28.

Khinduka, S. K. (1971). Social work in the Third World. *Social Science Review , 45.*

Mazibuko, F., McKendrick, B., & Patel, L. (1992). Social work in South Africa: coping with apartheid and change. In Hokenstad, Jr., M.C., Khinduka S., & Midgley, J. (Eds.). *Profiles in International Social Work.* Washington, D.C.: NASW Press, National Association of Social Workers.

McKendrick, B. (1990). Beyond apartheid: an alphabet of challenges for social work education. *Maatskaplike Werk/Social Work, 26,* 241–250.

Midgley, J. (1981). *Professional imperialism: social work in the Third World.* London: Heinemann.

Organization of African Unity (OAU). (1985). *Africa's Priority Programme for Economic Recovery,1986-1990.* Geneva: United Nations Food and Agricultural Organization (FAO).

Patel, L. (1987). Towards a critical theory and practice in social work with reference to South Africa. *International Social Work, 30,* 221–236.

Quartey-Papafio, E. (1977). Use of the community as a laboratory for training. In *Education for family welfare: a component of development.* New York: International Association of Schools of Social Work, pp. 75–77.

Rao, V. & Kendall, K. A. (1984). *World Guide to Social Work Education.* New York: Council on Social Work Education for International Association of Schools of Social Work.

Sawyer, A. (1990). *The Political Dimension of Structural Adjustment Programs in Sub-Saharan Africa.* Accra, Ghana: Ghana Universities Press.

Shawky, A. (1972). Social work education in Africa. *International Social Work, 15,* 3–16.

Tesfaye, A. (1974). Social work education in Africa: trends and prospects in relation to national development. In *Relationship Between Social Work Education and National Social Development Planning.* Addis Ababa: Association for Social Work Education in Africa (ASWEA), pp. 14–39.

Trends in world social development: the social progress of nations, 1970-1987, (Book review). (1991). *Journal of Social Development in Africa, 6,* 98–100.

UNICEF. (1993). *The State of the World's Children, 1993.* New York.

United Nations. (1968). *Report of the Inter-Regional Expert Meeting on Social Welfare Organization and Administration.* New York: UN publication, sales no. E.68.IV.8.

United Nations. (1969). *Proceedings of the International Conference of Ministers Responsible for Social Welfare.* New York: UN publication, Sales No. E. 69.IV.4.

United Nations. (1970). *Social Welfare Planning in the Context of National Development Plans.* New York: UN publication, sales No. E.70.IV.ll.

United Nations. (1971). *Training for Social Welfare: Fifth International Survey: New Approaches in Meeting Manpower Needs.* (ST/SOA/105). New York: United Nations, Department of Economic and Social Affairs.

United Nations. (1980). *Development at Grass Roots: Training of Front-Line Personnel in Social Welfare.* (ST/ESA/104). New York: United NationsDepartment of International Economic and Social Affairs.

United Nations. (1986). Social development in Africa (Special issue). *Social Development Newsletter,* 1 (23).

United Nations. (1990). *Strategies for children in the 1990's.* New York.

Walton, R. G. & Abo El Nasr. (1988). Indigenization and authentization in terms of social work in Egypt. *International Social Work, 31,* 135–144.

Wicker, E. R. (1958). Colonial development and welfare, 1929-1957. *Social and Economic Studies, 7,* 170–192.

Yiman, A. (1976). The need for social development training in a changing Africa. *Social Work Education in Africa, 2,* 11.

14

ZIMBABWE

Joseph Hampson, S.J.

INTRODUCTION

For many anglophone countries in Africa, the history of social work services is the history of British social work influence, more or less transplanted wholesale and with little adaptation to local circumstances. Typically social services were designed for the white communities of these countries, and at independence the services were ill prepared for national expansion. Rhodesia (the name of Zimbabwe before independence) was an extreme example of the use of social services oriented for the white community, so the early days of establishing the first and still the only social work education institution in the country were very difficult; right from the start the School of Social Work was designed for the education of social workers in a nonracial (open to all races) society. Over twenty-five years ago its first curriculum consisted of courses in group work and had a largely urban orientation. The current focus of social work education in Zimbabwe is on social development, so that social workers can be prepared for forms of intervention appropriate to a young, Third World African state.

HISTORY OF SOCIAL WORK EDUCATION IN ZIMBABWE

Early Days

The first institution in then Southern Rhodesia to train social workers opened its doors in January 1964, as the School of Social Service. It was established by a Jesuit priest, Fr. Edward ("Ted") Rogers. The school was nondenominational and nonracial and occupied temporary premises in the Old Morgan High School in the capital city. In the first year eighteen students took part in a full-time year's course for group workers, designed to train workers in group activities in clubs, welfare centers, and industrial and mining complexes, especially in urban conditions. Also established in that first year was a part-time course in social work (two nights per week for six months), designed to give background instruction for persons in voluntary agencies, or those interested in such work. A third part-time course was also launched for training in committee work and bookkeeping for members of credit unions.

During the course of that first year, the need for a higher level of full-time training became clear. There had been contact with the Oppenheimer College of Social Service in Zambia (later to become part of the University of Zambia), but the political climate of the time, moving towards Rhodesia's Unilateral Declaration of Independence to come in November 1965, meant that there would be no possibility of Rhodesian students going to study at Oppenheimer, so it became clear that serious full-time programs of study from an institution of social work education were required. In preparation for closer links with the university, there was launched in 1966 a three year diploma in social work, with O level entry qualifications gained after four years of secondary education. As a nongraduate course it had been debated whether a two or a three year diploma course was the better option, but the choice of a three year program seems to have been made as a result of the successful experiences with a three year program at Oppenheimer in Zambia. The first intake of eighteen on this diploma was complemented by a group of sixteen students following the one year group work course. The following year, 1967, had twenty-two new students for the diploma, and a further sixteen students in the group work course. This was to be the final year in which the one year group work course was run, as the school began to concentrate its energies on the diploma program and negotiated for university recognition of the diploma.

In these early days the emphasis was on group work as a professional technique: a paper produced by the principal said that:

> in the UK, social work training has traditionally stressed the casework approach. This means that it stresses the problems of the individual and of the family.... However, in a developing country such as Rhodesia, there are other problems of a wider nature which can best be tackled by what is called the "Group Work Technique." The School of Social Service, adapting its training program to the needs of the country, has decided to lay equal stress upon casework and group work. (Rogers, 1966)

Closer University Links

In 1969 the school changed its name to the School of Social Work and became the first associate college of the University of Rhodesia, with students being awarded a university diploma in social work after a three year program. The first year of study consisted of casework, group work, psychology, social administration, socioeconomic development, and public health. In the second year students followed university courses in sociology and psychology, as well as further school courses in health and ethics taught at the School of Social Work; in the final year they completed higher levels in the subjects introduced in the first year. In addition, fieldwork was taken in all three years.

By 1970, seven years in operation, the School of Social Work had produced eighty-six social workers who were working in various parts of the country. At this time, too, the new Board of Governors had been established, consisting of representatives from the Jesuit order, the university, the Department of Social Welfare, the Ministry of Education, and persons of standing in social work.

In early 1974 the school moved into new premises which had been built through donations from overseas organizations, principally Misereor of Germany. The following year the discussions by the joint Board of Studies for the school and the university culminated in a new degree program, bachelor of social work: the first three years for the diploma in social work were to be part I of the degree, and part II was the fourth year of university studies. The school's input for the fourth year was initially limited to fieldwork and dissertation, but later included teaching for the fourth year courses, mainly to ensure the professional nature of the BSW qualification, by having considerable social work content in the fourth year. In that first year of the bachelor of social work, 1975, there were nine students following the part II program, and some forty-three in the three years of the diploma.

War of Independence

Toward the end of the 1970s, the country of Rhodesia was suffering tremendously as the liberation war, initially confined to remote rural areas, began to dominate national life everywhere. There was more suffering among rural families, and more influx of refugees into urban areas. As the conflict intensified, the social work needs of many groups became great. In 1978 the school decided to complement its focus on specialized and professional social work education by introducing (or really reintroducing) a one year certificate program for paraprofessional workers to help refugee and displaced groups. There were two options on this program, a social work certificate in community work and a social work certificate in rehabilitation, which were combined the following year to become the social work certificate in community work. Fieldwork experiences concentrated on refugee needs, and eventually the school set up a fieldwork unit within a squatter settlement camp on the outskirts of the capital. The building was a multipurpose community center, erected in consultation with the Residents' Association: programs at the center were mainly concerned with preschool groups, adult literacy and skills training. As the country moved toward majority rule it also became clear that the needs of young people were very great. As hopes for independence grew the school felt that youth workers could be very much involved in helping the unemployed, the young out of school (as the whole educational system had almost collapsed at the height of the war), and returning refugees, and so a youth workers course was initiated just at the time of independence in 1980. The one year certificate in youth work course ran for two years.

At graduation day in Zimbabwe's year of independence, 1980, the school was able to note that 258 social workers had been trained at various levels. Graduates had been involved in many types of employment, and among the audience that day was the minister of foreign affairs in the new government, Dr. Mangwende, himself a former student of the school.

The vast changes brought about by majority rule did not lessen the needs in social work training and education but did introduce a new emphasis on social development. Fr. Rogers, the former principal of the School of Social Work, stressed participation in social policy as a prime prerequisite for full development.

> For a long time social work has helped the misfits of society, those disabled physically and mentally. This is a valuable service but is it enough. . . ? Social Work is palliative and in developing countries can be a luxury. The social worker must offer his services in development. . . . At a recent workshop for social workers from all over Rhodesia this was the message—with greater stress being made on rural development. . . . The social worker can offer his skills in group and community work as a team member in a group of agriculturists, technicians, administrators, and health personnel towards overall developmental assistance. (Rogers, 1978:22)

Postgraduate and Specialist Qualifications

The arrangements whereby School of Social Work staff taught university recognized courses brought up the questions of master's programs, specialist programs, and research capabilities at the school. In 1978 the desirability of a master's degree program was first expressed, for there were no facilities for master's degrees in social work in sub-Saharan Africa (excluding South Africa), yet it took five years for the school and the university to launch an MSW program to provide for higher levels of social work in research, in administration, and in social work education. This master's level followed the British model of postgraduate qualification, that is, a qualification that could entitle the bearer to teach at university level or provide higher level supervision in management or research activities.

At independence, too, the need for social workers who were specialized in mental health issues became pressing. In 1982 a BSW (Bachelor of Social Work with Honors) degree in clinical social work was started as a two year postgraduate diploma program to provide for the training of social workers who wish to specialize in the care of people with psychiatric problems.

In 1984 the school, in conjunction with the International Labor Organization (ILO), launched a course for training the trainers of community rehabilitation workers. The certificate in rehabilitation was a one year course intended to cover all aspects of community rehabilitation, and the first recruitment was from the SADCC region countries and Ethiopia. The ILO had seconded some teaching staff for the course, but the school also made use of its own teaching staff. The following year, in association with the University of Zimbabwe, the school launched a bachelor of science (social rehabilitation) degree as the second stage of the ILO sponsored program of training community rehabilitation workers. The main purpose of this course was to train higher level community rehabilitation professionals who would be involved in the planning and implementation of services for disabled persons and would assist and supervise lower-level community rehabilitation workers. Although the degree program was sponsored by the ILO initially, they withdrew after the second year, and the University of Zimbabwe and the School of Social Work then ran the program independently.

Currently, because of the great increase in secondary school opportunities in the country, the diploma in social work program attracts some three thousand applications for thirty to forty places each year. A majority of the successful applicants would possess A level qualifications, and almost all the successful applicants have had some work experience: generally students would be over twenty-one years old.

International Training

Postgraduate and specialist degrees at the Harare School of Social Work became popular not only with Zimbabwean social workers, but with social workers from many other parts of the Southern Africa region, as the school was the only institution in sub-Saharan Africa providing such specialist training. The ILO contacts meant that governments in Ethiopia, Malawi, Botswana, Zambia, Lesotho, Swaziland, Mozambique, Tanzania and Kenya, and South African liberation movements, could send students for training. The Harare School of Social Work also proved a popular venue for the training of paraprofessional social workers whose own countries lacked either university qualifications or training opportunities. The certificate courses annually have enrolled students from most of the neighboring front-line states, and even farther afield.

CULTURE AND VALUES

In its indigenous form, social work philosophy finds much support in Zimbabwean cultural and traditional values. Although social work motivation can find its origins in charitable and religious ideas in an individualist Christian tradition, the later emphasis on community values and the importance of community fit in well with a Zimbabwean perspective on the fundamental nature of community for individual and for family life, as well as finding religious support in the Christian tradition of community.

Yet, some social work values do challenge local traditional values—for example, the role of the disabled or those suffering mental illness, people who in local cultures could sometimes be marginalized because of fear (Jackson & Mupedziswa, 1988). Other challenges to local values can be seen in the corrupted *lobola,* or bride wealth, tradition. In traditional Zimbabwe marriage has been seen as a contract between two families, and the sealing of the contract involves *lobola,* or bride price, "paid from the family cattle herd of the son-in-law into the family herd of the father-in-law" (Bourdillon, 1976: 52). Nowadays cash has become the preferred form of payment rather than cattle, and in this purely monetary form *lobola* places women in secondary roles, seen as objects of trade. It also seriously affects widows' and orphans' rights of inheritance, for when a man dies his family often argue that since *lobola* has been paid the widow's goods are their goods. Folta and Deck (1987), describing a study of elderly black widows in rural Zimbabwe, note that "in many cases widows were told that they were 'strangers'—'not one of our family'—'not of our totem' and 'therefore had no rights of inheritance.'"

On the other hand, traditional structures have provided help for particularly vulnerable groups in times of community stress like drought: the very old and the very young were assisted through mechanisms such as work parties and village levies. What has proved difficult is, for example, the introduction of the practice of adoption, for its legal requirements in a country such as Zimbabwe do not fit well with the feelings and practices of traditional communities. Adoption challenges the assumptions of such communities because it does not need to know anything about the patrilineal background of the child—and indeed adoptive parents are often denied access to such information. Traditional communities define all individuals within a clearly classified set of relationships, which not only place the individual in the community but define his or her links with the ancestors. A child of unknown ancestry has no *mutupo,* or clan name, and therefore in a literal sense no place in the community. Yet experiments along the lines of extended fostering as is done in Mozambique show that there are compromises that allow social workers to introduce innovations in acceptable ways.

Equally intractable has been the deteriorating socioeconomic situation of some elderly, in spite of a cultural framework that would accord great respect to the elderly (Hampson, 1983, 1990). Here social work values would reinforce the respect traditional society believes due to the elderly, while also challenging the modern practices that in effect have corrupted the original values and resulted in the marginalization of elderly, through pauperization, through social and cultural exclusion and through low planning priority.

Local values have also posed challenges to the presumed universality of some social work values. For example, confidentiality as a universally valid value in casework is not often controverted: one study on values in social work said unambiguously, "That affairs should be treated as confidential by social workers has always been firmly emphasized by the profession" (Central Council for Education and Training in Social Work [CCETSW], 1976: 35). Nevertheless, in Shona society local social work practitioners have sometimes found that such a value not only is impractical and can be impossible to attain, but may even be detrimental to the success of a particular intervention (Mukaro, 1976).

There is very little literature on value bases for social work in Africa, and work on the academic foundations of this value base still needs thorough investigation. There have been attempts by social work educators in North Africa, principally Egypt, to conceptualize social work as evincing Islamic religious values (e.g., Ragab [1980] uses the concept *authentization*), but there is little comparable work on cultural and religious values in southern Africa as they impact on the value base of social work. A social science ideology based, on the one extreme, on mechanistic principles, or even, at the other end, on psychoanalytic principles, would have great difficulty being incorporated by a social worker in an African tradition, who would wish to see community in very broad terms, both horizontally in terms of the extended family and vertically in terms of incorporation of ancestors of the extended family who still exercise influence over their relatives. This outlook places great emphasis on the goal of a harmonious community; such a value would imply, for example, that social work interventions using an individualist approach, bypassing family or other community structures, would face intrinsic difficulties.

The little local literature that is available has examined this issue. Ankrah (1987), in proposing a new and more relevant social work model for Africa, speaks about the importance of the value of communalism. In arguing against the universalist approach to social work values she says (1987: 9) that such universalism

> subtly downgrades values such as communalism, spiritualism, etc., which under-gird African social organizations. In fact. . .it removes them altogether from serious consideration as principles for guiding practice. . . .In taking on a mandate assigned from outside the region, African social work indeed conforms to the conditions defined by Midgley (1981) as *professional imperialism.*

Ankrah later argues that the extended family, clan obligations, mutual aid societies and traditional patterns of agricultural production will all have serious implications for social work roles in Africa: it is clear that the value base for these roles is equally seriously affected.

It is also important to advert to the very fluid situation in which African culture and values are being influenced. Urbanization is an inexorable process that has brought about irreversible changes to Zimbabwean culture: the impact of the war of independence, universal education and greater exposure to the mass media and to travel is among the factors that make it impossible to speak any longer of a pure, traditional African or Zimbabwean culture. Such is the context in which social work educators in Zimbabwe introduce social work students to value bases of the profession.

RANGE AND STRUCTURE OF EDUCATION

Range of Social Work Education

As it is the only institution in the country engaged in social work education, the School of Social Work has had to provide for a very wide range of needs and therefore has had to deal with varying educational levels. The entry qualifications for the diploma have remained at O level—the public exam level after four years of secondary education—but the increasingly large pool of qualified school leavers has meant de facto that most successful applicants now have A levels—exams taken after six years of secondary school and a requirement for university. However, because of the great desire for professionalism among social workers, it will already be noted from the school's history that there was considerable support for an upgrading of diploma to bachelor level, and the master's and PhD levels are natural developments of this need. Yet there has always been a tension between meeting these professional needs and also providing education to a cadre of workers at a lower level—the paraprofessional or social work assistant. As the acting principal wrote in 1982, "In the short term, Certificate level training courses are particularly valuable for a developing country which needs social workers at varying levels of skills and academic achievement" (Mkhando, 1982). He went on to argue that:

> front-line social workers have a particularly important role to play in situations where needs are great, resources are limited and social infrastructure is lacking. This is seen to be particularly true in Zimbabwe where large segments of the population are poorly served by major social services, the need for decentralization is evidenced, and rehabilitation and resettlement programs in the context of a massive program of rural development rank high in national development priorities. (1982:2)

Yet, the social work profession in the country, and the civil service, remained unconvinced of the need and the value of paraprofessional education. Brand (1982), in a follow-up study of certificate students, found that "the concept of the paraprofessional social worker is still a novel one that has not yet been accepted in Zimbabwe, and is regarded with a certain amount of suspicion by professionals and non-professionals alike." The study found that the government Department of Social Welfare had established posts of "public assistance investigator," designed for certificate graduates, but appointed those without such qualifications on the same basis as those with the certificate in social work. In response to the vast increase in educational opportunities during the 1980s, and the consequent large pool of school leavers with O levels, the Zimbabwe government has since required a minimum of five O levels for anyone to be employed in the civil service. This has meant the effective barring of paraprofessional social workers from employment by government.

Client Groups

The Department of Social Welfare is the largest single employer of social workers in Zimbabwe. Among its statutory duties are probation services; adoption and child welfare; relief of destitution through public assistance; administration of drought relief; counseling and marriage guidance; supervision of preschool, creche, children's and old people's homes; and repatriation. Thus social work education at the Harare School of Social Work has had to take cognizance of the needs of this employer as well as the less clearly defined, but no less relevant needs of the other bodies and nongovernmental organizations (NGOs). Social work graduates have found employment with a wide range of local authorities, industrial settings, and service ministries of government; nongovernmental organizations (NGOs) local and international, in both relief and in development work. They have engaged in different levels of activity using the three traditional methods of social work, casework, group work and community work but have also been concerned with research, policy planning and evaluation.

Funding Arrangements

Students

All Zimbabwean social work students in the diploma and bachelor program receive assistance from the government, half grant and half loan, that pays for school fees and fieldwork costs, book allowance, and living allowances. After graduation when the student starts employment, the loan component is to be repaid at a low rate of interest. In the paraprofessional or certificate level programs, students are usually seconded from their employers (city councils, national army, NGOs, etc.) and receive their salaries as well as a full scholarship. A number of funding agencies provide assistance to foreign students and pay their fees, including the Commonwealth Fund for Technical Cooperation, the European Community, ILO, UNDP, CAFOD, Misereor, and the Konrad Adenauer Foundation.

Courses

The School of Social Work has relied on a wide range of statutory and NGO financial links both for capital development and for operating costs. The university-recognized programs of diploma, bachelor's and master's levels have fixed fee structures set by the university. The Ministry of Education grants to Zimbabwean students cover payment of these university fees. The certificate courses are self-funding and hence require a higher fee structure.

Sometimes specialist courses attract particular help from relevant agencies. For a limited time the ILO, WHO, and NGOs interested in particular client groups—such as Helpage International, who are concerned with social work education for workers to help the elderly—are involved in sponsorship of courses and workshops that develop responses to training needs in social work.

The government, through a salary grant voted to the Department of Social Welfare, pays the salaries of all professional lecturing and library staff at the School of Social Work. It has also provided a percentage of building costs for new developments.

Status

The status of the social work profession is not particularly high in Zimbabwe. This is no doubt due to a complex of factors, some common to the profession everywhere, but among those applicable to Zimbabwe are the cultural understanding of marginal groups and those who work with them, the weakness of the social workers' professional association National Association of Social Workers (NASW), the small numbers of trained social workers, and the lack of formal accreditation procedures. However, in both statutory and voluntary agencies, there are a sense of growing self-understanding and a growing desire to work for closer relationships with other professionals, which is difficult to do when the status of social work is so low. The Department of Social Welfare, together with NASW, is currently assisting in drafting a Social Workers' Act, which is intended to legislate in questions of accreditation, ethics, discipline, and private social work practice.

QUALIFYING AND POSTQUALIFYING TRAINING

Very few structured postqualifying training opportunities exist for social workers in Zimbabwe. The School of Social Work provides annual workshops for fieldwork supervisors, but it is not always possible at such workshops to devote enough time to the needs of continuing education rather than the practical demands and experiences of supervision. From time to time specific short courses have been mounted for specific groups of staff: prison officers, local authority community workers, care givers in children's homes and in old people's homes. Although these have always proved extremely popular, financial, personnel and structural constraints have not allowed for any regular program or commitment by the school. Every study done on former graduates of the school (Brand, 1982) stresses the perceived importance of postqualifying and in-service training, but the realities of agency finances and responsibilities, particularly in the Department of Social Welfare, have not allowed for developments in this area.

ACCREDITATION

Both the diploma and the degrees in social work at the Harare School are professional as well as academic qualifications. Thanks to the emphasis on fieldwork, and the importance given to it in the overall assessment process, the qualifications have proved acceptable to other accreditation bodies, such as the Central Council for Education and Training in Social Work (CCETSW) in the United Kingdom. However, in Zimbabwe there is not yet any process of licensing social workers, though a bill is presently being drafted. Social workers in statutory agencies are deemed to be licensed by possession of the relevant school qualification. The Public Service Commission generally uses the school to assess whether foreign social work qualifications are deemed equivalent or not.

POLITICAL CLIMATE

The preindependence and postindependence periods in the country provide a neat division in an examination of Zimbabwe's social policy, practice and social work response. The Department of Social Welfare was established in 1948, initially to deal with the problem of juvenile delinquency within the white settler community. The first probation officer was an immigrant from the United Kingdom, an African probation officer was appointed in 1952 (Hampson & Kaseke, 1987: 281). Then in 1964 the department was made responsible for the administration of public assistance, though, as Kaseke pointed out (1991: 35), four years later there were only four hundred African families deemed eligible. From then until independence the department was used by the minority government to enact its racist policies or differential opportunities and rewards for white and black groups. Public assistance, assistance to children's and old people's homes, pensions, and probation hostels all had two sets of conditions, depending on whether the client group was white or black, just as all the other social services (health, housing, education) had differing sets of conditions and rewards. The black communities were regarded as urban dwellers to provide a labor pool, with no right of permanent residence; black rural areas, in spite of attempts to deny them infrastructure and services, were meant to provide for long-term security. Social workers were also forced to take on positions of social control, for example, in the administration of probation hostels for youngsters caught trying to join the liberation armies in Mozambique and Botswana. As Rogers—at the time School of Social Work principal—said:

> Rhodesian social policy has been influenced fundamentally by the position of a politically strong white elite determined to maintain its position, and by an emerging black majority clamoring for its place in the sun. The black majority has realized that no matter how ordered the country may be and what economic heights it may attain, without their active participation in decision-making social policy must inevitably favor the white elite group. (1978: 25)

At independence social work was able to adopt an unambiguous commitment to the policies of social justice and equity in health care, relief and resettlement programs, education, and personal social services intended to be free of racial and discriminatory practices. It was envisaged that the potential contribution of social work was great: at the 1981 graduation ceremony, the new leader of the country, Prime Minister Robert Mugabe, challenged social workers to become change agents in many fields of the country's developmental efforts. He said that the social worker is not merely a healer of the ills of society's deviants; they are "largely, or can be the inspirer, the motivator, or even the initiator of projects of social development." Agere and Hampson (1981) and Hampson (1983) speculated on the new possibilities for social workers to contribute their skills in social development programs, and there were calls for social workers to become involved in, for example, new low–cost housing projects, resettlement schemes and schools. Yet ten years later at the Department of Social Welfare—the largest provider of social services, and with 143 qualified social workers the largest employer—Kaseke concluded that their services were still largely curative and casework-oriented, though development agencies, particularly NGOs, employed social workers in social development programs.

One particularly important social work approach that became overlaid with very strong political connotations was that of community development. Before independence the minority government had tried to hijack the philosophy of community development for its own ends, but after 1980 the potential for the approach to be used was unlocked, though the new government was very cautious to move from its ideology of liberation to a philosophy of community self-help tainted by its Rhodesian use to justify racist policies (Madondo, 1985).

Recently, the government has decided to modify its socialist stance in favor of an *economic structural adjustment program.* The immediate severe effects of such a program were recognized (greater unemployment, higher prices), though it is argued that eventually all groups will benefit from this economic liberalization. In the meantime the Department of Social Welfare has been designated as the administrator of a "social fund," designed to cushion the most vulnerable from the harshest effects of this structural adjustment. The School of Social Work has responded, too, by arranging in conjunction with the International Association of Schools of Social Work (IASSW), for workshops for social work educators from different parts of Africa to come together and map out curriculum changes, so that new social workers can be better prepared to deal with these issues when they graduate.

CURRICULUM

The curriculum of all university approved courses at the School of Social Work (i.e., at diploma level and above) is set by a joint Board of Studies from the school and the university, and any alterations of curriculum require the approval of the Senate. Naturally, this means that changes are both cumbersome and time-consuming. In 1990, changes were introduced to the bachelor in social work, to allow for an honors degree and to do away with specialist degrees (clinical social work, rehabilitation) in favor of options within a generalist ordinary or honors bachelor's program, but the process, initiated by the school after long consultation with students, employing agencies, and the university, had taken a number of years. However, the changes have meant that many more diploma graduates can now qualify to complete a bachelor's (ordinary) degree in social work and that those who qualify for honors have more opportunity for research dissertations.

Many of the necessary adaptations to curriculum were dealt with in the areas of research, dissertation and fieldwork requirements. A list of BSW and MSW dissertations down the years shows how the interests of both lecturers and students have altered in the light of changed circumstances.

Sometimes the motivation for curriculum development was internal, such as the school's creation of a specialist degree in clinical social work, which established a strong link with mental health professionals both in academic and in field situations. Occasionally, external input brings about a stimulus for curriculum change or development. Such was the case with disability and rehabilitation education when the ILO approached the school in 1982 to consider the possibility of upgrading the training of social workers from the Southern African Development Coordinating Committee (SADCC) region who worked with the disabled. Sponsorships were obtained from the Finnish government, and in 1984 eleven students from neighboring countries and Zimbabweans representing those who would in turn train others in rehabilitation skills undertook a year's diploma course. Later, the program was upgraded to bachelor level, as the university approved the new syllabus for a degree in social rehabilitation. This development of specialist programs in the early 1980s (social rehabilitation, clinical social work, youth work, research, etc.) was later dropped in favor of a return to a strictly generic approach. Walton says that

> in the past social workers were trained mainly in the use of casework with individuals and families and were more likely to undertake assessment from the stance of deciding whether clients needed casework or not, tending to assume that if there was a need for service then casework was the appropriate form of help. This approach is no longer valid (quoted in Willmore. [1985: 30])

One of the main reasons for restressing a generic approach in Zimbabwe seems to have been Walton's argument, that of allowing the social worker to respond with the most appropriate method for the situation, rather than impose a method willy-nilly on whatever situation is met. This is an important consideration in Zimbabwe because social workers, no matter from what employing agency they come, will often be faced with client groups who have a wide range of basic social problems. In addition, it seems that a strict application of the psychotherapeutic model of casework treatment in the Zimbabwean context was not made by social workers; rather there was an eclectic use of a variety of counseling skills, leaving the deeper levels of psychotherapeutic interventions to be undertaken by psychiatric specialists.

This raises the question of the relevance of Western social work models in Third World settings, a question very much alive throughout the Harare School of Social Work's existence. A glance through the early prospectuses and course contents shows that, in spite of the presence of African lecturing staff, traditional and casework presentations seemed to be very prominent, probably because all those local lecturers were educated at European or American social work schools. Yet, as the Harare School began to recruit another generation of local staff, who were trained in Africa, the relationship of social work education to Third World and underdevelopment issues took on greater importance and relevance. Midgley's (1981) study showed that this tendency was universal, though he was generally pessimistic about the ability of Third World schools to adapt to more indigenous models. In a study of social workers qualified from the Harare School, Willmore (1985) concluded that:

although training at the School of Social Work is essentially presented as a generic training, there appears to be a *de facto* specialization in casework which is reflected in practice. Of the respondents in the sample only 18 percent overall indicated that they use all three methods in their current jobs. . . .Because of the particular situation of Zimbabwe, the present casework bias should be counteracted by a special emphasis on group work and community work. (1985: 121)

The school itself was not unaware of the de facto concentration on casework. In a mission statement in 1987 the handbook says that there are four general aims of social work education in any country:

1. To provide workers who can facilitate the use and mobilization of community resources, both human and economic, for the benefit of that community
2. To produce workers who, through their knowledge of the social services, can act as resource persons
3. To provide workers who, through their knowledge of and ability in using individual and group dynamics, can facilitate change, growth and development within individuals, groups and communities
4. To produce workers who can formulate, as well as administer in a meaningful way, programs of social services

It continues:

However, it is also extremely important to advert to the fact that Zimbabwean social work education takes place in Africa. . .in a continent where social problems are vast, where poverty is the norm for 60 percent of the rural population (who make up four-fifths of the continent's 400 million). . .and in Zimbabwe, a country where most of the population live in poverty in rural areas, ill-served by almost all types of resources. Hence, education at the School of Social Work is now focusing on *social development* in rural Zimbabwe. Social development is a response by social workers that encourages institutional change (as opposed to encouraging maintenance), and social work practitioners thus become involved in human development, in improvements of social conditions in health, housing, education, employment, agriculture, etc. The School of Social Work believes that the training of such agents of social change, especially in rural areas, will help policy-makers rely on the most valuable resource that Zimbabwe (and indeed any country) has-its people, the means and the end of socio-economic development.

The school established requirements that all diploma students would have at least one fieldwork placement in a rural area that lecturing staff would add a focus on rural development to their research and publications. One gathering of fieldwork supervisors and lecturing staff in schools of social work throughout the southern Africa region tried to develop and encourage both traditional and innovative rural fieldwork placements (Hampson & Willmore, 1986).

One fundamental difficulty in moving to a social development perspective for social work education in Africa is the paucity, or even complete absence, of local teaching materials. Though the Harare School of Social Work has not been alone in Africa in attempting such a shift of perspective, serious obstacles such as heavy teaching loads, bureaucratic difficulties in research, lack of resources, printing and distribution problems mitigate against the production of local materials. There is still quite a heavy reliance on British and American textbooks at the school, though the tremendous costs of purchase and importation constitute an additional motive for the localization of resources. The problems are not only practical, nor are they confined to Africa. Even after decades of social work education in India, one observer noted, "Not a single textbook exists. . .which takes into consideration indigenous, social, economic and political conditions" (Nagpaul, 1972: 3). The dominance of Western models is considerable. Yet some materials have been produced in an attempt to articulate the relevance of a local, social development model of social work: for example, student fieldwork reports have proved a rich and even underutilized source for case materials and class analysis. Academic papers and theses are another relatively untapped source. Publications such as the *Journal of Social Development in Africa* have begun to articulate some of the issues involved in a social development paradigm (for example, Ankrah, 1987; Muzaale, 1987; Ose-Hwedie, 1990).

ROLE OF RESEARCH

In a country where social policy issues are rarely examined in depth the role of research at the school is vitally important. A review of social work research in relation to social development argued that a greater emphasis on social work research could reduce dependence on non-African and nonrelevant research efforts; increase the little information already available, information necessary for formulation of policies and programs of development; and have an important role in introducing and assessing innovative program alternatives, because of its value-committed approach (Brand, 1986: 73). The institutional research capacity of the school was enhanced to allow for rural research and publication of results. Teaching of research methods took on added importance in the school curriculum, and staff were given greater opportunities and encouragement to conduct research. To this end the *Journal of Social Development in Africa* was established in 1986 as a twice annual journal publishing "critical analyses of social development issues as they affect the poor and marginalized in society. It deals with concerns especially but not exclusively relevant to Southern Africa." In the six years of its existence themes concerning popular participation, urban squatters, rural health care, informal sector in Harare, food crisis in Africa, acquired immunodeficiency syndrome (AIDS) and social work, literacy campaign, rural disabled, women in cooperatives, elderly in Zimbabwe, mental health and NGOs, and equity in access to health care have been tackled. Under the auspices of the journal a fieldwork manual for social work students, staff and supervisors was published in 1990 (Hall, 1990). Other research reports on equity in health (Willmore & Hall, 1989) and the elderly (Hampson, 1986) were produced by the school. A research unit has been formally established, and current issues have focused on refugees, the internally displaced, institutional care of the elderly, and social security policy issues. The school is very conscious that this research is not only to inform the education of student social workers, but, because it is one of the few research centers dealing with national social policy, to influence policy design and implementation.

CONCLUSION

There is no doubt that the first quarter century of the School of Social Work's history has been the story of preparation of a solid professional group of social workers. These professionals have faced the challenges of applying models of intervention more relevant to first world situations and having to adapt, explore and develop more appropriate models. Through feedback between the school and the practitioners, and through contacts with other neighboring countries' experiences, a new perspective and model of practice, based on the concept of social development, seem to be emerging. Zimbabwe now has a growing tertiary educational system, thanks to the success of her postindependence expansion of secondary education: there are two universities established in addition to the Harare University. Perhaps in the future the training needs of the social services will be met by other institutions in addition to the School of Social Work, but for the moment, as the only such institution in the country, the school has to serve the needs of not only Zimbabwe but neighboring states through a policy of gradual expansion without any compromise on quality. As the country faces the rigors of structural adjustment in the coming years there is no doubt that the demands on social workers and their skills will become more insistent and more important: it is hoped that the profession can respond in ways that will guarantee genuine socioeconomic development for all.

REFERENCES

Agere, A. & Hampson, J. (1981). Social development training in Zimbabwe. *Journal for Social Work Education in Africa*, *4*, 81–90.

Ankrah, M. (1987). Radicalizing roles for Africa's development. *Journal of Social Development in Africa*, *2*(2), 3–12.

Bourdillon, M. (1976). *The Shona Peoples*. Gweru: Mambo Press.

Brand, V. (1982). *Emergency Training for Front-Line Social Workers*. Harare: School of Social Work, Unpublished manuscript.

Brand, V. (1986). Social work research in relation to social development in Zimbabwe. *Journal of Social Development in Africa, 1*(1), 67-80.

CCETSW (1976). *Values in Social Work: A Discussion Paper Produced by the Working Party on the Teaching of the Value Bases of Social Work.* CCETSW Paper 13. London: Central Council for Education and Training in Social Work.

Folta, J. & Deck, E. (1987). Elderly black widows in rural Zimbabwe. *Journal of Cross-Cultural Gerontology, 2*, 321-342.

Hall, N. (1990). *Social Work Training in Africa: A Fieldwork Manual.* Harare: School of Social Work.

Hampson, J. (1983). A Zimbabwean perspective. In Yimam, A. (Ed.). *Organization and Delivery of Social Services to Rural Areas.* Addis Ababa: Association of Social Work Education in Africa, pp. 180–232..

Hampson, J. (Ed.). (1986). *Zimbabwe Action Plan on Elderly.* Harare: School of Social Work.

Hampson, J. (1990). Marginalization and rural elderly: a Shona case study. *Journal of Social Development in Africa, 5*(2), 5–23.

Hampson, J. & Kaseke, E. (1987). Zimbabwe. In Dixon, J. (Ed.). *Social Welfare in Africa.* London: Routledge, pp. 279–306.

Hampson, J. & Willmore, B. (1986). *Social Development and Rural Fieldwork.* Harare: School of Social Work.

Hlazo, C. (1977). The attitudes of staff towards causes of mental illness: a case study at Harare hospital psychiatric unit. Bachelor's thesis, University of Zimbabwe, Harare.

Jackson, H. & Mupedziswa, R. (1988). Disability and rehabilitation. *Journal of Social Development in Africa, 3*(1), 21–30.

Kaseke, E. (1991). Social work practice in Zimbabwe. *Journal of Social Development in Africa, 6*(1), 33–45.

Madondo, B. (1985). Community development: a quiet evaluation from Rhodesia to Zimbabwe. *Community Development Journal, 20*, 293–298.

Midgley, J. (1981). *Professional Imperialism.* London: Heinemann.

Mkhando, J. (1982). Points relevant to recognition of one year certificate in social work. Unpublished manuscript.

Mukaro, I. (1976). Confidentiality and Shona clients: highfields social work office. Bachelor's thesis, University of Zimbabwe, Harare.

Muzaale, P. (1987). Social development, rural poverty and implications for fieldwork practice. *Journal of Social Development in Africa, 2*(1), 75–85.

Nagpaul, H. (1972). The diffusion of American social work education to India: problems and issues. *International Social Work, 15*, 2–20.

Ose-Hwedie, K. (1990). Social work and the question of social development in Africa. *Journal of Social Development in Africa, 5*(2), 87–99.

Ragab, I. (1980). *Towards Authentization of Social Work in Developing Countries.* Cairo: Helwan University, Unpublished manuscript.

Rogers, E. (1966). *Social Work Training in Rhodesia.* Unpublished manuscript.

Rogers, E. (1978). Social policy and social work. *International Social Work, 20*, 20-25.

Sanders, D. (Ed.). (1982). *The Developmental Perspective in Social Work.* Honolulu: University of Hawaii School of Social Work.

Savanhu, T. (1985). *Adaptations in social work education: a case study of a course for social rehabilitation workers in the SADCC region.* Master's thesis, University of Zimbabwe, Harare.

Walton, R. (1982). *Social Work 2000: The Future of Social Work in a Changing Society*. London: Longmans.

Willmore, B. (1985). Training for flexibility in choice of method in social work practice. Master's thesis, University of Zimbabwe, Harare.

Willmore, B. & Hall, N. (1989). *Health Manpower Issues in Relation to Equity in and Access to Health Services in Zimbabwe*. Harare: School of Social Work.

15

SOUTH AFRICA

Tembeka Ntusi

HISTORY OF SOCIAL WORK EDUCATION

The development of social work education and training in South Africa has its roots in the poor white problem (Helm, 1964; Marks, 1989). One of the major developments in the efforts to combat white poverty was the Carnegie Commission of Inquiry into the causes and solutions of the problem. Amongst other recommendations of the 1932 commission were the creation of a state bureau of social welfare and the training of professionals to deliver social welfare services (Helm, 1964; McKendrick, 1987)

From the very beginning, social work education and training were undertaken by university institutions, with few exceptions. The University of Cape Town was the first to establish a two year course in 1924, it was superseded by a three year bachelor's degree and a postgraduate diploma in social science.   By 1934, only the universities of Cape Town, Pretoria and Stellenbosch had ever enrolled any trainees.

In 1938, the University of Cape Town hosted an inter-university conference which had significant results for social work training in South Africa. The Joint Universities Committee on Social Studies (JUC) was established with the following objectives:

1. To promote and facilitate exchange of views and information on all matters affecting the teaching of social studies, with specific regard to curricula, courses, syllabi, research, public relations and professional aspects of social work
2. Generally to promote social studies in the Union of South Africa

By 1964, nine universities and five university colleges had enrolled social work trainees. The basic social work qualification was a bachelor's degree in the faculty of Arts or Social Sciences, (BASW or BASS) awarded after a minimum of three years study following matriculation (Helm, 1964 :2). This was the case until 1983, when the Council for Social and Associated Workers

(CSAW) set the minimum training period to qualify for registration as a social worker as four years.

CULTURE, VALUES AND RELIGION

From the beginning, social work education in South Africa was directed to solving problems. The problem then was poverty among whites. Education was provided to produce professionals motivated by humanism who would eliminate poverty. This humanitarian foundation resulted in a social work education system which produces persons who work for the welfare of human beings by reducing suffering and reforming laws about punishment.

Conservation and continuation of culture became integral to that professional education, focusing on refinement and interpretation of value principles into action through practice. This commitment to humanism and culture conservation resulted in a person-centered (poor white) rather than a problem–centered (poverty) education system (Marks, 1989: 165).

Social Work and Social Values

Two academics are linked with the development of social work education in this country, Professor Batson, who was the professor of sociology at the University of Cape Town, and Professor Verwoerd, also a professor of sociology at the University of Stellenbosch and later prime minister of the Republic of South Africa from 1958 to 1966. Batson and Verwoerd represented two different cultural values: Liberalism and Broederbond.

Liberalism focuses on the provision of services, rather than on the provider or recipient of that service (Leiby, 1985: 325). Missionary benevolence and focused welfare organizations were a product of liberal values. These organizations were non-denominational and often multicultural in the services they offered and were committed to the protection and guidance of individuals, irrespective of color, as the ideal. To achieve these goals, specialist training was considered necessary. The liberals developed an assimilationist strategy. (Marks, 1989: 175)

Broederbond was an underground unifying and organizing force in the ethnic strategy for Afrikaner advancement. Believing themselves to be the saviors of the Afrikaners and implicitly convinced of their assumed right to speak for the people, the Broederbond saw an explicit threat to their strategy in the cultural fusion that was occurring.

Dr. Verwoerd, a member of the Broederbond, set out with his "brothers" to create a nation. Professional social work practice and education were part of their means to this end (Marks, 1989: 170). The provision of social work services to the poor whites served two purposes. It unified and strengthened the ethnic boundaries and gave rise to a certified professional elite, loyal to the government and all out to achieve the government's goal of stamping out white poverty. It was in the Broederbond spirit that Verwoerd studied sociology and social work until he established a department of sociology and social work at the University of Stellenbosch in 1932. He pioneered a specific form of education for the new profession of social work.

Batson was a representative of the dominant colonial liberal establishment. He was arguing for diversity and openness as against Verwoerd's prophetic vision of Boers as the chosen children of God who are superior to other races and should protect their ethnic superiority by isolating themselves from contamination by inferior races. The diversity propounded by liberals faded and academic schooling within a bachelor's degree became entrenched as the only accepted form of social work qualification. When Verwoerd became the prime minister in 1958 he first encouraged subsidization of university education, which was followed by state influence on social work practice and education. The Afrikaans and English universities disagreed on cultural grounds on the type of education to be provided. The former perpetuated scientific charity focusing on nation building, while the latter espoused an implicit liberal philosophy.

It is noteworthy that the cultural and philosophical differences on which social work education in this country was founded have remained unchanged over the years. For instance, the original Carnegie Commission in which the University of Stellenbosch played so large a role focused on white poverty and produced social work education services that were related to protection of Afrikanerdom. The 1982 Second Carnegie Commission of Inquiry was based at the University of Cape Town. Typical of liberal university philosophy, the inquiry was not confined to any particular race group, although in the 1980s, poverty was endured primarily by blacks.

Social Work and Religion

There seems to be a close relationship between the profession and religion. For instance, Hough (1973: 35) suggested that social work has been human beings' answer to the Biblical question "Am I my brother's keeper?" By establishing a helping service, society accepts responsibility for those who are unable to provide for their survival needs.

Historically, social services grew out of a motivation of sympathy—some may call it the deep seated guilt feelings of the community's conscience—and out of the religious injunction to look after our fellow humans in need.

Action in social work has always had an orientation of giving alms to the poor and of providing help for nothing. Even Verwoerd, who pioneered social work education in this country, had religious considerations in his motives. He saw himself and his brothers as chosen children of God with the special mission of protecting and perpetuating Afrikanerdom.

Social work values that emphasize the dignity and worth of the human being imply that all humans have intrinsic value in the eyes of God. This represents Western religious orientation and belief in the everlasting existence of the human soul. From our Calvinistic orientation in this country, we tend to balance this feeling of patronizing charity and sympathy with a person's responsibility for himself/herself as against mere rights of individuals. However, it is uncertain how our national policy of racial discrimination affects the achievement of this ideal. We have ended up with a residual welfare system which comes into play only when the normal structures of supply break down.

RANGE AND STRUCTURE OF SOCIAL WORK EDUCATION

Social work practice covers a very wide range of social issues, such as protection of children and care of the aged, the disabled, the mentally ill and many others. Social work education of necessity has to prepare professionals to deliver services in that wide range. When the generalist education based on scientific charity superseded the diverse training espoused by Batson during the early 1960s, all qualifying courses prepared practitioners for service in all fields, settings and methods.

All qualifying education is now generalist in nature. Specialization is in practice only where social work is implemented by specialist agencies like the South African National Councils. As a result, specialist training is conducted by the agencies themselves in orientation courses, in-service training and specialized supervision services. Otherwise, all qualifying education for social work is located in university institutions and leads to a bachelor of arts in social work (BASW) or a bachelor of arts in social sciences (BASS) degree. Universities offer specialized courses at postqualifying level: clinical social work—Universities of Cape Town and Durban Westville; clinical social work in industry—Rand Afrikaans University and the University of Witwatersrand; medical social work—Universities of Durban, Westville, Pretoria and Stellenbosch; mental health—University of South Africa; social planning and administration—Universities of CapeTown and Port Elizabeth; supervision—Universities of Pretoria and Stellenbosch (SACSW, 1991).

Most of the universities offering qualifying courses also offer postqualifying courses such as the general master's degree and the PhD in social work. Master's and doctoral programs usually entail a dissertation or thesis. These are specialized courses since a student carries out intensive research on a specific area of interest. Even those postgraduate programs that have course work offer specialized fields.

There are universities that offer special courses for marriage guidance counselors which are sometimes a requirement for employment by some agencies, such as the Family and Marriage Association of South Africa (FAMSA). Residential workers are usually oriented in the various residential settings. Probation officers are sometimes expected to have a course in criminology or some other law courses, for example, family law or law of persons.

Basically, all university education is state subsidized. The National Study Loan and Bursary Act 89 of 1964 provided for the establishment of a committee to discuss matters relating to the fund and make recommendations to the government on how the funds should be allocated. The Department of Education and Training does not award bursaries and loans to individual students from the fund but makes amounts available annually to all universities. Applications for financial assistance are therefore directed to the university where a student intends to study (Department of Education, 1980).

Not all students qualify for state subsidies. Funds from private welfare agencies are awarded to applicants according to merit. There are also other bursaries from institutions, such as the South African Council of Churches (SACC), the South African Institute of Race Relations. and other overseas embassies and institutes, such as the South African Education Programs (SAEP) and International Institute of Education (IIE) which usually grant funds for postgraduate studies tenable in overseas institutions only. It is common for most social work students to be funded solely by their parents at undergraduate level, especially in the predominantly black universities.

Social work qualifying education carries the prestige of being a university degree. This is not the case with other human service professions such as nursing. This should place social work on a higher pedestal, but in actual practice, that is not the case. Professions are judged by the general public according to the quality of services they offer. Lack of resources cripples the delivery of social work services, especially for blacks. On the other hand, health services are fairly developed and well established, and as a result practitioners in that field are capable of providing more meaningful services. Generally social work is not greatly respected in university campuses, but there are shared courses with more established disciplines like sociology and psychology and their faculty teach on social work programs.

According to section 3 of Act 110 of 1978 it is the responsibility of the council to promote the image, status and prestige of social work as a profession. To this end, the CSAW focused its attention on several issues such as improvement of conditions of service. The CSAW Annual Report (1981: 27) states that the council believes that conditions of service are of great importance and is concerned that this profession is considerably behind comparable professions in this regard. The council was convinced that, unless this was reme-died, it could in the long run cause serious damage to the status, prestige and acceptability of social work as a profession. In 1982, the council appointed a work group to investigate salaries and other conditions of service with a view to improvement.

The council also enforced the registration of social work students for the protection of the client's rights and maintenance of professional standards of conduct. This, the council stated, was in keeping with practice in other human service professions, such as nursing. In 1983, a work group was appointed to formulate a generally acceptable course of conduct for social work. This was also directed toward improvement of the image and status of the profession. In general, the Council for Social and Associated Workers (CSAW) is involved in various efforts to improve the status and relationship of social work to other human service professions. In 1989 it changed its name to the South African Council for Social Work (SACSW).

QUALIFYING AND POST QUALIFYING TRAINING

From the beginning, social work education in this country has been under-taken in university institutions, exceptions are the programs of the following nonuniversity settings: Jan Hofmeyr, South African Railways, Huguenot College, Minnie Hofmeyr, DeColigny Training Institution, Strydom Training School and Friedenheim College.

Postqualifying training took place only at universities which granted either a postgraduate diploma or an honor's degree, a master's degree or a doctorate in social work. Some social university institutions with financial assistance from overseas embassies and/or other institutes.

There is no certified agency training so far. It is only recently that agencies have been empowered to train social auxiliary workers who will write an examination determined by the council before qualifying for registration with the council.

Agencies such as Life Line have designed their own training programs. These courses are usually taken by qualified social workers and only enable them to meet the employment requirements for those agencies. These can be classified as post-qualifying courses but specializing in specific client groups. Some universities currently offer specializing courses and all these are at post-graduate level or are post qualifying courses.

GATEKEEPING TO THE PROFESSION

Gatekeeping is one of the most prominent steps in the development of a profession. It is exercised by the closing of the ranks of the profession by means of a system of statutory registration. The introduction of Act 110 of 1978 made provision for social work to:

- set specified conditions for admission to the profession
- limit the use of the professional title and the practicing of the profession to those who satisfy the set conditions
- subject the continued use of the title and the practicing of the profession to the fulfillment of specific requirements and rules of conduct (CSAW, 1982:9)

The first goal of this gatekeeping is to protect the *community*, the consumers of the services the profession renders against those who practice the profession illegally and against the practitioners of the profession who practice it in an unprofessional or improper manner. The second goal is to protect the *profession* by creating mechanisms to regulate the training for admission to and practicing of the profession. Thus, the prestige of the profession is increased and a certain status and dignity given to it. The third goal is to protect the individual *practitioner* by defining the terrain of his or her own activities and thereby granting him or her recognition.

Accreditation

When the Joint Universities Committee (JUC) on Social Work Education was established, one of its objectives was to promote and facilitate the exchange of information among the university institutions of South Africa on all matters affecting the teaching of social studies. This exchange formed the foundation of arrangements for accreditation of qualifying courses. The JUC, however, did not campaign for exact uniformity of curricula and syllabi for all institutions. Instead, it agreed on some basic courses that should be included in each training program. Also it did not agree on the content of these courses. Nevertheless, it laid the ground for further discussion. As a result, when the CSAW was established, it took over where the JUC had left off. In 1983, the CSAW decided to form a committee on tuition and training. The council so far has prescribed the duration to be four year's training in the subject of social work (CSAW, 1985: 15).

To date, no requirements have been determined for the nature and content of curricula for academic tuition and practical training. Views of training institutions and other relevant persons and organizations have been sought in this regard. The council has compiled a document on proposed minimum standards which has not yet been finalized for prescription and implementation. The formation of the standing committee on tuition and training signaled the council's opinion that the time has arrived to work in the direction of setting accreditation criteria for social work courses.

Licensing of Professionals

Section 3(a) of Act 110 of 1978 relates to admission to the practice of social work (1) by determining the qualifications for registration as a social worker and (2) by regulating the practice of the profession of social work and the registration of the social workers.

In 1985, the original Act was amended considerably for the sake of clarity. The amended section 15 (1) states the following:

> No person shall, for gain, directly or indirectly, in any manner whatsoever, practice the profession of social work, unless he has been registered under this Act as a social worker or is deemed to have been so registered. No person shall give instruction on any aspect of the subject, social work, at a training institution unless he has been registered under this Act as a social worker or is a person who is not a permanent resident in R.S.A. and who, with the approval of the Council, can give instruction in an aspect of the subject, social work, determined by the Council at a training institution in the Republic determined by the Council. No person shall in any manner pretend to be a social worker, student or associated worker, while he has not been registered under this Act. (CSAW, 1985: 12).

This statement, in no uncertain terms, makes it illegal for anyone to practice, teach or even study the profession of social work without prior registration with the council.

Licensing of Social Workers in Private Practice

A newcomer in the social work practice scene in this country is private practice for profit. This sector has grown in strength and number to such an extent that there is now a recognized association for social workers in private practice which keeps a register of such professionals. This association has also developed some guidelines for private practice, standardized charges and other criteria guarding and directing private practice. Although this is a voluntary organization, registration with it improves the prestige and status of a social worker in private practice. The association now boasts a membership of about two hundred social workers, which is 2 percent of all registered social workers.

The South African Council for Social Work (SACSW) resolved in 1990 that it would not institute a separate register for social workers in private practice; these workers would be required to obtain and maintain registration as social workers with the council to legitimize their practice. The council further resolved that should a social worker in private practice be charged with alleged unprofessional and improper conduct in the running of his or her practice, the council's disciplinary committee would investigate such a complaint on the basis of existing legislation and would also be guided by the guidelines set by the association. The association was encouraged to enter into negotiations with the Representative Association of Medical Aid Schemes with a view to recognition of social work services for medical aid benefits (SACSW, 1990).

Malpractice

A work group was appointed by the council in 1983 to formulate a set of accepted standards of conduct. In 1984, they produced the first document, which has gone through various revisions. The current rules are published in the *Government Gazette* 11133 as Notice R164 (CSAW, 1988: 5).

Frequency and Incidence of Malpractice

Before 1985 there were no cases reported. For later years the cases indicated in Table 15-1 were recorded. No further cases have been recorded:

Table 15-1
Incidence of Malpractice Cases 1985-1988

Year	No. of Cases	Guilty	Not Guilty	Accusations Withdrawn	No Findings	NonSocial Workers
1985/6	9	0	1	1	4	3
1986/7	5	1	2	1	1	0
1987/8	6	0	1	0	0	5

(CSAW, 1988: 34).

POLITCAL CLIMATE

The politics of a nation have a direct bearing on its welfare policy. South African society with its emphasis on racial and cultural discrimination is no exception to this rule.

The profession was established in order to solve white poverty, as a result, the needs of whites, a legally protected group, have come to be a major determining factor in the development of social work services (McKendrick, 1990a: 12). Thus, today, they have the greatest range of services available to them and of the highest quality. Even social work education shows this tendency in the numbers of qualified and registered social workers. In 1988, for instance, there were 6575 registered social workers—4439 were white, 1045 were black, 647 were colored and 344 Indian. The ratio of social workers to the whole population was 1:20,462 for blacks, 1:4827 for Colored, 1:2700 for Indians and 1:1116 for whites (Botha, 1989: 7).

This is worth noting in a racially segmented country where social workers are often required to serve people of the same population group as they. There has been a steady increase in the number of social workers qualifying. SACSW data indicated that there were 7006 social workers registered with the council in 1990 (SACSW, 1990: 12), while their 1994 statistics show a total of 8458 (926 male, 7532 female) registered social workers.

Social work education and training were also affected by the national policy of racial discrimination, for example, when the extension of University Education Act 45 of 1959 came into effect. One of the provisions of this act was for the establishment of universities to serve different racial and ethnic groups. The same act stipulated that no nonwhites might apply to enter into the open universities without the written consent of the responsible minister of state. This meant that the universities which admitted students of all races were limited by this act from doing so without such consent.

The creation of homeland governments for the different ethnic groups during the 1970s and 1980s also had a direct effect on social work education, 95 new universities offering social work were established in those homelands that had not had them.

When the council was instituted in 1979, its jurisdiction was in a way confined to the republic, to the exclusion of independent homelands. This led to a state where the council could not fully enforce its rules beyond the borders of the Republic of South Africa. Such requirements as registration of all social workers became optional for people in the independent homelands.

For some reason, though, the council had a firm grip on the universities, even those in the homelands. As a result, social work educators may not offer any tuition without being registered with the council; otherwise, the certificates they award will be invalid. Presently, very few social workers from the homelands are registered and this is no breach of law, since Act 110 of 1978 is not enforceable there. This has led to a state where the council is unable to keep a complete register of qualified or practicing social workers, since the Council registration is not a prerequisite in the independent homelands. For instance, in 1989, of the national total of 536 registered fourth year students, only 398 had registered with the council by September 30, 1990 (SACSW, 1990).

Role of the Government in the Profession

Legislation concerning the organization of welfare services in South Africa consists of three acts: the National Welfare Act 100 of 1978, the Fund Raising Act 107 of 1978 and the Social and Associated Workers Act 110 of 1978. The acts amended the 1965 National Welfare Act.

The Council for Social and Associated Workers was established in accordance with Act 110 of 1978. This council is a partly elective statutory yet autonomous body with a legal personality which in the interests of the community, works for the protection and the promotion of the profession of social work. The objects of the SACSW are fully outlined in Section 3 of the Social Workers Act. The council consists of twelve members, all of whom should be registered social workers.

Eight of the members are elected by the voting members of the profession, while four are nominated by the minister of health, welfare and pensions. The term of office for both nominated and elected members is three years.

The council has the following objectives:

- Determine standards of training
- Promote the status and prestige of the profession
- Protect the interests of the social work profession
- Determine and maintain standards of professional conduct
- Determine qualifications for registration as social worker
- Control professional conduct
- Encourage study of social work
- Organize practice of the profession and registration of social workers
- Promote efficiency of social work services
- Advise the minister on social work matters
- Support social control and its implications

From the very early stages of development, social work education set out to prepare "persons who would build a specific society " (Marks, 1989: 171). The Verwoerd model of social work education produced social workers who were loyal to the government, committed to nation building, advocating changing people rather than changing situations. Even at a later stage, social work education emphasized therapeutic and rehabilitative models, rather than developmental models. As McKendrick (1990a: 243) observes, the main function of

South African social work has been to maintain the established social order. This was achieved by excluding social workers from policy formulation and planning positions. They were mainly confined to service delivery roles. These did not enable them to design relevant services nor curricula, but instead compelled them to adhere to the expectations of the government officials who did the planning and policy formulation.

When government subsidies were provided for social workers and students, it became difficult for the profession to raise any objections to the social control models, as this would be tantamount to "biting the hand that feeds you."

Only now are social workers beginning to look critically at their roles and functions. They are also making their voices heard for the establishment of a democratic welfare policy that will be more developmentally oriented than therapeutic. Social work practice which attempts to change people even when the causes of their problems are elsewhere is now seen to be less effective. It is recommended that social work education prepare professionals who will deal both with people and their environment. As Hough (1973: 48) observes, "What we need are techniques of working with man in the context of, and in close interaction with his fellow men, as well as with his physical environment" also pleaded for action in a new approach which would prepare social workers for a more active part in community development. Hough (1973: 56) further notes that this should be effectively facilitated by government authorities, by including social workers at the crucial points of policy making in our body politic.

CURRICULA AND THE SOCIOPOLITICAL CONTEXT

The basic requirement for qualifying as a social worker is a four year undergraduate social work course which leads to a BASW or BASS degree. Although there are common elements such as intensive social science theory and extensive field instruction, there is a wide diversity in the actual content of the social work courses offered by South African universities. There is no specific focus on women's issues. Some rural dimensions related to concurrent practica are included, especially in the homeland universities located in rural areas.

The subjects required for a degree or diploma are as follows:

- Four year courses in social work
- Three year courses in sociology or psychology
- Two year courses in sociology or psychology
- One year courses in two other subjects such as law or economics, criminology, anthropology and a language. (SACSW, n. d.)

JUC has held discussions on this issue. The government also tried to standardize qualifying requirements for subsidization. When the council was established, one of its objectives was to look into the issue of course content. A
lot of investigations have been carried out, and so far there is only a proposal for
minimum standards which has not yet been implemented. Training institutions,
employing agencies, practitioners and other related bodies have been consulted
and the result would reflect a concerted effort of all the involved parties.

McKendrick (1990b: 18) states that the over-emphasis on helping people to
adjust to their existing circumstances has limited the impact of the profession on
achieving a better life for people. Instead, it has left itself open to accusations of
being an agent of oppression. Indeed, the curriculum focuses on theoretical
issues instead of practical problems. Therapeutic and rehabilitative models are
mostly used without paying any attention to the causes of social problems. This
is more evident in the type of research investigations carried out by social
workers. These are usually for further studies carried out under the auspices of
university institutions. Most of these address issues that are far removed from
the sociopolitical context of the country. As Chinkanda (1988: 4) has also
observed, this reflects a complete insensitivity of researchers to the current
sociopolitical context.

An effort has been made by some universities to address local issues. This is
evident in courses in child abuse, social welfare law, counseling of ex-detainees
and returning exiles taught by individual staff members or generated by local
pressures are included easily because the departments still decide on the content
oftheir courses. The need for indigenization of social work literature is
recognized by some universities and an effort is made, but a lot of work still
needs to be done in this area.

Although basic social work knowledge, methodology and skill are universal,
it is necessary to develop curriculum content and literature for the understanding
of local social circumstances, cultures and values.

When major sociopolitical changes took place in 1990, there were new pressures on the profession that made it difficult for practitioners to remain apoliti-
cal. Dealing with casualties of political violence, analyzing the proposed welfare policy, providing services for returning exiles, counseling former political
prisoners and many other activities brought social workers into direct confrontation with the realities of the South African community. Certain professional
organizations and individuals identified themselves with the changes and saw
the need to develop services to meet the current needs. Development is the key
concept. As Hough (1973: 47) had indicated

The whole community must become the object and main focus of our efforts, not
merely the small number of cast offs, who may or may not be vaguely rehabilitated
and who in our fantasy may become healthy and contributing members of the society
again. Perhaps it is high time that social work in developing societies bravely refuse

to be wholly preoccupied with the dregs of society. Social work education cannot afford to overlook the need for curriculum that focuses on the current sociopolitical changes.

Direct practice with individuals experiencing problems need not be replaced by societal change or developmental practice. As McKendrick (1990a: 15) states, "Not all problems in living are caused by forces outside the person." The greatest challenge to social work education therefore is to integrate the treatment and developmental models according to the demands of each situation.

Role of the Student

South African social work education does not leave room for the contribution of students to the planning and presentation of the curriculum, especially at the undergraduate level. Students are at the receiving end of those curricula which they find in the universities. If there is any input, it is very minor and probably through the course evaluation comments, which are optional and voluntary. Postgraduate students in postqualifying courses may have some input on what they learn through choice of topics and methods for research.

Theory and Practice

Social work education depends greatly on American and European publications. This trend transfers foreign theoretical models to South African social work practice. This is functional as long as they address universal issues relating to poverty, growth, grief and other human factors. When foreign theoretical models are used to solve local problems, then they become completely irrelevant. There has always been severe criticism of this transportation of foreign theories to local problems that have local causes. It is only now that indigenous literature is sprouting out, but it is still not extensive enough to cover all social issues.

Schools and departments of social work are characterized by a theoretical approach to the curriculum. As a result, when students enter practice, they usually have problems adapting this theoretical knowledge to realities of the local communities. Some beginning social workers have been complained that the theory they learn at university is irrelevant to practice. Sensitive to this complaint, most agencies expose their beginning social workers to extensive orientation sessions to close the wide gap between theory and practice. Actually, the experienced social workers have mastered the skill of integrating theory and practice in the field. The sad fact is that they have not been able to commit their professional experiences to publications that would help the beginning social worker.

Social work educators appreciate the value of experience as a practitioner. As a result, no social worker is allowed to qualify without extensive practical work under the supervision of experienced practitioners. This in every way confirms the need for integrating theory to practice.

The social work educators involved in fieldwork supervision do sometimes come across some local models of practice that are either original or adaptations of foreign models to meet local situations. For instance, the past two years have seen traditional counseling techniques being refined to meet the needs of former political detainees and returning exiles. Community development and social action strategies have been adapted to meet local needs and solve particular social problems of racial discrimination. These valuable anecdotes, unfortunately, rarely are published for use by social work educators. They die a natural death in the wake of new interests, or they are sometimes rediscovered by younger practitioners and go out of fashion as agencies change directors or points of focus. A sad reality indeed.

The Medical Model

The therapeutic and rehabilitative models have their place in social work practice. They can never be devalued. In a situation like the one prevailing in this country, though, it becomes very difficult to rely on the medical model for the majority of human problems that are caused by factors outside the persons. Then it becomes necessary to think about democratic means of delivering professional services. It also becomes necessary to think about uprooting the policies that cause disadvantage and disability among some racial or ethnic groups. Factors that affect the well being of human beings such as gross national product demand attention before the medical model can be implanted on a wide scale.

ROLE OF RESEARCH

Research is a very important component of social work practice. In this country, the need for social work research was acknowledged when the Carnegie Commission of Inquiry into the poor white problem was instituted. Causes of white poverty were investigated with the aim of finding solutions. Social work practice therefore has to continue investigating and studying social problems, in order to find solutions. As Thomas (1986: 98) advises, social work research activities should be directed to solving problems confronting the practitioner, not merely at verifying or refuting theories that are of interest to the researcher only.

Training for Research

All social work qualifying courses have a research component built into them. The extent depends on individual schools or departments. However, this does not seem to prepare social workers enough for full integration of research into practice. As a result, most social work research takes place at university institutions or research institutes outside the agencies, usually for the purpose of obtaining higher qualifications. Aside from this, only social work educators engage in research activity. These research reports are often useless to the practitioner who has not been schooled in understanding complex statistical analyses. Epstein (1986: 158) notes that social work research is beset by a number of practical problems that stem from the particular circumstances of social work practice, such as "social conditions changing too fast for yesterday's social research predictions to have much meaning for tomorrow's problems" (Maas, 1968: 45).

Also, ethical issues make it difficult to subject research subjects to some conditions and therefore complete control of variables becomes impracticable sometimes. Social work education therefore needs to design research courses that are sensitive to these issues and prepare practitioners for active research that will improve the practice of the profession.

South African universities have been for the greater part teaching universities; as a result social work educators have not been affected by the venerable dictum "publish or perish." Promotions, status and recognition have depended on teaching experience and not on research and publication. It is only recently that research and publication has been encouraged and even used in some cases as criteria for promotion. Commitment and hard work have enabled some social work educators to be good teachers while involved in practice and research. Probably it is important to strike a good balance between these equally important academic activities so that one does not excel or suffer at the cost of the other. The ascendancy of research over teaching is highly possible especially if there are incentives for research involvement and none for teaching excellence.

Need for Research

The need for research is irrefutable. Indeed, it is by looking again that we can identify what is happening, how and why, and it is only when we have answers to these questions that we can hope to find solutions to contemporary social problems. This country, with its peculiar conditions and continuous changes, cannot do without ongoing research. Professional practice that is not based on concurrent research studies is sure to be outdated, irrelevant and ineffective.

Empirical and Methodological Debates

There are various designs in social research. The choice of a design is decided by the nature of information to be gathered. In historical research, for instance, the task involves the systematic collection and critical evaluation of data relating to past events. Louw (1983) and Marks (1989) are examples of historical investigations. Social work practice and education are informed by historical studies like these. As a result, planning for future practice or education can be refined after an in-depth analysis of past events in both areas.

Exploratory research is meant to acquaint the researcher with the characteristics of the research target. The main aim is to refine the definition of concepts in preparation for further research. A study by Louw (1982), "Social Work in the Western Cape," is an example of exploratory research. Most social work research investigations are descriptive in nature. They give both quantitative and qualitative descriptions of the subjects studied.

Experimental research which requires manipulation of variables aims at discovering cause and effect relationships among variables. As Collins (1987: 258) notes, examples of experimental social work research are extremely sparse in the literature. This is due probably to ethical issues that make it difficult to subject social work clients to strict empirical conditions that may be inhuman, detrimental or contrary to the basic principles of the profession.

SUMMARY

McKendrick (1990b: 13) notes that South African social work education is generally of a high standard. Graduates may and do go anywhere in the world, and they readily are accepted into highly competitive postgraduate programs of most prestigious universities or obtain appointments to senior positions. Probably this means that our graduates are more prepared for universal practice than for practice in South Africa, per se.

The establishment of the CSAW was a milestone in the development of the profession. This step has given direction and guidance to social work practice and education. As long as racial discrimination is the order of the day, it may be necessary for the council to make sure that each race group is represented it.

Typical of the field the world over, most social work students are female. This has caused the profession to be seen as "womanly." The few men who enter social work are promoted into senior positions sooner than their female counterparts. Professional education needs to pay more attention to practice focused research in order to encourage practitioners to integrate research into their everyday practice activities. It is hoped that the newly formed minimum standard proposals will pay specific attention to adoption of locally relevant curricula with a universal touch that will continue to enable social workers trained in this country to fit in well with international standards of practice.

REFERENCES

Bosman, F. (1982). *Social Welfare Law*. Johannesburg: LexPatria.

Botha, N. J. (1989). The future of social work in South Africa. *South African Council for Social Work Newsletter*, 8(2).

Chinkanda, E. (1988). Social work research in South Africa--as I see it. *The Social Work Practitioner Researcher*, 1(1), 2-6.

Collins, K. (1987). Social work research. In McKendrick, B.W. (Ed.). *Introduction to Social Work in South Africa*. Pinetown: Owen Burgess.

Council for Social and Associated Workers Newsletters/Annual Reports. (1981 to 1991).

Department of Education, Republic of South Africa. (1980). *Annual Report*. Pretoria: Government Printer.

Epstein, W.M. (1986). Science and social work. *Social Service Review*, March, 145–160.

Gray, M. (1989) Community development: has social work met the challenge? *Social Work/Maatskaplike Werk*, 25(1), 44-67.

Helm, B. (1964). *Thirty years of social work training in South Africa, 1934-1964*. Capetown: Board of Sociological Research, University of Cape Town, South Africa.

Higgins, J. B. (1977). Reflections on the education of black social workers in South Africa. Inaugural address delivered at the University of Zululand on November 30. South Africa, Kwa Dlangezwa.

Hough, M. A. (1973). Social Work in developing communities. In *Social Work in Contemporary South African Society*. Pretoria: Department of Social Work, University of South Africa.

Leiby, J. (1985). Moral foundations, social welfare and social work: a historical review. *Social Work* (NASW), July/August, 323-330.

Louw, L. R. (1982). Social work in the Western Cape. *Social Work/Maatskaplike Werk*, 18(3), 192-195.

Louw, L. (1983). The anatomy of underdevelopment: implications for social work training in South Africa. Master's thesis, University of Cape Town, South Africa.

Lowe, G. (1985). Is American social work education relevant toSouth African social work education: some thoughts on professional imperialism. *Social Work/Maatskaplike Werk*, 21(4), 231-234.

Maas, D.T. (1968). Social work knowledge and social responsibility. *Journal of Education for Social Work*, 4,45.

Marks, C. (1989). *A contextual commentary on social work in South Africa*. Master's thesis, University of CapeTown, South Africa.

McKendrick, B.W. (1987). (Ed.). *Introduction to Social Work in South Africa*. Pinetown: Owen Burgess.

McKendrick, B.W. (1990:a). Beyond Apartheid: an alphabet of challenges for social work education.*Social Work/Maatskaplike Werk*, *26*(3), 241-250.

McKendrick, B.W. (1990:b). The future of social work in South Africa. *Social Work/Maatskaplike Werk*, *26*(1), 10-18

O'Meara, D. (1983). *Volskapitalisme*. Johannesburg: Ravan.

Powers, G. T., Meenaghan, T. M., & Toomey, B. G. (1985). *Practiced Focused Research: Integrating Human Service Practice and Research*. Englewood Cliffs, N.J.: Prentice Hall.

Small, A. (1987). Thoughts on making social work education relevant to South African needs. *Social Work/Maatskaplike Werk*, *23*(1), 5-12.

South African Council for Social Workers Publication: *A Profession of Our Time*.

Thomas, A. (1986). Research and practice in social work: a source of strain. *Social Work/Maatskaplike Werk*, *22*(2), 96-100.

IV
MIDDLE EAST

16

MIDDLE EAST AND EGYPT

Ibrahim A. Ragab

INTRODUCTION

Social work education in the Middle East differs in a very important way from its counterpart in Western industrialized countries. The two systems differ on where each stands on a continuum of spontaneity of development versus emulation of foreign models. It is generally assumed that programs for the training of social workers in Western industrialized countries emerged spontaneously, as a genuine response to a societal need. The development of these training programs thus reflected the broader social, political, and economic forces at work in these countries (Hammoud, 1988). Naturally, the basic philosophy around which these programs evolved was thus inherently congruent with dominant cultural values and national sentiment, or at least with significant parts thereof.

By contrast, the development of social work education in the Middle East—as in the rest of the developing world—can hardly be described as spontaneous. It could best be conceived of in terms of "transfer of social technology" or "diffusion of innovation," with all the attending nuances of these processes. Recognition of the need to create such training programs resided with a few individuals with some influence, who had some exposure to similar programs in England and the United States of America. Programs were emulated from foreign-grown models. In most cases, they were copied in toto, with very little regard to the extent of their appropriateness for application under the local conditions, or their congruence with the prevailing culture of the region.

The diffusion of the Western model of social work education into the region—with the exception of the former French colonial territories—could be better understood as a "two-stage" process. In the initial stage, beginning in 1935, the American model was successfully transplanted into Egypt, a trendsetter among the countries of the Middle East. Once the new training programs gained widespread acceptance, they rapidly proliferated. Graduates of schools of social work were soon in high demand—and not only at home. With the advent of the oil industry and the era of ambitious development plans in many

Arab countries, especially in the Gulf area, a vast new market for the skills of trained Egyptian social workers—from the front–line worker to the highly qualified consultant—was wide open.

The host countries later felt the need to create local training programs to prepare their own citizens to replace the expatriates. In this second stage of the diffusion process, beginning in the early 1960s, it was only natural for these Arab countries to fashion their new training programs after the Egyptian experience—when Egyptian social work educators were called upon to help. In the process, the American model was indirectly transplanted into most of the other countries of the region—speaking in the Arabic tongue, in the Egyptian dialect!

But if the concept of a two-stage diffusion of innovation does help us understand the evolution of social work education in most countries of the Middle East, it may not be sufficient for an adequate understanding of more recent developments. After more than a half-century of social work education and practice in Egypt (and lesser durations in other countries), certain trends are emerging—and continuing to unfold—that may point to a process of "reverse diffusion," which may also be two-staged!

One manifestation of this process is the *indigenization of social work* movement. Since the early 1960s most social work educators in the region have taken indigenization to be the remedy of choice to the earlier "blind emulation" syndrome (Ragab, 1990). However, this idea of "adapting or adjusting [the American model of] the profession in accordance with the conditions and requirements of the society in which it is being practiced" (Osman et al., 1984) did not prove to be a potent enough medicine.

Since the early 1980s a new trend, emanating this time from the Gulf region (or getting strong support from its universities), has been gaining momentum and is rapidly supplanting the indigenization concept. Reference is made here to the *Islamic reorientation of social work* movement currently in vogue in the region. Beginning hardly a decade ago, it is increasingly accepted as a viable alternative to the traditional conceptions of social work. Practitioners in the Gulf area—especially in Saudi Arabia—have been for years encountering difficulties applying these traditional Western models. Social work educators detected major incongruencies between the fundamental assumptions upon which such models are built and the basic tenets of Islam, the predominant religion in the region. They realized that effective practice and education, of necessity, require a more intimate alignment of social work theory and practice with the basic Islamic conceptions of humankind, society and the universe.

This call found very receptive ears among many social work educators in Egypt, who had also been sensing the incompatibilities but had hoped that indigenization of social work would solve their problems. Islamic reorientation came to be seen as the ultimate indigenization stance. The Egyptians were now beginning to learn from their ex-students. But is it possible for the tide of this "reverse diffusion" to reach the shores of the countries of origin of professional social work? Some think that this may not be as far-fetched as it sounds. A good idea promulgated fifty years ago, through the vehicle of reverse diffusion, may turn out to be even better.

The main thrust of the Islamic reorientation of social work movement, after all, is the need to correct the traditional bias against religion in the social work profession, the process identified by Martin Marty (1980) as the "secularization of social work." The main objective of this movement is to reinstate the spiritual aspects of the clients' lives, and the religious values of society, as major causal factors in our theoretical models for understanding and effecting change in human behavior. We are told that many Western social work educators are increasingly subscribing to that very same idea (Spencer, 1957; Coughlin, 1970; Hess, 1980; Joseph, 1988; Loewenberg, 1988; Canda, 1988, 1989; Dudley & Helfgott, 1990).

In the remainder of this chapter, the historical background to these developments will be dealt with in some detail. Naturally, the Egyptian experience with social work education will be given the lion's share of that account because of its centrality to our understanding of developments in the other countries. The range and structure of social work education in the region will be described. Other pertinent aspects, related to accreditation, curricula, and the role of research, will also be discussed, to present the most accurate picture of the social work educational system in the region possible—given the limitations of space and time. The Middle East, however, is a vast area. We will concern ourselves here only with what *Encyclopedia Britannica* (1975) defines as its "inner core, that of the Muslim Arab world."

HISTORICAL BACKGROUND

Diffusion: Phase One

The first social work training institution in the Middle East, the Cairo School of Social Work, was established in 1936. Two foreign-born social workers (one trained in the United States and the other in Switzerland) and a professor from the American University in Cairo initiated the idea and were able to muster enough support to bring it to fruition (Owais, 1973).

Time, in fact, was ripe. Egypt had in that same year finally achieved recognition as an independent nation, after fifty years of stifling British colonial rule. The call of the day was to find ways to combat the myriad social problems plaguing the country, and then to embark on the business of national reconstruction and development. Social work was introduced as the exact answer to that calling. In less than two years, these two social workers were instrumental in bringing together a group of Egyptian nationals, of the politician-reformer-scholar type, to start the Egyptian Society for Social Studies. They were all convinced that postcolonial problems could only be dealt with if social reform were firmly grounded in sound scientific inquiry. Establishing the Cairo School of Social Work was for that reason their first important accomplishment. The school was an instant success, for it could draw upon a vast pool of potential students. The country was teeming with idealistic, enthusiastic youth searching for a role in national reconstruction and development.

Only a year earlier, in 1935, the Greek community in Alexandria, the second largest city in Egypt, started a short-lived one year program for the training of social workers to cater to the needs of their own sectarian social agencies. Classes were taught in the French language. The idea did not work, and in 1937, the program was replaced by an Arabic-language School of Social Work on the same lines as the Cairo School. The idea of professional training for social workers was firmly established. The Cairo School became the prototype for others. In the beginning, high school graduates were admitted to that school for a one year program of courses and field instruction, but it was soon extended to two years of training. The graduates of the schools were granted a diploma of social work.

Many graduates of the Cairo School (ten out of thirty of the class of 1940) found their way to the United States to complete their graduate studies in social work. Returning with advanced degrees from leading schools of social work in the American universities, they became the pioneers of American-style social work education in Egypt, and later in other Arab countries as well. The dye was cast, and the model they enthusiastically promoted called for the establishment of either independent or university based-schools of social work.

By 1946, the movement toward specialized training for social work received government recognition and support. The Ministry of Education established the Higher Institute of Social Work for Girls; study in that institute and in the other two schools was also extended to three years. In 1946, civil service job classification systems formally recognized "social worker" as a separate occupational category. In 1953, all schools of social work adopted a four year program of courses and fieldwork ending with a higher diploma, equivalent to the bachelor's degree in social work.

Demand for the services of trained social workers dramatically increased as a result of the introduction of free public education in Egypt in 1950. Prior to that date, graduates from schools of social work were mainly employed by the Ministry of Social Affairs (established in 1939). With the need for teachers to staff the newly founded public schools, large numbers of social workers were appointed in schools nationwide to free for teaching tasks those teachers previously assigned part-time "counseling" loads (Hassanein, 1982). Since then, the Ministry of Education has become by far the leading employer of trained social workers in Egypt—a trend later duplicated by countries all over the region.

The leaders of the 1952 revolution in Egypt vowed to extend health, education, and social welfare services to all citizens. At one point, four hundred new schools were built a year. The increased demand on the skills of social workers prompted the creation of a new type of training at the junior college level. In 1952, a two year program, which grants an associate degree in social work, was created in Cairo. Alexandria and Aswan soon followed suit. Graduates were employed by different governmental agencies in the position of assistant social worker. In many cases they assumed the functions of social worker after a few years of experience on the job.

In 1961, graduates of all four year programs were granted a bachelor's degree in social work . In 1968, the government–affiliated Higher Institute of Social Work in Cairo (formerly "for Girls") started its graduate program at the MA and the PhD levels.

During the 1970s four more Higher Institutes of Social Work were founded by voluntary associations mainly interested in providing university education to students in governorates other than Cairo and Alexandria. These institutes were all fashioned after the Cairo School of Social Work, with four year programs at the undergraduate level. Even departments of sociology in Egyptian universities began to offer a few courses in social work and a little fieldwork to bank on the availability of social work jobs in government.

It was not until 1975, however, that social work education became part of the Egyptian universities, when the Higher Institute of Social Work in Cairo became part of the newly established Helwan University and was renamed the Faculty of Social Work. The oldest secular university in Egypt—Cairo University—followed suit and established the second university-based school of social work, in its Fayoum campus. This latter school has since its inception had both undergraduate and graduate programs. In 1993 Al-Azhar University—maybe the oldest university in the world—started two departments of social work, one in Cairo and the other in Assiut. The significance of this development lies in the recognition of the importance of Islamic concepts to social work education in a Muslim country.

Diffusion: Phase Two

In the 1950s, only a trickle of Egyptian trained social workers found their way to other Arab countries to work. During the 1960s, larger numbers served in different capacities in a variety of settings at the request of governmental bodies in these countries. Experienced consultants were called upon to design and implement new programs or reorganize old ones. Front line workers were also needed to staff these programs. By the 1980s, the trickle almost became a torrent. The Directorate of School Social Work in Kuwait in 1975, for example, hired 392 persons, mostly social workers (Al-Ibrahim & Hafiz, 1988); naturally most were Egyptians or others trained in Egypt. In 1981, the Saudi Arabian Ministry of Education hired 702 mostly Egyptian social workers, and the

Ministry of Health employed another 150 (Hassanein, 1982). This pattern had close parallels in other Gulf states and also in Libya—although numbers were not as large.

Another important route for this second-phase diffusion of the Egyptian version of the American model into other countries in the region was the training of students from these countries in Egyptian schools of social work. Some of these students returned back to their countries as early as 1961 and were very effective interpreting social work to their compatriots and very active promoting practice along the same lines that they had already learned (Hussein, 1989).

Certain factors common to conditions in these countries contributed to this rapid expansion in the utilization of Egyptian social workers. By 1970, every country in the region had established a Ministry of Social Affairs, theoretically at least identified with social work professionals as core staff. Even more important was the establishment within Ministries of Education of directorates for "social education" or "social activities," roughly corresponding to school social work sections. One of the missions of these national bodies was to assure the deployment of social workers in every secondary, intermediate, and even primary school. The discovery of oil in these countries made it possible to expand school systems and to provide high-quality services to students, including social work services.

With this kind of dependence on expatriates in large numbers to fill social work positions, host countries felt an urgent need to train local nationals to take over. In these mostly conservative countries, it was difficult for ordinary citizens to tolerate "strangers" poking their noses into their private lives. There was also a general feeling that no one could really have an insight into local problems and their solutions in the same way a citizen of the concerned country could. These kinds of sensitivities prodded officials into starting whatever sort of local training facilities they could, at whatever level possible under the circumstances.

In Saudi Arabia, the Institute of Social Work was established as early as 1961. Civil servants with only junior-high school education were admitted into this program of night classes for the duration of three years, to obtain a diploma in social work—equivalent to the general secondary school certificate. The institute was discontinued in 1974, when the University of Riyadh opened its Department of Sociology and Social Work. That department started a four year program at the undergraduate level. Other Saudi universities followed suit. In time, some universities came to realize the need for creating separate departments of social work. The common training pattern today is a four year program of courses and fieldwork leading to the BSW degree. A more significant development yet was the founding in Riyadh in 1975 of a separate school of social work, the Higher Institute of Social Work for Girls. The need to train sufficient numbers of women to perform social work functions with their female compatriots had long been considered a top priority in the kingdom, for social and religious reasons. That Higher Institute (now the Faculty of Social Work) soon started its own graduate program offering MSW and PhD degrees.

Libya went through a very similar course. Since 1964, seven high school–level three year (later extended to four) programs were established. These institutes grant their graduates an intermediate diploma in social work equivalent to the secondary school certificate. In 1969, a specialization in social work was offered within the Department of Social Studies in the Faculty of Education at the University of Tripoli. In 1972, the full-fledged Department of Social Work was opened in that university. Today, the seven intermediate diploma programs are still functioning—alongside the baccalaureate program in the university.

Social work education in Iraq has always had its ups and downs, reflecting the vicissitudes of the political climate in that country. Training programs for social workers started in 1951 with the establishment of the Department of Social Work in the Girls College in Baghdad, with some assistance from the UN. That college was closed in five years' time by 1956 but was again reopened in 1958. In 1968, the Department of Social Work became part of the Faculty of Arts, Baghdad University. However, it was merged in 1971 into the Department of Sociology (Shihab, 1982). With the Iraq-Iran war, however, two departments of social work were established, one in the University of Mosul and the other in the University of Quadisiya. Syria, sharing in basically the same radical traditions, had in the mid-1960s closed its only Egyptian-patterned Higher Institute of Social Work (Abdul-Aal, 1990).

Like Saudi Arabia, other Gulf states—Qatar, Kuwait, and the United Arab Emirates—have followed a pattern (since 1974) in which training takes place at the undergraduate level, in combined departments of sociology and social work, or in separate departments of social work within the university system.

Other Tributaries

Two additional factors deeply affected the development of programs for social work education in the remaining parts of the region. First were the technical assistance provided by regional and international bodies and the adoption by some countries of models of training advocated and supported by these bodies. Second was the adherence to the French and British models of training for social work–related functions, which drastically influenced the former French colonies and at least one former British colony.

Influence of International and Regional Organizations

It may be reasonable to assume that regional bodies (such as the Arab League) and international organizations (such as UNICEF and the UN Development Program) tend to adopt policies that approximate the lowest common denominator of training for social work in the region, rather than push for the highest possible standard. There may be some justification for that tendency, on the basis of political, organizational or financial considerations. But the consequences of this bias, nevertheless, can be felt in terms of the weakness of the training programs they advocate.

Two manifestations of this tendency can be easily observed. the encouragement by these organizations of Associate degree levels of training (two years after high school) and the focus on in-service training for persons without (or with some) formal training who are assigned social work functions. A case in point is the role of UNICEF in the establishment in 1965 of the Institute of Social Work, later renamed the Social Work Community College (SWCC) in Amman, Jordan (SWCC, n.d.). The college provides two separate programs, one for the training of social workers, and the other for the training of special education workers. After two years of courses and fieldwork, high school graduates who join the college receive a diploma in either specialty. But the college also offers a variety of in-service training and continuous education programs. On the other hand, the Arab League's Department of Social Development has invariably supported in-service training programs, especially in the fields of social development, but has hardly encouraged degreed training.

The Influence of the French and the British Models

Traditionally, the French model in social work practice and education has not resulted in the development of a strong sense of professionalism similar to that found in the United States. Rather, the identification of those carrying out social work functions is with specific fields of practice, such as health services, family welfare, and industrial social services (Birks, 1987). Although the situation, according to Birks, may be changing of late, it is the old patterns of deployment and education of workers that still influence the former French colonies, particularly in the North African Maghrib area.

Social work education in Tunisia, Algeria, and Morocco still follows in the footsteps of the French traditional patterns. It basically consists of training programs with a duration of somewhere between one and three years to which high school-level graduates are admitted (Al-Saud, 1988).

Sudan represents a very special case, in that the influence of the traditional British model of social work education is preserved, alongside the influence of technical assistance from UN organizations. The University of Khartoum, through its Extramural Studies department, offers training programs in social work to those already engaged in social work activities in the government. Close ties are maintained with the British, who are regularly involved in program design and evaluation (Al-Hassan, 1990). However, the establishment of undergraduate and graduate programs in social work through the Department of Sociology and Social Work in Omdurman Islamic University clearly shows the growing influence of the American model.

CULTURAL AND RELIGIOUS INFLUENCES

The advent of professional social work practice and education in the Middle East coincided with the closing chapter in its people's struggle for independence and for freedom from colonial rule. These were turbulent times, with their own peculiar contradictions and ambivalence. People were carrying arms against their European oppressors. Yet, dazed by the immensity of the problems left behind in the aftermath of their evacuation, they were looking to their ex-tormentors for inspiration as to how to reconstruct and develop their own countries. On the face of it, people in the region seemed to have had the upper hand. After all, they had finally succeeded in driving away foreign occupation forces. Inside, however, people were defeated, feeling helpless as they became aware of the pathetic situation in their countries compared with the levels of material achievement in the Western world.

For most people, the solution seemed very simple: "Emulate the West!" was the call of the day—despite rhetoric to the contrary by the likes of Nasser of Egypt. Advanced Western science and technology—material and social—seemed to offer the best hope for the inhabitants of the region to catch up with the modern world. In that climate, when social work was introduced as a means of solving social problems—on a "scientific" basis, it was wholeheartedly embraced by the earlier generations of social workers and social work educators. The general feeling prevailing in these formative years was that what proved good for the United States should be good for everybody. These were not times for questioning, but for learning from those who were more success-ful.

After years of practice in accordance with the emulated American model, many social workers discovered that they had serious problems with local ap-plications. Certain practices seemed to be completely out of alignment with the general cultural configuration. Later, questions of effectiveness of social work began to be seriously raised. Even questions of "appropriateness" were consid-ered in different respects and at different levels. At a more benign level, the appropriateness of the emphasis on working with individuals versus using broader methods of intervention was the focus of debate. At the other extreme, even the need for social work as a profession was itself questioned, in the so-called socialist transformation era in the early sixties.

In any case, it began to dawn on many practitioners and educators that there were indeed significant differences between the social, economic and political conditions prevalent in the industrialized countries where social work models evolved and those prevalent in the developing world. Ignoring these differences, it was thought, may have been responsible for those failures of application. The *indigenization of social work* movement was born, and it seemed to provide *the* solution. According to the proponents of this movement, all that social work educators—as the pioneers and leaders of the profession—have to do is identify and make the necessary adjustments in the American model to make it more compatible with the local conditions. But this was only the beginning of a more radical process of self-searching in quest for identity. Transplanted social work did not seem to take roots in the local soil. But again, it was still doing a lot of good, and it was rapidly proliferating—on faith, or inertia, or both!

A number of developments later converged to cause a renewed pride in, and a closer identification with, Islam and its values in the region—as in all of the Muslim world. Some of these developments took place in the Western world it-self, incidentally, leading to a similar religious revival among the adherents of Christianity and other religions (Midgley & Sazenbach, 1989). Other developments were native to the region.

It is beyond the scope of this discussion to elaborate on these two types of developments in detail. Suffice it to point out a few of the trends that are shaping this new awareness.

1. The emergence of the new paradigm in physics pioneered by Einstein's work on relativity and Niels Bohr and Werner Heisenberg's work on quantum theory (Augros & Stanciu, 1984) provided a "New Vision of Reality" according to Capra (1982) that departed from the traditional materialistic biases of modern Western civilization. Capra tells us that classical physics was based on a mechanistic view of the world. "Matter was thought to be the basis of all existence, and the material world was seen as a multitude of separate objects assembled into a huge machine." Twentieth century physics brought about such conceptual revolutions that revealed the limitations of that mechanistic worldview. "The universe is no longer seen as a machine. . .but appears as a harmonious indivisible whole; *a network of dynamic relationships that include the human observer and his or her consciousness in an essential way*" (italics mine) (pp. 31–32).
2. The profound disillusionment with the cult of growth at any price and the surfacing of "the limits to growth" concept (Meadows et al., 1972) led to a questioning of the Western value system, which guides the development of its economic, political and social institutions.
3. The region became disillusioned with both the socialist and the liberal secularist systems of government after the dismal failures of both to improve the lot of the people. Gone with that was the naive infatuation with all that was Western.

Naturally, the only viable ideology to turn to was Islam, the religion of the majority of the population. Islam is an institutional religion: In Islam salvation requires that people live under the right institutional arrangements, just as it depends on the right beliefs and the right personal conduct (Ragab, 1980). So, although a Muslim is enjoined to be his brother's keeper voluntarily, this commandment is translated into legally binding commitments when necessary. (For example if a person starves to death in a specific community, all inhabitants share the responsibility for causing him to die because of their callousness. They communally have to pay his blood money). This, however, does not mean that Islam envisions a naive classless society. Private ownership of property is staunchly protected. But people are vehemently exhorted to give generously for the satisfaction of basic needs for all. However, as a safeguard against any reluctance to do so voluntarily, a legally binding minimum of 2.5 percent of their savings should be given as a religious duty to charitable purposes (*Zakat*).

Islam, then, has a lot to say about social work, because it has a lot to say about humankind, societal arrangements, and the universe in which humans live. Naturally, social work practice and education in the region—with this new self-confidence and sense of identity—had to turn to Islam for guidance. Humans, according to Islam, are created by *the One God* of all celestial religions. God is omniscient, omnipotent, and most merciful. He is in control over all of what He created, and He requires submission (*Islam*) to what he has prescribed for the benefit of humankind. The spiritual aspect of the human being (i.e., the way humans relate to their creator) is crucial to accurate understanding, or effective modification of their behavior. The relationship between humans and their Creator is a direct one—no priest or middleman is allowed. So, the quality of human life on earth or the fate of human beings in the hereafter basically depends on the quality of their faith, their conduct, as well as the grace of *the* Merciful God.

The Islamic reorientation of social work movement sought a synthesis between this sublime conception of humankind and their place in the universe on the one side, and the best of what the behavioral/social sciences have to say in this regard on the other. However, only rigorously verified observations and generalizations of these sciences would be accepted. Theoretical frameworks—basically conjecture and guesswork—are taken for what they really are and are replaced by more solid concepts derived from revelation. The Quran is directly attributed to God, as revealed to the Prophet Muhammad, with no scripture writers, narrators or translators tampering with the text. No serious researcher could question its validity as far as the way it reached us today from the early days of Islam. However, interpretation of the text is open to scholarship of jurists or any learned lay persons, with no self-assigned authority of a hierarchy of priests. So insights gained through this modified methodology could be a better guide for the practitioners—the advocates of this view feel (Ragab, 1993).

A lot of work has yet to be done before the results of this paradigmatic shift can be seen. The proponents of this new development in the field of social work education in the Middle East feel they may be at the threshold of a real scientific revolution, with all the dimensions and nuances associated with the emergence of such revolutions, as Kuhn (1962) has aptly described them.

RANGE AND STRUCTURE OF SOCIAL WORK EDUCATION

It should be clear from the foregoing historical review that very wide variations in the range and structure of social work education do exist among the different countries of the region. On the one extreme, we find countries like Egypt (and to some extent Saudi Arabia) with a full range of training programs from the associate of arts (AA) level to the PhD degree. On the other extreme, we find other countries such as Jordan with programs at the AA level only, or countries like Syria and Algeria with no formal identification with social work education as such. As far as numbers are concerned, we would find countries with systems that annually turn out thousands of qualified social workers, as is the case with Egypt; hundreds as with Saudi Arabia; or only scores of graduates, as is the case with some Gulf states. To prevent repetition, we will start with a somewhat detailed description of the current scene in Egypt, which will be followed by brief comparisons with the situation in other countries.

The Current Scene: Egypt

Independent Private Schools

Social work education in Egypt at its lower end is represented by four private Intermediate Institutes of social work. One of these is located in Cairo and another in Alexandria; both accept only female students. The other two institutes are located in Aswan and Suhag (upper Egypt) and are coeducational. These institutes offer an associate degree in social work to high school graduates after completion of two years of study. More than twenty-eight hundred assistant social workers graduated from these programs in 1991.[1] The better graduates of these institutes (with a grade level of 75 % or better) are allowed to continue their studies to obtain the BSW degree from Helwan University.

On a different plane, there are six private Higher Institutes of Social Work which offer the bachelor's degree in social work, after four years of courses and fieldwork. These institutes are independent of the university system. However, the Ministry of Higher Education regulates and supervises their activities. The degrees they confer are recognized as equivalent to those offered by Egyptian universities.

These institutes depend on the university-based schools to lend them lecturers to supplement their own limited number of faculty members. As private institutions sponsored by nonprofit organizations, they charge their students for tuition—which is kept artificially low by the government. This naturally reflects on the performance of these institutions. It shows in their perennially crowded classes and in the very large numbers of students assigned to each field instructor responsible for supervision of their fieldwork. Close to forty-four hundred persons graduated from these institutes in 1991, in comparison with only six hundred who graduated from university-based schools.[2]

University-Based Schools

Two schools of social work operate within the Egyptian university system, one in Helwan University and the other in Cairo University. Additionally, Alexandria University, through its graduate-level Institute of Social Sciences, offers advanced degrees in social work. The oldest and the more influential school is Helwan University's Faculty of Social Work in Cairo. The organizational structure of the school follows the traditional "methods" lines, consisting of departments of casework, group work, community organization and social planning. In addition, there is a catchall subdivision called the "fields of practice" department. However, the school offers its graduates a generic baccalaureate in social work which prepares them as general practitioners. Around three hundred students graduate from this school annually.

The Helwan school launched its graduate program, the oldest in the region, in 1968. This program offers the following degrees:

1. The higher diploma: Social workers with a BSW and some job experience join this program to further their knowledge in their chosen field of specialization. After one year of courses, they are granted the higher diploma in one of the major fields of practice, such as school social work, or medical social work. Graduates are seen as specialists in their chosen field.
2. The master's degree in social work: This program is comparable to similar MSW programs in the United States in some respects. Two years of course work, followed by an average of two years of work on a master's thesis, is required for completion of the degree. Students, however, specialize in one of the traditional methods: casework, group work, community organization or social planning.
3. The PhD degree in social work: Requirements for this degree include two years of course work and the preparation of a dissertation. Students are again expected to specialize in one of the traditional methods. Graduates of this program constitute the bulk of social work educators in the private higher institutes of social work in Egypt, in the Gulf states and in many countries in the region. At the same time, this school still sends a few junior faculty members for graduate education in the United States. This is meant to ensure that the school keeps abreast of developments in the field in that country.

The second school of social work operating within the Egyptian university system is Cairo University's Faculty of Social Work at Fayoum. Since inception, Cairo University has adhered to the European academic traditions. Its school of social work thus differs in many respects from the social work training institutions mentioned previously. Also, the school's recent origin (established 1984) has allowed it to experiment with some rather unconventional, and somewhat controversial ideas.

The Fayoum school, for example, comprises four departments: the methods, the fields, the community development and the social and behavioral sciences departments. The undergraduate program consists of two years of core courses, followed by two years of specialization courses in one of the first three departments (methods, fields, or community development). This constitutes a radical departure from the general practitioner model followed by all other schools.

The graduate program of that school also offers a higher diploma, the MSW and the PhD degree. The higher diploma is similar to that of Helwan University. The master's degree in one of the three specializations is conferred upon the completion of two years of courses and the preparation of a master's thesis. The doctoral program, however, is drastically different. No course work is required. The preparation of the dissertation is the only requirement for the PhD degree, again in one of the three specializations.

The University of Alexandria's Institute for Social Studies, a graduate studies organ of that university, offers a subspecialty in social work. It offers the MA and the PhD degrees in social work. Understaffed, and with no undergraduate program of its own to build upon, it has been able to attract only a very small number of students.

The newly established Departments of Social Work in Al-Azhar University differ from the patterns described in terms of the content of the curriculum, not the structure. The emphasis of these departments is on integrating Islamic concepts with modern scholarship in the field of social work. However, this reflects the intent, rather than the present content, of teaching in these departments.

Preservice and In-Service Training

Thus far, this discussion has focused on formal educational programs, now a word on preservice and in-service training. It was noted earlier that the backbone of professional social work practice in Egypt is the baccalaureate level worker. Because all BSW programs are geared to prepare their graduates to carry out general practitioner responsibilities, the major employers of these workers (Ministries of Social Affairs, Education, and Health) had to create their own training programs to orient newcomers to their field of practice and later to upgrade their skills on the job.

The Ministry of Social Affairs organizes a preservice training program that comprises fourteen weeks of lectures, with a focus on the mission of the ministry, its structure and the services it provides. In addition, the program includes two months of practical experience in the ministry's field offices. Two levels of in-service training are also organized, one for the front line workers and the other for supervisors and administrators (Badran, 1975).

The Ministries of Education and Health organize similar programs, but of much shorter duration. Because of the in-house nature of all of these training programs, undue emphasis is given to the day-to-day routines of doing the job, thereby perpetuating traditional ways of doing things. This pattern seems to strengthen the bureaucratic aspects of the job and to dampen innovation.

The Current Scene: The Gulf Area

Social work educational programs in Saudi Arabia are similar to those of Egypt, with a few differences. The baccalaureate is the basic training level in the kingdom. This degree, however, is offered through departments of social work or sociology and social work in the universities rather than in professional schools. Imam University in Riyadh, for example, has its own Department of Social Work, which turns out around forty BSWs annually. King Saud University in Riyadh has a Department of Social Studies, from which about 170 students graduate annually. Om-Alqura University in Mecca has also started its own Department of Social Work, which turns out a few score graduates a year—male and female.

A major exception to that rule is the Faculty of Social Work for Girls in Riyadh, a separate school which is part of a national governmental body for girls' education. This school trains around one hundred BSWs a year. Moreover, it has a graduate program, which annually enrolls about ten MSW students. Eleven PhD degrees have been awarded to graduates of the school as of 1995. King Saud University in Riyadh also has its own graduate program, which normally enrolls around fifteen students in its MSW program annually. It is also starting its new doctoral program in 1995.

The pattern in other Gulf States is also the same as far as the focus on the baccalaureate is concerned and in that social work education is provided through departments of social work or of sociology and social work. No graduate programs, however, exist in these countries. Most Gulf countries prefer to send their future faculty members to complete their graduate studies in the United States or England, rather than train them locally.

The Current Scene: Other Countries

Libya has seven intermediate institutes of social work. These institutes admit persons with junior high school education into a program of study for four years. They are granted an intermediate diploma, equivalent to the general high school certificate, which qualifies them to hold social work positions in the Ministry of Social Affairs. At a different level, BSW training takes place in the School of Applied Social Sciences in Alfatih University in Tripoli. This program replaces the social work department of the same university, which used to enroll the largest number of students in any department of social work in the region—outside Egypt. In 1982, for example, it enrolled more than 250 students (Hassanein, 1982).

The Sudan has a diversity of programs. University of Khartoum's Extramural Studies, through its Center of Social Work, organizes what is basically in-service training for government employees. It has two levels of programs. The first is the associate degree level which enrolls people with high school certificates. The duration of study is two years. The second is a one year program for people with an undifferentiated bachelor's degree (regardless of the specialization in their undergraduate years). These are granted a higher diploma in social work.

Omdurman Islamic University has a Department of Sociology and Social Work in its Girls College. This department offers the BSW, MSW and PhD degrees. At present the first PhD candidate is now preparing to complete the requirements of her degree. A program which helped staff many of Sudan's social work positions, however, is Cairo University's Khartoum Branch through its Department of Sociology, which offers its students only a single course in social work. A private institution, Al–Ahfad Community College for Girls, does the same through its Department of Family Studies.

Social work education in Lebanon takes place in and outside the universities at the BA level. Beirut University College offers—through its Department of Social Sciences—a degree in social work. École Sociale also offers social work training in the French language. The Lebanese University has recently started an undergraduate program which is identified with health care.

The emphasis in Jordan is on the associate degree in social work, which requires two years of study after high school. The Social Work Community College in Amman, recently renamed Princess Rahmah College of Social Work, is the only social work education facility in Jordan today.

Regional and International Assistance

Most regional and international assistance in the region is geared to preservice and in-service training of employees of the Ministries of Labor and Social Affairs. Under the umbrella of the Arab League, the Meeting of Ministers Responsible for Social Affairs in 1979 adopted the Strategy for Arab Social Action. In a report suggesting programs to implement that strategy, the Arab League's Department on Social Affairs concluded that "only qualified and specialized manpower can ensure the realization of the Strategy's ends. This is the real key to effective social action" (Arab League, 1983). But the report notes at the same time that data formally supplied by Arab countries reveal a general lack of qualified personnel in the field of social action and social work. To remedy the situation partially, the department only suggested and designed a variety of in-service training programs to be supported between 1984 and 1990.

United Nations organizations, particularly UNESCO and UNDP, have helped establish regional training and research centers in the region. Most salient among the activities of these centers is in-service training in the fields of social welfare and social development. UNESCO started with adult education but moved to community development as the organizing concept for its regional training centers. UNDP, in contrast, was interested in training for community development, but ended doing, in addition, a lot of training covering the whole range of social welfare service , in the most general sense of the term.

ACCREDITATION, CURRICULA AND RELATED ISSUES

Gatekeeping to the Profession

Since most social work education in the region takes place in governmental or government-supported institutions, no real accreditation issue arises. Degrees conferred by universities, or by other government sponsored programs, are automatically recognized by employers without further examination. Private schools of social work are regulated and supervised by Ministries of Higher Education. No independent bodies for accreditation exist.

Decisions pertaining to degree requirements, structure and sequencing of courses, or course contents reside with university and school administrative bodies, assisted by faculty committees—within the general framework of the applicable rules in the by-laws. Such formal rules give students no say in the process. Only the more progressive schools do informally seek some sort of feedback from the students. The tenure system allows faculty members to stay with the university permanently if they choose to, with no regard whatsoever to student enrollment in their courses. Promotions depend (almost) solely on published work.

In the case of the private schools of social work, Ministries of Higher Education perform most of the functions described, setting the rules for running the schools' educational program. The schools do not normally resent this. In return, the degrees they confer receive the same status and respectability as university degrees—as long as they are endorsed by the ministry.

Such stamp of government approval and recognition normally is enough for the employers of holders of these degrees—because most of the employers are themselves government agencies. The situation can best be seen as reflecting "demand," rather than "market" characteristics. Hardly any scrutiny of the differential quality of graduates of various schools is really done. The customer government agencies can order whatever number of degree holders they deem necessary. If budgets allow, graduates are employed on the presentation of proof of the degree. Some agencies may insist on interviewing job applicants, but only to screen out the more flagrant cases of unemployability. In very rare cases, a specific school may gain some reputation for excellence, in which case employers may give preference to graduates of that particular school.

Professional organizations are either nonexistent, or seriously diluted by the forced inclusion into their membership (by government decree) of graduates of sociology departments. In the more conservative countries of the region, anything remotely resembling unionization is politically suspect. In other, more liberal societies, however, because of political considerations, holders of other than social work degrees are grouped into the same professional organizations.

Many Gulf States are in the first category, with no professional organizations for social workers. Egypt exemplifies the second category. Although the first professional group, The Egyptian Society for Social Workers, was founded as early as 1940, that organization was unable to muster enough clout with the government to achieve formal recognition as "the" professional association of social workers. Pressure from sociology departments and their graduates, inter alia, prevented that organization from achieving any degree of control on licensing in the field.

A compromise solution was later reached with the creation by the government of the so-called Association of Social Professions. Membership in that organization is granted equally to holders of sociology and social work degrees. It is still a loosely organized group, with factional and personality considerations looming large among its interests. In some cases, it did intervene on behalf of some of its members facing unjustified charges by others. Rarely did this organization become involved in any malpractice cases, because malpractice charges rarely are contemplated against social workers. Clients are mostly underprivileged and inarticulate—and are hardly aware of any rights granted their "benefactors." This, however, may be an oversimplification of the situation, it may not hold for some countries. But in cases of misconduct by social workers in "primary" social agencies, the case is normally dealt with by administrators. In host settings, the normal procedures for dealing with allegations of misconduct by other personnel are applied to social workers, without intervention from outside bodies—except in highly controversial situations.

Curricula and Related Issues

The professional degree required for practice in most countries in the region is the baccalaureate. Even a cursory look at course offerings, course contents or textbooks used in undergraduate programs in the region would reveal plain similarities with what could be found in American universities, a quarter century ago! This should come as no surprise to anyone, in the light of the "diffusion" or "social technology transfer" hypothesis discussed earlier.

In the beginning phase of transfer, social work educators in the region found the American model of curriculum structuring very convenient, ready for copying. American textbooks also served as a basic source for Arabic language texts. These, however, neither were straightforward translations of specific texts, nor could possibly be authentic books written on the basis of indigenous experience or research. When applied in practice, concepts contained in such Arabized texts seemed remote, with a foreign, unpalatable taste. Practitioners were left on their own, trying and erring, with very little opportunity for accumulation of home-grown concepts or principles. The weakness of professional organizations did not help, either. Very little communication or professional exchange was taking place. So, the umbilical cord to the "mother" arena of practice and conceptual development in the United States had to be kept connected—as far as possible. Dependence on this source of professional knowledge became a fact of life for social work educators. However, after a few solid Arabic language textbooks appeared and after they became very widely used, the motivation for continuing to follow new developments in the field abroad waned. Books became stale and repetitive. The situation was exacerbated when very few scholarships for study abroad were available (particularly in Egypt) because of hard currency shortages—while no "effective" practice was taking place at home that could help generate a viable alternative. The same could be said with regard to course design and content. As the schools gained recognition by the government, they tended to continue on the same old path, with little incentive for change. Curriculum development in these schools receives little attention.

The standard BSW program today provides its students with the equivalent of three semesters of social and behavioral science courses. These consist of "separate" courses in psychology, sociology, social psychology, economics, political sciences and health sciences. Very little effort is directed to the integration of their concepts. It should be noted here that when the program is part of a sociology department (or even of a combined sociology and social work department) the curriculum is usually lopsided, becoming oversaturated with narrowly defined sociological courses.

These social/behavioral courses are supplemented with other courses designed to introduce students to basic cultural and ideological concepts commensurate with the particular political climate in the country under consideration. The contents of these courses range from factual-historical to political indoctrination. In some countries, basic Islamic religious concepts are stressed. In others nationalist sentiments are the focus of the courses.

The rest of the curriculum is devoted to professional courses and fieldwork. Professional courses follow the traditional "methods" and "fields of practice " model. So, invariably, programs include one or several courses each on casework, group work, community organization, administration and research. Also, there are courses in fields such as school social work, medical social work, family and child welfare, occupational social work, work with the handicapped, delinquency and crime, and so on. Other fields of practice are stressed in some countries but not in others.

The content of both types of courses, the social/behavioral sciences and the professional (social welfare/social work), is rather traditional. It hardly catches up with the new developments and insights in the courses' respective fields. It seems that the forces at work in the case of social/behavioral sciences are similar to those described in the case of social work. Even where newer perspectives are included, the "integration" of social work methods, for example, they are often misrepresented, or only given lip service without even grappling with their implications for education or practice. Although "methods" courses are each given an equal share of the curriculum, instructors and students relate more to direct practice courses. These courses are richer in case material. Local practice episodes are readily cited in class. Community work courses seem rather hollow and remote, lacking in indigenous experiences as referents.

Fieldwork receives somewhere between 15 % and 25 % of the total required hours. In most countries a "concurrent" rather than "block" field placement is used. Normally, third and fourth year students spend two days a week in social welfare agencies selected as fieldwork settings. Schools share with the agencies the responsibility for supervision of students in the field. Because very few social workers in the agencies qualify as instructors, faculty members from the schools are expected to contribute more actively to field "instruction." Agency workers are expected to provide to students opportunities for observation, give them access to direct work with clients, give some advice on the spot, and record hours spent in training.

Training for Research

The BSW is basically seen as a practice, rather than a research-oriented degree. Undergraduate curricula normally include at least one introductory course in social work research. Sometimes this is followed by a research practicum where students are required to design and actually implement empirical research under the guidance of their instructors.

In contrast, graduate work is research-oriented. The MSW and the PhD are basically the graduate student's visa for university teaching and research positions. In some universities with Continental traditions, the only requirement for the PhD degree is the completion of research work for the dissertation. Doctoral students in countries with graduate-level education in the region face a real challenge. They are expected to do social work research, rather than merely social research. But social work practice in these countries can hardly provide them with the pool of rich and meaningful practice experiences needed to do that kind of specialized research. In many cases , students first have to create their own practice "experiments" as their research focus. Those who are not willing to do so have to select research problems hardly distinguishable from those selected by their colleagues in psychology or sociology departments.

Arabic language textbooks on research widely used in the region are steeped in the traditional "empiricist" perspective. But in recent years, dissatisfaction with this tradition has been steadily mounting. The basic criticism directed to that empiricist orientation is its neglect of a significant segment of reality which is part and parcel of the human experience: that is, the spiritual aspects of the human being. In contrast, a human being, according to the Islamic religion, is an amalgam of nonempirical and empirical components. For that reason—the critics say—the traditional methods of science which succeeded magnificently in the study of the empirical physical world have failed miserably in the study of humans.

The basic assumptions on which the emerging alternative paradigm rests can be summed up in the following statements: "True" revelation can provide a theoretical guide to the explanation of the nonempirical aspects of humans. Hypotheses derived from this theoretical framework can be tested in the "total" reality, rather than the "empirical" reality. This should, of course, entail devising new and more relevant research methods and techniques sensitive to both types of phenomena—either directly or indirectly. If hypotheses are corroborated, then the theory gains in validity. If they are refuted, then two types of critical reviews are warranted. First, methodological procedures should be checked and rechecked for possible errors or flaws. Then, if the methodology proves impeccable, our human "understanding" of "true" revelation may be the reason for inconsistency. It should be revised to accommodate the "valid" observations (Ragab, 1991).

The basic assumption here is that there can be no conflict between "true" revelation and "valid" observations. This reminds us of the logic extended by Maimonides (c. 1190) to the effect that there can be no conflict between reason and faith "because both come from God" (Levi, 1975). One may risk adding that these insights may furnish the way to the cherished unification of the human experience: its mundane and its transcendental aspects. It should help researchers achieve epistemological integration and avoid the compartmentalization of self into the worldly and the religious. Although this may seem far-fetched, this approach may even gradually help religions shed some of the more flagrant inconsistencies with *total* reality, accumulated over millennia. All this, however, seems to hinge upon our ingenuity in tapping this total reality.

SUMMARY AND CONCLUSION

This chapter has dealt with the evolution of social work education in the Middle East. It is limited to the Muslim Arab core of that region. The influence of the American model of social work practice and education has been treated in some detail. The transfer of that model into the region is described in terms of a two-stage diffusion process, whereby concepts and institutions were first transferred from the United States to Egypt, and then later traveled from Egypt to most countries of the region—with the salient exception of some North African countries. It has been shown, on the other hand, that a process of reverse diffusion may now be taking place. With the application of Western models of practice in the Gulf area, they were found not to fit the local cultural realities—largely shaped by Islamic ideals. The "indigenization" movement matured into an Islamic reorientation of social work movement, which was exported back to Egypt, and is rapidly influencing social work education in that country.

The structure of social work educational systems in the region has been described in some detail. Most training programs in the region are university–based with a focus on the baccalaureate degree in social work, the basic entry level for practice. Curriculum organization, course content and textbook material have been shown to lag behind those found in the United States. At least a quarter century separates them.

A paradigmatic shift, however, that may be of broader interest seems to be taking place now. If social work education in the Middle East may have something to contribute to social work education in other countries of the world, it is to point out the inevitability of reconciling the human being's soul and body. Social work can hardly achieve its long-sought "effectiveness" in dealing with the problems of humankind by ignoring a major component of humans. Social work research and practice should strive to reach that true unification of the human being. Some Western social workers and psychotherapists have recently been coming to that realization (Maslow, 1977; Hess, 1980; Bergin, 1980,1983; Canda, 1988, Peile, 1988). However, evolutionist and secularist convictions held and expressed by many of those authors may have hampered a fuller exploration of the potential of these insights or their extension to reach their ultimate, logical end. The Middle East, the cradle of all celestial religions, may be once again trying to reach out to help humans in their eternal search for meaning and happiness.

NOTES

1. Data compiled by author, calculated on the basis of the Egyptian Ministry of Higher Education records.

2. Data compiled by author.

REFERENCES

Abdul-Aal, A.H.R. (1990). Recent trends in social work education and practice in the Arab World. In *Social Work in the Arab World and the Future.* Proceedings of the Third Annual Conference of the Faculty of Social Work in Fayoum (in Arabic) Fayoum, Egypt. In Arabic.

Al-Hassan, O.M. (1990) Contemporary issues in social work: the Sudanese experience. Proceedings of the Fourth Annual Conference, Faculty of Social Work, Helwan University, Cairo. In Arabic.

Al-Ibrahim, F.Y. & Hafiz, Z.A. (1988). Indigenization of school social work in Kuwait. Proceedings of the Second Annual Conference of the Faculty of Social Work, Helwan University, Cairo. In Arabic.

Al-Saud, A.F.T, (1988). *Social Work in Saudi Arabia.* Master's Thesis, Department of Social Studies, King Saud University, Riyadh. In Arabic.

Arab League. (1983). *Proposed programs towards implementation of the Strategy for Arab Social Action 1984-1990.* Tunis and Cairo: General Directorate for Social Affairs. In Arabic.

Augros, R.M. & Stanciu, G.N. (1984). *The New Story of Science.* Chicago: Gateway Editions.

Badran, H. (1975). Egypt's social service system. In Thurz, D. & Vigilante, J.L. (Eds.). *Meeting Human Needs.* London: George Allen & Unwin, pp. 28–68.

Bergin, A. (1980). Psychotherapy and religious values. *Journal of Consulting and Clinical Psychology, . 48*, 95–105.

Bergin, A. (1983). Religiosity and mental health. *Professional Psychology, 14*, 170–184.

Birks, C. (1987). Social welfare provision in France. In Ford, R. & Chakrabarti, M. (Eds.). *Welfare Abroad.* Edinburgh: Scottish Academic Press, pp. 66–98.

Canda, E.R. (1988). Spirituality, religious diversity and social work practice. *Social Casework, 69* , 238–247.

Canda, E.R. (1989). Religious content in social work education: a comparative approach. *Journal of Social Work Education, 25*, 1, 36–45.

Capra, F. (1982). *The Turning Point: Science, Society and the Rising Culture.* New York: Simon & Schuster.

Coughlin, B.J. (1970). Religious values and child welfare. *Social Casework, 51* 82–90.

Dudley, J.R. & Helfgott, C. (1990). Exploring a place for spirituality in the social work curriculum. *Journal of Social Work Education, 26*, 3, 287–294.

Encyclopedia Britannica. (1975). "The Middle East." Chicago: Encyclopedia Britannica.

Hammoud, H. (1988). Social work education in developing countries. *International Social Work, 31*, 195–210.

Hassanein, S.A. (1982*). Introduction to social work.* Cairo: Tigara. In Arabic.

Hess, J. (1980). Social work's identity crisis. *Social Thought, 6*, 59–62.

Hussein, S.A. (1989). *Models of Social Work.* Kuwait: Al-Moalla. In Arabic.

Joseph, M.V. (1988). Religion and social work practice. *Social Casework, 69,* 443–452.

Kuhn, T.S (1962). *The Structure of Scientific Revolutions.* Chicago: University of Chicago Press.

Levi, A.W. (1975). History of western philosophy. In *The New Encyclopedia Britannica,* 15th ed. Chicago: Encyclopedia Britannia.

Loewenberg, F.M. (1988). *Religion and Social Work Practice in Contemporary American Society.* New York: Columbia University Press.

Marty, M. (1980). Social service: godly and godless. *Social Service Review, 54,* 463 - 481.

Maslow, A.(1977). A theory of metamotivation: the biological rooting of the value-life. In Chang, Hung-Min (Ed). *The Healthy Personality,* 2nd ed. New York: Van Nostrand, pp. 28–48.

Meadows, D.H. et al. (1972). *The Limits to Growth.* New York: Universe Books.

Midgley, J. and Sazenbach, P. (1989). Social work, religion and the global challenge of fundamentalism. *International Social Work, 32,* 273–278.

Osman, A.F., Ismael, M.H., & Abdul-Aal, A.R. (1984). *Introduction to Social Work.* Cairo: Anglo-Egyptian. In Arabic.

Owais, S. (1973). *The Emergence of the Social Work Profession in Egypt: A Personal History.* Cairo. In Arabic.

Peile, C. (1988). Research paradigms in social work: from stalemate to creative synthesis. *Social Service Review, 62,* 1–19.

Ragab, I. (1980). Islam and development. *World Development, 8,* 513–521.

Ragab, I. (1990). How can social work really take roots in developing countries. *Social Development Issues, 12,* (3).

Ragab, I. (1991). The scientific method from an Islamic perspective. Paper presented at the seminar on Islamic Perspectives on Social Work. Cairo: International Institute for Islamic Thought. In Arabic.

Ragab, I. (1993). Islamic perspectives on theory building in the social sciences. *The American Journal of Islamic Social Sciences, 10,* 2–22.

Shihab, Bahigah A., (1982). *Introduction to Social Work.* Musol: University of Musol Press.

Social Work Community College Manual. Jordan: Amman. In Arabic.

Spencer, S.W. (1957). Religious and spiritual values in social casework practice. *Social Casework, 38,* 519–528.

17

ISRAEL

David Guttmann and Ben-Zion Cohen

HISTORY OF SOCIAL WORK AND SOCIAL WORK EDUCATION IN ISRAEL

The end of the past decade and the beginning of the present one have witnessed major demographic and social changes in Israel. Between 1989 and 1991 the population grew by 10 percent, mostly because of mass immigration of Jews from the Soviet Union and Ethiopia. Since its establishment in 1948, Israel has maintained an open-door, instant citizenship policy with regard to Jewish immigration. This policy, known as "the in gathering of the exiles," has resulted in sporadic and often unanticipated waves of immigration over the years, with the social work establishment providing services and many of the necessary resources for the newcomers. From 600,000 in 1948, Israel's population has grown to over five million. Many of the immigrants have been refugees from persecution and most have arrived lacking basic educational, vocational, and social resources. They have engaged the social services not only in the immediate sphere of immigrant absorption, but in the related areas of economic aid, health, mental health, criminal justice, housing, employment, and services to special populations and age groups.

Before the period of modern Jewish settlement began in the last quarter of the nineteenth century, the small Jewish communities in Palestine were concentrated almost exclusively in the holy cities of Jerusalem, Safed, Tiberias, and Hebron. These communities of pious Jews survived mainly on charity collected from Jewish communities abroad. As the first Zionist pioneers arrived, driven by the dream of redeeming the ancient homeland, they established an ethic of self-reliance and, rejecting the notions of charity prevalent among the older communities, established a labor union and collected funds from all workers for mutual assistance. At this time, the first women's associations for self-help and child care were created; these groups laid the foundations for the extensive system of day care and preschool kindergartens, health and maternity care, which are an important force for social welfare in Israel to the present day. The women who worked in these organizations to improve the circumstances of women and their children were the first modern social workers in this country (Neipriss, 1989).

With the approach of the Great Depression, the Jewish population in Palestine, numbering some 400,000 souls, experienced unexpected poverty, unemployment, and lack of adequate shelter for many of the victims of the 1929 Arab uprising. The economic outlook was bleak and the leaders of the Jewish community decided on a major innovation: they invited Henrietta Szold, a well-known American social worker and Zionist leader, in 1931, to become a member of the provisional government and to establish a department of social welfare. Szold introduced modern American and British welfare concepts to the area and built a system of service delivery based on these concepts. Principles such as the sharing of responsibility for the welfare of the poor with the local authorities date back to that time.

Henrietta Szold placed great value on the work of volunteers but insisted that the welfare departments be staffed by trained professionals. With the help of leading social workers from the United States and Germany, she opened the first training course for social workers in 1934. The course was for one year and aimed at preparing its graduates for work in public welfare and immigrant absorption. At the same time, she established a tradition of annual social work conferences for the exchange of ideas and the strengthening of the collective commitment to the profession and its values. At these conferences Henrietta Szold outlined her professional creed, emphasizing human rights, social security, and the centrality of the family.

In 1948 the state of Israel came into being. Immediately, seven Arab countries attacked. As the War of Independence raged, great waves of refugees from the Holocaust and from Arab countries flooded the gates. Clearly, the existing social workers, even with an additional dozen completing the training program each year, could not possibly meet the challenge. The young state was fighting for survival, but somehow resources were mobilized to send tens of students to France and to the United States for training in social work.

Ten years after statehood, in 1958, the Hebrew University in Jerusalem opened the first university-based school of social work in Israel. This event signified that social work had attained the status of a profession to be taken seriously by the other helping professions and by Israeli society. It also reflected awareness by Israel's social workers themselves of the need for university training.

The Hebrew University invited Eileen Blackey, a noted social work educator from the United States, to organize the curriculum, recruit faculty from local talent and potential immigrants, and help launch the BSW program. Professor Blackey organized a team of instructors, nearly all of whom had advanced social work degrees from the United States, and twenty students were admitted to the first class, thus initiating academic training for social workers in Israel.

The first group of social work educators at the Hebrew University built a curriculum emphasizing the role of social work as society's instrument for promoting social justice, particularly distributive justice. Their aim was to train students who would use their knowledge and skills to improve the quality of life for all citizens, protect the weak and helpless, and serve the special needs of disadvantaged populations. Consequently, the curriculum, and especially the first two years of the three year program, concentrated on teaching social structure and dynamics, political economy and poverty-related issues; the theoretical bases of practice, social policy, research and statistics; and the methods, skills, and values of generalist social work practice. The third year of studies centered on a problem area, such as family welfare, criminal justice, rehabilitation, physical and mental health, or community work. For example, the third year family welfare concentration offered courses in personality theory, cultural aspects of family life, family dynamics and research, social policy on family issues, family dynamics and research, and intervention techniques with families. Social science concepts and knowledge related to intervention skills were taught at all levels of the program, moving from the general to the particular.

During the 1960s three more schools of social work were opened at Israeli universities (Tel-Aviv, Bar-Ilan, and Haifa) and in 1982 a fifth, at Ben Gurion University in Beer-Sheva, serving the southern part of Israel, was established. As the new schools opened their doors, and as Israeli society became more middle-class-oriented, clinical emphases in the curriculum began to compete with the older social justice emphases. This process, taking place at all of the schools, is a source of much debate to the present day.

The shift in orientation toward greater emphasis on clinical practice and mental health has been analyzed by Abraham Doron, one of the pioneer social work educators at the Hebrew University. Doron (1989) attributes the growing preoccupation with mental health to four factors:

1. The attempt by front-line social workers in public welfare to escape the harsh conditions still prevailing in many of the agencies
2. The influence of American social work with its emphasis on medical-model and psychiatric approaches to care
3. The growing impact of the free-market economy on social work, favoring clients who can pay for services
4. The erosion of social work's basic values, along with a general decline in prestige for the services provided by the Israeli version of the welfare state

Regarding this last factor, Guttmann and Cohen (1992) have written:

By 1970 [in Israel] the welfare-state structure of entitlements was firmly in place. The working- and middle-class population consumed the services eagerly, despite chronic grumbling about bureaucratic inefficiencies in the delivery of services. During the 1970's, as the society shifted subtly in the direction of a market economy, the welfare system was consistently de-emphasized (the Ministry of Welfare was merged with the Ministry of Labor in 1977). On the other hand, the government encouraged the accelerated development of privatized and informal social support networks as cost–effective instruments for providing services to persons in need (Auslander & Litwin, 1988; Fischer, 1982; Biegel, 1985; Meyer, 1985). This was the environment in which today's social work students were growing up, well fed, well clothed, well housed, and unaware that other children were growing up differently.

Indeed, the pressure for greater clinical content seems to come largely from students and from the field. Many of the faculty would prefer a stronger emphasis on the social justice aspects of social work.

One of the blessings of the move toward a more clinical orientation has been a quickening of the process of professionalization. This development, along with the growing number of graduates and the corresponding growth of the professional association (which today numbers some seven thousand), precipitated the introduction of higher degrees in social work education. For each of the four veteran schools of social work MA (MSW) programs were approved in rapid succession by the Council on Higher Education.

JEWISH TRADITION AND SOCIAL WORK

Many of the underlying principles of modern social work and social welfare can be traced to the Jewish teachings on social justice, human rights, and mutual responsibility as expounded in Biblical, Talmudic, and Rabbinic texts over the centuries. Five of the Ten Commandments aim directly at the regulation of relations between persons; they have been regarded in Jewish law and tradition as foundations of both justice and caring. The Fifth Commandment, for example, directing us to honor father and mother, is universally accepted as the basis of filial responsibility for elderly parents. In Jewish tradition, however, to "honor" parents entails more than fulfilling financial obligations and providing physical care. The method in which these acts are performed, the psychological and emotional aspects of care, are no less crucial. The concept of "honor" includes the obligation that both giver and receiver feel the respect which is mutually bestowed. Care must be rooted in sensitivity; food may keep an old person alive, but only respect and reverence will make his or her life meaningful in old age (Blech, 1977).

The Prophet Micah (6:8) presents the Divine command that every human being perform good deeds and virtuous behavior, practice justice and love kindness. The Torah and the Prophets as well as the Codes of Jewish Law place individual and communal responsibility for the poor, the ill, the aged, the orphan, the widow, and the stranger at the center of the social and religious obligations of the nation. According to the Ethics of the Fathers (1:2), the three pillars of existence are <u>Torah</u> (learning), <u>Avoda</u> (worship), and <u>Gmilut Has-sadim</u> (righteous deeds). The latter concept refers not to voluntary beneficence but, like learning and worship, to fulfillment of a Commandment. This commandment is not limited to contributing money. According to the Rabbinic literature, it also includes feeding the hungry, clothing the naked, burying the dead and comforting mourners, visiting the sick, redeeming the captive, educating the orphan and sheltering the homeless, and providing dowries for poor maidens. The notion of "charity," in the sense of giving when not obligated, is foreign to Jewish thought. In Jewish Law giving to the needy is an obligation; they have a right to help from the more fortunate.

Maimonides (1135–1204) taught that there are eight levels of giving to the needy, ranked according to virtuousness:

1. The first, least virtuous, is to give, but grudgingly
2. To give, ungrudgingly, but less than you can afford
3. To give, but only after being asked
4. To give before being asked
5. To give without knowing the identity of the beneficiary
6. To give without the beneficiary knowing the identity of the benefactor
7. To give, without the beneficiary or the benefactor knowing the identity of the other
8. To enable the needy to become self-supporting, by arranging a gift or loan, procuring work, or entering into partnership (Maimonides, 1180).

Maimonides' eighth and highest form of giving contains the seed of the modern concept of rehabilitation. The records of Jewish communities throughout the world, from medieval to modern times, indicate that many of the communal efforts were indeed conceived in that spirit; one of the most persistent features of Jewish communal life has been the free loan fund. These free loan funds are active to the present day, particularly in the religious community, and many of them loan not only cash but also such necessities as home medical equipment (Jaffe et al., 1991).

The influence of Jewish thought on social work values and principles has been mostly via Christianity and secular ethical teachings. The question of direct impact–whether there has been or should be a distinctly Jewish social work–has not been resolved. A much-debated paper on this topic was published in 1982 by Harris Chaiklin, an influential American-Jewish social worker who is a frequent visitor to Israel. Chaiklin, after a critical review of social work and social work education in Israel, writes of "the failure to develop a social work education founded in the Jewish ethic. Western oriented literature stresses such concepts as individualism and confidentiality. A Jewish oriented social worker 'should' stress family, community, and openness" (p.40). Published (Gidron, 1983; Mittwoch, 1983; Prager, 1988) and unpublished responses to Chaiklin's criticisms and suggestions debated both his assumption that a social work based on Jewish ethics was needed and his notions of how, if invented, it might differ from Western social work. In practice, some of the BSW programs include a course on Jewish values as they relate to social work, and the school at Bar-Ilan, the only university in Israel under religious auspices, requires a full year of Jewish studies before social work studies commence.

THE RANGE AND STRUCTURE OF SOCIAL WORK EDUCATION IN ISRAEL

All universities in Israel are state-supported, their budgets distributed by the Council on Higher Education. The council is a public forum of academic and nonacademic representatives, meeting together and in subcommittees, anchored in the Ministry of Education; its composition and functions are determined by law. The council's approval is necessary for all new academic departments and degree granting programs within the existing universities, as well as for the creation of new universities. The gatekeeping function of the council, as well as its generally conservative orientation, have resulted in an overall lack of budgetary support for program innovation and curriculum development. The schools obtain financial support for these functions through such revenue-generating activities as continuing education and their own fund-raising efforts. Recent grants from foundations include funding for developing a new community-organization curriculum and for planning a new PhD program at one of the universities.

The MA programs have been growing steadily in size and importance since the Baerwald School in Jerusalem initiated the first graduate program in social work in 1970. The enrollments of the four MA programs (Hebrew, Tel-Aviv, Haifa, Bar-Ilan Universities) increased 300 to 400 percent during the 1980s and there are presently some five hundred students in Israel working toward the MA. Haifa University, for example, where the MA program began in 1974, had 180 students in its MSW program in the 1991–92 academic year; the School of Social Work had the second largest master's program in the university. At Haifa, each year a few outstanding BSW graduates are admitted directly into the MA program, but otherwise the graduate student is nearly always a person who has acquired several years of field experience and has received his or her employer's consent for time off (and in some cases, tuition aid) to enable him or her to return to the university and undertake graduate studies while continuing to work. To accommodate these working students, the MA programs attempt to concentrate the scheduling of courses so as to minimize commuting to and from home, work, and school.

Although there has been significant variation across time and among schools, in contrast to the BSW curriculum, which has most often proceeded according to a generalist model, the MSW programs have typically provided for specialization by fields of practice. In part, this has been in response to the need to plan courses that will address the practice needs of advanced practitioners. These courses must also provide intellectual stimulation, strengthen and enrich the base of social work knowledge, and–despite the fact that they are taught by much of the same faculty–not recycle the course content of the BSW program. Virtually all the MA students have completed the BSW just a few years before and justifiably expect course content to be both original and more advanced than the material they studied as undergraduates.

At Haifa University the MA curriculum includes four specializations: clinical social work, family, organization/administration, and health/rehabilitation. Within each specialization are thesis-track students, who must complete thirty-eight hours of coursework and a thesis, and non-thesis-track students, who do fifty semester hours of courses and a comprehensive final examination. The courses encompass research, administration, and social sciences as well as required and elective courses within the field of specialization. All MA students must also complete a two semester practicum with fifty hours of individual supervision; in most cases they are allowed to choose both the setting and the supervisor, contingent upon approval by the responsible faculty person. The supervisors are paid by the school and are required to submit periodic evaluations. Within the clinical specialization, in the late 1980s a subspecialization in family therapy was developed. Students enrolled in this program take not only special courses in family therapy, but also a more extensive practicum: they must complete 125 hours of supervised fieldwork in settings devoted exclusively to family therapy. This meets the requirement of the Israel Family Therapy Association, which credentials family therapists. Practicum grades are pass/fail and the practicum does not carry academic credits.

The family therapy program at Haifa is an exception to Chaiklin's (1982) observation that the graduate programs at Israeli schools of social work prepare neither advanced practitioners (they are not, in Chaiklin's view, sufficiently practice–oriented) nor future faculty members (they are not a gateway to doctoral studies). All the schools now require a doctorate from candidates for faculty appointments, although some of the veteran faculty members were hired with MA or MSW degrees and were subsequently granted tenure.

Most Israeli social workers holding doctoral degrees have obtained them abroad but in recent years the number of doctoral degrees in social work granted in Israel has been increasing. In some Israeli universities, doctoral studies are conducted on the American model; thus, the doctoral programs in social work at Bar-Ilan and Tel-Aviv universities represent the third degree level at the respective schools of social work. At the Hebrew University in Jerusalem, where doctoral studies are reminiscent of the European model, the doctoral student submits a proposal to the university and his or her program of study and research is individually tailored, with departmental boundaries largely irrelevant and with no preplanned curriculum.

CONTINUING EDUCATION

During the past decade all five schools of social work have expanded their continuing education programs, reflecting the needs of social workers to update and revitalize their knowledge and skills, broaden their horizons, and gain access to new materials for use in practice. A growing body of practitioners attend courses, lectures, workshops and seminars within the framework of continuing education. Regular faculty teach many of the courses, but the continuing education departments also use the services of visiting professors, administrators, advanced practitioners, and faculty from other schools of social work.

The offerings vary from school to school, but all offer both long- and short-term programs, usually on a one-day-per-week basis. There are, for example, two year programs providing specialized training for family therapists, group facilitators, and administrators of institutional facilities for the elderly; one year programs for social workers who work with specific age cohorts or special populations, such as violent spouses, the retarded or the addicted, or who work with paraprofessionals or volunteers; and, a wide variety of one semester courses offering in-depth analysis of policy issues or innovative models of intervention. Workshops and seminars are most often devoted to a specific topic such as techniques of written communication for practitioners.

Participants in continuing education pay tuition, frequently provided or subsidized by their employers, which covers part of the cost. The more ambitious programs, however, are most often supported by outside funding agencies such as government ministries, municipal welfare departments, the Israel Association of Social Workers, organizations such as the Association for Development of Services to the Aged, and a wide range of social service agencies. The funds generated by the continuing education programs are an important source of revenue for the schools. Successful completion of continuing education programs also entitles the practitioner to modest monetary benefits in most instances.

Continuing education also contributes to maintaining the two-way relationship between the schools and the field. Educators, administrators, and practitioners meeting under the umbrella of continuing education work together in a shared effort to   develop new knowledge, contribute to existing knowledge, expand and enrich practice skills, deepen the commitment of the profession to ethics and values, and enhance accountability for quality practice.

THE STUDENT BODY

All applicants to the undergraduate programs at the five schools of social work must take the Inter-University Psychometric Entrance Examination. Each school, in addition, may establish an admissions committee which sets the minimum passing grade on the psychometric examination and may also establish procedures for additional screening of applicants with respect to their suitability for social work studies. Applicants must also pass an English proficiency examination; if they do not, they take additional English language courses when they begin their social work studies.

Thirty years ago no one doubted that students entered social work school because they had decided to become social workers. They went to the university because that is where one learns to be a social worker. Today, motivation is a moot subject. Many of our students appear to be the sons and daughters (about 75 % daughters) of middle-class families whose routine life-course includes a period of university studies. Once having decided to attend university, they choose among the majors the university offers and for which they can qualify. They do not arrive on our doorstep burning with ambition to become social workers. Thus, the instilling of that ambition and the ideals of the profession has become a major challenge to social work education, along with socialization to the profession and the imparting of knowledge and skills.

A study of undergraduate social work students in Israel (Guttmann & Cohen, 1992) found that only one-quarter regarded the promotion of social justice as their goal in becoming social workers. The desire to do casework in a clinical setting was the most prominent motivation. In their perceptions of poverty, its causes and cures, the social work students were not significantly different from other students at the university.

Minorities are represented in social work education in approximately the same proportion as in the general population. Arab students are generally younger than their Jewish counterparts because they are exempt from the military service which nearly all Jewish students do (two years for females, three years for males) before entering university. According to Guttmann and Cohen (1992), the Arab students rank themselves as lower in socioeconomic status than do the Jewish students, their parents have less education, they come from larger families, and the percentage of male students among them is considerably higher than among the Jews. In their perceptions of poverty the Arab students, like the Jews, exhibit great ambivalence, but their attitudes are quite different. While 25.6 percent of the Jews ranked poverty as the leading social problem, only 8.3 percent of the Arabs made this choice (ironically, this reflects both long-term acceptance of poverty in the Arab community and steady economic progress in recent years). On the other hand, 26.0 percent of the Jewish students, but only 7.9 percent of the Arabs regarded the major cause of poverty as the poor themselves. Similarly, more Jewish (83.7 %) than Arab (59.0%) students blamed the unemployed for their plight.

THE FACULTY

Most of the social work educators in Israel received their undergraduate training at the local schools, some also did their MA degrees here, but most attained their doctorates abroad, mostly in the United States, Canada, and England. University standards require a steady flow of research and publication, and the struggle for tenure (after five years of successful service) is as harsh and demanding as in any American or European university. A good command of the English language is a necessity because publication in Hebrew, as it reaches a limited audience, is less valued.

A special problem affecting all the schools of social work is the shortage of senior faculty: associate and full professors. The first generation of social work educators is now reaching retirement age (sixty-eight) and their replacement by younger faculty advancing to these levels is not sufficient to meet the needs of the expanding schools. As a result, the competition among the schools in recruiting senior faculty is keen. As more "homegrown" PhDs enter the system, this problem may be alleviated. Meanwhile, the schools try to compensate for the present shortage by "importing" visiting professors from abroad, many of whom arrive for up to one year with the support of the Fulbright Commission's program for faculty exchange and development. Usually, these professors do not teach undergraduates because of the language problem, but in the MA programs some courses are taught in English by the visiting faculty.

It should be noted here that most social work faculty in Israel are on the academic track and their universities expect them to publish regularly in Israel and abroad. The quantity of academic and professional books and papers published each year is impressive, but only a small fraction is on the topic of social work education.

About ten years ago the Israel Council of Social Work Education came into being. The members are the five heads of the schools and a representative of the American Joint Distribution Committee (a philanthropic institution which funds many special activities of the council, such as the publication of social work textbooks in Hebrew), a secretary and a treasurer. The participants meet monthly and share information on new programs and resources. The council also sponsors conferences, on an annual or biannual basis, for social work educators and field instructors.

The schools are independent with respect to programs and funding, and the decisions reached by the council are nonbinding recommendations. Nevertheless, the prevailing atmosphere is one of close cooperation and the council has initiated a range of projects important to all the schools. One example is the survey completed in 1993 on personnel needs for the coming decade.

The member schools pay an annual fee to the council (currently about $650). These funds are used for the regular functioning of the council and as support for participation of its representative in the various meetings of the International Association of Schools of Social Work.

RESEARCH AND SOCIAL WORK EDUCATION IN ISRAEL

Research plays an important role in social work education in Israel. Undergraduate programs have traditionally required six semester hours of research and at least two of statistics (Lazar, 1991). The sequence is designed to provide the student with the knowledge and skills necessary to consume research intelligently and to conduct the less sophisticated forms of survey and evaluation research projects. Because research is important not only for these practical reasons, but also because the study of research promotes the use of scientific method and its inherent logic, many faculty members would like to see more research courses at all levels of social work education. According to this viewpoint, social work should not be content to present itself to the university community as a profession; we need to establish our credentials as a profession anchored in a discipline. An enhanced role for research in social work education would advance this cause.

At the MA level, the research component is clearly more important for thesis-track students than for those on the nonthesis track. The former will typically have required courses in advanced research method, advanced statistics, and computer applications, as well as a prethesis seminar. Nonthesis students will also be expected to participate in some research courses. At Haifa University the required course for nonthesis MA students is called "Applied Research," and while it varies in form and content according to the faculty member teaching it, it is usually conceived as an extension of the undergraduate research sequence. The expectations of the thesis student are far less ambiguous; he or she needs to be provided with the basic tools for the thesis research. The nonthesis student has no such clearly defined need and in many cases is not highly motivated for additional study of research method.

SOCIAL WORK EDUCATION AND THE PROFESSION IN ISRAEL

There is no licensing procedure for social workers in Israel as exists, for example, for psychologists. The subject has been under discussion at least since the Vitkon Committee recommended in 1984 that the licensing of social workers be part of a legislation package to establish standards for the profession

(Spiro, 1991). Various groups within the social work establishment are presently considering a proposal that a social work license be granted to those who successfully complete a one year post-BSW supervised, paid internship. The Israel Association of Social Workers, which functions as both trade union and professional association, is actively involved in the planning of this innovation. Meanwhile, pending additional legislation regarding the licensing of psychotherapists, social workers in private practice are not permitted to present themselves as psychotherapists and third party payments are allowed or disallowed at the discretion of the third party. Nevertheless, the number of social workers in private practice has been increasing slowly but steadily.

The Ministry of Labor and Social Affairs maintains a registry of social workers, with registration contingent on receipt of a degree from one of the five schools of social work in Israel or from a recognized institution abroad. According to official policy, governmental and government supported bodies may employ only social workers who are listed in the registry. Implementation, however, is lax and many qualified social workers are unaware of the existence of the government registry. In the nongovernmental sector, including many municipal and local organizations, registration is not required for hiring. Within the public sector in Israel, where nearly all our graduates seek employment, the beginning salaries of BSW social workers compare favorably with those of other professionals with undergraduate training. This is particularly true in the municipalities, where many of the public welfare offices are now offering increased salaries and benefits. Unlike most other professionals, however, social workers face very limited opportunity to move into for-profit workplaces where salaries are higher. Moreover, because the profession has consistently emphasized starting salaries over many years of wage negotiations, the wages in the upper part of the scale do not compare favorably with those of other professional groups. In any case, it seems that low wages have become part of the lore of social work, and the belief that they will forever be underpaid and overworked is part of what students acquire in social work school.

Changing the image of social work as a low paid occupation, as well as changing the reality of unsatisfactory compensation for veteran public sector social workers, is hampered by the predominance of women in the profession. At least 80 percent of social workers in Israel are women and few of them are primary wage earners in their families. The tax structure (Israel has one of the highest income taxes in the world) renders the size of a second salary in a middle-class family less than crucial to the family's standard of living. The lack of progress in improving the salary situation has, in turn, had an adverse effect on the size and quality of the recruitment pool for social work training.

The consumerist attitudes taking hold in Israel in recent years have increased the pressure on social workers for more direct accountability to their client constituencies. Simultaneously, the accelerated penetration of the social services by information technology has created more pressure for accountability to the bureaucrats and money managers of the political establishment. Some veteran social workers regard these developments as a pull away from independence; others have seen them as a push toward greater responsibility. In either case, today's social workers need professional rather than instrumental authority to enhance their status and advance their cause. The demand for greater opportunities for graduate and continuing education reflects their understanding of this reality.

Malpractice suits against professionals are not as widespread in Israel as they are, for example, in the United States. Only an occasional case is reported in the press, and typically it will be for gross incompetence by a physician or medical facility. Scandals and unethical behavior, on the other hand, are daily fare for the printed and electronic media. Lawyers, politicians, bankers, and corporate managers are the most frequent players in the scandals that may involve theft or embezzlement, illicit sex or violence, abuse of authority, or conspiratorial behavior against the public interest. Social workers, although many occupy positions of power with considerable opportunity for abuse, have virtually never been tainted by scandal. This may be because of the type of person attracted to the profession, but it may be attributable, at least in part, to the accent on ethics in social work education.

CONTEMPORARY CURRENTS IN ISRAEL AND SOCIAL WORK EDUCATION

Recent developments in the political economy of Israel, including privatization of industries previously under governmental control and liberalization of currency and trade regulations, have reflected changes in the ideological position of many of Israel's citizens and leaders. Capitalistic attitudes and programs are more acceptable today than they were in the past. On the other hand, many of the socialist beliefs survive. Thus, while public agencies are now encouraged to contract with private firms providing privatized services to such populations as the elderly, the disabled, and the addicted, there has also been an increased sensitivity, prodded by the media, to the plight of the victims of capitalist enterprise, particularly the unemployed.

Despite double digit unemployment, one rarely hears of an unemployed social worker in Israel. Indeed, many positions are vacant, especially in outlying areas. Social workers, like most Israelis, are reluctant to move out of the big cities. The move is even less likely to take place if the social worker is the secondary wage earner. One response of the schools of social work has been retraining programs for university educated new immigrants from the Soviet Union. Many of the immigrants have professions not suitable for Israel (forestry engineers, for example) and since they presumably do not have roots in the overpopulated cities, the programs are retraining them for social work positions in the hope that they will be attracted to the small towns and rural areas where social workers are most needed.

The network of social services in Israel is staffed almost exclusively by university trained social workers and it is, relative to most Western countries, a wide net. It includes much of the criminal justice system, such as probation, parole, and community corrections functions, as well as a wide range of mental health services in institutions, in the community, and in the military. The graduates of schools of social work occupy positions at all levels, from direct service providers to top level executives. Although social work, as a profession, has not been particularly effective as a political pressure group, many individual social workers have been politically active in causes related to their work (Cohen, 1987). Moreover, a number of social workers have entered political life and attained prominence as municipal councilors, mayors, and members of the Knesset (the parliament of Israel). One trained social worker, Dr. Israel Katz, was minister of welfare from 1977 to 1980.

Assuming present trends continue, we can expect the next decade to be a time of consolidation and continued progress for social work and social work education in Israel. The distinction between BSW and MA level practitioners is sharpening both in the profession, as a new salary scale is being negotiated and job stratification within agencies increases, and in the academic communities, as the universities expand their advanced degree programs at the schools of social work. It would appear that the future structure of the profession here will diverge considerably from that of those Western countries where advanced degrees most often signify movement into administration or private practice. In Israel we are witnessing the emergence of a cadre of advanced practitioners in the public sector, many of whom take on supervisory responsibilities without abandoning direct practice.

This model seems to have special appeal for middle range developing countries. Israeli social work educators are becoming increasingly active in Third World and Eastern European countries and in international bodies such as the International Association of Schools of Social Work, the International Federation of Social Workers, and the International Association of Social Welfare. As these trends continue and as more "homegrown" PhDs join the faculties of the schools of social work, we hope to see the social work profession in Israel gain prestige and status for the mutual benefit of educators, practitioners and, most importantly, our clients.

REFERENCES

Auslander, G.K. & Litwin, H. (1988). Social networks and the poor: toward effective policy and practice. *Social Work, 33*, 234–238.

Biegel, D.E. (1985). The application of network theory and research to the field of aging. In Sauer, W. & Coward, R. (Eds.). *Social Support Networks and the Care of the Elderly.* New York: Springer-Verlag, pp. 251-273.

Blech, B. (1977). Judaism and gerontology. *Tradition, 16*(4), 62–78.

Chaiklin, H. (1982). Social work education in Israel: an analysis and some suggestions. *Journal of Jewish Communal Service, 59,* 35–42.

Cohen, B.Z. (1987). Political activism of social workers: a cross-national replication. *Journal of Social Work and Policy in Israel, 1,* 51–64.

Doron, A. (1989). The social image of social work. *Society and Welfare* (Hebrew), 10, 170–178.

Fischer, C. (1982). *To Dwell Among Friends: personal Networks in Town and City.* Chicago: University of Chicago Press.

Gidron, B. (1983). Comment on "Social work education in Israel: An analysis and some suggestions." *Journal of Jewish Communal Service, 59,* 259–262.

Guttmann, D. & Cohen, B.Z. (1992). Teaching about poverty in Israeli schools of social work. *International Social Work, 35,* 49–63.

Jaffe, E.D. et al. (1991). The free loan funds of Jerusalem: a social and economic network for providing supplemental income. *Society and Welfare* (Hebrew), *12,* 74–90.

Lazar, A. (1991). Faculty, practitioners, and student attitudes toward research. *Journal of Social Work Education, 27,* 34–40.

Maimonides. (1180). Hilchot matnot aniyim (Laws of giving to the needy). In *Mishneh Torah,* Ch. X, paragraphs 7–14.

Meyer, C. (1985). Social supports and social workers: collaboration or conflict? (editorial). *Social Work, 30,* 291.

Mittwoch, F. (1983). An exchange on Israeli social work education (letter). *Journal of Jewish Communal Service, 59,* 361–362.

Neipriss, J. (1989). *Social services and social work in the pre-state period. Meda'os* (Hebrew), May, 5–9.

Prager, E. (1988). American social work imperialism: consequences for professional education in Israel. In Ben-Shahak, I., Berger, R., & Kadman, Y. (Eds.). *Social Work in Israel.* Tel-Aviv: Israel Association of Social Workers.

Spiro, S. (1991). Trends and needs in training for social work: towards the year 2000. Paper presented at the meeting of the Israel Council of Schools of Social Work, Safed, Israel.

V

ASIA AND THE PACIFIC

18

ASIA AND THE PACIFIC

David Cox

This chapter presents an introduction to and general overview of social work education in the Asia-Pacific region. The region is a vast and complex one, and no brief chapter like this will convey fully the variety of contexts in which social work education is developing or is still to develop.

Social work education exists in at least nineteen countries in the region, with a slightly higher number of countries where it does not exist. Dividing the region into subregions, the situation is as follows. In the South Asia subregion, there are schools in Bangladesh, India, Pakistan and Sri Lanka, but no schools in Afghanistan, Bhutan, Maldives, Myanmar and Nepal. In the southeast Asia subregion, there are schools in Indonesia, Malaysia, Philippines, Singapore and Thailand, but none in Brunei, Kampuchea, Laos and Vietnam. In East Asia, there are schools in Hong Kong, Japan, People's Republic of China, South Korea and Taiwan, but not in North Korea. In Australasia there are schools in Australia and New Zealand. In the vast area of the Pacific, schools exist only in Guam, Hawaii and Papau New Guinea (of course Hawaii is a state of the United States). There are thus virtually no schools in the vast sweep of Melanesia, Micronesia and Polynesia.

THE REGION AS CONTEXT

To understand social work education in this region—its history, format, emphases and issues—one must appreciate its context, or, more accurately, its contexts. For in this region there are great contrasts. In population terms, some countries face dilemmas in welfare relating to their massive populations, while others, with fewer than 100,000 inhabitants, are limited in their development potential by their smallness. The region contains countries with widespread and severe poverty, and others with great affluence. Within the region are some of the highest population growth rates in the world and some of the lowest. In religious terms, the region contains the world's largest Islamic countries, the great majority of the world's Buddhists and Hindus, large Christian populations and a large number of religious groups that fall outside the world's major religions. This religious diversity reflects a wide cultural diversity in relation to all aspects of life.

Development is a major concern in the region. Some of the countries are classified as least developed countries and face enormous problems. Others have achieved high growth rates but are plagued by serious inequalities in the distribution of the fruits of development, frequently due in part to social stratification based on caste, class, ethnicity, race and religion. The process of development in some countries has resulted in tremendous rural poverty while in some of the same countries and in others the high rate of urbanization has resulted in vast urban squatter and slum areas.

Various aspects of the region's economic, political and social development have resulted in major migration movements, with repercussions for ongoing development. Internal migration is often massive and is characterized mainly as rural to urban; the drain of particularly the better educated to Western countries is a serious problem; the region's very large, as well as smaller refugee movements continue to cause grave concern; some millions of people from the region have joined the contract labor or migrant worker movements, with significant economic and social consequences; and, finally, illegal migrations resulting from a lack of access to official migration programs presents an additional set of dilemmas.

While this presentation of the region is extremely limited, it may help in part to explain the state of social work education as we find it today. Certainly, the aspects described are important in the contemporary debates around the role and nature of social work education in the region. Many within and without the profession are asking whether social work education is producing graduates likely to work at levels of intervention appropriate to the region's needs, with knowledge and skills relevant to the major presenting challenges and generally able to contribute significantly to the region's development.

NATIONAL CHARACTERISTICS AND THE DEVELOPMENT OF SOCIAL WORK EDUCATION

With some forty countries in the region, only half of which have introduced social work education, it is appropriate to ask which factors are associated with that introduction. In terms of population size, there seems to be no relationship between the number of schools and graduates and the size of the population. It does seem, however, that schools are not introduced, or seem unlikely to be introduced, in the region's very small countries. Whether this is related to size as such, or to actual and potential economic development partly as a consequence of size, is difficult to say.

It may well be assumed that the establishment of schools will reflect the stage of economic development, but this does not seem to be entirely the case. Some of the least developed countries have schools while most of them do not. On the other hand, some reasonably developed countries have a much higher ratio of schools and graduates to population than have others. On the whole, there seems to be some relationship between the existence of schools and the processes of development and modernization, and yet little evidence suggests that increasing levels of both result invariably in extensions in social work education. For example, social work education in Malaysia and Thailand has remained fairly static and at a comparatively low level during a period of considerable economic and social development. All this suggests that social work is not readily perceived as playing a significant role in development.

A third possible correlation is between social work education and the extent of need in identified areas. Where large-scale rural or urban poverty exists, delinquency and crime rates are rising quickly, large-scale rehabilitation programs are called for, and so on, one might expect to see an increasing emphasis on social work. That this is not obviously the case suggests that most in positions of authority do not, for whatever reasons, see social work as playing a significant role in such situations, perhaps because the profession has not demonstrated clearly that it can play a role.

The final linkage to consider is that between social work and culture, for it is generally agreed that social work has its origins in Western culture. Given the cultural diversity of the region, is there any evident link between the development of social work education and culture? It does seem that social work has flourished more in countries strongly reflecting Judaeo-Christian values (e.g., Australia, New Zealand and the Philippines). It is also true that the organizations and persons behind the introduction of social work education often represented Western values. There is some evidence for this in, for example, South Korea, Japan, India and Sri Lanka. On the other hand, beyond Western, and often colonial, influences in the introduction of social work education, and excluding Australasia, there is little evidence suggesting that social work finds roots more easily in Buddhist, Hindu, Muslim or any other particular cultural milieu. Given, however, that social work relates far more to the modern than to the traditional sector in most countries, the dominant culture in the traditional sector may be at least a partial explanation of this phenomenon. While many commentators complain that social work is far too focused on the modern urban sector, the extent to which this is due to cultural factors seems not to have been considered.

The introduction of social work education does seem, therefore, to bear at most a limited relationship to population size, development stage and culture; however, there is no clear evidence that it arises and flourishes in one type of culture more than another or more at one particular period in a country's development than at others.

FACTORS IN THE INTRODUCTION AND DEVELOPMENT OF SOCIAL WORK EDUCATION

If the rise of social work education does not closely relate to the national characteristics discussed, to what does it relate? This is an important question in the consideration of the existing and potential relevance of social work education to the region.

The rise of social work education would seem to have its roots in the development process, in the sense that without some development beyond the traditional life-styles there is no soil in which social work can take root. In the traditional situation, welfare needs are handled in traditional ways, and there is little if any scope for the employment of trained welfare personnel. Any such work that is done in the traditional sector tends to be a part of development aid. It is only as a country begins to modernize that demand and supply factors render the introduction of social work possible. For with modernization come both the need for outside intervention, as traditional responses are rendered less effective, and the resources for it, as central government strengthens and incorporates a welfare focus.

If modernization is the initial essential factor, the second and related factor is a government response to the needs arising from modernization. In many countries of the region, social work education has grown out of an embryonic public welfare sector. With the establishment of such a sector, the need to provide training for its employees frequently constitutes the origins of a school of social work. Hence it is not surprising that the focus of social work education will then be on the modern sector, and on the addressing of needs that lie beyond the scope of traditional welfare responses.

The preceding factors provide the context for the introduction of social work education, but its introduction is not automatic. It seems that a third and final factor is a personal one: that is, a person decides that social work education can contribute to the evolving situation. That person may be a private individual, such as Clifford Manshardt, whose initiative led to the establishment of the first school in India; or it may be a government official who related training needs to an understanding of the role of social work. In other words, while the need for appropriate personnel to staff an emerging public welfare sector soon becomes obvious, at what point that need is related to professional social work is a matter almost of chance. In a sense, the concept of social work is simply too alien to the region for it to represent the automatic response to emerging welfare needs. Accordingly, throughout this region there remains a need for social work to publicize and demonstrate its capacity to contribute significantly to any country's move into the modern sector.

This raises the critical question of whether modern social work has significant potential to relate to the traditional sector. Rather than representing only a response to the social needs arising from the modern sector, does social work have the potential to buttress the traditional sector in such a way that the strengths inherent in that situation, which have long met welfare needs, can be adapted to the changing situation and continue to serve society? As little attention has been devoted by the profession to this matter, it remains an open question.

PATTERNS IN THE EMERGENCE OF SOCIAL WORK EDUCATION IN THE REGION

From the material available, it seems that social work education has been introduced in the region in three major ways.

One development pattern has been the introduction by government of a public welfare sector, and the establishment within that of an in-service training system which eventually may evolve into a school of social work. We can see this in the Bandung School of Social Welfare in Indonesia, established in 1957 to provide training for government personnel and still under the control of the ministry. The same situation applies in Sri Lanka, where the Ceylon Institute of Social Work was established in 1953, later became a school of social work under the Ministry of Social Services, and recently received a degree of autonomy, thought its director is still appointed by the government. It remains the only school of social work in Sri Lanka. In some countries, such as Singapore, the in-service training in the Ministry of Social Affairs never developed into a fully fledged school and remains an alternative training arrangement to the school of social work within the National University of Singapore.

In the second development pattern an individual or organization establishes a private college which focuses exclusively on or includes a course in social work. There are such colleges in many countries, including Hong Kong, India, Indonesia, Japan, the Philippines and South Korea. Such schools are independent of government, vary considerably in the extent to which they reflect professional social work and sometimes reflect the values (often religious) of their founders. While some of these colleges have strong foundations, unfortunately many are relatively poorly funded, take in few students and are very limited in their faculty and training facilities.

In the third development pattern a tertiary education institution establishes a school of social work. This pattern is characteristic of Australia, Hong Kong, India, New Zealand and the People's Republic of China, while in Malaysia, Papua New Guinea and Thailand the sole school is situated within a university. The origins of such schools are for the most part unclear. Was it personal initiative, Western influence, government policy or some other factor that led to their incorporation in institutional profiles?

There is thus no single pattern in the establishment of social work education in the region, but the patterns that have emerged can be significant. It would seem that, for the most part and for at least an initial period, a "ministry school" will focus on basic skills training of lower level functionaries. For example, in Indonesia even today the junior ranks of the welfare sector are filled with social work graduates, especially from the Bandung school, while the upper levels are occupied mainly by the graduates of public administration and similar courses. Such schools have found it difficult to reflect the profession of social work, to give it status in areas like policy development and implementation, or to incorporate higher degree studies. This situation is well exemplified in the history of the Sri Lankan school. By and large this pattern in itself has not been conducive to the establishment of the range of roles for social work either characteristic of Western countries or potentially relevant to the wider field of social development.

The college model, with a few notable exceptions, has played a minor role in the region. One suspects that the number of graduates of such schools has been relatively small, that their employment has been often in the nongovernment sector, and that their overall expertise has been at a low to average level. If this is correct, it is not surprising that we see little evidence that such colleges have exerted any significant influence on developments in either the profession or their respective countries.

The effectiveness of social work education when based in recognized tertiary institutions would seem to have varied greatly. In some countries, such social work schools have had relatively high status, produced competent graduates, offered advanced training opportunities and so contributed to leadership in the human services field, and been productive in research, publications and general development of teaching materials. In other countries, however, university status has not resulted in these outcomes, so that university status is not sufficient to ensure well-developed social work education.

Of course, it is not the case that all countries have relied exclusively on the one model. Indonesia is one country where all three of the patterns exist together (together with a high school model inherited from the Dutch), although the potential complementary character of this arrangement does not seem to have been recognized. Nor is it the case that the models need to be mutually exclusive. Papua New Guinea and the People's Republic of China are two countries where university-based schools provide in-service training for government personnel, and this would seem to be an eminently logical arrangement, although one with the potential to inhibit academic freedom. Nor is it out of the question that college schools might provide some specialized training or emphases while working in close collaboration with university schools, thus incorporating their particular contribution while obviating the necessity that they cover the complete curriculum if their resources are limited.

If, then, the role of social work education is largely to contribute personnel for the service delivery sections of the public welfare sector, government-run training centers could be seen to be the preferred model because the training would be very focused and, being limited, less expensive. On the other hand, if the roles of social work extend into social research, planning, policy development and administration—at the levels where it can play a leading role in social development—then almost certainly a sound academic base such as a university might best provide is required. It is not, however, quite as simple as this. The literature on social work education in the region refers repeatedly to developments which, on the one hand, buttress the academic standards of the university model of social work education but which may, on the other hand, detract from the effectiveness of the final product in the local context. The developments referred to include academics, receiving their higher degrees in the West; a desire in schools to replicate Western models and receive international recognition; the establishment of curricula that are Western in structure, draw on theory developed largely in a Western context, and use Western texts in teaching; a tendency for academics to publish in Western journals material of international interest and stature; and so, in general, a propensity to relate externally to the development of the profession internationally, rather than internally to the needs and challenges of the local environment.

The phenomenon of university schools, seeking to be international in this sense may well mean that neither the ministry model nor the university model inspires confidence in government authorities and others involved in development, the former model because of its low level training and the latter because of its often irrelevant training. Hence it is possible that social work education in much of the region has yet to find a model capable of preparing social work graduates for the range of roles that they play in the West, and for playing those roles in a manner consistent with the region's context. Finding such a model might not be difficult if there existed a clear and widely accepted view of the roles which social work could and should play in the region. The current lack of clarity on this matter has left schools of social work to develop on the basis of either chance or imported Western models. A clear vision of the potential of social work in the region, and therefore of the type of social work education called for, is desperately needed.

The diverse national social work education profiles that have emerged in the region suggest a few tentative conclusions.

1. Nowhere does social work seem to have emerged from or related to traditional approaches in handling welfare needs.
2. Countries in which public welfare is poorly developed, or reasonably developed but relatively unrelated to professional standards and planning, present low levels

of social work education in terms of both extent of development and training levels.
3. Countries which are characterized by considerable development in welfare along relatively modern lines, but within a struggling economy, revealconsiderable development in social work education but with a strong emphasis on the para-professional level of training.
4. Countries with a modern welfare sector in Western terms, buttressed by a strong economy, present a strong and modern (Western) system of social work education.

Modern social work education, functioning at levels relevant to a country's population size and needs, seems to require a modern or professional approach to welfare and the economic strength to sustain it. Where either or both conditions are lacking, social work education will be nonexistent, present but poorly developed in every sense, or well-developed in terms of size but not in terms of higher levels or standards of education. Very few countries in the region possess both conditions, and very few therefore contain a modern social work education system—perhaps still only Australia, Hong Kong, New Zealand and Singapore, but with others beginning to emerge.

Moreover, if these conditions are the essential prerequisites for a relevant social work education system that they seem to be, one would have to anticipate very slow future progress. It may be the case, however, that these are not pre-requisites for a strong and appropriate social work education system only for a modern system along Western lines. It is likely that many of the region's countries will not be able to sustain either a modern professional welfare system or a modern Western social work education system. As we examine in the next section the issues facing social work education in the Asia-Pacific region, we may come to realize that much of the region calls for an approach to both wel-fare services and preparation of welfare personnel that is distinctive to the re-gion, consistent with the region's predominant needs and resources profiles, and therefore different from the systems which prevail in the West. The region's tardiness in developing social work education may thus be a product largely of a lack of fit between the commonly espoused model and prevailing realities.

Issues and Problems Confronting Social Work Education in the Region

Dependence on an Imported Western Model

It is very common to see and hear it asserted that a major problem facing social work education in the region is its adoption from the beginning of a Western model. What is required, it is said, is for social work education to de-velop its own practice models, introduce more local content, indigenize the curriculum, and so on. What precisely is meant by such assertions?

Sometimes the assertion implies that social work education in this region should exclude from the curriculum, or at least deemphasize, casework. Because of the mass nature of most situations of need, any focus on the individual is unrealistic, if not also culturally and politically unacceptable. The alternatives to casework suggested are most commonly community and social development, usually with no precise specification of the way in which these approaches to social work represent alternatives to casework.

With other commentators, the starting point is not the models adopted by social work but the social problems dominating the region. Unless, it is said, social work can apply itself to the eradication of poverty, to the needs within rural development, to the rapidly growing urban squatter settlements, and so on, it has little to contribute to the region. Whatever the models adopted, and perhaps they have yet to be found, such social problems must constitute major targets of social work practice. Yet, it is claimed, the schools do little to prepare social workers for such roles.

A third way of presenting this issue is to focus on the value base of social work. Claiming that the current value base is Western, and therefore largely only in the emerging modern sector, it is said that social work in the region must reflect Asian–Pacific cultures if it is to play a significant role. Some authors list the Western and local values, but seldom go on to show how a social work curriculum can reflect the alternative local list. It is sometimes also claimed that there exists an internationally accepted set of values, representing part of the common base of social work wherever it flourishes, but that this value set needs always to be adapted to local realities.

A fourth criticism of social work in the region concerns its predominant level of intervention. It is said that the curriculum prepares workers to work with individuals in an urban context, or in other words with those who are or are striving to be in the mainstream of development within the process of modernization. The alternative to this approach most frequently presented is that social workers' role is to work at a grass-roots level with marginalized populations for whom exclusion from both the process and the benefits of modernization is the norm. The implications of adopting this alternative focus, especially for schools of social work, are not explored.

Is social work education in the region a foreign import, a product of professional imperialism? Has it introduced practice models that are inappropriate to the region? Is the profession largely alien to the region because it rests on a Western values foundation? Is it focusing on problems and levels of intervention that are not the critical concerns of the region? Or, alternatively, do social work education and practice have the inherent capacity to be adapted to the region's circumstances, providing that some of the other issues commonly identified are resolved? Let us leave open this series of questions until we consider some of these other issues.

The Status of Social Work Schools and Graduates

It is very common to hear it said that social work in the region has a very low status; and while it is clearly less true in Australasia, Hong Kong and Singapore as elsewhere, there is ample evidence suggesting that the statement accurately assesses most of the region. Why is this the case and what restrictions does it impose on the profession?

Perceived reasons for the low status of social work vary greatly. Some see it as reflecting the low training levels, so they argue the need for schools to be based in universities and incorporating higher degree studies. Sometimes the perceived reason is cultural—for example, a cultural reaction to those who "sacrifice their future" to assist the disadvantaged. For others low status derives from the profession's inability, for whatever reasons, to contribute to the significant debates and developments of the day.

It would seem to be true theoretically that schools of social work can either train students for low levels of intervention and low–status positions or, alternatively, educate them for participation in the higher–status positions of administration, planning, research and professional supervision of service development. In practice, however, schools must work with the resources available to them (faculty, quality of applicants and physical resources) and prepare students for the prevailing employment market. Many schools are also subject to considerable government influence on this matter. In addition to such factors, however, the profession is frequently so ambivalent about its role that developing an appropriate and acceptable curriculum presents major difficulties.

It is clearly true both that low status imposes restrictions on any profession's potential to contribute and that the prevailing status level originates with the education system preparing the professional. If the schools are preparing low level welfare functionaries, then its graduates will have this status and possess neither the expertise nor the status to participate significantly in guiding the development process. Yet it is logical that those who are closest to the problems emanating from underdevelopment should have much to contribute to the development process, provided that they are able to translate their experience into policy and planning terms. But is it asking the impossible to expect the one profession to work effectively at both these ends of the development process and the schools to prepare graduates adequately for the implied diversity of roles? Again, let us leave this question for the moment.

Resources Available to Schools

A major issue for the region is the relative lack of the resources necessary for servicing the curriculum, particularly staff and teaching materials.

The availability of appropriate faculty is a major issue. In countries where social work is in its infancy, faculty with higher social work degrees and appropriate practice experience are inevitably the product of foreign, and usually Western, universities. Without local training, research and experience their value must be questioned. Even where social work is not in its infancy, the absence of higher degree programs and faculty appointment systems can present difficulties. Moreover, even when appropriate programs are available, the capacity of the country to avoid losing the best graduates through emigration or of the profession to avoid losing the best to higher status and better paid professions may be limited.

Some work is under way in the region to raise faculty levels and more could be done. The Sri Lankan–Canadian Joint Project included some staff development; the social work education project between the University of Hong Kong and Zhongshan University in the People's Republic of China (Nan et al., 1990) focused in part on this issue. The role of APASWE and the IASSW in the general development of social work education in the People's Republic of China is a good example of the potential contribution in this area of associations of schools of social work, and the development at La Trobe University in Australia of higher degree courses related to the region's development (Cox, 1991) is a further relevant measure. Faculty levels are critical to the future of social work education in the region.

The common complaints regarding teaching materials are that there are few materials with local content, that library holdings are usually small and outdated, that students are expected to do most of their study in the English language, and that there is a dearth of material addressing the key development concerns of the region. Whether true or not, the common perception is that the curriculum is driven largely by the availability of teaching materials. If the literature is largely Western, or focuses on microsystems, or reflects other specific emphases, then the curriculum too will possess these emphases.

There is certainly by now considerable practice experience available in the region. The task, however, of reflecting that experience in writings is frustrated by work pressures, the need in most countries to publish in English and the scarcity of publishing avenues. It is hoped that the establishment of some publishing firms in the region and the recent introduction of a regional journal of social work in Singapore will eventually assist in this area, but the smallness of the social work market will continue for some time to present problems.

There are undoubtedly resource problems in the region, and often very serious ones, and while there have also been efforts to address these problems, there is little evidence to suggest that schools of social work will hold the better educated members of faculty, that the extent and quality of local teaching material can be readily improved, or that the typical school in the region will be able to meet the high cost of a relatively comprehensive library, especially given the low status of social work. Does this mean that most schools of social work in the region will never progress? Not necessarily, for it may be that appropriate strategies at regional or subregional levels could go a considerable distance in meeting these needs.

CHALLENGES FOR THE FUTURE

Although there are other issues confronting social work education in the region, let us summarize major points before exploring potential strategies for tackling them:

1. Does social work in the region require a distinctive character, in terms of practice models, values, orientation, and so on, or can social work as it has evolved in the West be adapted to the region?
2. Can social work in the region span the range of roles often attributed to it, namely from a role at the grass-roots level of development, to a casework role in areas such as rehabilitation, to a role in the formulation of social policy and the development, introduction and administration of social programs? This implies availability of schools that cover this breadth of roles.
3. Assuming that schools at the national level will not be able to overcome the pre-vailing resource problems, especially in the short term, can social work education at the regional level develop strategies to address resource deficiencies?

At the heart of these issues is the question of whether social work has a uni-versal core. An examination of the nature of social work, and of the profession's experience to date, confirms the existence of several universal aspects. First, back in 1976 social workers from around the world, meeting in Puerto Rico, affirmed a core of values for the profession, an international code of ethics (Alexander, 1982) which has since been reaffirmed. A second aspect of a universal core to social work is the roles adopted by the profession. Everywhere it seems that social work is involved in responding to human need in a direct manner, in advocating that others (especially governments) respond appropriately to those needs, and in contributing to the development of a social environment that will maximize the potential for human development. The balance among these roles, the precise ways in which they are pursued, and the extent to which they are buttressed by additional roles will vary from place to place.

The third universal aspect of social work is the methods it adopts in the pur-suit of its roles. Everywhere, methods such as those that come under the rubric of casework and group work enable social workers to intervene effectively at the level of individuals, families and groups; other methods form the basis of work with communities. Finally, at the societal level social work encompasses methods relevant to social planning and social policy development. Yet, of course, the methods selected by the profession to teach and practice will vary, at least in emphasis, with the context and the roles that social work is largely playing in that context.

There is, therefore, a universal core to social work. The precise manner in which that core is reflected in a national context, however, is dependent largely on how social work education chooses to reflect in its curriculum both the universal nature of social work and the characteristics of the local context. It is the existence of the core, however, that enables the profession internationally and regionally to assist schools of social work in any country to emerge and confront the challenges outlined.

Looking at the Asia-Pacific region as a whole, it is clear that in much of it social work education suffers from low status, inadequate supports and few resources, while in over 50 percent of the region's states it does not even exist. How does and can the profession internationally respond to this situation? Several strategies have in effect been tried over the years, and we need to evaluate the ineffectiveness carefully. However, it is already clear that additional or new strategies are called for.

A common strategy to date has been for social work education in the region to draw on the facilities developed in the West. Many countries have sent individuals off to the West for basic and higher education in social work. Several countries have brought in social work educators from the West to teach, while others have employed them as consultants on curriculum development and other matters. Some schools have, to a very limited degree, drawn on external aid to fund the establishment of facilities such as libraries. How effective have these methods been? It has presumably varied, depending in each case on the knowledge, understanding, cultural sensitivity, and so on, of the individuals involved. Commonly, however, it is regarded within the region as resulting in inappropriate emphases, and loss of potential leadership through emigration and, generally, in contributing little to the major challenge of establishing social work education as a vital force in the region.

These outcomes would seem to suggest that the development of social work education should be within the region, with supports available on a regional basis and closely reflecting significant regional realities. Among such supports should be opportunities for social work educators to pursue study opportunities within the region that will equip them for the task of establishing strong schools with curricula relevant to their national contexts. In the past, such opportunities have existed mainly in Australia, Hong Kong, India, New Zealand and the Philippines. Such arrangements largely reflect the specific location and usually fail to capitalize on the wisdom and expertise scattered through the region. It seems logical to suggest that social work higher degree courses in the region either be located in one country but reflect the region in its staffing, curriculum and student population or be developed as regional courses, perhaps using several campuses. Either approach would facilitate the involvement of a network of people as teachers, necessitate the development of a regionally focused curriculum, and encourage research and writing relevant to social work education and practice in the region.

A second strategy might be the establishment of mechanisms for clarifying the roles of social work in relation to the region's major needs and for promoting, especially within governments, the utilization of social workers in those roles. This suggests the need for a center or centers committed to exploring this matter, with a particular emphasis on the roles of social work in poverty alleviation, rural and urban development, migration, social policy and human resource development. Only when such roles are more adequately understood will it be possible to devise curricula that prepare social workers appropriately for such roles.

A third desirable strategy involves measures to support social work education at the national level during its early stages of development. During this stage, a school may lack appropriately trained staff, a well-devised curriculum and resources of various kinds. Measures such as those employed recently by IASSW and APASWE in relation to the People's Republic of China can be highly beneficial. Ideally, such supports should not come from a lone (or even several) consultant with inevitably a limited perspective, but from a diversity of regional inputs, thus presenting a school with a sense of the range of options available and enabling it to develop the option most relevant to its context. This strategy should ideally go beyond the provision of direct support to an emerging social work education system. It should, together with that emerging system, build a relationship with the relevant organs of government, and perhaps others, and engage in the promotion of social work roles in relation to identified areas of national concern. For often a newly formed school lacks the status, and even the expertise, to initiate and carry through such discussions. The reality is also that the social work profession does not strike most of the people in positions of authority in this region as an obvious response to social needs; therefore, a well-based public relations strategy is essential, not merely to promote social work but to promote the social work perspective on the response to human needs.

In essence, the three strategies referred to are (1) provision within the region of appropriate educational courses, especially at the higher degree level; (2) regional research capacity; and (3) mechanisms for providing guidance and support to national level development. The implementation of these three strategies necessitates the following:

1. Strong regional associations for social work and social work education, preferably backed by strong international associations
2. A few good social work research and development centers in the region
3. Attraction of international aid by demonstration that the programs being promoted will play a significant role in the region's development.

The potential for all three elements is there. The challenge for the future is to realize that potential, and so ensure that social work education and practice can contribute effectively to development throughout the Asia-Pacific region.

SOCIAL WORK EDUCATION IN THE ASIA-PACIFIC REGION

Table 18-1

Areas of Emphasis and Neglect of Social Work Education in the Region

Areas Emphasized	Areas Neglected
Modern sector	Traditional sector
Upwardly mobile populations	Marginalised disadvantaged populations
Urban sector	Social planning and human services management
Direct service provision	

The profile of social work education set out in Table 18-1 is due largely to the relationship between the emergence of a government welfare service and that of social work. This association, rather than the influence of the region's developmental needs, has determined the direction taken by social work education. Not only have selected aspects of development been largely ignored in curriculum terms by the schools of social work, but little expertise has been developed around how social work might respond to the region's developmental needs—this despite the frequent rhetoric that it should be covering these areas.

An examination of social development in the region suggests three areas on which social work practice and education should focus:

1. The needs at a grass-roots level in relation to poverty, deprivation and alienation
2. The needs arising from rapid social change, and the breakdown of traditional patterns, especially those due to internal migration and urbanization, refugee movements, and civil and international war
3. The all-important demands for appropriate social policy, arising largely from the situations described

It is not, however, a matter of choosing among these areas of emphasis. All three areas are interrelated and require, therefore, a coordinated response, especially if that response is to be developmental in nature.

The question that arises is whether social work practice and education have the capacity to span such a broad range of activities. If it is to develop such a capacity, certain implications for education would seem to arise. The first is the necessity to prepare graduates for three basic levels of intervention:

1. Certificate or diploma courses for grass-roots intervention
2. Bachelor's degree level courses for graduates who will work with families and communities affected by social change
3. Master's and doctoral degree courses for graduates moving into the areas of social planning, social policy and social administration

Academically these three levels of training should not become too distinct, for they share such features as a common knowledge base. In professional terms also they should not be too distinct in that articulation of the levels is important both for career development and for merging of work at the grass–roots level with, for example, social policy development.

In curriculum terms, diploma courses would focus on basic knowledge and skills; bachelor level education would be broad and generic, covering the normal range of social work methods; higher degree courses would provide opportunities for specialization. At the same time, however, the curriculum at all three levels would need to reflect the regional context, and not just the knowledge base, skills and methods common to social work curricula in the West. The social work roles and their educational requirements, in situations such as extreme mass poverty and very low self–esteem, massive and impoverished urban squatter settlements, large-scale youth delinquency flowing from large-scale unemployment, and rapid erosion of traditional welfare structures, have, for the most part, yet to be determined. Such roles may prove to be adaptations of traditional Western roles or they may be new creations. More importantly, they will not emerge until the research capacity of social work in the region is strengthened.

The pattern of three levels of social work education, embracing a curriculum that is relevant and buttressed by research, has emerged in only a few countries in the region. In each such case the country has included a strong modern sector to which social work has largely related. Is such a pattern feasible in the less developed countries? If its emergence relies on resources available within such countries, then the answer is clearly no. Nor, increasingly, will such countries be interested in importing a Western pattern, should such a package be offered to them in terms of overseas training opportunities for educators and curriculum consultants oriented to Western conditions.

The future of social work education in this region requires a regional response that should initially embrace

1. research into the potential roles of social work
2. the development of a curriculum appropriate to those roles
3. higher degree education opportunities for those who will play a leadership role in developing both the profession and its educational foundations

In the longer term, social work education in much of the region will require the support of strong regional associations and centers able to work with governments at a planning level, facilitate the development of training materials, provide appropriate opportunities for the exchange of experience and knowledge, offer short-term training courses on relevant topics, and generally do everything possible to encourage ongoing research into and support of an educational system responsive to the region's needs.

REFERENCES

Alexander, C.A. (1982). The international code of ethics for the professional social worker. In Sanders, D.G.,. Kurren, O. & Fisher, J. (Eds.). *Fundamentals of Social Work Practice.* Belmont, Calif:: Wadsworth.

Asia and Pacific Association of Social Work Educators and Sociology Department of Peking University of China. (1991). *Status-Quo: Challenge and Prospect.* Beijing: Peking University Press.

Asian and Pacific Association of Social Work Educators. (1985). *Report of the 8th Asia Pacific Regional Seminar on Social Work.* Penang, Malaysia.

Billups, J.O. (1990). Towards social development as an organising concept for social work. *Social Development Issues, 12,* 3.

Brigham, T.M. (1984). Social work education in five developing countries. In Guzzetta, C., Katz, A.J., & English,R.A. (Eds.). *Education for Social Work Practice: Some International Models.* New York: Council for Social Work Education.

Burgess, M.D.R. (1983). Principles of social casework and the Third World. *International Social Work, XXVI,* 3.

Chow, N.W.S. (1987). Western and Chinese ideas of social welfare. *International Social Work,* Vol. 30.

Cox, D.R. (1991). Social word education in Asia-Pacific region. *Asia Pacific Journal of Social Work, 1,* 1.

Cox, D.R., & Britto, G.A. (1986). Social work curriculum development in Asia and the Pacific. APASWE Report. Melbourne: Department of Social Work, University of Melbourne.

Dixon, J. & Kim, H.S. (Eds.). (1985). *Social Welfare in Asia.* Bechenham Kent: Croon Helm.

Hammoud, H.R. (1988). Social work education in developing countries: issues and problems in undergraduate curriculum. *International Social Work,* Vol. 31.

Kendall, K.A. (1986). Social work education in the 1980s: accent on change. *International Social Work,* Vol. 29.

Mandal, K.S. (1989). American influence on social work education in India and its impact. *International Social Work,* Vol. 32.

Nann, R.C., Zhao-Fa, He, & Cho-Bun Leung, J., (1990). *Introducing Social Work and Social Work Education in the People's Republic of China.* Hong Kong: University of Hong Kong.

Ragab, I.A. (1990). How Social Work Can Take Root in Developing Countries. *Social Development Issues, 12,* 3.

19

AUSTRALIA

John Lawrence

THE AUSTRALIAN CONTEXT

Australia is a large, geographically isolated country, with a relatively small population of about 17 million, most of whom live a comfortable suburban existence in large coastal cities. The greater part of the land is arid; less than 15 percent of the people live in rural areas (Withers, 1989; *Year Book Australia*, 1989: 121).

During the last forty years, Australia's population has doubled. Immigration, carefully controlled, has accounted for about half of the population growth and has resulted in a substantial change in the ethnic composition of the society. The Anglo-Celt (British) group remain numerically dominant at almost 75 percent (almost 90 percent in 1947), but now almost 20 percent come from other European cultures, and 4.5 percent are of Asian origin (compared with less than 1 percent in 1947) (*National Agenda*, 1989: 2-3). Australians and their national government have recently become much more aware of the extent to which theirs has become a multicultural society. (*National Agenda*, 1989; Jupp, 1988, 1989). It is, however, a multiculturalism made up of a remarkable diversity of small groups—over one hundred of them (Borrie, 1988). Since the late 1960s, the well-being of Aboriginal Australians has become prominent on the national political agenda, although they now constitute only about 1 percent of the population (Bennett,1989).

At the last census, in 1986, 73 percent of the population nominated some form of Christianity as their religion (26 percent Catholic, 24 percent Anglican); only 2 percent were followers of non-Christian religions; and 13 percent did not subscribe to any religion (*National Agenda*, 1989: 5-6).

Australia was the first country to have fully representative government based on free, equal and universal suffrage. However, as in other Western democracies, "state intervention to protect the disadvantaged is tempered by a disinclination to interfere with property rights" (Aitkin & Castles, 1989: 208). The country has been organized politically as a nation only since federation in 1901. It has demonstrated remarkable, if rather dull, political stability. The society has been a particularly patriarchal society, but the women's movement has had a significant impact over the last couple of decades.

SOCIAL WORK EDUCATION

The Concept

In Australia, there were in 1991 fifteen schools which recognize their prime function as the initial and further education of social workers; others are being planned. All are located in large, public, tertiary educational institutions, which since 1974 have depended almost entirely on federal government funding which are now being encouraged to supplement this from other sources. Almost all these institutions are universities, although for some, it is a newly acquired status.

Each of the social work schools ensures that its basic education program meets at least the minimum standards prescribed for membership eligibility of the Australian Association of Social Workers (AASW). Most employers accept this as the minimum standard for social work employment, and indeed there is no other generally recognized standard. It has been AASW policy for its branches to pursue registration of social workers by title, but so far this has only succeeded in the Northern Territory, although active negotiations are proceeding with state governments in New South Wales, Western Australia, and Queensland (AASW, 1991; AASW-NSW, 1990).

It will become obvious in the story about to be told what a crucial role the AASW has played in Australia in determining who is now called a "social worker." Especially since about the 1960s, the term *social work* has not generally been used as a broad generic label to cover all social welfare or social service work. Instead, it has referred to a particular occupational group organized along professional lines—that is, one based on shared values, knowledge and skills, initially developed in universities, and further developed and sustained by subsequent professional association.

The shared value base of the occupation is a commitment to enhance human well-being through assisting people to lead more satisfying lives and by seeking to redress social injustice. An Australian school of social work states that currently it stresses "an empowerment approach," having emphasized in turn over its fifty-year history casework, generic models which included group work and community work, a research-oriented basis of practice, and radical social work and associated structural perspectives (*Profiles and Priorities*, 1990).

The Working Product

Australian social work graduates are employed at all levels of government—federal, state, and local—and in a wide range of nongovernment welfare organizations (religious and secular). A small number work in industrial settings, and a small but increasing number in private practice (AASW-NSW, 1991). The great majority continues to be female. The work of social workers covers an extensive range of functions. Some administer agencies and programs of various sizes; some undertake research; some work with communities, others with particular client groups both singly and collectively; and many concentrate generally on individual clients, while others focus on families.

The Early Years

The first Australian social work courses appeared in the deeply troubled decade prior to the Second World War. For the training bodies, it was a period of struggle—to find appropriate standards, to gain community acceptance, and to stay solvent. General training bodies in Sydney (1929), Melbourne (1933), and Adelaide (1936) established two year undergraduate diplomas, seen as appropriate for every type of social worker. These courses included both a wide range of background subjects and classroom teaching of professional (then, primarily social casework) skills, together with considerable prescribed "fieldwork"—a pattern which has persisted to the present. One year hospital almoner diplomas were also established in Melbourne and Sydney. By 1940, the product of this first pioneering decade was about 120 qualified social workers, with just 12 in Adelaide and the rest split evenly between Sydney and Melbourne.

The Australian Council of Schools of Social Work was formed in 1938 but did not survive the onset of the war and the movement of the courses into the universities. The case for university education for social work had been made successfully many years before in both Britain and the United States (Macadam, 1925: 50-57), and from the outset, each of the Australian independent general training bodies had a firm connection with its local university. In the early years of the war, these universities were persuaded to assume full responsibility for the social work courses—Sydney University in 1940, Melbourne University in 1941, and University of Adelaide in 1943.

During the war years, 1940-45, an additional 149 social workers were qualified, 79 in Sydney, only 40 in Melbourne, and 30 in Adelaide. The product of the two postdiploma almoner courses was 58 women. Only 3 men completed the general diploma, partly because the federal government refused to reserve male social work students from being called up for military service.

In the immediate postwar period, 1946-51, the three existing university courses qualified 436 social workers (16 percent men), almost three times the product of the war years, but this figure dropped back to 258 (14 percent men) in the subsequent six years. In the period 1946-57, Melbourne University produced only 132 qualified social workers, compared with 403 from the University of Sydney.

A National Professional Association

In 1946, the AASW, a national general association, was formed with the purpose of uniting professional social workers throughout the country, but also because of the growth of national and international social welfare programs in the postwar reconstruction period. It was a federal body with state branches and saw itself as having educational, social action, and industrial functions. In addition to the educational accreditation function, the AASW has performed its educational function through biennial national conferences, local conferences, regular meetings, seminars, workshops, newsletters, and a national professional journal. In 1949 it had about 300 members; by 1974, 1700 (17 percent were male); and in 1991, 3254.

By the early 1960s, the movement for social work education in Australia had made solid but not spectacular progress. The three longer-standing courses had extended to three year undergraduate diplomas—Melbourne University in 1947, University of Adelaide in 1957, and Sydney University finally in 1959, after a brief experiment with a two year postgraduate diploma. A new school, at the University of Queensland in Brisbane, pointed the way by establishing in 1957 a four year professional degree (Pavlin, 1981). Since many social work students combined their social work (or social studies) diploma and an arts degree with substantial content in the social and behavioral sciences, and considerable overlap was permitted, this was an obvious next step. Without degree-status education, the schools could not yet be full members of their academic communities, and genuinely postgraduate professional education in social work could not be developed.

After about thirty years, the total output from the social work courses was not much more than one thousand qualified social workers. About 88 percent were women, and many did not remain in professional practice. Yet despite the low numbers of practicing qualified social workers, the university schools still apparently had no serious competition from other narrower training schemes.

A Decade of Rapid Expansion from the Mid-1960s

Dramatic changes occurred in the decade from about the mid-1960s, and especially during the period of the social reform Whitlam government, 1972-75.

Preparation for the changes occurred in the Murray Report (1957), which had led to federal government financing of universities, matching state grants, and to the Australian Universities Commission. In addition, the Martin Report (1964-65) suggested universities should discard subgraduate courses. One of its chapters was on social work, which was described as "a discipline with a developing body of theory sufficient to justify provision for initial professional training." It asserted, "Preparation for social work demands interdisciplinary studies of a kind and standard which a university can best provide." The Martin Report also stressed, however, the need to finance and develop institutes of technology. A commission, established in 1965, popularized the idea of a college of advanced education (CAE), a multipurpose technological institution. A binary system of tertiary education was, in fact, established, with little clarity about the respective roles of the two parts. The CAEs catered to the swelling numbers of matriculated students who could not be accommodated by the universities, even though they, too, were considerably expanded.

For both the new CAEs and the more recently established universities, social work education was attractive. "The high rate of attrition from the workforce of the female majority of qualified social workers" (Martin, 1990: 168) meant a continuing employer demand, and this was greatly strengthened by "the surge of demand" (1990: 168) for statutory and other social services. Employer-provided in-service training, which some state welfare departments had introduced, was not a satisfactory substitute for professional education, to tackle the more difficult social service tasks.

In just over a decade, 1965-76, Australia moved from four to thirteen schools of social work and remained at this figure until a further round of development which began in the late 1980s. Five were new university schools—at the University of New South Wales (UNSW) in Sydney (1965); the University of Western Australia in Perth (1965); the Flinders University in Adelaide (1965), a transfer of the former University of Adelaide school; Monash (1974) and La Trobe (1975) Universities, both in Melbourne; and James Cook University of Northern Queensland in Townsville (1976).
These joined the existing schools at the Universities of Sydney, Melbourne, and Queensland.

A new feature in Australian social work education was the emergence of social work schools at four CAEs—at the South Australian Institute of Technology (SAIT) in Adelaide (1966); at the Western Australian Institute of Technology (WAIT) in Perth (1967); at the Preston Institute of Technology (PIT) in Melbourne (1973); and at the Tasmanian CAE in Hobart (1973), but subsequently relocated to Launceston (1981).

In the late 1960s and early 1970s, the AASW clarified its procedures, both for consultations with institutions establishing social work courses and for assessment of them once established. Consultations with both SAIT and WAIT, and with others, were often difficult and confused. Full AASW accreditation for the SAIT course was not provided until 1971; and for the WAIT course, not until 1973 (Ladbrook & Kunnen, 1988). The next round of consultations in the early 1970s took place within an organized national system, with the new courses being developed in consultation with the AASW, often through social work educators who were active AASW members.

The three new social work schools established in Melbourne were encouraged by a study of the shortage of qualified social workers (Malseed & Schuyers, 1973) and by special funding from the federal Whitlam Labor government. That government also funded the new Tasmanian course, and in 1975, provided thirty postgraduate social work awards, to stimulate further the postgraduate programs that had begun in at least some of the schools. Given the schools' dismal offerings of genuine postgraduate social work education and the great recent expansion of social work schools and courses, Australia had a desperate shortage of qualified social work educators (Boss, 1986). Recruitment from overseas, especially from Britain and the United States, was an obvious but sometimes controversial route to follow.

In 1964, the combined yearly product of the Australian schools was 107 graduates. In 1974, it had risen to 353 (23 percent males), although by then the schools had still produced only 8 social workers with an advanced social work qualification. By 1976, the yearly product of the schools was about 540 graduates, more than a five fold increase since 1964, and all now held a four year degree qualification in social work, the minimum AASW standard from 1974.

There were now two main educational patterns among the schools of social work. In the four year "integrated" degree, the school planned and taught most, if not all, of the full four years. In contrast, was the 2+2 or 2+3 pattern, whereby a two year undergraduate social work degree built on a relevant first degree or at least two years of a relevant first degree. Roughly, the courses at UNSW, UQ, SAIT, WAIT, and PIT followed the former "integrated" pattern, which tended to require a larger school, and more detailed planning and administration. The educational merits of each pattern continue to be argued. Clearly for prospective students, it is an advantage to have both available.

In 1964, no head of the then four university schools was at a full professorial level, a key indicator to the university status of the schools and their senior staff. In 1975, eight of the university schools were headed by professors—two from Britain, two from the United States, and one from Sri Lanka. Despite the gender composition of the student body and the emerging profession, only one of the professors was female.

Seeking and Establishing New National Structures

In the mid-1960s, an attempt to establish a formal association of schools was foiled by a vice-chancellor who opposed a university department's having membership in an outside body. Instead, in 1967, an association of teachers was formed. For a time, it held periodic workshops, usually adjacent to AASW and Australian Council of Social Service conferences, and it was a joint sponsor with these two bodies of an inquiry into social welfare education in Australia, 1968-71. This inquiry revealed, in addition to social work courses, a great variety of specific welfare courses run by educational institutions or by employing agencies (*Social Welfare Education*, 1973), and in the immediately ensuing period further welfare courses were to be added, for example, both in the technical education system and in some of the CAEs. Educational planning issues were becoming increasingly obvious and acute and in typical Australian fashion were complicated by problems of federal-state relationships.

The idea of a national council on social work or social welfare education was strongly mooted, but various initiatives proved abortive. In 1975, the heads of the social work schools established a standing committee (SCHSSWA), at least partly to make an effective social work contribution to the Learner Inquiry, set up by the Social Welfare Commission to examine the desirability and feasibility of a national social welfare education body. The Learner Report identified a number of educationally neglected areas: work with Aboriginal people; work with ethnic groups; residential care; probation, parole and corrective services; welfare in industry; and welfare for disabled persons. Its recommendation for a broad statutory national council was, however, not acted upon (Learner, 1979). The government and the political climate had changed. Also, other national bodies, such as the Australian Association for Social Work Education (AASWE) and the UNSW Social Welfare (later, Social Policy) Research Center, were beginning to assume some of the functions prescribed for the proposed statutory council. On the initiative of SCHSSWA, AASWE was firmly established in 1979 and held the first of its biennial national conferences the following year. The aims were to enhance social work education and to participate in appropriate structures and processes for accreditation.

In 1978-79, on the initiative of SCHSSWA, a moratorium on AASW accreditation and reaccreditation occurred, to enable a joint working party of the educators and the professional association to revise AASW accreditation assessment criteria and procedures.

Parallel with these social work developments was the emergence in 1972 of a national organization covering welfare workers, the Australian Institute of Welfare Officers (AIWO, changed later to the Australian Institute of Welfare and Community Workers, AIWCW). The Learner Report commented on the proliferation of categories of welfare workers which had created problems in role differentiation and deployment (Learner, 1979: 65,136).

Recent Developments

Australian Association for Social Work and Welfare Education

Throughout the 1980s, teachers in the welfare courses could attend AASWE conferences but did not have full AASWE membership. In 1989, AASWE became the Australian Association for Social Work and Welfare Education (AASWWE), with a General Council and two standing committees, one for social work education, the other for welfare work education. The former standing committee had virtually the same aims and structure as the former AASWE.

Each school is represented by its head, an elected staff member, a student, and a field educator. Early AASWWE initiatives included a working party on field education (*Field Education*, 1990), and, with the Standing Committee of Social Welfare Administrators, a joint working party on education and training for public welfare practice (*Education and Training*, 1990).

A National System of Industry Training Boards

With the Victorian government giving the lead (*Industry Training Plan*, 1990), a new set of government advisory structures is developing to examine the training needs of the community services "industry" throughout the country. All categories of "training" are included (Brown & Ryan, 1990).

The Abolition of the Binary System

In the late 1980s, the federal government decided to abolish the binary system in higher education, by forcing amalgamations between universities and CAEs, or combining CAEs to form new universities. At the same time, overall student numbers were to be substantially increased, and priority was to be given to what were seen to be economically productive areas of education such as engineering, business studies and Asian studies.

When the federal government assumed full financial responsibility for the universities and CAEs in 1974 and student fees were abolished, it had acquired considerable potential power over the higher education sector. In the later 1980s, this was being used out of concern for the Australian economy, although the Hawke Labor government also had a concern for increasing access to higher education. To help fund higher education, an administration charge of $250 pesannum was introduced in 1986, replaced in 1989 by a higher education contribution of almost $2000 p.a., which could be deferred until a graduate was in employment (Harman, 1990).

Social work education as an integral part of higher education was, of course, affected by these various national developments. Three of the CAE schools became university schools—as WAIT became the Curtin University of Technology, SAIT became the University of South Australia, and the Tasmanian CAE at Launceston became the University of Tasmania at Launceston. In 1991, the Phillip (formerly Preston) Institute of Technology. was still engaged in amalgamation talks with La Trobe University. One obvious result of the change to university status has been an increased emphasis for the social work educators involved to be engaged in research, as well as teaching and professional activity in the community.

Another Round of New Schools; Extended Campuses; Distance Education

After a considerable lull, another round of new schools has begun, with AASW consultants being actively utilized. In addition, a number of existing schools have extended their BSW programs to rural areas.

Extended Programs

Induced by Victorian state government funds, the four Melbourne-based schools have recently extended their BSW programs to rural campuses. In Queensland, James Cook University established a Cairns Campus in 1987, and the first two years of its BSW degree can now be undertaken there. Since 1992, students have been able to complete the University of Tasmania's BSW in Hobart, not just at Launceston.

New Schools

A fifth school is getting under way in Melbourne—at the Victorian University of Technology. In Sydney, a third school is being developed at the University of Western Sydney from an existing community welfare program. At Newcastle, north of Sydney, the University of Newcastle in 1991 commenced an imaginative social work program which is using a system of experienced-based learning to integrate the theory, practice and values of social work in each of the four years of the course. Other disciplines in the university have adopted a similar approach to learning (*Submission*, 1991). Also in New South Wales is another interesting new development at the Charles Sturt University, which was established in 1989 from three geographically dispersed CAE campuses, at Wagga Wagga, Albury-Wodonga, and Bathurst. Since 1991, it has offered a BSW degree with students able to take the second half by distance education over four years. The planned distance education mode is unique in Australian social work education (*Bachelor of Social Work*, 1990).

The Northern Territory University has initiated a BSW degree in 1992, but as yet no school has been established in the Australian Capital Territory, although Canberra University (a former CAE) has indicated some interest.

The Pressure on the Universities and Their Staffs

In addition to these new developments, student numbers in the established social work courses generally increased—in 1989, 576 graduated; in 1990, 652 (Brown & Ryan, 1990). But there was no commensurate increase in financial resources. In the recent period, Australian social work educators, like their colleagues in the rest of the tertiary education sector, have been under increasing pressure to teach more students, produce more research, fill out more forms, and at the same time be less financially rewarded. Recent unprecedented nationwide industrial action by the nation's academics has indicated the extent of current concerns.

The Australian System of Social Work Education Accreditation

The Australian model for the assessment and accreditation of social work courses recognizes that education is a central feature and responsibility of the organized profession, not a separate vaguely related activity, and it helps current social work practitioners and social work educators to recognize their interdependence (Lawrence, 1986: 22).

In 1990, after consultation with SCHSSWA, the AASW further revised its educational accreditation policy and procedures to keep them relevant to changing circumstances. What, briefly, are the current AASW standards which a basic Australian social work course is expected to meet?

Current Accreditation Standards

The course must have clear, written, communicated objectives, which are evident in the implementation of the curriculum (AASW, 1990). The primary objective must be to produce graduates capable of critical analysis, committed to social justice, and competent to begin social work practice. The course must provide a sound general foundation for such practice and be a basis for continuing education and incorporation of new practice ideas. Social work graduates must have completed at least four years of full-time degree-level tertiary study, or its part-time equivalent, the major part in subjects of direct relevance to social work. The tertiary study must lead to a distinct qualification in social work, and this must be acceptable as an avenue of entry to advanced social work education.

The content of the four years of study must include at least six major components, appropriately balanced and integrated: the study of the individual in society, the study of society, the study of social welfare systems and social policy, the study of the sociopolitical context, the study of social work research methods, and the study and application of social work theory and practice. The AASW indicates briefly what each of these components should contain. The last component must extend over at least four semesters and must include the study of values, theories, methods and fields of social work practice. Ethics, with reference to the AASW Code of Ethics, must be taught and integrated with practice subjects. General social work theory and a range of method/models of intervention must be taught, and taught by social workers.

The content of the social work theory and method subjects must be demonstrably integrated with the field education. There must be an identifiable field education unit within the school, responsible for field education policy and the establishment and maintenance of links between practice settings and the school. Students must spend at least 980 hours in at least two field placements. These can be taken in blocks, or two to three days a week concurrent with classroom teaching. Field teachers must be suitably qualified and experienced social workers. In certain circumstances, the supervision can be off-site.

A student's field education must provide experience in at least two settings, and two fields of practice, and experience in interpersonal helping and other recognized professional intervention methods. Criteria for assessment in field education need to be identified at the commencement of each placement. A member of the school's staff should make regular visits to the field education agency to evaluate a student's progress and provide consultation as required.

In addition to these various standards, AASW insists on a school's being an identifiable structural unit, with levels of autonomy proper to a professional school. It must be headed by a social worker and have relevantly qualified teachers. Teachers and students must have appropriate opportunities to participate in the school's decision making. Finally, the school must have sufficient relevant resources to attain its educational purposes.

An AASW assessment team consists of at least three members, at least two of whom must be experienced social work educators. None of the team can be from the same state as the course being assessed. Courses are reviewed by the AASW every five years, earlier if necessary. A process of formal consultancy and provisional approval is available to a new school.

Continuing Education, Higher Degrees and Research

Continuing Education

Australian social workers have a wide range of opportunities to continue their professional education. These may be provided by their employing agencies, by the schools, by the AASW, or by a multitude of community and professional bodies operating in their various fields of interest, and the opportunities may be local, national, or international.

Higher Degrees in Social Work

Most of the schools of social work are involved in various forms of continuing education. Of particular note is the now very evident, if belated development of genuine postgraduate social work qualifications. Each of the established schools now offers a master's degree in social work, and many a research doctoral degree. There is no standard pattern for the MSW, although all require a first degree in social work and some professional experience. The MSW may be primarily a research degree, it may be primarily a course-work degree, or it may be a mix of the two. The course-work component may be heavily specialized, by method or field of practice, or may emphasize a common core necessary for all advanced practice. It may or may not have a practicum component. The desire to make available a wide range of educational options at an advanced level has been clearly held in check by the relatively small numbers of students and limited teaching resources.

Schools have not had the staff capacity to provide adequate supervision for many students to undertake primarily research degrees, particularly at the doctoral level. However, the situation is changing in at least some schools. For example, in 1990, of the twenty-one academic staff in the UNSW school, thirteen had doctorates. (This school produced Australia's first PhD graduate in social work, in the early 1980s.)

Research

The present generation of social work students and their teachers are generally much better educated than their predecessors in relation to matters of research. All students now undertake the study of social work research methods to enable them to participate in and evaluate research projects, and further research learning occurs in all the advanced social work degree programs, not just the research degree programs.

The academic staffs of the schools, especially the universities, have been under heavy pressure to publish as part of their academic responsibilities as well as to attain academic advancement. In addition, the growth in the local social work education market has made it more attractive to publishers in Australia. Recent years have seen a considerable growth in Australian social work literature, much of it produced by social work educators (see for example; *Advances in Social Work/Welfare Education,* 1986, 1988, 1989; Chamberlain, 1988; Cox,1989; Petruchinia & Thorpe, 1990; Donovan & Jackson, 1991; Rees, 1991). The traditional heavy reliance on teaching materials published in North America and Britain is noticeably reduced.

Final Comment

The Economic Environment

The new round of development in Australian social work education, unlike the earlier round beginning in the mid-1960s, is not sustained by much in the way of increased financial resources, for the Australian economy continues to be in bad shape and the general national policy debate and climate are dominated by economic rationalists (Pusey, 1991). Even with a federal Labor government, the unemployment rate was more than 10 percent in 1991, and economic "recovery" was being defined as a return to a 5 to 6 percent unemployment rate. The serious social impact of long-term unemployment is only beginning to be understood. An occupation with an historic commitment to the most disadvantaged and vulnerable sections of society, and an espousal of a social justice philosophy, has a particularly significant role to play in the present circumstances of Australian society.

Current Tasks

Tasks facing the current generation of social work educators include the following:

- Ensure that the emerging political emphasis on "competence" and "skills" is not used to eliminate occupational identity
- Interact with other professional and paraprofessional occupations, guided by a "public interest" ethic
- Encourage graduates to retain a long-term commitment to social work
- Distinguish between what is universal and what is culturally specific in the educational programs
- Encourage social work graduates to see themselves as part of a worldwide occupation
- Develop further a range of opportunities for continuing professional education
- Take full advantage of audiovisual and computer technology
- Encourage more women to become qualified for senior appointments
- Ensure that the schools prepare social workers for senior administrative positions
- Develop the capacity to teach ethics as a core subject and cooperate with the AASW's new national network of ethics committees (Lawrence, 1991)
- Devote more scholarly resources to examining Australian social work education

NOTE

The account up to the mid-1970s is based on Lawrence (1965, 1976). Heads of schools here kindly provided material mainly on the current situation.

REFERENCES

Advances in social work/welfare education. (1986, 1988, 1989). Sydney: The Heads of Schools of Social Work in Australia & UNSW School of Social Work.
Aitkin, D. & Castles, F. G. (1988). Democracy untrammeled: the Australian political experience since federation. In Hancock, K., (Ed.). *Australian Society.* Cambridge: Cambridge University Press, pp. 208-227.
Australian Association of Social Workers Ltd. (AASW). (1990). *Eligibility for Membership of AASW: Policy and Procedures for the Review of Australian Social Work Courses.* Canberra.
Australian Association of Social Workers Ltd. (AASW). (1991). *National Information Bulletin, 1, 2.*
Australian Association of Social Workers Ltd., New South Wales Branch (AASW-NSW). (1990). *Submission on the Registration of Social Workers by Title in N.S.W.* Surry Hills, New South Wales.
Australian Association of Social Workers Ltd., New South Wales Branch (AASW-NSW). (1991). Social Work in Private Practice. *Newsletter, 2.*
Bachelor of Social Work: Course Document. (1990). Wagga Wagga: Charles Sturt University.
Bennett, S. (1989). *Aborigines and Political Power.* Sydney: Allen & Unwin.
Borrie, W. D. (1988). The population. In Hancock, K., (Ed.). *Australian Society.* Cambridge: Cambridge Uuniversity Press, pp. 119-142.
Boss, P. (1986). *Social Work Education at Monash University: The First Twelve Years—a Personal Recollection (1974-1986).* Clayton, Victoria: Monash University, Department of Social Work.
Brown, T. & Ryan, M. (1990). *The National B.S.W. Graduate Employment Study for 1989.* Typescript.
Chamberlain, E. (Ed.). (1988). *Change and Continuity in Australian Social Work.* Melbourne: Longman Cheshire.
Cox, D. (1989). *Welfare Practice in a Multicultural Society.* Sydney: Prentice Hall.
Donovan, F. & Jackson, A. (1991). *Managing Human Service Organisations.* Sydney: Prentice Hall.
Education and Training for Public Welfare. (1990). Report of the Standing Committee of Social Welfare Administrators & Australian Association for Social Work & Welfare Education.
Field Education in the 1990's: Policy and Curriculum. (1990). Sydney: Australian Association for Social Work and Welfare Education.
Gardner, J. (1990). *Looking Back: Reflections on 25 Years 1965 to 1990.* Nedlands: Department of Social Work and Social Administration, University of Western Australia.

Harman, G. S. (1990). The Universities in Australia. In *Commonwealth Universities Yearbook*. London: Association of Commonwealth Universities.

Industry Training Plan. (1990). Hawthorn, Victoria: Social and Community Services Industry Training Board.

Jupp, J. (Ed.). (1988). *The Australian People*. North Ryde, New South Wales: Angus & Robertson.

Jupp, J. (Ed.). (1989). *The Challenge of Diversity: Policy Options for a Multicultural Australia*. Canberra: Australian Government Publishing Service.

Ladbrook, D. & Kunnen, N. (1988). *The Evolution of Social Work Education at the Western Australian Institute of Technology, 1967-1986* (Report of a grant project). Perth: Curtin University of Technology.

Lawrence, J. (1986). Future directions for social work education. *Australian Social Work, 39*(4), 19-26.

Lawrence, J. (1991). Ethics in social work practice: how serious are we? *Proceedings of the 22nd AASW National Conference*. City unknown.

Lawrence, R. J. (1965). *Professional social work in Australia*. Canberra: Australian National University.

Lawrence, R. J. (1976). Australian social work: in historical, international and social welfare context. In Boas, P. J. & Crawley, J. (Eds.). *Social Work in Australia: Responses to a Changing Context*. Melbourne: Australia International Press, pp.1-37.

Learner, E. (1979). *Education and Training for Social Welfare Personnel in Australia*. Canberra: Australian Government Publishing Service.

Macadam, E. (1925). *Equipment of the Social Worker*. London: George Allen & Unwin.

Malseed, E. & Schuyers, G. (1973). *The Demand for Professionally Trained Social Workers in Victoria, 1972-1982*. Melbourne: University of Melbourne, Institute of Applied Economic and Social Research.

Martin, E.M.W. (1990). Gender, demand and domain: the social work profession in South Australia 1935-1980. Doctoral thesis, University of Melbourne.

National Agenda for a Multicultural Australia. (1989). Canberra: Department of the Prime Minister and Cabinet, Office of Multicultural Affairs.

Petruchinia, J. & Thorpe, R. (Eds.) (1990). *Social Change and Social Welfare Practice*. Sydney: Hale & Iremonger.

Pavlin, H. (1981). *Social Work in the University of Queensland: The First Twenty-Five Years 1956-1981*. St. Lucia: University of Queensland, Department of Social Work.

Profiles and Priorities. (1990). Sydney: University of Sydney, Department of Social Work & Social Policy.

Pusey, M. (1991). *Economic Rationalism in Canberra: A Nation Building State Changes Its Mind*. Melbourne: Cambridge University Press.

Rees, S. (1991). *Achieving Power: Practice and Policy in Social Welfare*. Sydney: Allen & Unwin.

Social Welfare Education in Australia. (1973). Sydney: ACOSS.

Submission for Accreditation of the Bachelor of Social Work Degree. (1991). Newcastle: University of Newcastle, Department of Social Work.

Withers, G. (1989). Living and working in Australia. In Hancock, K. (Ed.). *Australian Society*. Cambridge: Cambridge University Press, pp. 1-22.

Year Book Australia. (1989). Canberra: Australian Bureau of Statistics.

20

INDIA

Kalyan Sankar Mandal

INTRODUCTION

The development of professional social work education in India can be viewed in terms of three stages. The first stage is a period of relatively indigenous inception of professional social work education in India in the preindependence period (1936–47). The second stage is the period after independence (i.e., after 1947), when professional social work education in India took shape under American influence. The third phase is a reaction to the inadequacies of the emerged curative model of social work education in India, when suggestions for reforming social work education have been mooted. Thus, in this chapter, we shall discuss the development of professional social work education in India, in three sections in terms of these three stages.

Professional Social Work Education in India in the Preindependence Period (1936–47)

Clifford Manshardt, an American missionary, a graduate in theology from the University of Chicago, went to India in 1925 through the American Marathi Mission, a Protestant Christian organization. This organization decided to undertake social work in slums and, with that objective, founded the Nagpada Neighbourhood House in Bombay in 1926, headed by Manshardt. While working in the industrial metropolis of Bombay, the highly industrialized commercial capital of India, Manshardt felt the need of trained personnel for social work. Thus, when opportunity arose with financing from the Sir Dorabji Tata Trust, Manshardt founded the Sir Dorabji Tata Graduate School of Social Work in Bombay in 1936. This was the beginning of professional social work education in India[1]. Thus, professional social work in India has been initiated through a combination of the religious impulse of charity and the modern scientific orientation of Tata, a pioneer in the field of industry in India (Ranade, 1987).

To illustrate the nature of social work education in India in the preinde-pendence period, in this section we make the following points.

Clifford Manshardt, the American missionary who played an important role in the shaping of social work education in India at its inception, while narrating his first social work experience among the industrial workers in Chicago, observed, "It did not take long to realize that welfare work is not a substitute for social action which aims at creating working conditions which are conducive to human welfare, and that social legislation and its enforcement are at times the most basic form of social work." (Manshardt, 1967). This observation suggests that probably this American initiator of social work education in India was not part of the American influence, which, as has been argued, resulted in adequate emphasis on social action, and curative social work practice in India.

Manshardt observed that at the inception, the social work training program in India was based on experience (1967). In fact Manshardt's establishment of the first school resulted from his felt need for trained social workers during his ten years of social work experience in Bombay. Manshardt further stated that when the social work training program was introduced in India, every attempt was made to make it relevant to India. Moreover, in deciding about the subjects to be taught in this program, a combination of American as well as British social work education was attempted.

Finally, the inception of social work education in India was influenced by an American idea which has been articulated by Gore and Gore (1977) as follows:

> The idea that social work requires training was not particularly American; but that the variety of jobs that go under the name of social work have a certain common content, that they call for study ranging beyond the learning of specific skills through apprenticeship and that a minimum basis of general education up to the graduate level is necessary for professional preparation, was an idea nurtured largely in the United States. The choice of post-graduate education for social work was purely due to the fact that the founder of the first school of social work was an American.

After the initiation of social work education in India, the Sir Dorabji Tata Graduate School of Social Work, renamed Tata Institute of Social Sciences in 1944, remained the only school for professional social work education for ten years, from 1936 to 1946[2]. Other schools of professional social work education came into being only after independence in 1947.

SHAPING OF SOCIAL WORK EDUCATION IN INDIA AFTER INDEPENDENCE

After independence, the second school of social work was established at Delhi in 1947–48. This was a significant step because it was the first school to be established as a part of a university and thus contributed to the academic recognition of social work education in India. The school was organized at postgraduate level. In 1950 another school was established, as a part of University of Boroda. This school was not only a part of the university but constituted an independent faculty (Gore, 1965). Subsequently, several other schools came into being, including the social work school in Madras and Lucknow in 1954 and another institution in Bombay in 1955. By 1975, when the Second Review Committee for Social Work Education appointed by the University Grants Commission undertook a survey, there were thirty-four institutions of social work education in the country. Geographical distribution of these institutions is very uneven. Thus, while Maharashtra had eight institutions and Tamil Nadu six, states in the extreme north and northeast had none. Generally, these projects include community centers, family agency, foster care, adoption and school social work. They are used by the institutions for demonstration, experimentation, field training and research (Desai, 1987).

Under American influence, social work education in India is generally offered at the university level. The trend is to provide the first education in social work at the master's level and then go beyond it to MPhil and PhD level. As a result a majority of these institutions are urban based. Most are affiliated to state universities (Desai, 1987).

In the period following independence, an attempt was made to develop professional social work in India through promoting American sponsored study tours for Indian social workers and appointing American trained social workers on the faculties of schools of social work in India. One important scheme in this regard was the US government's Technical Co-Operation Mission and Council of Social Work Education Exchange Programme. Under this program, during 1957–62, American social work educators worked as consultants or conducted faculty development programs in the Indian schools of social work. In exchange, faculty members for Indian schools of social work went for study to the schools of social work in the United States (Pathak, 1975). A corollary was the extensive use of American books and journals in schools of social work (Nagpal, 1986).

Social work education in India was a generic course in the preindependence period (1936–46). The introduction of specialization in social work emerged in the postindependence period, primarily under American influence and partly as a result of felt need. An examination of the process of introduction of specialization at the Tata Institute of Social Sciences, the pioneer of social work education in India, suggests that when a specialization was introduced at the Tata Institute, either it was designed and developed by an American social work educator at the initial stage and handed over to an Indian social work educator trained in the United States, or an Indian social work educator was sent to the United States to take training in a particular specialization in India (Desai, 1987).[3] This resulted in the correspondence of social work curriculum at the

Tata Institute with American social work education. What is more important, the Tata Institute, as the forerunner of social work education in India, was closely followed by other schools in designing their curriculum. Thus, American influence of social work education in India become widespread.

However, there are some viewpoints which to an extent counter the preceding argument. For instance, Kulkarni (1993) argues that professional social work in India has a very distinct model of its own, in spite of adopting and adapting a lot from other countries. Further it should be noted that some developments in social work education in India were a departure from American social work (see Gore & Gore, 1977). Besides, from time to time some changes to the existing pattern of social work education in India have been suggested (e.g., UGC Review Committee Reports, 1965, 1980). Whatever small changes have been generated, in terms of those suggestions, they, in general, are not in the tradition of Americanization of social work; rather they are to the contrary. However, the fact remains that, in spite of these departures from American social work, dominance of American influence on social work education in India persists.

It should be noted here that this American influence in the shaping of social work education in India is not a unique development. It has been pointed out that social education in the developing countries in general has been influenced by the American model of social work. For instance, comparing social work education in five developing countries, Bringham (1984) noted that these countries which were predominantly rural had adopted an American urban model of social work education.

Here, it is important to review the shaping of social work education in India under American influence. Indian social work educators have reflected on it on several occasions. Some of these observations are presented here to highlight their core content.

Gore and Gore (1977) observe that as social work education in the United States leaned heavily on curative social work mainly through casework, the American influence made social work education in India more concerned with method and techniques of work. It deemphasized the needs of social and economic development, promotion of preventative services and social action—the prime need of the country in the postindependence era.

Pathak (1975) observes that it "led to the curtailment of the social science content, inadequate emphasis on social action, alienation of a group of trained social workers from the *sarvodaya* social workers and neglect of social reform."

In pointing out the inappropriateness of the American model for India and other South Asian societies, Nagpaul (1980, 1986) observes that American history and culture are influenced by ideologies such as capitalism, social Darwinism, the Portestant ethic and individualism. These ideologies emphasize the individual's responsibility in shaping his or her own welfare; public responsibility arises only when the individual grossly fails to benefit from the existing social system. However, during the Great Depression of 1919, these ideologies had a setback and there was a reorientation of social work strategies which led to widening its scope. But, this reorientation of the American model retained the general framework of psychological orientation and casework principles. The American model of social work with the characteristics cited is unfit for India and other developing societies whose problems and developmental needs are substantially different from those of a developed capitalist society. A similar point has also been made by some others (e.g., Ranade, 1975).

Finally, one consequence of the shaping of social work education in an irrelevant manner is that it limited the employability of social workers and consequently affected the development of the profession in India (Ranade, 1975; Nagpaul, 1986).

It should be pointed out here that it is not that social work education has been shaped inappropriately under American influence in India only. It has been argued that social work education in developing countries in general has thus been shaped inappropriately because the American model does not suit the situation of the developing countries (Brigham, 1984; Midgley, 1981.) It is argued that social work education should take shape in the societal context. Thus, Humphreys and Dineman (1984) have pointed out that even within the United States, the definition of social work has evolved as society's need for and definitions of professions have changed in response to changing social conditions and values.

Further, one gets the impression that American social work is concerned only with the curative function. It should be noted that social work in America has been influenced by curative as well as preventive, "residual" as well as "institutional" ideas of social welfare (Wilensky & Lebeaux, 1958). However, the fact remains, as is obvious in the assertion of the Indian social work educators, that American social work has remained primarily oriented to a curative model and it is mainly this curative part of American social work which has influenced social work education in India. This has made it irrelevant to the prime need of Indian society. However, this conclusion does not imply that there was no positive contribution of American influence on social work education in India. Pathak (1975) and Gore and Gore (1977), for instance, have also pointed out the benefits of American sponsoring of social work education in India.

SUGGESTIONS FOR REFORMING SOCIAL WORK EDUCATION IN INDIA

We have seen how social work education in India has been shaped by close contact with American social work education. We have also documented the observations of social work educators on that influence. It is evident that there is a widespread feeling among social work educators that the influence of the curative and microbased school of American social work has made social work education irrelevant to the needs of Indian society. Thus, it is not surprising that social work educators gave several suggestions for reforming social work education. For instance, as a result of American influence, social work education in India is mainly developed at the postgraduate level. It has been suggested that social work training should be provided at various levels and there should be a ladder program of social work education (Desai, 1975). The need for training paraprofessionals has been emphasized. The urban bias of social work education has been deplored and the need for rural social work emphasized. However, apart from these reforms, the prominent suggestions for remodeling social work education in India have been in terms of a social development orientation of social work and promotional social work.

SOCIAL DEVELOPMENT ORIENTATION OF SOCIAL WORK

The most prominent viewpoint regarding the remodeling of social work education is that it should take on a social developmental orientation. Time and again, it has been argued that social work education in India requires a social development orientation. However, this concern has been characterized by the fact that the meaning of social development orientation remained vague. Thus, Gore (1981) cautioned, "I am afraid that unless we can think through clearly what social development means and what role social workers can play in bringing out such development, we only use the word as part of a rhetoric, without stating pragmatic implication for social work."

One discovers that exactly that is happening. Though the need for social developmental orientation in social work has been voiced on several occasions, the type of change that will be required in social work curriculum to equip social workers to perform a social developmental role or the steps that will be required to make social work development oriented has rarely been outlined.

One such rare exercise was undertaken by Sugata Dasgupta (1976) in an article where he provided an outline for a social development model of social work education. In this article Dasgupta argued that the nature of social work in India, in fact in all the less developed countries, should be different from that of the developed industrial countries. In a developed country, the concern of social work is helping the marginal section of "deviant" individuals or groups adjust to the society, whereas in a less developed country the main concern should be to bring about changes in society that will mitigate the problems of the disadvantaged.

Having made this point, Dasgupta did not suggest any change in the major components of what he calls "the classical model of social work education," consisting of (1) classroom instruction, (2) fieldwork, (3) supervisory conferences, and (4) research, though he does suggest modifications in the substantive content. We briefly present Dasgupta's suggestions in this regard.

Dasgupta (1976) suggested that the subjects to be taught under social development model of social work education needed to be grouped under three broad categories. The first will include those subjects which help understanding of the society and of the individual in the broader context of their being the creatures of this planet and the products of history. Second, social work should teach subjects which concentrate on the change process and on the whats and whys of this change, as well as the how-tos of it. This will be the course on method. Third, social work should deal with planning, decentralization, technology, irrigation, family planning and a substantial reorientation of the traditional fields of practice. This will require a reorganization of theories which would involve inclusion of courses on cultural history, methods of change, social philosophy, political sociology, environmental sciences, and others. This curriculum will train change agents and should lean heavily on "case studies" that depict the process of change.

Gore (1977, 1981) has expressed his disagreement with Dasgupta's suggestions on at least two occasions, once in the journal that published Dasgupta's article and in an expression of his view on social development orientation in social work. Gore is of the opinion that social workers should address themselves to a limited area of social development:

> The distinguishing characteristic of social work lies not in its social know-how or even in its skills in interpersonal relations, but in its concern for those in need of help—the deprived, the unprivileged, the unadjusted and the handicapped. Our interest in social policy is in terms of preventing this suffering and promoting rehabilitation. (1981: 9–10)

Gore further adds:

> The wider field of social development in all its aspects can at best be added...as tertiary area adjacent to the area of professional concern to social workers. In this perspective, social work practice may be said to have three types of foci and settings: (1) the core area of "welfare" services directly oriented to "handicapped" sections of the population: (2) the secondary area of social service in which social work skills can be practiced either fully as in medical social work, school social work and personnel social work or peripherally as in the planning and administration of these services for "handicapped" segments of the population; and (3) the tertiary area of general social planning where social workers have to call upon their resources as social scientists more than on their professional skills as social workers. (Gore 1981: 12)

Gore feels that to attain social development orientation, a restructuring of social work curricula is needed:

The undergraduate program should be developed to equip the students primarily to take the responsibilities of preventive and generalized care services. The post-graduate program should be strengthened in the areas of social sciences and social policy and should primarily equip a person for clinical and guidance type of work with individuals, some type of group work, the whole sphere of community work, welfare planning and administration. The program beyond Master's degree level should aim at equipping a person for social developmental tasks in the areas of social welfare and in the allied fields of social service and for teaching and research. (pp. 12–13)

Thus, we have observed that there is a viewpoint which holds that social work education in India should take social development orientation and it is felt that the said orientation can be achieved within the existing frame of social work education with some modifications in its course content.

PROMOTIONAL SOCIAL WORK

"Activists" or "action groups" have gained prominence in India particularly since the 1970s. Their emergence as a model of social work has had a sys-tematic expression in a project undertaken by Ramachandran (1989) at the Tata Institute of Social Science, Bombay. This project enumerated views of social work alumni of that institute on developing plans and programs for meeting the future needs of social work training. Analyzing the views expressed by this group, graduating between 1956 and 1981, Ramachandran concludes that there exists a "Great Divide" in the perspective of social work training. There are two positions on the question of the nature of the relationship between social work and social change. The models of social work we have discussed so far belong to one side of this divide. According to Ramachandran (1989), these models of social work are committed to retaining the existing form of training system and institution, subject only to some redistribution of teaching courses and loads, and consequently, some modification in the content of the existing training program. They are "in favor of *perpetuating the system*, i.e., that professional social work must continue to be concerned with responding to social change and on such of its fallout on society as have been the traditional concern of professional social workers in India" (emphasis in the original). Ramachandran calls this position curative social work.

The other side of this divide, which Ramachandran calls promotional social work, is strongly of the view that "the role of professional social work is to ac-tively participate in *reforming the system*, a stance reflecting the belief that the role of professional social work should be to initiate such social changes as are desirable for one and beneficial to society—especially, to its marginalized sec-tions" (emphasis in the original).

Thus, Ramachandran proposes that there should be two major streams of social work training—curative social work and promotional social work. One may, however, keep moving from one stream of activity to the other, and preferably training for both the streams should be offered in the same institution for social work education.

What is new in Ramachandran's suggestion is this stream of promotional social work. Ramachandran (1989) outlines the content of the promotional social work training program:

> This will address itself more pointedly to promoting equality, social justice, and working for human rights. The emphasis in training will be more on analyzing and understanding the oppressive structure in which society lives, the inequality structures—old and new—the macro dimension of social problems, exploitation, social conflicts and non-party interactions. Problem focused discussion, people's participation, theory and strategies for change, social movement, politicization, critical analysis of various facilities offered by different agencies and understanding of distortions in Indian developmental models are other areas of emphasis in promotional social work.
>
> Field work would involve greater exposure to projects which reflect the developmental situations, with direct experiences in different settings. Though the base of this work may be in a formal setting, it is not unforeseen that the trainees may be placed in such specific situations as may provide the necessary learning experiences for promotional work—non-structural settings or crises situations. There would be a greater degree of freedom given to teachers and students to experiment. Hence, there would be more flexible interaction between theory and practice, and by implication, a less rigid time-table of work.

The key component of this model is social reform action. According to Ramachandran (1989) *social reform action* involves awakening of the "marginalized to their condition, so that they can be helped to grow out of it through their own collective sense—not necessarily through a political party formation, but perhaps, through people's own movements."

Thus, we observe that there is a school of thought which proposes such changes that cannot be accomplished within the existing frame of social work curriculum. Thus, a separate stream of social work training has been proposed. The purpose of the proposed stream of social work training will be to prepare persons for social reform action.

To conclude, in India a relatively indigenous beginning of social work education was made in the preindependence period. After independence, professional social work education in India has been shaped by American influence. Reflecting the need of that country, social work curriculum in America is predominantly curative. Being shaped under the influence of this curative model of American social work, social work education in India has become predominantly curative. However, as the social work needs of a developing country like

India are quite different from those of America, the predominantly curative social work model, developed under American influence, misfit Indian society.
Thus, social work educators in India have expressed their dissatisfaction with
the predominantly curative social work curriculum in India and have suggested
remodeling social work education in India in terms of social development orientation and social action orientation. Both these models of social work have
been widely debated and they have prompted some changes in the social work
curriculum in India. However, it is still predominantly curative and the social
work profession in India remains a shortcoming of the inadequate emphasis on
broader developmental issues.

NOTES

The first two sections of this chapter are based on Mandal (1989).

1. Gore and Gore (1977) have pointed out that though part-time training courses in
    social work were in operation in India before 1936, they cannot be considered the
    forerunner of professional social work education in India.
2. It may be mentioned here that when professional social work education was
    initiated in India, a different brand of social work movement was growing outside
    professional social work under the leadership of Mahatma Gandhi. This was a
    nonpolitical component of the nationalist movement and was termed Constructive
    Work. This included the development of *khadi* (handloomed cloth) and village
    industries, village sanitation, removal of untouchability, improvement of women's
    status, improvement in the condition of the hill and forest peoples, service of
    leprosy affected persons and development of new life–oriented as opposed to
    book-oriented education. Unlike professional social work, which had an urban
    orientation and which tended to focus on specific problem groups, constructive
    work had a rural and more generalized orientation to the problems of the commu-
    nity—general poverty, illiteracy, low standards of sanitation, public health, living
    conditions of "deprived" groups, such as women and untouchables (Gore, 1988).
3. For a detailed account of the process of introduction of social work specialization
    at the Tata Institute of Social Sciences, see Mandal (1989).

REFERENCES

Brigham, T. M. (1984). Social work education in five developing countries. In
    Education for Social Work Practice: Selected International Models. Vienna:
    International Association for Schools of Social Work.
Dasgupta, S. (1976). Social work education: a critique of the classical model. *Journal
    of Higher Education*, I (3), 358–366.
Desai, M. (1987). *Emergence and Debate Concerning Social Work Specializations*.
    Tata Institute of Social Sciences, Bombay. Unpublished manuscript.

Gore, M. S. (1965). *Social work and social work education* (pp. 86-96). Bombay: Asia Publishing House.

Gore, M. S. (1977). Social work education. *Journal of Higher education, 2* (3), 413–415.

Gore, M. S. (1981). The scope of social work practice. In Krishnan Niar, T. (Ed.). *Social Work Education and Social Work Practice in India.* Madras: Association of Schools of Social Work in India, pp. 1–31.

Gore, M.S. (1988). Levels of social work provisions in relation to needs in a developing society. *The Indian Journal of Social Work, XLIX* (4), 1–9.

Gore, P. & Gore, M.S. (1977). Social work education in India. In Ganguli, B. N. (Ed.). *Social development.* New Delhi: Sterling, pp. 260–290.

Humphreys, N.S. & Dineman, N. (1984). Professionalizing social work. In Dineman, M. & Geismar, L. L. (Eds.). *A Quarter Century of Social Work Education.* National Association of Social Workers, Washington, D. C., pp. 181–16.

Kulkarni, P. D. (1993). The indigenous base of social work profession in India. *The Indian Journal of Social Work, LIV* (4), 555–565.

Mandal, K. S. (1989). American influence on social work education in India and its impact. *International Social Work, 32,* 303–309.

Manshardt, C. (1967). *Pioneering on Social Frontiers in India.* Bombay: Lalvani.

Midgley, J. (1981). *Professional imperialism: social work in the Third World.* London: Heinemann.

Nagpaul, H. (1972). *A sociological Analysis of Social Welfare and Social Work Education.* New Delhi: S. Chand.

Nagpaul, H. (1980). *Culture, Education and Social Welfare.* New Delhi: S. Chand.

Nagpaul, H. (1986). Highlights on the paper on the diffusion of Americanism: a case study of social work education in India and its dilemmas. Paper presented at the XI World Congress of Sociology, August. New Delhi.

Pathak, S. H. (1975). A quarter century of professional social work in India. In Gokhale, S. D. (Ed.). *Social Welfare--Legend and Legacy.* Bombay: Popular, pp. 171–178.

Ramachandran, P. (1989). *Perspective for Social Work Training: 2000 A.D.* Tata Institute of Social Sciences, Bombay, unpublished manuscript.

Ranade, S. N. (1975). Social work education in India. In Gokhale, S. D. (Ed.). *Social Welfare--Legend and Legacy.* Bombay: Popular, pp. 194–195.

Ranade, S. N. (1987). Social work. In *Encyclopedia of Social Work in India, vol. III,* Delhi: Ministry of Welfare, Government of India, p. 141.

University Grants Commission. (1965). *Social Work Education in Indian Universities.* New Delhi: UGC.

University Grants Commission. (1980). *Review of Social Work Education in India--Retrospect and Prospect, Report of the Second Review Committee.* New Delhi UGC.

Wilenski, H. L. & Lebeaux, C. N. (1958). *Industrial Society and Social Welfare.* New York, Russell Sage Foundation.

21

BANGLADESH

Abdul Hakim Sarker and A. K. Ahmadullah

INTRODUCTION

Even before the growth of tribes and the advent of religion, as the anthropologists and sociologists agree, there were among the people a sense of fellow feeling, a sense of belonging and a readiness to provide mutual protection, along with a tendency, in some cases, to dominate the weaker sections by the stronger. With the rise of religion, the priests and the preachers of religion assumed leadership in providing services for those in need, i.e. helping widows, orphans, the sick, and others (Friedlander,1968). The powerful incentive behind charity and benevolence is evident in many ancient religions, that is the Vendidad and Hindu philosophy in Assyrian, Babylonian, and Egyptian codes; and Greek and Roman customs (Friedlander, 1968). In ancient India (of which Bangladesh is culturally and politically a part) there were sporadic and, in some cases, organized efforts to help the needy and victims of natural calamities not only in terms of material assistance but also through education or assurance of assistance (Rahman,1990). The advent of Islam, needless to say, brought about a renaissance among the relatively lower caste population in India under a conversion process (Karim, 1991). Islam, in a comparatively stable form, institutionalized charity work through systems like *Zakat, Baitulmal, Sadquah,* and *Karze Hasana.* Thus in the name of social service, some forms of social welfare activities have evolved and have been in practice in our society as elsewhere in the world.

"A good hearted person with wealth and desire to serve the distressed, the destitute and the abandoned is generally regarded as a social worker; no professional qualification or experience, is a requirement. He or she may practice charity, do reform work and be useful to any person or an institution designed to render social service" (Rashid, 1964). In an unsophisticated society, such magnanimity and will to help individuals or groups (religiously oriented or humanely concerned) solved the problems of the distressed and temporarily met certain material needs of the disadvantaged.

Since the inception of capitalism a substantial change has occurred in social structures (Akbar,1986). As the society became more complex, problems of human life began to take new shapes and became more complicated; varied, interwoven, intermingled and multidimensional (Hussain and Alauddin,1970). As a consequence, problems which were previously easy to cope with for persons with a philanthropic bend, got beyond their control. This gave rise to the need for more systematic methods of helping and scientific techniques of intervention. Thus, the concept of "enabling people to help themselves" emerged, decreasing reliance on sporadic charity. This is how social work as a profession appeared on the scene in response to certain pressing conditions and experiences, not as an outcome of some theory (Hussain & Alauddin, 1970). Based on the recognition for self-reliance social work started making a definite move toward "self help" projects related to the needs and situations prevailing in a specific society (Ahmadullah, 1964). The culmination of social work, what is done and needs to be done, in the context of social service, and the attainment of its objectives, often entails pooling of national and international views toward a professional standard. Social work was organized as a profession after the second decade of the present century. The two world wars and the Depression of the 1930s greatly hastened its systematization not only at the level of government but also at the private level (Hussain & Alauddin, 1970).

THE PROJECT OUT OF WHICH SOCIAL WORK AROSE IN BANGLADESH

The history of social work in Bangladesh originated in the Pakistan regime. Under the slogan "A new profession for a new nation in a new age" recommendations were made by a UN expert for the establishment of a program of professional education for social welfare practice in erstwhile East Pakistan, now Bangladesh. The first step and core of this program would be an independent institution for graduate professional study and research. The institution was thought to be of special interest to the province of East Pakistan in the then federal structure, similar to such programs in the other part of Pakistan (there was a wide geographic difference between two parts of Pakistan). Student, staff and educational programs were designed to be international in character.

Professional education for social welfare practice in the country was on the basis of two key observations. First was the compelling need for scientific leadership in the solution of acute and large-scale social problems, expressed in a variety of training ventures locally undertaken which would perhaps continue. The question was what the nature of such training would be. Second was the extensive social welfare structure existing in response to various types of human needs, which required professional leadership to criticize the operation and to guide the future development of the program (Moore, 1958).

Dr. J.J.O. Moore, the UN expert, was assigned in 1958 to prepare a report, which received serious consideration from individuals and groups, particularly a few professionally trained social workers, volunteer workers, and from education and industry, on whose generous interest, initiative and support, the government must rely on for the success of the programs.

BACKGROUND OF SOCIAL WELFARE PRACTICE

The background of social welfare (considerable confusion surrounds the meaning of the terms social welfare and social work) is related, for historic reasons, to Pakistan. Continuous and multifaceted development has been underway for more than half a decade. In the period 1952–58 a few UN advisers (among them Dr. J.J.O. Moore, who spearheaded the establishment of professional social work education in Bangladesh) dealt with the disciplines of social administration, medical social work, institutional management and family welfare, social welfare development and administration, and urban community development (Moore, 1958).

Such efforts, however, began in West Pakistan. An introductory course in social work of three months' duration was first started in East Pakistan (now Bangladesh) in 1953. Then, particularly in 1955–56, professional education in social work was introduced as a nine month training course in community development and medical social work at Dhaka. In 1957, with the completion of the nine month on-the-job training course under an urban community development project, the establishment of a school of social work at Dhaka University was proposed and the appointment of an adviser was advocated in the latter part of 1957 (Moore, 1958). Moore was thus appointed with the purpose of investigating the need for and feasibility of such an institution. The feasibility study findings confirmed the need for a social work school and Moore recommended advising the appropriate ministry and departments of the government to establish a training program at Dhaka University and assist the proposed school of social work in conducting the training course; analyzing conditions and needs for training in specialized fields; developing courses and fieldwork and related projects for training purposes; participating in the training program and related activities; assisting in selection of local staff for the faculty and fellows for training abroad under UN auspices; and assisting in negotiations with educational institutions to participate in the training programs of the school (Moore, 1958).

In the course of his assignment in Bangladesh (then East Pakistan) the adviser found situations favorable and unfavorable to the establishment of the proposed school. The central and provincial governments as well as Dhaka University agreed, in principle, to establish a school disagreed about the extent of importance to be assigned to social welfare in this context. However, for fiscal year 1957–58, the Ministry of Works budgeted an amount to Dhaka University as a grant for the school. Unfortunately, the fund was misdirected because of communication gaps and scattered interests about the proposed school among the concerned authorities. The UN expert, in his attempt to develop a professional school and to advise the government on welfare training in general, was mostly consulted informally by officials on a number of related matters. Thus the role of the expert was to some extent circumscribed. However, the influence of the consultant was neutralized to a considerable extent, because of his potential usefulness to the program (Moore, 1958).

The nine month on-the-job-training course which was conducted by the Urban Community Development project was viewed as a short–term course in social welfare training but was subsequently seen as a social welfare training institute. Under such dismal conditions, this course posed a threat to the proposed school and confused the issue of the professional school in the minds of responsible persons, weakening the support for a long–term educational program (Moore, 1958). One senior central government officer (M. Akber Kabir) often came to the rescue of the proposed school at Dhaka whenever it was deemed necessary.

BANGLADESH: GEOGRAPHY AND SOCIOCULTURAL CONDITIONS

Bangladesh is a delta country, interconnected with rivers and canals, and its climate is tropical. It has an area of 143,998 square Kilometers and about 110 million people, of whom about 90 percent are Muslims; others are Hindus, Buddhists and Christians. There is a steady increase in population. More than 80 percent live below the poverty line. The literacy rate is estimated to be around 25 percent. It is predominantly an agricultural country, industrial development is gradual, industrial zones have been developed around city or town areas. Thus, marked changes have taken place in the organization of urban society. In 1958, the total population of the capital city of Dhaka was almost half a million; today it is about five million. Tea, jute, hides and skin, and garments are the chief export items. It is a land of natural disasters—flood, cyclone, and tidal bore almost every year.

In terms of health, people are the victims of dysenteric disorders, such as diarrheal diseases and typhoid. Epidemics, particularly those related to diarrheal diseases, are quite common.

Housing in more than 80 percent of urban situations is notably bad and of very poor quality. Streets are narrow and full of potholes. In Dhaka over one–third of the residents live in poverty clusters; the density of population is as high as two thousand persons per acre. An estimated 70 to 80 percent of city dwellers cannot afford even the smallest unit of conventional housing (Camp, 1981). Chronic social conditions of unemployment and underemployment largely act as push factors for the rural people to move to urban areas, aggravating the problems of housing, transportation, employment opportunities, and so forth. Education, health and recreational facilities are inadequate.

Added to these basic conditions are institutionalized problems such as beggary, prostitution and abuse of children and women. Child neglect, desertion, delinquency and gangsterism, along with many other problems, such as physical, mental and social handicaps, are quite common.

In Bangladesh, after partition of India in 1947, alarming problems and circumstances including the refugee problem; of about 1 million refugees approximately 250,000 were without security and political status (Carlson, 1958). Much was attempted by the government but no systematic and comprehensive plan for development was initiated in the first five year (1955–1960) plan (Government of Pakistan, 1958). Attention was given to developing material resources and bettering economic conditions. Human dignity development of human services to raise the standard of living were found to be tied almost solely to economic development. But there appeared to be no clear understanding of the extent to which economic development depended upon the ability and the will of the people, which needed to be emphasized. For developing human power resources the two propositions were (1) empowering people to improve their own economic conditions and (2) improving economic conditions to enhance human potential. These are equally important and are interdependent.

The key to the success of a country like Bangladesh lies in the improvement of its economic and industrial growth, which is influenced by social factors such as ignorance, malnutrition, unsanitary conditions, and overpopulation. According to the first UN expert's appraisal, the social welfare programs undertaken or encouraged, were characterized by insufficient thought about how they could contribute to economic productivity and insufficient attention to establishing priorities in relief and rehabilitation (Moore, 1958). According to him, the urban population, though it was only about 10 percent of the country's population, had disproportionate significance. Loss of values; weakening of parental authority, and family and social ties; issues related to the responsibilities and status of women; antisocial behavior; loss of protection against unemployment; old-age problems; deterioration of the family system; absence of recreation, among other factors, were the results of urbanization (National Report, 1956). And the effect of urbanization was so important that UNICEF sought, during that time, to improve the lot of mothers and children by turning its attention in some countries including Bangladesh to an entirely new set of dangers arising from the growth of cities—new health hazards, the denial of basic education to children through formal schooling and the destabilizing influence of the city environment (United Nations, 1958). The slums of cities are veritable cesspools of humanity, which can only be described as cancers on the body politic (Moore, 1958). Whatever forces are generated in cities usually affect the villages. Cultural diffusion tends to be from urban areas outward rather than vice versa.

IMPLICATIONS OF SOCIAL WELFARE IN BANGLADESH

Large-scale and acute problems existed (and still exist) in primary and secondary poverty, disease, ignorance, unstable employment conditions, inadequate housing, indebtedness, unemployment and underemployment in addition to some institutionalized problems. Thus, a major number of human families were in misery, social instability and danger of self-annihilation (Moore, 1958).

While social planning, large scale relief and rehabilitative measures were viewed as potential solutions to the multiproblem conditions, a greater difficulty yet to be surmounted resided in motivating the people to participate in developmental projects (Moore, 1958). Thus, on the basis of overall situations it has been suggested that solutions to these problems require a greater emphasis on human resources, the gearing up of rehabilitative measures to productive ends, and the balancing of work in rural and urban areas. And this required modifications in policies for coping with certain attitudes, and for overcoming limitation, and improving certain practices in public affairs (Moore, 1958). It was suggested that this could be met through the establishment of centers for the development of basic scientific knowledge and for constant experimentation in their application; centers thus created would provide a necessary exchange of information and ideas with other parts of Asia. These required a new policy, in particular to develop a new professional leadership with an obligation to humanity.

On an examination and analysis it was found necessary to deal with some popular misconceptions of social welfare. Social welfare was often viewed (is still viewed) in terms of the present alone and as a preestablished area of activity. This view always deprives us of the indispensable benefit of seeing it in relation to its historical development and in its dynamic aspects (Moore, 1958).

THE STUDY PLAN AND ACTION FOR SOCIAL WORK

In view of the circumstances, how a program of professional training could be initiated in Bangladesh was a basic question to the UN expert. It was, however, not difficult to reach the conclusion that training for social welfare of some nature was urgently needed and that it would continue to be developed by other UN advisers. Dr. Moore, accordingly, proposed a plan of action with some broad objectives and had it approved by the UN. The major objectives were to coordinate and channel existing interest in the establishment of a formal school for giving training; to secure all possible information bearing on it; to bring together those persons whose thinking and support were vital to it; to move forward as far as possible with concrete planning and action and especially to secure answers to some queries of professional interest.

Keeping these points in view, the project was conceived of as in the nature of action research, assuming that (1) social work practice is based on a scientific approach to human problems, and the establishment of social work training programs must at least incorporate the objective observation which is a part of scientific method; (2) simple transplantation of social work education from Western countries to this country is not valid; the commodity of value that the Western expert brings is objectivity and scientific method, and with this as a starting point, the specifics of programs must evolve from local resources; (3) a program of social work education has value in itself, but it will not achieve its full value unless there are built into it both local understanding of it and local responsibility for it. The inquiry, the participation, the sharing in decisions and the development of responsibility were accomplished through direct observation of social conditions, observation of social welfare programs, study of related professional programs, study of established schools of social welfare, study of relevant literature, consultations and discussions with interested individuals, and discussions with key groups comprising professionally trained workers, industrialists, educators, volunteers and government officials.

THE PROGRESS ASSESSMENT

According to this large order of business, attempts were successful, though there were special difficulties inherent in the situation. Among the difficulties, some were accounted for by the unwillingness of government officials to facilitate the work of the project because of preconceptions about the value of social welfare. Nevertheless as a result of the courtesy of Dhaka University in offering to accept the initial grant and to act as the "banker" for the project, release of funds was secured. The continuing question had been whether or not the government was prepared or able to support the project. It was, however, favorably resolved, in a verbal commitment of the then central government to continue to finance the project (Mr. Akber Kabir in the central government was of great help in this matter) and in an agreement to vest continued control of the proposed institution in an independent board/council. However, substantial concentration on substantive problems of the proposed school was possible only from about February 20, 1958, and an attempt was made to start the school in the early fall and a target date established.

After examination and reexamination of the social situation it was suggested that social welfare is applicable to all as a conscious, organized effort to meet human needs and is distinguished from social services because it is believed to be in harmony with the historical development of social welfare and with modern conceptions of humans and their social organization as an interrelated whole. According to sociocultural values underlying the then state principles, the welfare programs showed that the social welfare structure could absorb the trained personnel who would be the graduates of the proposed institution for professional education.

In view of the considerations elaborated, it was recommended that the institution be established in Dhaka, to known as the College of Social Welfare and Research Center. The proposed college was assumed to be a reservoir of knowledge of human behavior and its practical application; to encourage, through separate endeavor or in collaboration with existing bodies, the refinement of existing knowledge and the development of new knowledge, including basic research and the collection of social data; to stimulate the use of tested knowledge and techniques in the extensive administrative machinery for social welfare existing in the country and yet to be developed; to prepare practitioners for administrative, supervisory, or other positions in social welfare organizations; to collaborate with other professional training institutions on matters of mutual concern, in particular to give consultation and assistance, where requested, in strengthening the human management and administrative content of the teaching programs of such institutions; to advise and assist in respect to subprofessional courses of training and to guide social service organizations in the discharge of their teaching responsibilities; to maintain contacts with similar and related institutions throughout the world for the exchange of knowledge, data and techniques, and to take an active part in strengthening and extending, national, regional and international communities of spirit, thought and action.

The control of the institution was vested in a council closely tied to the university and with representatives from government and from interested citizenry and agency groups. Thus, a seven member council was formed with the vice-chancellor, Dhaka University, as its chairperson.

The college was initially sponsored by the Ministry of Health, Labor and Social Welfare of the then federal government for the purpose of producing competent and qualified social workers for shouldering responsibilities of organizing and administering the various social welfare programs launched by the government as well as by private agencies. From 1962–1963 the provincial government accepted the responsibility of meeting all the financial requirements of the college and later provided a suitable campus of about seven acres of land with three buildings (Ahmadullah, 1964). The College of Social Welfare and Research Center commenced its educational program in the academic year 1958–59 with fifteen students registered for an MA degree in social welfare at Dhaka University (Ahmadullah, 1986). The college was merged with the Dhaka University as the Institute of Social Welfare and Research in 1973. In 1963, it may be noted, another college of social work was established at Rajshahi for the same purpose, subsequently in 1972 it became a department under the Faculty of Arts at Rajshahi University. It started with honors in the subject, followed by a master's degree (Momen, 1964). This is how training in social welfare and social work came to be a university program.

TRAINING CONTENTS

Considering the generally accepted nature of social welfare practices and the special requirement of the country, it was proposed that the content of training would consist of fundamental problems, values, individual and group behavior, social institutions, social problems and social policy and social investigations; problems of social welfare practice, the process of work with communities, groups and individuals; auxiliary practice problems, administration and research; and problems of special settings (Moore, 1958).

Figure 21-1

A Diagrammatic View of the Content of the Training

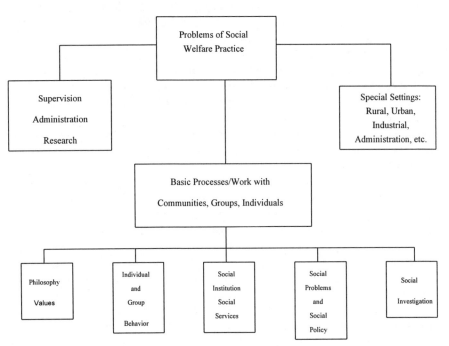

The training would be provided with a provision for field instruction to help students with principles and techniques of practice as the real world counterpart of classroom instruction. Field instruction and classroom instruction would be complementary, each contributing uniquely to the education of the students.

After Moore, who spearheaded the establishment of professional social work education, some other UN experts, as earlier indicated, contributed to the development of this professional education program. Dr. Arthur J. Robins (1962) endeavored to evaluate activities of voluntary social welfare agencies in Dhaka, among other assignments, to ascertain and understand the extent to which they had been meeting the needs that prompted their establishment (evaluation in relation to ends) and the way they were carrying out their functions (evaluation in relation to means). This study was conducted under the joint auspices of the Social Welfare College and the then East Pakistan Council of Social Welfare with a view to enhancing and modernizing the functioning of the agencies with a bearing on the responsibility of administering the grants-in-aid program. The study was also to decide, on their behalf, the appropriateness of the services; to engage the interest of businesspersons in social welfare programs; to utilize the civic-mindedness of the business community and to train the direct service volunteers, an activity in which the college and the council might share responsibility. The council which was an active association of voluntary agencies, scrutinized the findings of the study. Among others, they invited Frances Maria Yasas to contribute (during 1962–63) to the development of social welfare training. Her principal work involved advising the concerned ministry or departments in carrying out a training program for social welfare personnel at the college,, as a consultant on fieldwork and other matters; assisting in developing practical training materials, reference material and other aids required in training welfare personnel at various levels (Yasas, 1963). Yasas ascertained certain special needs of the College of Social Welfare: growth of the college faculty in depth; development of research and indigenous literature; preparation of a directory of social welfare agencies; inclusion of rural social welfare in the teaching program; a suggestion for a ten day camp in a village in the training program; closer cooperation of the college with other training institutions; strengthening of the contents of the human growth and development course and of the medical social work course; need to study the effect of cultural patterns on social work; need to study the relationship of Islamic values and social work (Yasas, 1963).

The values of social work as a profession should be linked with those of the culture but not necessarily at every point, for in social work the process is more important than results (Williams, 1958). At one time there was a survey of activities of the members of the teaching staff designed to make them more conscious of their responsibility in the college; similar to this endeavor, a special fieldwork workshop was organized and held in the Bangladesh Academy for Rural Development at Comilla (when Mr. Giffard was UN adviser) to chalk out ways and means for conducting fieldwork practice in a meaningful way so that it could yield extensive indigenous teaching materials.

The course on fieldwork was noted several times in relation to issues of agency problems, their appropriateness, supervision facilities at the agency's end, and the components of education the students could receive in a professional perspective.

To investigate the prospects and problems of the social welfare course at the BA (pass) level, principals of major colleges were invited in 1966 to a seminar by the authorities of the College of Social Welfare. (A.K. Ahmadullah spearheaded the project uniquely through his contributions in this respect. Vice-Chancellor Dr. M.O. Ghani's contribution in this respect deserves to be recorded.) Inaugurating the seminar, Vice-Chancellor of the University (the late) Ghani pointed out that the society might prevent, if not cure, a score of social problems by providing the right type of education to the students and people at large. He added, "There comes to the fore the importance of social welfare as a discipline." Professor Ahmadullah pointed out that the members of the faculty were trying to compensate for the deficiency in existing study material by means of fieldwork experience, research findings and use of those insights inherent in the Bangla literature. A publication program was introduced for publishing books in English and Bangla which might be useful for the students at BA (pass) level (Yasas, 1963). The Asia Foundation at Dhaka, showing a keen interest in the development of social work education, came forward to assist financially and by donations of books. Both universities and colleges benefited from this support. The question of library development had always been attended to seriously. There were more than five thousand books and about five hundred bound periodicals of back issues and every day the number was rising through gifts. Professor Ahmadullah deserves credit for most of the library development work.

ADMISSION OF THE STUDENTS

A group test, a verbal reasoning (VR) and language usage test, differential aptitude tests (DAT), and an interview to assess motivation of an applicant for social work are administered to students. Aspects of the college program requiring further attention were, according to Dr. Yasas, curriculum planning and development, field work, development of teaching materials related to local settings and research. She recommended that the college take the initiative in arranging for faculty to become members of boards of agencies; arranging for faculty to be invited to speak to outside groups; getting the staff together for a two or three day retreat during the summer vacation at some quiet spot outside Dhaka where the faculty as a group could evaluate what was done during the year; sending representatives to attend international conferences, and encouraging the staff to write for professional and semiprofessional social work journals. A teacher's job description might include joining the association of social workers and, ideally, assuming leadership responsibilities in it; joining the Council on Social Work Education; playing a role in the National Council of Social Welfare in planning and program formulation stages; talking to prospective employers to sell the idea that persons with social work training can best do the job; establishing contact with the Child Welfare Training Center.

In light of the suggestions, the National Conference of Social Work Educators was organized in Dhaka in 1964 for further development of social work education. The goals and objectives of this conference were mainly to share experiences in all areas of social work with special emphasis on major issues confronting social work education for exploring the possibilities of strengthening and improving the educational programs and facilities available to professional social workers (Ahmadullah, 1964). In order to achieve balanced development of society, social welfare as a special field of activity received recognition from the beginning in the national plans which provided it with the necessary administrative and organizational framework (Momen, 1964). With the growing need for trained personnel and emphasis on the type and quality of training, social welfare was introduced as a subject of study in the university. By the year 1964 it was introduced in the Dhaka University as a full-fledged course of studies at the BA (hons); the subject had been taught at the MA level since late 1958. The subject was introduced in some colleges at the BA (pass) level under Dhaka University as one of the elective courses for preparing students for professional training and for meeting the overwhelming demand for trained workers (Momen, 1964) (see Table 21-1).

Table 21-1

Affiliated Colleges in Different Universities and Colleges Offering Social Welfare/Work Courses

Dhaka University		Rajashahi University		Chittagong University	
Number of Colleges	Number of Colleges having social welfare	Number of Colleges	Number of Colleges having social welfare	Number of Colleges	Number of Colleges having social welfare
245	101	135	22	216	17

ACADEMIC AND PROFESSIONAL DEVELOPMENT OF THE COURSE

The National Conference of Social Work Educators in 1964 was a landmark in the history of the development of social work in the country. The main thrust of the conference was on problems and prospects of social work education; development of courses based on local needs, study material and indigenous literature; selection, admission and evaluation of students; and staff development. By sharing experiences in various areas of social work education; considering ways and means by which the existing supply of social work educators could best contribute to the planned extension of social work education; endeavoring to have some uniformity in the curricula of social work, the conference attempted to reach certain conclusions in respect to training curricula (Ashraf, 1964).

The recommendations about the objectives, applicability, and levels of social work education were that the School of Social Work should have a committee consisting of teachers and agency workers for developing indigenous materials. The schools should undertake programs such as youth clubs, nursery schools, and recreation centers as a laboratory for experimentation of social work methods. Survey and research reports on social problems and experiences of workers in the field should be used in teaching.

About the foundation and background courses, undergraduate courses and fields of special interest, the major recommendations were to select such courses as sociology, economics, psychology, philosophy, political science, statistics, concepts in relevant Islamic studies, criminology, and demography. It was also suggested that the teaching of the background courses should be undertaken, as far as possible, by social welfare teachers.

The theme of the interrelationships of social work methods and fieldwork practice was highlighted; research should be conducted to find out the consistency or lack of it between religious values and social work values and the everyday practice of people in society. As regards admission and evaluation of students, it was suggested that personal contact should be made with social work agencies and educational institutions to inform and educate them about social work; that relations should be established with various employment agencies by providing booklets/pamphlets and other literature containing information on social work training; that employers of the various organizations should be encouraged to send their workers for social work training; that alumni members of various schools working in the field should also be requested to refer suitable candidates for admission; that evaluation of students should employ a written test, personal interview, psychological test, group test and medical examination.

In respect to staff development, the suggestions were that the role of the international consultants should be mainly advisory, providing technical knowledge in developing social work expertise. They might take on limited teaching responsibility primarily to help the country teacher in his or her professional development (Yasas 1963).

In relation to selection of faculty members it was suggested that no fresh graduates should be appointed as faculty members until they had had approximately two years of field experience. Exchange of faculty and field staff was suggested. It was advocated that local teachers be sent abroad for advanced training when they have acquired basic professional training and had some teaching experience.

Only after social work became relatively clear at the government level from a conceptual viewpoint did the training program gain momentum and start marching forward along the professional path. Studies in social welfare/social work courses at BA (pass), BA (hons) and master's level in the country were being carried on in that spirit up to the beginning of the liberation war (a mass upsurge against Pakistani rule began in late 1969). During the period from 1971 to 1973 the new government had to take steps to reorganize the war-ravaged country in various aspects of national life including education. During this period educational institutions, particularly at the intermediate and degree levels, sprang up like mushrooms. At this time the College of Social Welfare and Research Center at Dhaka merged with the Dhaka University as an institute (1973). The proposal for merger was initiated quite some time before at the planning board level. This merger (in the opinion of the authors) greatly impeded the college's autonomy in regard to maintaining the professional identity of the course. In respect to the Institute at Dhaka University, situations hindering professional autonomy are easily understood. Other Institutes at Dhaka University had been enjoying considerable autonomy and continued to exercise independent control over selection and admission of students and other areas of administration. Selection and admission of students at the honors level at the Social Welfare Institute are controlled by the faculties concerned (Faculty of Arts and Faculty of Social Sciences). One of the reasons seems to be that in no other institute is there provision for teaching honors level courses.

The professional practice of social work in Bangladesh was primarily a response to certain needs and circumstances facing the changing society at the onset of industrialization and urbanization. The Directorate of Social Welfare (DSW) dealing with these needs and problems, in principle, began to meet its human power requirement exclusively with the graduates in social welfare/social work. It continued to follow this principle, as far as possible, up to 1973. Toward early 1974 in order to cope with postwar social problems and amid disorganization due to unemployment and malpractice in the academic arena, policymakers and planners were found to be apathetic toward the professional implementation of social welfare programs. Consequent upon this view, a sharp change took place in the recruitment policy. Any person having a master's degree in social work or any social science subject is eligible to compete for professional jobs in social welfare. It is worth noting that some programs after 1982 (when H. M. Ershad assumed power) were renamed: the urban community development program became the municipal social service, and medical social work was designated hospital social service. According to Recruitment Rules formulated in 1985, for employment of personnel in hospital social service, research and publication, and various institutional programs, the minimum qualification is a second class master's degree in any discipline, preferably a master's in social welfare, sociology and social work (Government of Bangladesh, 1985).

The gradual weakening of the status of social work may also be attributed to other situations, such as the creation of separate departments for youth and women, which were initially controlled by DSW. At present DSW runs programs for youth and women with limited or nominal responsibility. Relief and rehabilitation, rural development, family planning, health education, and labor welfare issues have been outside the domain of social welfare from the very beginning. As such, the limited programs of DSW have become more limited, rather more squeezed (Mia, 1990). But generally it is agreed, and was endorsed by the National Conference of Social Work Educators (1964) that in a developing country like Bangladesh, to establish social work as a profession on a firm footing, persons involved in training and those working in professional jobs should jointly endeavor to enrich knowledge and experience and at the same time advocate professionalizing the discipline. The renaming of the department from Social Welfare to Social Service indicates a trend of attributing decreasing importance to professionalism, for there are certain ever–existing sociopathological problems in every society (loss of both parents, vagrancy and juvenile crime, prostitution and physical or mental handicaps) which demand service-oriented programs such as those that have long existed. Another important fact is that the internal training center, the Social Service Academy, has widened its scope and responsibility according to departmental requirements for imparting fundamental training for social workers on the job. The Rural Social Service (RSS) program, launched mostly under the financial patronage of one nongovernmental organization (NGO) in 1974, could not until recently obtain any results that could be differentiated from those of other allied programs. The Upa-Zilla Social Service Officers, who are mainly concerned with RSS, are also assigned to many other responsibilities, including those of probation officer, police, court, and prison officials (Sarker, 1989).

To look into structural constraints surrounding social work and the role of social work educator, a second National Conference of Bangladesh Social Work Teachers' Association was held in 1986. After Bangladesh became independent in 1971, it was expected that every public service, including social welfare, would be more systematized and the skills and methods of social work would be applied in appropriate fields in a scientific manner. It should be mentioned that the poverty alleviation program not only is highly emphasized in our national planning process, but has also been the continuing slogan since the Pakistan

regime.   Hidden at the roots, poverty, unemployment and systematic
exploitation have created socioeconomic problems with the result that the primary concern of the government has been to work with the poorest sections of
the poor. In such a situation, the so-called development programs taken up by
the government or NGOs are for all practical purposes circling around the outer
periphery of people's needs. The endeavors of these programs may be termed as
mostly present need–oriented or circumscribed. Social surveys and research on
many relevant issues are undertaken, reports are prepared, but, in many cases,
they are not used in the formulation of plans and programs for development.
Such plans and programs are also not implemented effectively. So, the aims of
social work in such circumstances as the avowed policy of the Department of
Social Service (DSS) of selecting and training social work personnel, are being
threatened and, perhaps, destroyed.   Moreover, if we examine the budget
allocation or amounts spent for social welfare programs in different national
plan periods we can determine the government's evaluation of the program of
social welfare (see Table 21-2).

Table 21-2

Budgeted Allocation in Different Plan Periods

Plan	Allocated Amount against Social Welfare (TK. in crore)	Amount Spent (TK in Crore)	%
First five-year plan	12.28	12.28	0.2/7
Two-year plan	13.60	11.30	---
Third five-year plan (1980–85)	59.00	39.11	0.2/4
Fourth five-year plan (1991–94)	133.00	---	0.8/6

Source: Planning Commission, Ministry of Planning, Government of Bangladesh,
           Dhaka.

Note: Some internal changes might have taken place.

The programs of social welfare are currently confined to rural social service, welfare of the physically and mentally handicapped, child welfare, control of vagrancy, the social service academy and grants-in-aid for voluntary social welfare agencies (Momen, 1990). Programs relating to corrections of juvenile offenders and rehabilitation of released prisoners are neglected, though they are among the oldest programs of the DSW. The program of school social work was abandoned a few years ago. Mental illness is taken care of by the psychiatric wards in a few important hospitals in addition to the Mental Hospital at Pabna.

REVIEW OF SOCIAL WORK EDUCATION AT UNIVERSITY AND COLLEGE LEVEL

Any discipline at the university level must have its syllabi, with earmarked reading materials and books or references. A discipline like social work also needs fieldwork practice and research activities with a view to developing reading materials and thereby meeting the demands of the changing society. At the time of writing this chapter, as indicated, under the guidance and supervision of UN experts/teachers, a curriculum of an international standard was framed for courses on social welfare. Today, after about thirty years, some changes and adjustments in the curriculum have been made by local experts having exposure to the Western situation. But, compared to our needs, to what extent these are sufficient is a matter of close scrutiny, critical evaluation and objective assessment (Momen, 1990).

Since independence a serious dearth of textbooks in Bangla, the predominant medium of instruction, has been observed. In this situation the textbooks or notes written by college level teachers to meet college level needs have become more or less key resources for those who are studying at the degree, honors degree and master's level. Indigenous reading material, which should have been developed through use of case materials screened out of field practices of students, research and survey reports, case studies, on-the-spot observation or some action oriented programs to this end, as was recommended as far back in 1964, has still not been implemented to a satisfactory extent. Furthermore, sufficient attempts have not been made to modify or update our curricula according to the changing needs of the society together with emphasis on indigenous material. As a consequence, teaching of these courses remains confined to the stereotyped content although the society has changed a lot in the meantime.

Social work as an elective subject was introduced at the college level (BA pass) about twenty-five years back (see Table 21-3). The question as to whether it could be taught at the college level in a general manner needs to be resolved. As indicated, the number of colleges in which social welfare/work is offered compared to the total number of colleges in the country gives an impression of the popularity of the subject. But the teacher/student ratio is very uneven. The number of teachers compared to that of students is deplorably inadequate; in a few colleges teachers with no social welfare/work qualification are temporarily teaching this course (Talukder, 1990). In such a situation, social welfare/work as an elective subject has also been introduced at the intermediate level (because of its popularity as a subject) under the various higher secondary boards in the country (see Table 21-3).

Table 21-3

Distribution of Courses in Social Work at Different Stages

(According to Dhaka University curriculum up to Degree Hons. Level. Other information as provided are common)

Stage	Term	Number of Courses	Marks		Total Marks		
		Theoretical	Pract.	Compre-hensive	Credit	Non-Credit	
Master's (Final)		4 (with social research and statistics com-bined)	1	1	600	—	600
Master's (Prely)	1	4 (with social research and statistics com-bined)	1	1	600	—	600
Degree (Hons.)	(courses are complet ed in 3 parts in 3 years)	7 (taking 2 courses as 1 in second and third years)	1	2	900	600	1500
Degree (pass)	2	3	—	—	300	—	300
Interme-diate (H.S.C.)	2	2	—	—	200	—	200

Note: Those who obtain Honors degree of 3 years' duration go directly to the Master's (Final) course while those with a Bachelor's degree of 2 year's duration must be admitted initially to Master's (Ply) course of one year duration and only on successful completion of that course one can be admitted to the Master's (Final) course.

It is an admitted fact that in a modern state among many welfare programs social welfare/work is crucial but not the most important program (Maurice, 1974). Social work is basically a helping profession aiming at guiding individuals singly or in groups toward solving the problems they encounter. People of Bangladesh generally face problems—social, economic and psychological—mainly created by mass poverty. So the main objective of social work should be to assist the poor and the destitute in such a manner that they can play their social roles ably. Since individuals and groups are the universal concern of social work, it is the prime duty of social workers to develop a systematic process and strategy under which they may be encouraged to take initiative and be productive in their efforts. As has been indicated, a theoretical framework of social work is yet to be developed in Bangladesh, and the professional persons or agencies concerned need to be aware of it before formulating the curriculum as well as social work activity programs. So we should give serious attention to analyzing the following: knowledge about humans and society, critical examination and review of various social service communities, and training at field level to obtain knowledge and skills at the grass-roots level for drawing up a plan for study and formulation of activity programs. Social work supports the proposition that if people are guided, and are given material assistance, and if favorable opportunities are created for them, many will become responsible and productive citizens. To this end, the task of a trained social worker is to establish rapport with people, identify their needs, form work groups, sensitize people, utilize resources, restore latent potentialities and encourage will and initiatives (Akbar, 1990).

In order to accomplish this, all that needs be done cannot be implemented by the social work educators alone. The responsibility for carrying out such an enormous but most important professional task cannot and need not be shouldered by the social workers or educators alone. This responsibility lies with all those who are concerned about the social work professional, the users, the beneficiaries, as well as the funding agencies and, in a country like ours, the government. In the final analysis, all those who are affected directly, or indirectly or who have any concern about the quantity and quality of delivery of human services—which are the products of common endeavors of people needing human services, people ably providing such services and people working in close collaboration and cooperation—should work as equal partners toward attainment of human welfare goals. For this, what is needed most is a public relations system, well organized and competently handled. The mechanism would be constant educating, learning, mutual exchange of views and information, a sense of partnership, equality and mutual respect. Not only are these to be encouraged and valued but are essential and, therefore, deserve to be the focus of all concerned at all times.

REFERENCES

Ahmadullah, A.K. (1964). Address of welcome in the National Conference of Social Work Educators of Pakistan, Dhaka.

Ahmadullah, A.K. (1986). Problems and prospects of social welfare education in Pakistan. In Momen, M.A. (Ed.). Report of theNational Conference of Social Work Educators of Pakistan, Dhaka.

Ahmadullah, A.K. (1986). Presidential address, Report of the Seminar of Bangladesh Social Work Teachers Association, Dhaka.

Akbar, Muhammad Ali. (1990). Social work education in the socio-economic context of Bangladesh. Seminar report of Bangladesh Social Work Teachers Association, 1986, Dhaka.

Akbar, Muhammad Ali.(1990) Role and contribution of population control program and agencies in social work education. In Mia et. al. (Eds.). Social work and social development *(bangla)*. Rajshahi: Bangladesh Social Work Teachers Association, p. 91.

Ashraf, Shareef. (1964). First National Conference of Social Work Educators: an evaluation. Report of the First National Conference of Social Work Educators of Pakistan, Dhaka.

Camp, Sharon L. (Ed.). (1981). *Draper Fund Report*, No. 10. Washington, D.C. p. 17.

Carlson, Victor D. (1958). *Current Activities Report* (to UNTAA) for the period February 16 to March 31 (1958) as referred to in the *Report and the Project from which It Arose* by Dr. J.J.O. Moore.

Friedlander, Walter A. (1968). *Introduction to Social Welfare*, 3rd. ed. Englewood Cliffs, N.J.: Prentice Hall, pp. 9–10.

Government of Bangladesh. (1985). *Bangladesh Gazettes*, Extra, Jan, 23. *The First 5-Year Plans* (a 2-Year Plan included) Planning Commission, Ministry of Planning, Dhaka.

Government of Pakistan. (1956). National Report of the Pakistan Conference of Social Work for the Eighth International Conference of Social Work. Munich.

Government of Pakistan. (1958). *The First 5-Year Plan (1955-1960)*, vols. I, II. Karachi: Government of Pakistan Press.

Hussain, Noorul & Alauddin, M. (1970). *Introduction to Social Work Methods*, Dhaka: College of Social Welfare and Research Center, pp. 1-2.

Karim, Nehal. (1991). Quest for cultural identity of Bangalee Muslims. In Chowdhury, A. & Momen (Ed.). *The Dhaka University Studies*, Part A, Dhaka: University of Dhaka, Vol. 48, No. 1, p. 121.

Maurice, Bruce. (1974). *The Coming of Welfare State*. London: B.T. Betsford, p. 90.

Mia, Ahmadullah. (1990). Social problems, social welfare planning and training in Akbar, Muhammad Ali et al. (Eds.). *Social Work and Social Development (Bangla)*. Rajshahi: Bangladesh Social Work Teachers' Association, p. 15.

Momen, M. Abdul. (1964). Editorial. Report of the First National Conference of Social Work Educators of Pakistan, Dhaka.

Momen, M. Abdul. (1990). Social work education - university level akbar. Muhammad Ali et al. (Eds.). *Social Work and Social Development, Bangladesh Social Work Teachers Association,* Rajshahi: Bangladesh Social Work Teachers' Association, p. 116.

Momen, M. Abdul. (1964). Seminar report of the First National Conference of Social Work Educators of Pakistan, Dhaka.

Moore, J.J.O. (1958). *The Report and the Project from Which It Arose: A Tentative and Unpublished Report.* Prepared for the Government of Pakistan, Dhaka.

Rahman, Atiqur M. (1990). *Degree Social Welfare (Bangla)* Dhaka: Quran Mahal, p. 236.

Rashid, Rifaat. (1964). Problems and prospects of social work education in Pakistan. *Report of the National Conference of Social Work Educators of Pakistan*, College of Social Welfare and Research Center, Dhaka, p. 11.

Robins, Arthur J. (1962). *Voluntary social welfare agencies in Dhaka: a critical appraisal*, Social Welfare Studies, Dhaka: No. 1 College of Social Welfare and Research Center.

Sarker, Abdul Hakim. (1989). Probation in Bangladesh: problems and prospects. In Qamruddin, K.A.A. (Ed.). *The Dhaka University Studies*, Part F, vol. 1. no. 1. Dhaka: University of Dhaka.

Talukder, Abdul Huq. (1990). Social work education at college level. In Akbar et al. (Eds.). *Social Work and Social Development (Bangla)*. Rajshahi: Bangladesh Social Work Teachers' Association, p. 119.

United Nations (1958) UNICEFs work in Africa - changing cultural patterns. *United Nations News Letter*, March 16.

Williams, Robin M. (1958). Value orientation in American society. In Stein, Herman D. & Cloward, Richard A. (Eds.). *Social Perspective on Behaviour,* Glencoe, Ill.: Free Press.

Yasas, Frances Maria. (1962-1963). *Role of United Nations Social Welfare Training Advisor in East Pakistan with Special Reference to the College of Social Welfare and Research Center*, Dhaka.

22

JAPAN

Kei Kudo Maeda

HISTORY OF SOCIAL WORK EDUCATION IN JAPAN

Japan exemplifies rapid industrial growth and economic prosperity in today's world, but at the middle of the nineteenth century it was an isolated nation. Let us first look at how it started and developed the system of social work education.

Apprenticeship Training

Since 1639, Japan had been maintaining self-imposed isolation, which ended in 1853 with the visit of American fleets that requested Japan to trade. The subsequent uprisings led to the establishment of a new government under the Meiji emperor in 1868. This marks the beginning of modern Japan. The Meiji government promoted active political, economic and cultural exchanges with Western countries. The real changes the government leaders tried to make were the abandonment of the feudal structure of Tokugawa society and the adaptation of Western institutions of modern centralized rule (Reischauer, 1981).

Compulsory education in Japan began in 1872. There was a strong interest in the education of children among the families of all social classes. By 1900, the enrollment in elementary schools reached 80 percent. This figure was equal to the enrollment record of England in the same year (Foreign Press Center, 1988).

Now let us look at the field of social services. The native Japanese religion Sinto, "the way of gods," centered around the worship of nature, fertility, reverence for ancestral deities. It did not play any significant role in charitable work. The Buddhist religion was introduced into Japan from China in the sixth century. Since then, it had played various important roles in providing care to the needy either by the work of faithful Buddhist among the imperial families or by the Buddhist temples. But the modernization of the governmental policies had given a new dimension to social services.

In 1873, the government abolished the policy of prohibition of the Christian faith that was adopted in 1587. Within the following few years, Christian missionaries had built many high schools and seminaries. Among the graduates of those schools were some very active social service workers who made large contributions to the development of social work education. With the help of Christian churches some of them had opportunities to visit the United States and Europe in the early 1900s. They committed themselves to improve Japanese social services and the educational system for the workers in those services along with the Buddhist people.

The organized relief work in Japan in the nineteenth century was developed out of the needs created by repeated natural disasters and the wars against China (1896 to 1897) and Russia (1904 to 1905).

The first program of social work education may be traced to 1908. In that year, the national government begun an educational program, the Training Course for Workers in Correction and Relief (Kanka Kyusai Jigyo Koshukai). It lasted for fifteen years until the local governments started their training programs in 1922. They taught a variety of subjects in the training courses, including mental health, child psychology, administration of institutions, and treatment programs. The total number of participants of this national program was 6296 (Kikuchi & Sakano, 1980).

Yet the length of the course itself was very short. It varied from year to year, from only ten days to three weeks. Therefore, the training of those who were engaged in social services had to depend largely on apprenticeship. By 1911, there were 494 private social service agencies or organizations, 130 were of Buddhist and 80 Christian (Namae, 1931). Others were supported by charitable individuals and by donations from the Imperial families. Except in the field of education for the disabled, there was no tax-supported social service institution in those days.

Beginning of University-Based Education

In 1911, Taisho University, a Buddhist university in Tokyo, set up a study center for social work. In 1918 that university started the first course in social work on the university level in Japan. By 1932, eleven Buddhist and Christian colleges and universities had begun courses in social work. They taught their students about social problems and social service programs both at home and abroad. Though not all the graduates of those courses found jobs in social services, some of them worked as pioneers in settlements, children's homes, training schools for the delinquent, or youth organizations such as YMCA or YWCA.

In 1928, the Central Social Work Association (Chuoh Shakai Jigyo Kyokai), the forerunner of the National Council of Social Welfare, started a one year training course for university graduates. Though far from ideal, it may be regarded as Japan's first attempt to establish a graduate school for social work students (Kida, 1967). In the same year the First International Conference of Social Work was held in Paris. Sixteen Japanese participated in that conference after many weeks of travel by boat. Japan was getting ready to join the rest of the world in the assertion that social work requires professionally trained personnel. Yet the tide within the nation was about to turn against democracy.

The effect of the Great Depression was prevalent in Japan, and in 1932 the government started a public assistance program. About this program the government documents stated that the "law was formulated on a different basis from those of foreign countries." It explained that individuals who applied for assistance did not have rights, though the national and local governments had responsibilities to help needy individuals (Okamoto, 1983). When we look at this logic in historical perspective, we can see that such paternalistic ideology was closely related to the politically necessary image of the Emperor. He was to be looked upon as the responsible and protective head of the whole Japanese family.

In 1933 Japan withdrew from the League of Nations and started to walk on a road toward nationalism and totalitarianism. The government began to control state socialism and tried to change any expression that contained the word *social*. In 1938 the Ministry of Internal Affairs changed the name of its Bureau of Social Work to Kosei-Kyoku. (The literal translation of *kosei* means to make life of people healthy and enriched.) The colleges and universities that had social work departments also changed the name of their department to Kosei Department or something else.

In 1943, because of World War II, the "graduate course" in the Central Social Work Association was closed. In the sixteen years of its existence, there were 174 graduates of that course. Many of them became government officials in social service administration or social work teachers after the end of World War II.

New Orientation for Professional Education

World War II was over for Japan in August 1945. Japan was occupied by the Allied Forces with General MacArthur of the American army as the head of the administration. The Japanese people faced the problems of survival. With the joint efforts of staff members of the Supreme Commander for the Allied Powers (SCAP) and Japanese government officials, they established various social welfare policies that laid the foundation for the postwar Japanese social welfare systems. According to Mr. Yoshisuke Kasai, then vice minister of the Ministry of Health and Welfare, there was mutual respect and trust in their teamwork (Shakai Fukushi Kenkyujo, 1978).

The SCAP staff urged the earliest possible establishment of a training school for public assistance workers. Dr. Donald V. Wilson, who formerly taught at Louisiana State University, was in charge of the social work training branch of Public Health and Welfare Section in SCAP and helped the Ministry of Health and Welfare establish and finance the training school. The school started in 1946 and later developed into the Japan College of Social Work in Tokyo, the only school in the country with complete financial support by the Ministry of Health and Welfare.

The curriculum of this college of social work in the beginning stage was patterned after a prewar one year graduate course held by the Central Council of Social Work. The college also offered new courses such as social casework and group work. To some social work teachers and social workers, those methods courses were the symbol of "professional education," while to others they were the symbol of "straight " importation of Western theories.

Many universities whose social work departments suffered from lack of support during the war were gradually getting ready to reestablish themselves. In 1950, Doshisha University in Kyoto set up the first master's program in social work. In 1951, the U.S.-Japan Peace Treaty was concluded and Japan was an independent nation again.

In 1955 the Japanese Association of Schools of Social Work (JASSW [Nihon Shakai jigyo Gakko Renmei]) was organized with nine schools; soon three more schools joined. Not all those schools identified themselves as offering professional social work education. Whether university education for social work should prepare its students for professional practice became a long-standing subject of debate. Very often, the term *professionals* was taken to mean specialists. Some people believed that the university should not try to train their students to become "specialists." They said the university should help them understand human suffering and be critical of existing service programs. On the other hand, other people believed that the university should train students as professionals to help people with their problems of living. The differences of opinion were often rooted in ideological differences, reflecting the political cold war between the Western countries and socialistic countries that was taking place at that time.

Antiprofessionalism Influenced by the Student Movement

In the 1960s social welfare services were expanding while the Japanese economy developed. The governments and voluntary organizations worked to set up various social service programs for different population groups. Many people pointed out the need for better qualified social workers at social work conferences and at professional meetings.

On the other hand, there was a new current in the world of young people. In the early 1970s, joining the arising student movements in Western countries, an antiestablishment movement in Japan began in the Psychiatric Department of the School of Medicine in Tokyo University. The student leaders challenged their professors and criticized their practices as a violation of human rights in the name of "profession." Students of other Japanese universities followed suit, demanding that university professors and administrators institute various reforms.

In some departments of social work, activist students demanded revision of their curriculum because they thought it was "too Western." The faculty members could not readily reach any conclusion about taking united action in response to the requests of the student leaders. They found themselves deeply split between social reform interests and direct service or methodological interests.

The student movement also influenced the leadership of professional organizations. The Association of Psychiatric Social Workers devalued "professional" training, and the Japanese Association of Medical Social Workers changed its membership requirement to include nonsocial workers. They formally changed their name to the Japanese Association of Medical Social Work. In the 1970s the place of *social worker*, the title *social welfare laborer* gained popularity.

In 1976, in responding to the increasing need for qualified workers, the Central Advisory Council on Social Welfare of the Ministry of Health and Welfare made a draft for a law to regulate social workers. Yet, mainly reflecting the antiprofessionalism of the time, many social work organizations expressed negative views on the proposed act. After much debate, the proposal was withdrawn.

Beginning of Regulating Social Workers

The greatly expanded Japanese economy in the 1980s made the Japanese enjoy life in an affluent society. The social insurance programs and public welfare services greatly improved over the years, including the establishment of comprehensive national health and national pension programs. Yet the rapid social changes had brought many difficult human relations problems, which required different helping approaches from the traditional institutional care. Besides, there was an unforeseen rapid increase in the population of old people. The statistics showed that the Japanese people lived the longest in the world. (In 1991, the average life expectancy for women was 82.81 years, and for men 76.11 years.) New nursing homes and day care centers for the elderly had been built all over the country to meet the pressing needs, but many more were necessary. Foresighted planning for social welfare human power and service resources was needed to assure quality of services. Local councils of social welfare set up volunteer centers to promote citizen participation in various welfare programs. With a rising standard of living, citizens of all ages started to show an interest in volunteering. Those citizens obviously needed good supervision by professionals.

To meet these changing situations, JASSW started to formulate a curriculum policy by setting up a Special Task Committee in the mid-1980s. The committee studied the curricula of the member schools. The findings of the study indicated that in the diversity of the curriculum of social work education, one major characteristic was neglect of practice theory and fieldwork.

In 1987, the committee presented to the general meeting of JASSW, guidelines for the curriculum for social work education, which were approved. The point that the task committee emphasized was that the purpose of social work education was social work practice, and for that purpose a comprehensive and well-balanced curriculum was indispensable. The curriculum guidelines set up four areas: the foundation area, methods and skill area, fields of practice area, and seminars and practicum area. The guidelines stated that four weeks of practicum should be a part of required subjects. The guidelines also described qualifications of agency supervisors and faculty members who would lead fieldwork seminars at the school.

Though four weeks of practicum seemed far from sufficient, this was a big change for Japanese social work education, for it symbolized that JASSW did have a unified goal for the education of undergraduate students. JASSW finally held the position that social work education for baccalaureate students prepares them for the beginning level of professional practice. At that time there was hope that JASSW would issue certificates in the future for those who completed the educational programs established according to the JASSW guidelines (Hirata, 1986). But, before that idea was carried out, a new law to regulate social workers that oriented social work education to a new direction was passed.

In 1988, the new law, the Registered Social Worker and Registered Care Worker Law (Shakai Fukushishi oyobi Kaigo Fukushishi Ho), was implemented. We will look at the current picture in more detail later.

VALUES OF SOCIAL WORK

Emerging Democratic Values in the Taisho Period

For centuries, Japanese feudalistic society was under the influences of Buddhism and Confucianism. Japanese people considered filial piety the center of all virtues. Diligence and harmony were highly valued in farming culture, as the people in the community had to work together for the rice crop like a large extended family.

The modernization of Japan through industrialization and urbanization continued in the Taisho period (1912-1926), under Emperor Taisho, who had succeeded Emperor Meiji, his father. With the development of parliamentary power as well as higher education and mass media, there was a strong liberalizing tendency not only in the political system but in every aspect of life. This trend toward democracy was more clear in big cities, where traditional values of family solidarity and paternal authority were challenged by young people. They were called "mobo and moga," standing for modern boys and modern girls. Traditional arranged marriage was looked down upon by them. Many progressive college students became interested in the Marxist movement stimulated by the Russian Revolution.

As mentioned, the collapse of democracy was to follow soon in the Showa period, after the Taisho period. Before and during the World War II the militaristic and totalitarianism ideology emphasized the traditional culture of group-orientedness and vertical relationships. They adopted the idea of the family system in various organizations in the society, including the field of social services. The residents of social welfare institutions were thought of as a big family with the image of directors as fathers and the care takers as mothers. The concept of welfare rights was never heard of in those days.

Rights of Individuals

With Japan's defeat in 1945, the Allied Occupation undertook major restructuring to democratize the political, economic and social institutions of Japan. The constitution was completely revised in 1946. In its Article 25, it guarantees that the state has the responsibility to ensure that the people maintain a minimum standard of wholesome and cultural living. At a school of social work, some students named their club "25" to show their high respect for Article 25 of the constitution. This anecdote indicates that the very idea of the "right to life of individuals" was important to social work students. In fact, it was a central value that supported the welfare workers as advocates for poverty-stricken people in 1950s and 1960s.

The value of individual dignity was presented as a distinct countertheme to the wartime theme of "die for the country." Identified with Western culture in postwar Japan, many Christian social work leaders actively discussed values in their writing. For instance, one wrote, "The greatest lesson that the Japanese people got from the last World War was about the values of human dignity . . . The human personality is above the nation, and it should direct the nation for its actions" (Shimada,1980). In a way, however, this value was the reemergence of the old value of Taisho democracy, which provided a solid foundation for postwar democratic Japan.

In the 1970s and 1980s, Japanese social workers adopted such Western concepts as self-realization and quality of life in their work. This does not mean
that Japanese people merely imported foreign ideas. Rather, these concepts
expressed ideas which Japanese social workers were seeking to formulate their
new goal.

Various welfare programs and systems centered around the institutional
services were already well developed by that time to meet the basic needs of
people in crisis. But many social workers were not satisfied with that level of
service. The concept of normalization, for instance, expressed exactly what
many Japanese social workers were seeking in their work. When this concept
was introduced, Japanese social workers recognized that their counterparts
overseas were seeking the same goal.

Various United Nations actions to promote rights of the disabled helped
Japanese citizens deepen their understanding of the equal rights of disabled
persons. Supported with the values of individual dignity, the social service
system in Japan has been gradually changing its emphasis from traditional institutional care to community-based care in recent decades.

In 1986, the Japanese Association of Social Workers formulated the Code of
Ethics for its members. It included the respect for the value of human dignity
and other cardinal values of social work that were also valued in Western
countries. At schools of social work in Japan these values are taught to students,
yet social work teachers need to improve their methods of teaching how to
operationalize these values in day to day social work practice.

Current Issues Related to Values

In recent years, advocacy for consumer rights by various professional and
citizen groups is making people more sensitive to their rights. Newspapers frequently discuss the right of patients and their families to informed consent or
informed choice in health services. Progress in medicine is raising many
complicated value-related problems that cannot be solved with the simple notion
of "self-determination" of patients.

The right to privacy of citizens is also an issue with the advancement of
computer technology. Many local governments are forming ethical committees
to establish rules for the information in computers and often social workers are
among such committee members.

Another major issue related to values is the rapid internationalization of the
labor market in Japanese society. Particularly in the past few years because of
the shortage of labor force, many unskilled laborers have been entering Japan
legally or illegally to work. They are making big cities multicultural communities. To most Japanese people, including social workers, this presents a new
experience. Can we truly respect individual differences and diversity in our

daily living, given them precedence over traditionally valued harmony and group unity? These suggest that in Japanese social work education, more down-to-earth discussions of values are necessary in the classrooms and professional meetings.

RANGE AND STRUCTURE OF SOCIAL WORK EDUCATION

Overview of School Education

Let us first take an overview of the Japanese educational system and its trends. Under Japan's compulsory education system, all children have the right to six years of elementary school and three years of junior high school free. The enrollment rate in those schools in 1991 was 99.99 percent (Ministry of Education, 1991). The ratio of students going on to senior high school was 95.4 percent in 1991. The ratio of senior high school graduates who entered colleges or universities in 1992 was 38.9 percent.

The competition for the "good" universities is very fierce and aspiring students have to study hard for many years to enter universities of their choice. Because Japanese companies usually employ their workers for a lifetime, it is commonly believed that good universities open doors to good workplaces with lifelong security. Some universities of high academic status that offer social work education are influenced by this trend. Some of their students choose the Social Work Department because admission is easier for them than in other departments. They are merely interested in getting a diploma from that university. Fortunately, there are other seriously motivated social work students. The 1983 Study on Social Work Students showed that 73.4 percent of Japanese social work students in the BS program were seriously considering working in the field of social work (Nihon Shakai Jigyo Gakko Renmei, 1988).

Currently, there are 514 universities that grant a baccalaureate degree with four years of education. The total number of university students is nearly two million, and about 30 percent of these are women. The number of women students is steadily increasing every year.

As for social work, thirty-nine universities and colleges are currently members of JASSW. The total number of students in social work courses or departments in those schools is estimated to be around thirteen thousand. There are more women than men in social work programs.

Eleven junior colleges are also members of JASSW. There are many other colleges that offer training for child care workers, but these are not members of the association.

What about the situation of graduate schools? In Japan, the role of the graduate school has been traditionally regarded as that of training academic researchers and future university teachers. Except in the field of medicine and a few others, the graduate schools have played a small role in professional education. One reason is that because of the lifelong employment system, employing organizations preferred to give their own training to their employees so they will develop an identification with their organizations. They give systematic and continuing training on the job. With the advancement of science and technology, this situation is gradually changing. Increasing numbers of adult learners are entering graduate schools to upgrade their professional knowledge and skills.

Currently in Japan 219 schools offer doctoral and master's programs and ninety-four offer only masters programs. The total number of students in the Japanese graduate schools is about ninety thousand. As for social work, only nineteen universities offer master's programs and twelve offer doctoral programs. The number of graduate students in social work is about 150.

To meet the changing situation, the Ministry of Education plans to double the number of graduate students by the year 2000. So the graduate schools of social work will see some changes in this decade.

Vocational School and Junior College Programs

Vocational school and junior college education offers training programs for care workers. Currently there are two kinds of specialized programs for care work personnel: child welfare and care of the disabled and aged.

The Child Welfare Law of 1947 provides that child care workers must be qualified either by graduating from a recognized two year training school after a high school education or by passing the public examination given by the local governments for high school graduates. As the general level of education advances, the people of the latter category are decreasing. As of 1991, there were 330 vocational schools for child care workers. Most of the graduates of these schools work at children's day care centers for working parents. These centers are well developed and located all over Japan. Other graduates are employed in various kinds of child welfare institutions as care workers.

In 1988, the Diet passed the Registered Social Worker and Registered Care Worker Law mentioned earlier. The care workers this law describes are those workers who take care of physically disabled and elderly persons. The law provides that those who graduate from recognized vocational schools for care workers for the disabled and the aged can register as qualified care workers (Kaigo fukushishi). As of 1991, there were 119 such schools for high school graduates that offered two years of education.

There is another category of junior colleges, which aim at educating not care workers but social workers. These are members of JASSW. With the introduction of a national examination system for registered social workers, these junior colleges are finding themselves in a difficult position because the title of *social workers* is to be given to the baccalaureate graduates. Though there is a way for junior college graduates to take the national examination after two years of work experience as social workers, some junior colleges are trying to change their status to become four year universities.

Baccalaureate Programs

The Registered Social Worker and Care Worker Law clearly shows that the basic professional social work qualification is baccalaureate education. This law protects the title of the registered social worker. To receive that title, an individual must pass the national examination. To be eligible to take the examination, one must have completed the courses designated by the minister of health and welfare, including at least four weeks of practicum.

The examination is given annually. The applicants are tested on their knowledge on specified subjects: theories and principles of social welfare, welfare services for the aged, welfare services for the disabled, child welfare services, social security, public assistance, community welfare services, social work practice, psychology, sociology, law, medical knowledge, and care work for adults.

By spring 1991, three national examinations for registered social workers had been held. At the third examination, of 2565 applicants, 528 persons, or 20.6 percent of the total applicants, passed the examination. So far, this system has produced 1086 qualified workers who can register as social workers. With the introduction of the national examination, the curriculum of JASSW member schools is beginning to have some common courses.

Apart from the required courses for the national examination, many schools are creatively responding to the needs of the time. One recent unique development in the curriculum of these social work departments is the provision of international experiences for their students. Some schools place their students in agencies overseas, some others organize work camps for their students in developing countries, others take their students on a study trip to visit social work agencies in European and North American countries. Various other forms of international collaboration are also taking place (Bogo & Maeda, 1990).

The graduates of baccalaureate programs find work in a wide range of social services. Government services, child welfare services, services for the disabled, services for the elderly are traditional fields. Hospitals and health centers, community agencies and youth organizations also employ those graduates. In recent years, there are more job openings than available students seeking social work jobs.

Graduate Schools

In graduate schools, students prepare themselves to be specialized clinical workers, social work educators, or researchers. Though each school has unique characteristics in its educational goals, JASSW does not yet have a unified curriculum policy for graduate education.

When compared with the level of North American schools of social work, Japanese graduate schools of social work show a need for considerable improvement. For instance, many graduate schools can only admit a few students, five or ten each year. To catch up to the advancement in science and to meet the human power need for social workers of high quality, they have to enroll more students. The graduate schools have to have more creative programs to enroll experienced workers in advanced studies. They have to improve their skills training programs for their students, including good practicum placement. Similarly in the area of training researchers, improvement seems urgent.

These improvements cannot be made by the effort of graduate schools alone, since the Ministry of Education has the administrative power to recognize the educational programs of the schools. We will look at the role of the Ministry later.

In-Service Training

Most social service agencies and organizations carry active in-service training programs severally or jointly. The national and local governments also provide programs for training social workers. For instance, the Ministry of Health and Welfare is giving in-service training programs for medical social workers every year that run for several weeks. In recent years, over two-thirds of prefectural governments have a Training Institute to provide organized continuing education for workers in social welfare agencies in their region. The National Council of Social Welfare also has various in-service training programs including one for agency administrators. Often local governments give subsidies or grants to social service agencies to encourage them to hold continuing staff-development programs. Continuing educational programs for the workers in social services are actively operated throughout the country. A shortage of personnel in social services is anticipated. In October 1993 the National Council of Social Welfare set up the Center for Manpower Development within its organization. It aims to help prefectural councils actively promote their labor force development programs, which include training for home helpers as well as for volunteers of all ages in various fields.

Various professional organizations, such as the Japanese Association of Social Workers, the Family Therapy Association, and the Group Psychotherapy Association also have annual workshops of many kinds, and their programs seem to be well attended. In recent years, the interest of social workers in learning from the programs and practice of social workers overseas is increasing. Various organizations are sponsoring trips abroad for social workers to meet this need. On the other hand, various Japanese organizations and social work agencies are inviting social workers from overseas to have them experience Japanese social services and learn from them.

The Role of the Ministry of Education

In Japan, the Ministry of Education is responsible for determining whether the colleges and universities are meeting its standards and regulations. Such standards relate to financial status, land and buildings and other facilities of the educational institutions. The Ministry of Education also reviews educational programs with respect to educational aims, curriculum, and number and qualification of faculty members. Each year, educational institutions have to report their curriculum and school regulations and financial status. Whenever universities and colleges want to make changes, such as in departmental organization or student enrollment, they have to consult the ministry and present the required documents. Then the ministry seeks the opinions of the Advisory Committee on College Establishment (Daigaku Secchi Iinkai). That committee always includes a few social work professors appointed by the ministry when social work programs are under review.

The role of the Ministry of Education is not sufficient to function as gatekeeper for the profession. There is no periodic review as is practiced in the United States by the Council on Social Work Education in their accreditation procedures. It is hoped that in the future, Japanese social workers will have an organization similar to that council to improve the accreditation system. In social work courses, students' tuition is a funding source to the university, but its percentage of the total income of the educational institution varies from one school to another. Some schools are partly supported by religious organizations. The national government gives a lump sum subsidy to most private colleges and universities every year, based on the evaluation of the government-funded foundation Shigaku Shinko Zaidan. The foundation gives special subsidies to many unique educational projects of the schools such as extension programs for citizens in the community. The foundation also gives subsidies to schools if they have disabled students.

As already mentioned, there is an increasing interest among people of all ages in participating in various social services. The Ministry of Education is promoting social welfare education for schoolchildren by giving subsidies to schools for their volunteer projects. In the social education programs in local communities themes related to social welfare are popular. Both the Ministry of Health and Welfare and the Ministry of Education are helping the local governments finance these educational programs for the community, and university social work teachers are taking an active role in these programs.

Looking to the Future

In spite of a comparatively short history of social work education, Japan now has a distinct group of hard-working social work professionals.

As a nation, Japan is determined to play a responsible role in improving the quality of human life. It is hoped that in global partnership Japanese social workers will make a suitable contribution to that goal.

REFERENCES

Bogo, M. & Maeda, K. (1990). Collaboration in adaptation of knowledge for social work education for practice: a Canada/Japan experience. *International Social Work, 33*, 27-40.

Foreign Press Center/Japan. (1988). *Education in Japan.* About Japan series 8, Tokyo.

Hirata, T. (Ed.). (1986). *Guide to Japanese Social Work Education.* Tokyo: National Council of Social Welfare.

Kida, T. (1967). Shakaijigyo Kyoiku (Social work education). In Nihon Shakai Gigyo Daigaku (Ed.). *Sengo Nihon no Shakaijigyo* (Social work in post-war Japan), Tokyo: Keiso Shobo, pp. 393-404.

Kikuchi, M. & Sakano, M. (1980). *Nippon Kindai Shakaijigyo Kyoikushi no Kenkyu* (Study on the history of modern Japanese social work education). Tokyo: Aikawa Shobo.

Ministry of Education. (1991). *Monbu Tokei Yoran* (Statistics in educational administration). Tokyo: Daiichi Hoki.

Namae, T. (1931). *Nippon Kirisuto-kyo Shakai Jigyoshi* (History of Japanese Christian social work). Tokyo: Kyobunkan.

Nihon Shakai Jigyo Gakko Renmei (Ed.). (1988). *Shin-Shakai Fukushi o Manabu Hitono tameni* (New guide for those who want to study social welfare). Tokyo: National Council on Social Work.

Okamoto,.S. (1983). *Shakai Fukushi Genron* (Theories and principles of social welfare). Tokyo: Zenkoku Shakai Fukushi Kyogikai.

Reischauer, E. O. (1981). *The Story of a Nation.* New York: Alfred A. Knopf.

Shakai Fukushi Kenkyujo. (1978). *Senryoki ni okeru Shakai Fukushi Shiryo ni kansuru Kenkyu Hokokusho* (Report on studies of social welfare documents & data during the occupation of Japan). Tokyo.

Shimada, K. (1980). Shakai Fukushi Taikeiron (Systems of social welfare). Kyoto: Mineruba Shobo.

23

CHINA

Joe C. B. Leung

INTRODUCTION

In 1986, the writer had the opportunity to give a series of lectures, Introduction to Social Work, to a group of undergraduate sociology students in Guangzhou, the People's Republic of China (PRC).[1] After hearing the functions and qualities of a social worker, a student looked perplexed and confused. She said, "According to what you have said, our industrial workers and peasants are social workers too." In a sense, it is true to say that according to the cherished socialist values "to serve the people" and "mutual aid," all people in China are social workers. From another point of view, some American visitors in the 1970s perceived that China had already an effective social welfare system. Many social problems which preoccupied social workers in the West were virtually nonexistent. They concluded that professional social workers were not needed in China (Bacon, 1975; Sidel, 1974). Therefore, social work, by and large, has been an alien and unknown occupation in China, and a mythical entity of the people in the West. Yet, recent developments in China indicate that there is a glimpse of hope for the reemergence and revitalization of social work and social work education.

Reading a paper that purported to be about social work education in China, most readers would inevitably ask these basic questions: Does professional social work practice exist in socialist China? How are social workers with Chinese characteristics trained? To what extent can Western social work, which is rooted in the values of democracy and individual rights, have a place in a socialist country with primary emphasis on collective interest over individuality? There are no straightforward answers to these questions. This chapter is an attempt to present some recent developments of social work education in China. It is hoped that the descriptions may shed light on answers to these questions.

CHINA AS A SOCIALIST COUNTRY

China, with a fifth of the world population, avowedly and unswervingly socialist, is considered a Third World country. With a gross national product (GNP) per capita of U.S. $330 in 1988, China is ranked as one of the poorest countries in the world. However, social development in China in terms of life expectancy (69.5 years old), mortality rate (6.7 per thousand population), and literacy rate (70 percent of the population aged over fifteen years old) has already attained the level of the middle-income nation group (World Bank, 1989: 62-63).

Shortly after the inception of the People's Republic in 1949, China had to face a variety of social problems left behind by the previous feudalistic and traditional society. These included prostitution, gambling, venereal diseases, begging, crimes, low status of women, drug addiction, and unemployment. Ideological education and participation in productive labor were prescribed as effective means to rehabilitate people with these problems (Meng & Wang, 1986: 293-295; Fei, 1984: 350-355). Thereafter, the mentioning of social problems in China was regarded as an attack on, or denial of the superiority of the socialist system. It was believed that social problems could no longer exist in a socialist society where private property was abolished, class conflict and exploitation were absent, and the common people were masters of the production means.

However, with the rapid liberalization of the economic structure in the 1980s, social problems involving poverty, family breakdown, school dropout, unemployment, population pressure, prostitution, drug addiction, decadent life–style, juvenile delinquency, and care of abandoned children, the elderly, the physically disadvantaged, and the mentally ill have become more critical. With gradual relaxation of the policy on mass media and academic research studies, open recognition and discussion of these problems have become more acceptable. Some social problems are attributed both to corrupting influence of the West and to insufficient ideological education of the grass roots party units. Thus, the more recent interpretation of social problems does not deny their existence in a socialist society but makes the distinction that the socialist system is superior in solving social problems which cannot be solved satisfactorily in capitalistic societies (Chen, 1986: 15; Yuan, 1986; Ren, 1988: 347).

In the Third Plenum of the Central Committee of the 11th Party Congress in 1978, the Communist party advocated the construction of both a material and a spiritual civilization. Material civilization refers to the improvement of physical living standards and the quality of life, whereas spiritual civilization refers to the healthy culture of the society. The Communist leadership believes that impending social problems could be eliminated by the promotion of spiritual civilization through the practice of Communist ideals: self-sacrifice, selflessness, to serve the people, to love the country and the party, to love laboring, and to live a plain, frugal and austere life-style.

Although the Chinese Constitution (1982) has prescribed the rights of citizens to welfare protection by the state, the rights are mixed with obligations. Rather than seeing welfare rights as natural entitlements founded in human conditions, they are treated as grants given by the state to citizens to enable them to contribute their energies to the needs of the nation (Edwards et al. 1986: 125). In other words, individual rights will be respected so long as they are consistent with state policies of maintaining national stability, promoting economic productivity and building socialism. Coupled with the values of the work ethic and self-reliance, it is work rather than dependence on the state for assistance which would give a person dignity. Care for the weak is a gift to be received rather than a right to be claimed. In brief, the orientation espoused by the Chinese leaders in defining social problems means that all individual and personal problems should be viewed in the context of the need of the society, the country and the party. Under the emphasis on collectivity, self-oriented values would not be respected, and the individual would definitely not be the center of social work practice.

SOCIAL WELFARE SERVICES AND WELFARE PERSONNEL

As in the traditional Chinese society, the primary responsibility for personal problems and needs in Communist China still rests with the family (Chow, 1987; Leung, 1991). Other than the family, there are three major welfare institutions, namely the Civil Affairs Departments, the work units, and the neighborhoods. There are no official social work positions, per se, in these welfare institutions. The social welfare functions are carried out by cadres[2] in various government departments and mass organizations.[3] The following is a brief description of the activities and staffing of these welfare institutions.

The Civil Affairs Departments

Welfare services provided by the Civil Affairs Departments include material assistance to poverty-stricken households; residential care for the mentally ill, the mentally handicapped, the childless elderly and orphans; and job placement for the physically handicapped in welfare factories. Only the "three no" persons, that is, those without family support, working ability, and any source of income, are eligible for assistance.

Likewise, the other duties of the Civil Affairs Departments, such as relief work in natural calamities, management of funeral homes, marriage and society registration, demarcation of administrative regions, resettlement of migrants and ex-servicemen, are mainly administrative work, rather than direct social work practice. Working under tight budgets, civil affairs cadres are both low paid and poorly educated. It is estimated that among the 100,000 cadres of the civil affairs (1.13 million employees), only 5.2 percent have college education, and another 13.3 percent have junior secondary school education (*Social Security Bulletin*, 1989). The situation is further aggravated by the fact that a lot of the civil affairs cadres are veterans transferred from military units. The Ministry of Civil Affairs has recognized the urgent need to promote the quality of the staff since the Eighth National Convention on the Work of Civil Affairs in 1983. Of course, improving staff quality does not necessarily mean encouraging the development of professional social work.

The Work Units

Similar to the situation in other socialist countries, each individual work unit in China is the most important source of social services, including social security, medical benefits, housing, education, and even personal social services. Personal social services consist of mediating family disputes, providing material assistance to poverty-stricken households, counseling delinquents, implementing the single-child family policy and family life education, managing nurseries and kindergartens tens, organizing recreational and cultural activities, and caring for the elderly, the sick, the widowed, and the handicapped (Chow, 1988). The staff responsible for the tasks are cadres of the unions and the Communist Youth Leagues at the grass roots level. They are elected to the positions by their respective constituencies. On the top, the Ministry of Labor and its departments are responsible for the formulation and monitoring of the overall policy on labor welfare.

By 1989, there was a total of 589,000 grass roots unions, with 99.1 million members and 488,000 full-time union cadres (State Statistical Bureau [SSB], 1990: 807). On the other hand, the Communist Youth League had 56 million members and 208,000 full-time cadres in 1988 (SSB, 1990: 808). In a recent survey of the union executives at the grass roots level, 53 percent were over age fifty, and only 25 percent were less than forty years old. In terms of education, 70 percent were below the level of junior secondary school (Zhang, 1987: 64). By contrast, the cadres of the Communist Youth League were younger and better educated. Some 65.6 percent were secondary school graduates, and 26.1 percent had college education in 1986. In terms of age, 87.7 percent were under thirty years old (China Youth Work Annual Report Editorial Committee, 1989: 192).

It is noteworthy that comprehensive occupational welfare is only available to employees in state-owned enterprises, who comprise 18.3 percent of the economically active population (SSB, 1990: 113). The state policy on occupational welfare does not apply to employees in collectively owned enterprises, foreign joint ventures, and private enterprises. Of course, there is very little provision for rural laborers, temporary laborers, and individual entrepreneurs.

The Neighborhoods

A typical neighborhood structure in China consists of a street office (agent of the district people's government) and residents' committees in the city, and the county/town people's government and village committees in the rural areas. Financed by local economic enterprises, the street offices and county/town governments usually provide welfare services such as elderly homes, day care centers and shelter workshops for the mentally and physically handicapped and the mentally ill (Leung, 1990a, 1990b). According to the official regulations, cadres of the residents' committees and village committees are elected by the residents. They are usually retired people who are in charge of a number of personal social services similar to those in the work units. The work of providing care to the aged, the handicapped, and the destitute is guided by the Civil Affairs Departments, whereas the work in family and child care is assisted by the local Women's Federations. Neighborhoods have become an important source of help for those without work units, such as the peasants and the individual entrepreneurs.

By 1989, there was a total of 93,600 residents' committees with 366,000 full-time cadres, and 934,000 village committees with 3.8 million full-time cadres (*China Society*, 1990). Similar to the situation of the unions, these positions are often provided for demobilized soldiers, redundant staff transferred from other enterprises, and retired cadres. These cadres, by and large, are both old and poorly educated (Leung, 1990a: 202-203).

Overall, the Chinese welfare system is both segmented and decentralized. There is no coherent pattern for development among different welfare sectors. The government has given urgent priority in both the Eighth Five Year Plan (1991-1995) and the Ten-Year Development Program (1991-2000) to the reform of the existing social security system, which is becoming too expensive and ineffective in the context of demographic changes and economic reforms (*Beijing Review*, 1991: 21).

In addition, the development of the neighborhood-based welfare programs is to be promoted as a major source of help for people with welfare needs. China undoubtedly is also facing some of the impending social problems which are similar to those of the West. These problems are handled by a variety of personnel under different auspices. Specifically, the cadres in the work units, the neighborhoods, the government departments, and the mass organizations are in some ways performing social work functions like those of professional social workers in the West. Unlike in the West, however, these social work activities or tasks are often closely intermingle with political and economic functions. For instance, a welfare cadre is also responsible to convince the masses to accept government policies and transmit to them socialist and Communist values. Likewise, economic functions denote the need to develop profitable economic enterprises to finance welfare operations. Therefore, distinctive cadre positions solely responsible for social work and social welfare functions are rare.

The welfare cadres who engage in direct practice with clients have two distinctive features. First, they are nonprofessionals who largely have no specific training for their responsibilities. In staffing those welfare institutions, China relies heavily on nonprofessionals or laypeople with similar background to that of the working targets in the provision of personal social services. Instead of applying professional knowledge and systematic theories, the basis of help is usually providing mutual help, experiential advice, and informal support. Since these informal helpers are also officials representing the interests of the party and the government, informal help can, in some cases, be unfriendly and hostile (Leung, 1991). As a rule, the educational level of these cadres is low, and relevant training is not considered important.

Second, these cadres are administrative leaders and political representatives. Those who work at the grass roots level in the neighborhoods and work units are supposed to be elected by their constituencies to become the administrative leaders in charge of the units and then released from their previous production duties. In this case, preservice training of grass roots cadres seems difficult, and a career for them is not necessarily possible. In theory, if they are not reelected, they have to return to their previous job assignments. For example, a youth worker of the Communist Youth League has to transfer to work in other nonwelfare settings once he or she has attained the age of twenty-eight, which is the age limit for Youth League members.

Above all, as an elected representative of the constituency, the cadre is expected to provide leadership, guidance, and direction to his or her constituency. His or her authority is backed up by the control of administrative sanctions and rewards which determines the livelihood and life chances of the working target. From time to time, the cadre is expected to serve as a model in attitudes and behavior for subordinates. Instead of academic qualifications and job-related training, China considers correct political attitudes of supporting socialism and the party line, following the mass line working style, and living a plain and austere life-style as the pivotal qualities in effective performance of cadres (Leung, 1991: 20).

EARLY DEVELOPMENT IN SOCIAL WORK EDUCATION

Under the directorship of an American social worker, Ida Pruitt, a Social Service Department was established in a hospital in Beijing in 1921. Besides providing social casework, adoption, and rehabilitation services, the department was also an in-service training center for social workers. Later, with the assistance of professors from Princeton University in the United States, the Sociology Department in Yanjing University (now Beijing University) was established in 1922, and the department was renamed the Department of Sociology and Social Services in 1925.[4] The establishment of the training program was seen as a response to the staff training needs of voluntary welfare organizations established by American Christian missionaries in China, such as the Young Men's Christian Association and the Young Women's Christian Association. By the 1930s, social work studies were established in twelve universities.

A report prepared by the educators in 1948 for a United Nations international survey on social work training gave a general picture of social work functions in that period:

> Social work in China not only includes services rendered to needy persons but also includes helping individuals or groups of individuals to make social adjustments, remedying and preventing social illness, and promoting social welfare leading to peace and security. Social workers in China are engaged as administrators and practitioners in the following services and activities: general relief, child welfare, medical social work, psychiatric social work, employment, rehabilitation of handicapped persons, rural social work, labor welfare, social insurances, social settlement and institutional care for special groups (United Nations, 1950)

After the establishment of the Communist government in 1949, all social science subjects, including social work, were abolished in universities in 1952. Following the development in the Soviet Union, social science subjects were considered pseudosciences and bourgeois disciplines supporting the capitalistic system (Yuan, 1989: 72). As a result, social work education, based on American experiences, was completely abandoned, and for almost thirty years, China lost contact with Western social work. Not surprisingly, the report from a follow-up survey of social work training by the United Nations in 1955 showed only a question mark opposite "Mainland China" (United Nations, 1955).

The earlier development of social work in China was mainly based on a directly transplanted model from the United States. The concept of social work practice was largely urban-based clinical practice which mainly served the personnel needs of the voluntary agencies operated by the missionaries. Social work education was carried out mainly under the auspices of sociology in prestigious universities, particularly those established by Western missionaries. The Chinese critics attribute the failure of social work to take roots in China to the direct importation of Western social work without consideration of the actual local conditions. A recent conference report on Social Work Education in China concludes:

Social work education in the 1930s could not take root in China because it was basically imported from the United States. Learning from experiences in the past, a direct copy of Western models would not be effective. The establishment of social work and social work education with Chinese characteristics requires the insistence on socialist direction, the consideration of the reality in China, and the critical absorption of foreign ideas. (Ministry of Civil Affairs, 1989)

SOCIAL WORK EDUCATION IN THE PEOPLE'S REPUBLIC OF CHINA (PRC)

Even though formal social work training had been terminated, social welfare activities, such as relief of victims in natural calamities, mediation of family disputes, assistance to poverty-stricken households, and institutional care for the childless elderly and homeless handicapped people, continued. Yet, because it was dominated by political orientation and at the same time isolated from Western influences, there was hardly any attention given to the development of social welfare based on empirical research and systematic conceptualization. Welfare organizations were staffed by general cadres with no preservice training. Cadre colleges operated by the government ministries, the mass organizations, and the Communist party provided the main sources of in-service training for cadres. However, the focus of cadre colleges was mainly on ideological and leadership training.

It was only after 1979 that the government encouraged that social science subjects be reinstated in university curricula. By 1982, sociology departments existed in twelve universities. Problems encountered in the reinstatement included the lack of qualified teachers and teaching materials. With the opening of China to the outside world, international cooperation in research and teaching, though still limited, has facilitated the sending of students overseas for higher education in social sciences and the invitation of overseas academics to teach in China. Significantly, Western social science publications are now widely available in university libraries, and some of them have already been translated into Chinese.

Under the patronage of sociology, studies on social problems such as the causes of delinquency, the care of the elderly and the handicapped, urban and rural social security provisions, marriage and divorce, industrial relations, and demographic trends have been carried out. The severity of these social problems has been, for the first time, revealed publicly. For example, a national survey in 1987 identified 51.64 million people with various forms of physical and mental disabilities in China (SSB, 1989: 362).

The first indigenous textbook on sociology, which included a chapter on social work, was published in 1984. The book regarded social work as "applied sociology," which made use of sociological theories to study and analyze the causes of social problems and explore their solutions. The social work tasks are the following:

> Under the leadership of the Party and Government, social work mobilizes society efforts to manage welfare enterprises of the people. The focus is on helping those who have lost their ability to adjust to social life, and to rehabilitate them back to healthy living. The main task in social work is to maintain social order, and strengthen as well as develop the social system. (Fei, 1984: 336)

Eventually, some social work courses, such as "Introduction to social work", "Social Security," "Casework," and "Community Work," have been incorporated into the sociology curriculum. In 1988, four universities were approved by the State Education Commission to develop social work courses in their universities. Notably, there are limited numbers of qualified teachers in China to teach such courses. Existing social work teachers have a variety of backgrounds, including philosophy, sociology, economics, geography, political science, history, and law. Even some of the retired social workers, trained in the 1930s, have been redeployed as teachers. At the same time, books and journals with the term *social work* as the title have been published.[5] Not surprisingly, socialist ideologies have replaced Western social work values in these publications. With an absence of clear differentiation, the term *social work* is often confused with other disciplines such as Sociology, Social Services, Social Welfare, Civil Affairs, and Social Security. In the view of the ordinary people, "Social Work" is more commonly referred to as "voluntary work" which is outside one's employment, rather than an occupation, per se.

Among all the welfare institutions in China, only the Ministry of Civil Affairs has expressed an explicit desire to incorporate Western social work into its activities. Its interest is demonstrated by the following:

1. Sponsoring an undergraduate degree program in Social Work and Management in the Sociology Department of Beijing University in 1989.[6]
2. Setting up the Social Work Educational Center in 1988, composing of a core group of university professors to teach social work courses to teachers in civil affairs cadre colleges.
3. Proposing to establish a social work college, offering preservice undergraduate social work education.[7]
4. Communicating actively with overseas welfare agencies and universities on the development of social work education and social welfare services in China, and sending cadres for social work training in overseas universities and study tours in various countries.
5. Sponsoring and participating in international conferences on social welfare. Two of the conferences held in Beijing are the Conference on Social Work Education in the Asian and Pacific Region: Existing Patterns and Future Trends of Curriculum Development, 1988 and The Ninth Asia and Pacific Regional Conference of Rehabilitation International, 1990.

Finally, the China Social Workers' Association was formed in July 1991 under the patronage of the Ministry of Civil Affairs, and with the minister of civil affairs as the chairman of the association. In short, recent developments of social work education in China show that social work has been largely associated civil affairs activities.

THE CURRICULA OF SOCIAL WORK EDUCATION

Social work education is found now in fourteen civil affairs cadre training colleges and six universities. Specifically, the civil affairs cadre colleges are training staff for civil affairs work. At present there is neither an independent school of social work nor a social work department within the universities. Social work courses are included in the Sociology Departments of Zhongshan University, Beijing University, Shanghai University, and Jinin University; in the Faculty of Labor and Personnel Management of the People's University; and in the Philosophy Department of Xiamen University. Graduates of these universities are assigned to work in various fields, not necessarily related to social welfare. In terms of division of work, it is expected that cadre colleges would be for the lower-level cadres, whereas universities would be for the higher-level welfare personnel (*Social Security Bulletin*, 1989).

In Beijing University, a four year program on "social work and social management" was established in 1989, enrolling twenty students each year. This program consists of the following courses.[8]

1. Basic political courses (public courses): All university students take compulsory courses on political subjects, such as political economy, Marxism, history of the Chinese revolution, ethics, and logic.
2. Basic general courses: These subjects include social science disciplines such as sociology, statistics, political science, social psychology, and psychology, and other supplementary courses such as mathematics, computer usage, foreign languages, and official writing.
3. Basic social work courses: These subjects include social work methods, social security, social policy, social management, and social research.
4. Specializations: These subjects include working with youth, family, handicapped people, the elderly, and others. Since the program was only started in 1990, Specializations in the third and fourth years of the program have not yet been finalized.
5. Fieldwork: Fieldwork refers to field visits and research projects.

On the other hand, the Civil Affairs Administration Cadre College (Beijing) offers a two year program for existing civil affairs cadres with secondary school education and five years of relevant working experiences. Enrollment is eighty students each year. The program has three specializations: social work and social management, social administration, and welfare enterprise management. The courses can be divided into four main categories (*China Society*, 1991):

1. Political courses: philosophy, political economy, and history of the Chinese revolution
2. Basic courses: sports, foreign language, Chinese language, official writing, mathematics, and administrative laws
3. Social science courses: management, sociology, social psychology, social work, and civil affairs
4. Fields of civil affairs: grass roots political organ construction, administrative boundary demarcation, society management, marriage registration, funeral reforms, reception of migrants, social security, rural social insurance, relief work in natural calamities, community services, services for veterans, welfare production management, social welfare economics, civil affairs history, and marriage history.

Both political and basic courses are fundamental in cadre training and university education. The difference in the curriculum design between the Cadre College and Beijing University is the explicit emphasis by the former on the work of civil affairs, which therefore is more responsive to the need of training generic civil affairs cadres. On the other hand, the Beijing University curriculum, which apparently has more Western influence, seems to have the basic skeleton of a social work program.[9] The implementation of the curriculum design is largely dependent on the availability of qualified teachers for specific courses. Furthermore, designs of both institutions cannot clearly differentiate the responsibilities of the two levels or types of education.

Compared with the social work programs in the West, the Chinese training institutions only provide introductory courses on social sciences and social work methods. Other foundation courses in behavioral sciences, such as human growth and behavior, and specialized social work methods are relatively limited. Particularly in fieldwork, the idea of placing students in welfare agencies under qualified supervision has not been acknowledged. Unlike in the West, the priority on interpersonal intervention skills has evidently not been considered important. In short, the Chinese social work programs may be for welfare personnel, but definitely not for professional social workers, in the Western sense. Notwithstanding the experimental basis of the program in Beijing University which is sponsored by the Ministry of Civil Affairs, there is so far no definite commitment from the State Education Commission either to promote or to standardize the social work curricula in universities in the foreseeable future.

ISSUES IN SOCIAL WORK EDUCATION

Besides the need for qualified social work teachers, improved teaching methodologies,[10] and enriched teaching materials, several other issues have profound influence on the long road of professionalization and social work education development in China.

Education for Professional Social Workers Versus Political Educators

Influenced by the traditional emphasis on political and ideological education, the practice of "changing people" in China is based on the directive methods of giving guidance, instructions, and explanation, with the cadre defining and making judgments on what is right and what is wrong. According to the principle of "unity-criticism-unity" of Mao Zedong, a cadre would criticize the mistakes of the working target privately or openly, and persuade him or her to admit and make a self-criticism of his or her mistakes, and finally, accept the changes suggested or dictated by the cadre. Besides criticism and education, warning and threats backed by coercive administrative procedures and discipline are also employed by cadres to supplement the use of directive persuasion (Leung, 1991). Accordingly, the cadres are political educators from the Western perspective rather than professional change agents. The dogmatic and top-down approach is accepted by the Communist as wholly benign because presumably the party has the correct and absolute interpretation of the truth.

Political and ideological training would ensure that the cadres can make the correct decisions, follow the party line, and live as well as work as a model for ordinary people. Political and ideological work or propaganda work is considered paramount in unifying the thinking of the Communist party and the people of the whole country as well as enhancing education in adhering to the four cardinal principles and opposing bourgeois liberalization (*Beijing Review*, 1989: 5).

In contrast, Western professional training rejects any dogmatic imposition of defined and explicit political values. Rather, the Western model of social work practice would give preference to the values of acceptance, self-direction, neutrality, and a nonjudgmental approach to behavior. The individual rights of the clients to make self-chosen decisions would be respected. Hence, it is only when psychological and socioemotional needs of personal development and individual fulfillment can be recognized and perceived as important that Western social work can have a place in a Communist society. Otherwise, apart from ideological educators, what China needs are only social service personnel who take care of the physical needs of the disadvantaged. They may be occupational therapists, relief workers, home helpers, welfare planners and administrators, but not social workers per se.

Training for Micro Versus Macro Intervention Practice

In terms of the priority of needs of social work development in China, it is suggested that the types of social work knowledge required by China would not be sophisticated social work intervention methods at the microlevel, such as counseling and small group techniques, but macrolevel social science theories and practice methods, including community work, social planning, program implementation and evaluation, need studies, and policy analysis (He, 1989: 3). This differs from professional training in the West, which puts the emphasis on direct practice with clients.

Training for Professional Practice Versus Mobilization for Informal Care

The prevailing basis of operation of "social work with Chinese characteristics" is the informal network of mutual care. Following the mass line, the practice of the informal helpers is based on indigenous experience and wisdom as well as mobilization of informal support rather than systematic scientific knowledge. With millions of these informal helpers practicing in China, professionalization as a source of help and as a career is found to be both impractical and undesirable. Nevertheless, the strengths and weaknesses of the informal network should be evaluated, so that appropriate training of these informal helpers can be formulated. Again, this seems to support the preceding suggestion that the teaching of direct practice social work methods is not a priority. Yet, if it is desirable that the operation be supervised by well–qualified personnel, this implies that training for supervisors of the informal helpers with some forms of microlevel social work methods and skills would be advantageous, partly to facilitate the execution of their supervisory and teaching duties.

Training for General Practitioners Versus Cadres of the Civil Affairs

Of all the welfare sectors concerned, only the Ministry of Civil Affairs and its departments have shown explicit interest in and desire to accept professional social work training for their cadres. Thus, it seems that "professional social work," if it ever begins in China, will most likely emerge within the civil affairs system. However, the scope of the work of civil affairs is rather narrow, being mainly concerned with remedial welfare rather than social development. University educators do not like to equate social work with the work of civil affairs because it would both restrict the boundary of social work and the career choice of university graduates (He, 1989).

THE FUTURE OF SOCIAL WORK EDUCATION

Social work in China is far from being a profession, nor in fact a defined occupation. Although the road to professionalization is still uncertain, there is a clear consensus that training for welfare personnel is desirable. However, effective development of training and educational programs for the welfare personnel is largely determined by reforms in the existing civil service system as well as changes in policies on higher education. The Chinese civil service is plagued by the lack of institutionalized and rational procedures for selection, recruitment, dismissal, appraisal, training, appointment, promotion, and resignation (Burns, 1988). Under the present system of job allocation, it fails to ensure that individual interests and relevant training of students are respected and, seemingly, does not encourage a professional career.

Along this line, effective professionally/occupationally oriented curricula in training institutions can only be designed when defined welfare job positions and required qualifications are established. First and foremost, a review of the welfare personnel system with thorough job analysis and classifications, as well as long-term personnel planning, are urgently required. Multilevel training needs of welfare personnel can then be assessed before resources can be mobilized and allocated effectively to meet these needs. A further top priority is the training of competent and qualified social work teachers who can critically integrate Western social work knowledge with the Chinese situation.

Finally, what is the direction for the development of social work education in China? What is the meaning of professionalization of welfare personnel in China? To outsiders, what can Western social work offer to welfare development in China? It is too early and speculative to provide systematic and well-documented answers to these questions. Social work education in China has only taken the first step, and the future trends of social work and social work education remain uncertain.

Indeed, there is a need to promote better understanding between China and the West, to reduce the polarization based on the differences between social work with Chinese characteristics and Western professional social work. At this stage, both parties need to learn about whether some of their differences are in basic antagonistic conflict or are potentially complementary. It is believed that China can benefit from some of the scientific social science and social work knowledge/technologies, even some of the humanitarian and instrumental values behind social work practice. On the other hand, some of the distinctive characteristics and approaches to welfare in China can provide insights and stimulation to social welfare and social work development in developed and developing countries. The mission to determine the complementarity of the two social work approaches requires genuine cooperation, improved communication, and enhanced mutual understanding on equal terms between the training institutions and service agencies of China and the Western world. Fortunately, despite the prevailing conservative political climate, China is maintaining the open door policy of communicating with the West and is currently looking for outside assistance in the training of welfare personnel. It is hoped that Western social work technologies and values can in some ways be helpful to the development of social work and social work education in China.

NOTES

1   The opportunity to teach social work in China was part of a three year cooperative project in social work education between the University of Hong Kong and Zhongshan University, PRC. The write was the coordinator of the project (Leung, Nann, and He, 1990).

2. *Cadre* is a loose term referring to all governmental employees engaged in administrative, professional, and political tasks. Currently, there are 33 million cadres in China.

3. They are semigovernmental organizations under the auspices of the Communist party. Apart from being the bridges between the masses and party and the schools for the masses to learn socialism and Marxism, mass organizations also provide a variety of social services for their members. The more important ones include the trade unions, the Federation of Women, and the Communist Youth League.

4. The establishment of the Sociology Department of Yanjing University was assisted by Professor J. S. Burgese and Professor D. W. Edwards of Princeton University. The faculty consisted of six members from the United States (Lei and Shui, 1988). In the 1920s, there was a total of twenty-two universities in China, of which fourteen were established by overseas Christian churches. Besides being staffed mainly by overseas missionaries, these universities often adopted American university curricula (Cheng, 1987: 546).

5. *Chinese Social Work* by Lu (1991) and the journal *Social Work Studies* published by the Institute of Social Welfare and Social Progress (Beijing Civil Affairs Administration Cadre College) are examples.

6. Because of the June 4 Incident, 1989, all students enrolled in Beijing University in 1989 had to attend a compulsory one year military training program.

7. The proposed college in Chagsha has four specialized programs, including social work and management, social administration and management, welfare enterprise management, and social security. The proposal was turned down by the State Education Commission because teaching facilities were considered inadequate.

8. The curriculum was based on the description by a representative from Beijing University who participated in a social work training program, sponsored by the Asian and Pacific Association for Social Work Education, held in the University of Hong Kong, Hong Kong, in August 1991.

9. The program has been assisted in curriculum planning and program teaching by the staff of the School of Social Studies, Hong Kong Polytechnic.

10. Currently, the main method of teaching in university education is still lecturing. The use of simulation games, small group discussions, workshops, and case studies is unusual.

REFERENCES

Bacon, M. H. (1975). Social work in China., *Social Work, 20*(1), 68-69.

Beijing Review. (1989, July 31-Aug. 6; 1991, Feb. 18-March 3).

Burns, J. (1988). The Chinese civil service system. In Scott, I. & Burns, J. (Eds.). *The Hong Kong Civil Service and Its Future.* Hong Kong: Oxford University Press, pp. 204-220.

Chen, F. (1986). Introduction to social problems in Shanghai. In Yu, C. Y. & Pang, K. F.. (Eds.). *China Urban Welfare Development: Conference Papers.* Hong Kong: Hong Kong Social Workers' General Union, pp. 13-25.

Cheng, H. S. (1987). *New Edition of Introduction to Sociology.* Beijing: People's University Press.

China Society. (1990, August 5; 1991, March 5). China Youth Work Annual Report Editorial Committee. (1989). *Annual Report on Youth Work 1987.* Beijing: Youth Publishers.

Chow, N. (1987). Western and Chinese ideas of social welfare. *International Social Work, 30*, 31-41.

Chow, N. (1988). *The Administration and Financing of Social Security in China.* Hong Kong: Center of Asian Studies, University of Hong Kong.

Edwards, R. L., Henkin, L., & Nathan, A. (1986). *Human Rights in Contemporary China.* New York: Columbia University Press.

Fei, X. T. (1984). *Introduction to Sociology.* Tienjin: Tienjin People's Publishers.

He, X. F. (1989). The planning and prospect of social work education in China. *Social Security Bulletin,* October 27.

Lei, J. Q. & Shui, S. Z. (1988). Thirty years of social work education of Yanjing University. Paper presented in the Conference on Social Work Education in the Asian and Pacific Region: existing patterns and future trends of curriculum development, Beijing University, December.

Leung, J., Nann, R., & He, Z. F. (1990). *Introducing Social Work and Social Work Education in the People's Republic of China: A Report on a Three-Year Cooperative Project in Social Work Education and Research Between the University of Hong Kong and Zhongshan University.* Hong Kong: Department of Social Work and Social Administration, University of Hong Kong.

Leung, J. (1990a). The community-based social welfare system in urban China. *Community Development Journal, 25*(3), 196-205.

Leung, J. (1990b). Community-based social welfare provisions in rural China: mutual-help and self-protection. *Hong Kong Journal of Social Work, 24*, 11-24.

Leung, J. (1991). Family mediation with Chinese characteristics: a hybrid of formal and informal service in China. *Social Welfare in China Monograph Series, 1.* Hong Kong: Department of Social Work and Social Administration, University of Hong Kong.

Lu, M. H. (1991). *Chinese Social Work.* Beijing: China Society Publishers.

Meng, Z. H., & Wang, M. H. (1986). *The History of Civil Affairs in China*. Haerbin: Heinongjiang People's Publishers.

Ministry of Civil Affairs. (1989). *Report on the Seminar on Strategic Planning of Social Work Education in China*. Beijing: Ministry of Civil Affairs.

Ren, P. X. (1988). *Foundation of Sociology*. Zhongqiang: East West Teachers' Training College Publishers.

Sidel, R. (1974). *Families of Fengsheng: Urban Life in China*. Baltimore: Penguin Books.

Social Security Bulletin. (1989, September, 1; 1989, September, 22).

State Statistical Bureau. (1989). *China Population Yearbook*. Beijing: Science and Technology Publishers.

State Statistical Bureau. (1990). *China Statistical Annual Report*. Beijing: China Statistical Publishers.

United Nations, Department of Social Affairs. (1950, 1955). *Training for Social Work: An International Survey*. New York: Lake Success.

World Bank. (1989). *Social Indicators of Development 1989*. Baltimore: John Hopkins University Press.

Yuan, F. (1986). Civil affairs and sociology. In Civil Affairs Society. (Ed.). *Collection of Papers on Civil Affairs and Social Security*. Beijing: Civil Affairs Society and Social Welfare Research Society, pp. 8-19.

Yuan, F. (1990). Social work education and the construction of modern Chinese socialism. In Lu, X. Y. (Ed.). *The Chinese Sociology Report: 1979-1989*. Beijing: China Encyclopedia Publisher, pp. 69-77.

Zhang, Y. Q. (1987). *Talks on the Organizational Work of the Unions*. Beijing: Workers' Publishers.

VI

OVERVIEW

24

COMPARATIVE AND INTERNATIONAL OVERVIEW

Lynne M. Healy

INTRODUCTION

Social work education is almost a worldwide phenomenon. Social work training courses exist on six continents, in developing and more developed countries alike. Since the dissolution of Soviet communism, countries previously without social work, including the republics of the former Soviet Union, Hungary, and Bulgaria, have initiated social work training programs. Still the existence of social work as a worldwide profession is not reflected systematically in the curricula of social work courses around the world and the mention of international issues is sometimes totally lacking. Why has awareness of the potential of the global profession been so slow to develop among educators?

Curriculum in social work education is shaped by many factors. Events and trends in society at large influence the selection of priorities and content for social work programs. Ways in which potential content areas are defined over time open or close options for curriculum development. Social work education is also influenced by its own past. Thus, the present status of international content in social work education is best understood through an exploration of its evolution.

International and comparative content in social work education can best be traced through analyzing the purposes and directions of curriculum efforts at various points in time. As the history is discussed, it should be evident that social work education has a record of considerable international activity, but remains without a clear conceptualization of appropriate international roles for the profession to guide current efforts.

DEFINITIONAL ISSUES

An important unresolved issue in international social work content is the definition of international social work. If content relevant to international social work is to be taught in social work programs, what is international social work?

Definition is closely linked to clarity in establishing objectives for international content, both in general and in individual programs; therefore, definitional confusion impedes progress in internationalizing social work education.

In the literature on international social work education, numerous definitions of the term are stated or, more often, implied. Other terms, such as *cross-national, cross-cultural, comparative* and *global,* are also used and sometimes confused with *international,* which is best used as a broad, umbrella term referring to any aspect of social work involving two or more nations. When used more narrowly, it has legal/political connotations and refers specifically to dealings between nation-states (Sikkema, 1984). A useful broad definition of international social work was given by Sanders and Pederson, as those "social work activities and concerns that transcend national and cultural boundaries" (1984: xiv).

In distinguishing international from related words, the following definitions appear to be the most commonly used. *Comparative* is best used as a methodological word, referring to a method for organizing and analyzing information about several countries or cultures (Hokenstad, 1984). *Cross-cultural* applies to transactions between two or more cultures, either within or between nations. Cross-cultural therefore is not necessarily international, although understanding of cultural differences may be essential for international social work. *Cross-national* is sometimes used interchangeably with *international.* When differentiated, it has a narrower meaning, as limited to transactions or comparisons of several nations, with *international* used to apply to the study of phenomena across most or all nations (Estes, 1984). *Global* is a more recent term, when differentiated from *international,* it is reserved for those phenomena affecting the whole planet. It implies comprehensiveness in scope.

It is interesting that articles written on international content in social work education over several decades identify definitional confusion as an issue. Yet, little or no progress has been made in achieving clarity or consensus. Indeed, the authors of a recent book on international social work agree that definitional issues will persist (Hokenstad et al., 1992). In 1956, a working committee of the Council on Social Work Education developed a definition of international social work. They opted for a narrow definition emphasizing organized programs.

> It was the consensus of our sub-committee that the term "international social work" should properly be confined to programs of social work of international scope, such as those carried on by intergovernmental agencies, chiefly those of the United Nations; governmental; or non-governmental agencies with international programs. (Stein, 1957: 3).

In this paper describing the work of the committee, Stein noted that at least six different usages of the term *international social work* were uncovered, ranging from social workers working in other countries to refugee services to common professional concerns with social workers in other parts of the world. In describing the narrow definition adopted by the committee, he emphasized:

> From this understanding of international social work, such content as crosscultural information, the nature of programs in various countries of the world, and the comparative analysis of needs and resources would not warrant the term (Stein, 1957: 4).

An opposite point of view was expressed by Kimberly, who advocates keeping the term *international social work* open for broad interpretation (1984). He specifically argues against operationalizing the term as international practice. Instead, he recommends a grounded theory approach to this relatively new field of interest, explaining that "to be restrictive in our vision will create boundaries at a time when we should be attempting to transcend them" (Kimberly, 1984: 2).

The findings of a survey conducted over thirty years after the 1957 report confirm that definitional clarity has not been achieved. This global survey of the member schools of the International Association of Schools of Social Work (IASSW) identified the following concepts as essential to at least some educators' definitions of international social work: study of comparative social policy; cross-cultural understanding; knowledge of a worldwide common profession; intergovernmental activities in social welfare; international practice of social work; a sense of collegiality with social workers around the world; concern with global social problems; and a general worldview (Healy, 1990). Surprisingly few respondents agreed with the concepts endorsed by the 1956 subcommittee. Only about 16 percent identified intergovernmental social welfare as an essential concept, and international practice was selected as essential by fewer than 25 percent of the respondents. Three concepts were held essential to be by more than 50 percent of the respondents: cross-cultural understanding (58.9 percent), comparative social policy (56.9 percent), and concern with global social problems (54.5 percent). Views of educators from different world regions were surprisingly similar in selecting definitions of international social work. In four of the five IASSW regions, the three concepts identified here were most frequently selected as essential. Notable was deemphasis of comparative policy among North Americans who selected a general worldview as a more important concept. Other smaller differences were less enthusiasm about cross-cultural understanding in Asia and considerable support for a concept of a worldwide common profession among European educators (Healy, 1990).

In developing curriculum for international social work, the educator is left with a poorly defined concept. The emphasis on organized, internationally sponsored programs of social services suggested in the 1950s is no longer at the core of international interests. Instead, three separate threads are dominant—comparative social policy, cross-cultural understanding, and global social problems—with considerable support for building a general world view as an essential part of international social work (48.8 percent of responses). As these threads would each lead to quite different curriculum objectives and content, the impact of a lack of a clear sense of educational purpose is evident.

INTERNATIONAL EDUCATION EFFORTS: A BRIEF HISTORY

The history of the development of international curriculum content cannot be separated from the history of international efforts in social work education generally. As noted, curriculum priorities are often shaped by external events, both within the profession and in the environment generally.

Most social workers would be surprised to learn that the first U.S. technical assistance project was a social work education project. In 1939, after Congress passed the Technical Assistance to Foreign Countries Act, the Department of State, the Children's Bureau and the American Association of Schools of Social Work were involved in a project which brought fifteen directors of Latin American schools of social work to the United States for a training tour (Hilliard, 1965). This was the first of a series of efforts which involved U.S. social work educators in providing assistance to the development of schools of social work in Asia, Africa and Latin America.

The United Nations (UN) was perhaps the major force in the spread of social work education around the world and U.S. educators played significant roles in these efforts. The UN assumed major responsibility for starting schools of social work in developing nations and sponsored international seminars for social work educators (Younghusband, 1963). United Nations surveys of training for social work throughout the world were completed in 1950, 1955, 1959, 1965 and 1971 (United Nations, 1971, 1965, 1959, 1955, 1950). The UN also sponsored overseas study for social welfare officials in developing countries, contributing to the growing number of foreign students at U.S. schools of social work.

Thus, two international roles were defined early for social work education in the United States: (1) as educator of foreign students and (2) as expert consultant in the development of social work education in other, especially developing, countries. Schools of social work were actively involved with the Department of Health, Education and Welfare (DHEW) and with the U.S. Agency for International Development (USAID) in projects to increase the pool of trained social work personnel in developing countries (Pettis, 1964). It appears that other international roles were deemphasized during this time. Thus, throughout the 1950s and 1960s, international education was primarily viewed in terms of what the world could learn from the U.S. schools of social work. Americans were experts and the targets of influence were foreign nationals and foreign country institutions.

Conferences Advance Curriculum Development

International curriculum during this period was advanced through a series of conferences sponsored by the Council on Social Work Education to encourage the development of international and comparative social welfare curriculum for social work programs. These conferences, all held in the United States between 1959 and 1970, were the Interprofessional Conference on Training of Personnel for Overseas Service, held at Cornell University (1959); the Interprofessional Conference on Professional Training for Students from Other Countries, held in Boston in 1961 (1963); the Conference on International Social Welfare Manpower, Washington, D.C., 1964 (1965); the Inter-Cultural Seminar, held in Hawaii in 1966 (Intercultural Exploration, 1967); the Workshop on Teaching Comparative Social Welfare (Kendall, 1969); and the International Conference on Social Work Education, Population and Family Planning, held in 1970 at the East-West Center in Hawaii (Kendall, 1971). Through cosponsorships, these conferences represented substantial collaboration between social work education and the major intergovernmental and U.S. government agencies involved in international work. For example, the 1964 meeting was cosponsored by the United State Agency for International Development (USAID) and the U.S. Department of Health, Education and Welfare and included participants from the United Nations, the Organization of American States, and the Department of State. The 1970 family planning meeting was funded by USAID and guided by an advisory committee of representatives from the UN, UNICEF, USAID, Planned Parenthood-World Population, and the American Public Health Association (Healy, 1985).

The earlier conferences stressed curriculum development to support the dual themes of preparation for technical assistance and education of foreign students. Over time, an important shift occurred in the focus of the conferences to concern with international content for U.S. students. The later workshops addressed the importance of cross-cultural learning and comparative social welfare content for students in U.S. schools.

Council on Social Work Education Support

To support these international activities, the Council on Social Work Education created appropriate structures. In 1967, the council upgraded its long-standing international committee to establish the Commission on International Social Welfare Education. The Board of Directors adopted a program of international cooperation in social work education in March 1967 and created a Division of International Education within its structure to manage the program (Kendall, 1967). It should be noted that international cooperation was identified as one of the council's key functions in a bylaws amendment adopted in 1964 (Kendall, 1967). The work of the commission and division now supported three goals: the two identified, and the development of international content for all students. A staff article in the *Social Work Education Reporter* reported the "growing conviction that international perspective and comparative study are needed by all students" (International Highlights, 1968: 11).

The Retreat from Internationalism

This new goal emerged at an unfortunate point in the history of international education in social work. Both funding trends and other forces in the larger environment combined to create a more hostile climate for international social work content. Funding for programs in international social work education was anticipated to follow passage of the International Education Act of 1966 by the U.S. Congress. In a 1968 speech to the annual program meeting of CSWE, the assistant secretary for education at the Department of Health, Education and Welfare predicted that funds would flow for education of competent graduate-level specialists in international social work (Miller, 1968). The act, however, was never funded. Just as social work education's interest in developing international content for American students increased, funding for international study dwindled.

By this time, new forces were affecting social work education and the larger society. The Vietnam war brought a reintensification of antiimperialist sentiment and disillusionment with the U.S. role in international affairs. These feelings affected many Americans as well as citizens of the Third World countries. The result was intense questioning of the relevance of American contributions to international social work. The field was particularly vulnerable, as its familiar foci of overseas consultation and training of foreign students had put Americans in one-way, expert roles. It became suddenly suspect to be interested in international affairs. The literature on international social work published during the late 1960 's and 1970 's emphasizes this new negative evaluation of U.S. contributions and potential. Khinduka (1971), for example, wrote that "despite its abiding humanitarian concerns, the current conception of professional social work. . . is generally irrelevant and sometimes dysfunctional to the resolution of the major issues that beset the poor nations" (1971: 71). These sentiments were underscored by James Midgley in his 1981 *Professional Imperialism: Social Work in the Third World,* when he wrote, "The pervasive and powerful influence of American social work theory remains one of the greatest obstacles to the development of indigenous social work education in the Third World" (Midgley, 1981: 171). Simultaneously, domestic concerns pushed to the forefront of social work attention. Urban renewal, civil rights, student protests, and the war on poverty made domestic issues preeminent in importance and urgency.

Thus, just as the interest in developing international content seemed to heighten, international activities became unpopular, politically suspect, under-funded, and overshadowed by domestic events. Isolationism and focus on domestic events dampened interest in international study and language study across all disciplines. The 1970s saw a dramatic decline in these areas at all U.S. universities. Federal expenditures for research on foreign affairs, for example, dropped from $20.3 million in 1969 to $8.5 million in 1979, while the Ford Foundation funds for advanced training in international affairs dropped from $27 million annually from 1960-1967 to less than $3 million in 1978 (National Council on Foreign Language and International Studies, n.d.). Enrollments in courses in international and area studies and foreign language decreased substantially (President's Commission on Foreign Language and International Studies, 1979).

While the trends were felt in all disciplines, the impact on the place of American social work education on the international scene seems to have been particularly severe. Organizational support diminished as CSWE disbanded the International Division and Commission. The collaborative ventures with UN and U.S. government agencies on issues in international social work education also ceased. And, to the present, discussions of international social work activity are frequently accompanied by questions of relevancy and potential harm.

INTERNATIONAL CONTENT IN U.S. SCHOOLS OF SOCIAL WORK

Although the developments cited had a chilling effect on the advancement of international content in U.S. social work programs, some schools have continued to offer international courses or include international information or perspectives in required courses.

Models for International Content

The two dominant models for including international content in social work curricula are offering separate courses on international topics and infusing international content in existing courses. The infused content may be packaged as the addition of one or more sessions on international considerations or comparisons to a course, the inclusion of course readings which address international aspects of the topic, or use of international examples. Of interest here is planned infusion, in which the instructor purposefully designs international content into a course. "Informal infusion" may occur when an instructor or student introduces personal experiences into a course in an ad hoc way.

Other less commonly used models of incorporating international content in curricula are internationalization, specialization, and individual study. *Internationalization* refers to a comprehensive infusion of international content and perspectives into all major required aspects of the social work educational program, including practicum. Specialization permits some students to elect to concentrate their studies on international social work through an organized program of classes and practicum. While this rarely exists in a programmatic form, some schools permit students to specialize through individual study. Thus, in selection of topics for doctoral dissertations, or, less commonly, special projects and international field practicum sites, students may in effect create their own international specializations.

International Content in U.S. Schools

An early survey of international offerings in the United States and Canada was conducted in 1956 by a CSWE subcommittee. Among the thirty-two schools which responded, fourteen reported that they included international content in some of their courses, and seven had separate elective courses which focused on international social work or social welfare. Thus, twenty-one of thirty-two responding schools included some international content (65.6 percent). Most emphasized provision of information on social welfare programs in other countries (81 percent), alone or combined with encouraging the understanding of national differences (62 percent) (Stein, 1957).

By 1967, another CSWE survey revealed that twelve schools, or 35.3 percent of the respondents, then had separate courses on international social work (Prigmore, 1968). At this time, almost all schools (91.2 percent) had foreign students enrolled and over 41 percent had had faculty in recent overseas assignments. Prigmore concluded that schools of social work were engaged in largely one-way relationships with other countries emphasizing the education of foreign students and opportunities for faculty to provide technical assistance abroad (1968). Interest was focused on the developing nations of the Far East and Latin America. Fourteen schools identified each of these as their area of primary interest, with only six schools identifying Europe as their interest center. Through a counting of courses in catalogs issued from 1974 to 1977, Boehm also identified twelve courses on international social work at U.S. schools of social work (Boehm, 1980).

A survey conducted in 1982 showed a considerable increase in the number of international courses being offered. At that time, twenty-seven schools reported offering a total of thirty-nine separate courses emphasizing international issues in social work (Healy, 1986). The largest number of the courses (59 percent) were general surveys of policy and services cross-nationally, with a comparative social welfare focus. A shift toward emphasis on Western industrialized nations was evident, moving away from earlier focus on Third World nations. Other courses emphasized social or community development; particular social problems or service areas, such as women's status around the world or comparative approaches to health care; or a specific country, usually combined with a study tour.

A more recent article cites a study in which over eighty courses with international content being taught in graduate and undergraduate programs in the United States were identified by Estes (Garland and Escobar, 1988). This included both courses in which international content was infused as part of the content and separate offerings. Again, the authors note that this content is largely in the area of social policy.

There is little difference in the conclusion of Herman Stein in 1957 and later authors on the topic. Stein wrote that the response of social work education to international concerns had been "uneven, varied in direction and premises, and heavily dependent on the availability of interested and qualified faculty members" (1957: 1). The conclusion to the 1982 survey stated, "Despite the unexpected level of activity, the results do not indicate a strong institutional commitment to international social work or clarity of educational purpose in its inclusion in the curriculum" (Healy, 1986: 142).

The Global Status of International Content at Present

The studies discussed surveyed only schools in the United States, with the exception of the 1957 survey, which included Canada. More recently, a global survey which collected data on international curriculum at schools of social work and the opinions of social work educators on future directions and priorities for international activity and curriculum was completed (Healy, 1990).[1] Data from this study and other sources will be drawn upon to update the assessment of the number of schools, including international content and types of content covered around the world. The parallels between the findings of this global survey and those of earlier U.S. studies are particularly interesting.

Numbers of Schools Offering International Content

Of the 214 schools which responded to the survey described, 155, or 72.4 percent, reported that international content is included in their social work curricula. Almost all African schools (85 percent) reported inclusion of some international content, followed by North America (77 percent), Europe (75 percent), Asia (69 percent), and Latin America (50 percent). The approach taken by many schools is to infuse international content in existing courses. A number of schools, eighty-nine responding schools, or 42 percent, also offer one or more courses specifically devoted to international topics. The region with the highest percentage of schools offering special courses on international social welfare is North America, with over half the schools having such courses. When asked to estimate what percentage of the average student's course work was devoted to international content, however, North America reported the lowest percentage at 5.8 percent. Other regions ranged from a high of 18.8 percent in Africa to 14 percent in Asia, 8.8 percent in Latin America, and 7.3 percent in Europe (Healy, 1990). This suggests that the pattern in North America is overreliance on separate elective courses, which then diminishes the amount of international content received by the average student.

What Is Covered?

A reality which becomes both a positive and a negative for international content is that the field of potential curriculum material is vast. Within this vast array of possibilities, international content in social work programs has tended to focus on only a few areas, leaving other significant areas relatively untouched.

Most of the separate courses on international social work have emphasized comparative social welfare policy, usually with emphasis on the Western industrialized countries. And, when infused into required courses, international content has been most frequently found in social policy courses. Each of the surveys of international content in U.S. schools of social work has shown this pattern.

It is difficult to assess the whole world picture adequately, but there is some evidence to suggest that this is a worldwide pattern. In Japanese schools of social work, for example, where 50 percent report some international content, comparative social welfare policy is the most frequently covered international topic (Kojima, 1988). Among the forty-eight Japanese social work programs, eleven reported offering separate courses on international or comparative social work. Regardless of the titles, the objectives for these courses reflect heavy comparative policy emphasis: to understand comparative trends in social welfare (six courses); to identify the position of Japanese social welfare within international trends (four); to understand comparative social security systems (two) and to understand comparative historical development of welfare policies (two). Only a few other objectives were reported: to educate students with an international perspective to make them useful workers internationally (four courses); to provide exposure to world social problems (two); and to promote exchange programs (one) (Kojima, 1988).

While the comparative policy emphasis still predominates, courses have been developed more recently on such topics as practice with international populations, cross-cultural sensitivity in international perspective, and problems in development. Other courses treat special topics such as women's status around the world.

There have been no comprehensive efforts to define foundation or minimum content in the international arena. Therefore, what is infused into curricula covers quite a range and may seem haphazard. The IASSW member survey cited earlier, asked schools to indicate international social work topics that all or almost all of their students would cover during their courses of study. The most frequently covered topic is basic concepts of social and economic development, with over half the schools reporting that they include this content for most or all their students. Following development concepts, the content areas covered by the most schools are social policy issues of regional importance (45.5 percent); cross-cultural information and sensitivity (42.4 percent); and global social policy issues (33.9 percent). The topics least often covered were methods of cross-national research (9 percent) and content about the profession, including the functions of social work in other countries (18.8 percent) and the functions of the international social work organizations (12.6 percent). The North American schools were particularly low on coverage of the profession; only three schools included content on professional organizations or on social work in other countries. North America leads other regions in the percentage of schools addressing comparative social welfare policy (44.4 percent).

Topics covered do not necessarily reflect the views of educators on what is most essential. As noted, North America leads the world in the percentage of schools covering comparative social welfare policy. Yet, when asked in the same survey what concepts were most important in defining international social work, North Americans placed less emphasis on comparative social policy than respondents in any other region. Further study will be required to determine whether this represents a shift in curriculum priorities or merely reflects a somewhat confused state of international curriculum development.

In addition, topics covered do not always fit with identified regional social problems. In the Asia-Pacific region, only thirteen schools (18.6 percent) report that most students receive content on cross-cultural issues or cross-cultural understanding (18.6 percent). Yet, a regional survey (Mendoza, 1987) identified interethnic/intercultural conflict as a serious problem in most of the Asia-Pacific countries, including New Zealand, Malaysia, India, Singapore, Australia and Papua New Guinea.

Summary of Current International Curriculum Efforts

An examination of the current state of international curriculum content in schools of social work reveals a curriculum area in disarray. While there is considerable activity in both offering special courses and including elements of content in the required portions of social work curricula, there is little or no evidence of well-planned, comprehensive international curriculum development. International aspects of the curriculum most often appear peripheral to

mainstream curriculum; course objectives are poorly developed and not logi-
cally linked to broader educational priorities or regional needs; few schools have
incorporated internationally related objectives into their overall educational
plan; and the profession, as it exists in individual countries and as a worldwide
movement, has not thought through the nature of its international contribution.

Comparative policy content has dominated to the extent that many educators
have not considered the potential of other areas of international content. The
objectives that have been defined have been largely knowledge objectives,
stressing outcomes of knowledge rather than skill, and appreciation rather than
major attitude shift. Social work education continues to be hampered by a lack
of vision of the potential of social work as a worldwide professional movement.
The result is a set of learning outcomes which demand no personal or professional accountability of students and ultimately lead to no clear roles for social
work internationally.

ADVANCEMENTS FOR THE FUTURE

Reasonable recommendations for enhancing international content in social
work programs have been made by many authors. The Stein paper cited earlier
(1957); each of the major conferences on international social welfare, especially
the 1969 workshop on comparative and international content and the 1964
Conference on Professional Social Work Manpower, and many recent authors,
such as Sanders and Pederson (1984), have developed recommendations for
strengthening international curriculum which are highly relevant today. All
have been largely ignored. Why? It is important to analyze the obstacles which
continue to block significant advancements in international curriculum, before
offering recommendations.

Obstacles to Progress in Instituting International Content

There are many barriers to the development and implementation of international curriculum content. These include limited financial resources, questions
about the degree of faculty and student interest, scarcity of teaching and library
resources, established curriculum requirements which do not include international perspectives, lack of faculty competence to teach international content,
and, especially, competing priorities and limited time within the curriculum.
Although they seem overwhelming to the individual educator, these are relatively minor barriers in the context of three overarching conceptual obstacles.

Three overarching obstacles in the way the social work profession approaches international social work block major reform in international curriculum. These three interrelated obstacles are: (1) that social work has not come to

terms with the costs of international ignorance; (2) that international aspects of social work are treated as peripheral, not mainstream; and (3) that the profession has not defined its roles in the international context.

Many social workers and social work educators are not concerned with global ignorance. They do not recognize the relevance of knowledge about the profession, policy and practice beyond national borders. Even in the face of dramatic global social trends, including the increase in refugee movements and growing number of worldwide social problems such as drug abuse and acquired immunodeficiency syndrome (AIDS), the profession has been slow to appreciate the influence of international events on domestic practice. This national myopia may be particularly severe in the United States, where the security of a large, populous, relatively wealthy nation; a largely monolingual population and educational and media systems which often ignore the rest of the world produce young adults with an isolationist outlook. Thus, only a minority of social work educators are seriously interested in international content or enthusiastically support its inclusion in the curriculum.

When ignorance of the world is presumed to have no ill effects, international content in social work, as in many other fields, is viewed as peripheral. It is viewed as an add-on, a luxury, to be included only when all "mainstream objectives" have been met. This results from the failure of social workers to accept global interdependence as what development education experts term "an irrefutable fact of life upon which action must be based" (Joint Working Group on Development Education, 1984). Linkages between domestic and international social work practice and policy issues are overlooked. Thus, when presented, international content is treated separately rather than integrated with domestic concerns in a holistic manner.

This is understandable in the context of a profession which views itself as peripheral on the world scene. Although almost a worldwide profession, social work has not asserted its role and contribution internationally. Yet there are many arenas in which it could do so. As Sanders and Pederson (1984) note, "The major concerns in international social welfare such as the human consequences of hunger and poverty, refugee problems, issues of development, and unequal resource allocation and utilization in the global context necessitate the concerted effort of all nations." (p. xi). These issues present numerous opportunities to work in partnership with social workers in other nations. Social work could assert its leadership by addressing increasing numbers of intercountry cases needing social services; establishing a presence in international development work, through training staff for international development agencies; within each country, advocating for foreign policies which have humane social impact; and developing mechanisms to contribute social work expertise to the search for solutions to the most pressing human global social problems.

These actions would require a major reassessment of the global roles of social work and social work education. A new clarity of direction, relevant to the demands of the 1990s, is needed.

RECOMMENDATIONS FOR ACTION

To bring international content in from the social work periphery a major effort in strategic planning is needed to set directions, goals and objectives. This process can and should take place on many levels, from the broadest international level of the professional associations of IASSW and the International Federation of Social Workers (IFSW), to national committees and to the individual faculties of social work educational programs. (Note: A description of such an effort at a school of social work is provided in Rogers and Ramsey [1989] describing a planning process at the University of Calgary). Time should be taken to clarify what is expected from international content in terms of changed attitudes, knowledge, and action/skill development and to integrate the expectations with the overall goals of the profession and the educational program.

Some goals and objectives vary from country to country and the call to internationalize curricula may be answered in different ways in different places. In Asia, Africa and Latin America, the main agenda has been to indigenize social work curricula. To call for internationalization may seem contradictory. In fact, what is called for is a new understanding of international role and responsibility which provides a balance and a harmony between the indigenous and the international. As stated by Guzzetta (1987):

> Social work education must reflect ever-changing international reality but it will always be a product of the dominant social reality and cultural traditions of the localities in which it is taught and practiced. . . Social work education must have a set of priorities for preparing social workers to understand global movements and to recognize and work with them in many different, local forms. (1987: 38-39)

In North America and parts of Europe, the emphasis will be on moving away from perceiving one's national profession as superior and redefining international activity in terms of partnership. Through these efforts in both developed and developing nations, a holistic perspective which recognizes interdependence may finally be adopted.

Broad Objectives for Curriculum

While specific objectives may vary across nations, a starting place for all countries was provided in a 1969 presentation in which Konopka suggested two broad objectives for international content: (1) to improve the practice of social work in one's own country and (2) "to prepare for intelligent international cooperation in social work practice, theory and research" (Konopka, 1969: 1-3). The addition of the word *policy* to the second objective would provide a relatively complete foundation for building international curriculum and refining professional roles internationally. Thus, a major purpose of international content is to improve domestic practice. For many countries, this will require an international perspective on cross-cultural content to prepare for service to immigrant and refugee populations. In all, the concept of learning from innovations abroad would apply.

Intelligent international cooperation will require content on the profession as it exists in various countries and on the major international professional associations. These associations offer opportunities to exchange useful information and create networks of international colleagues. Cooperation in practice will include working together on the increasing numbers of intercountry cases involving adoption, custody, divorce, and civil, social and economic rights. Cooperation in policy will include each nation's responsibility to monitor and influence its own foreign and social policy for impact abroad, and concerted action to provide professional input to global social problems through United Nations and other channels. Cooperation in research and theory will provide opportunities to enhance social work throughout the world. Each of these purposes would stimulate curriculum development in new or underdeveloped aspects of international social work.

Remaining Issues

There are many other issues to be resolved in international and comparative content within each country. In the United States, cross-cultural content is very important. An undercurrent of tension between internationalists and minority group educators must be resolved to internationalize the teaching of cross-cultural content without diluting its powerful messages on oppression of domestic minority groups.

The appropriate educational level and expected educational outcomes for the teaching of comparative social welfare content should be defined. As mentioned throughout this chapter, comparative policy has dominated other aspects of international content at all levels of social work education. As traditionally taught, it may be most appropriate for doctoral level study, in which scholars can engage in cross-national research and can use knowledge about alternative policies to shape domestic policy. The role of comparative social welfare content in master's and baccalaureate curricula could be refocused. At these levels, comparative policy should include illustrations of the role of political, economic and social systems in shaping policy responses, and limited information about different approaches to policy. Minimum outcomes would be the appreciation of difference and knowledge that other, sometimes better, approaches to social problems exist. The policy curriculum should be enhanced through addition of content on global social problems and analysis of the impact of U.S. foreign and domestic social policy on conditions in other countries.

As comparative policy content is reassessed and reduced in centrality, other curriculum areas can be enriched by international content. This will require faculty development efforts, as faculty have largely overlooked the potential of international content outside the policy area. In one U.S. survey, educators were asked to rate the potential of international content to enhance learning in the various curriculum areas. Almost all respondents rated the potential con- tribution of international content to the social policy area as "substantial" (93 percent). In contrast, only 32 percent thought international content could make a substantial contribution to learning in the human behavior social environment area, and only 17.5 percent were positive about the potential contribution in the area of practice (Healy, 1985). To achieve objectives related to intercountry practice, practice with international populations, and professional cooperation will require, then, a redefinition of the place and purposes of international content and the development of new areas of content. As noted, a strong em- phasis on professional role and responsibility should be included.

While there are many other recommendations which could be added, none should detract from the importance of planning strategically for the profession's international role in the future. Having appropriately rejected the clearly fo- cused, but narrow, goals of educating foreign students and consultation abroad so prominent thirty years ago, it is now time to reject the confusion and lack of professional purpose characteristic of the recent past in international social work education. In the current global environment, national boundaries are becoming increasingly less important as determinants of human needs or as barriers to the spread of social problems. More social problems are global in scope and demand international, not national, solutions. Social work curriculum can respond through clearly establishing new purposes related to cross-cultural communication and knowledge, global social problems, and capacity for utili- zation of the worldwide profession and its networks. As curriculum develop- ment moves forward, the distinctions now sharply drawn between national and international content should begin to fade. The relevance of social work edu- cation in the world of the very near future depends upon success in these en- deavors.

NOTES

1. This study was a mail questionnaire survey, conducted in 1989-1990, of member schools of the International Association of Schools of Social Work (IASSW). The instrument was produced in English, French, Japanese and Spanish. Of the

444 member institutions at the time of the mailing, 214 usable responses were received (48.2 percent). Responses were received from forty-three countries in all five IASSW regions. Number of responses by region were Africa, twenty; Asia/Pacific, seventy; Europe, sixty-eight; North America, forty-eight; and Latin America, eight.

REFERENCES

Boehm, W.W. (1980). Teaching and learning international social welfare. *International Social Work, 23*(2), 17-24.

Estes, R.J. (1984). Education for international social welfare research. In Sanders, D. S. & Pederson, P. (Eds.). *Education for international social welfare.* Manoa: University of Hawaii

Garland, D.R. & Escobar, D. (1988). Education for cross-cultural social work practice. *Journal of Social Work Education, 24*(3), 229-241.

Guzzetta, C. (1987). An overview of the five world regions: Thinking globally, acting locally. In Kojima, Y. & Hosaka, T. (Eds.). Peace and social work education. Proceedings of the 23rd International Congress of Schools of Social Work. August, 1986, Tokyo. Vienna: IASSW, pp. 34-39.

Healy, L. M. (1985). The role of the international dimension in graduate social work education in the United States. Doctoral dissertation, Rutgers University, 1985. *Dissertation Abstracts International, 46*(3A), 794.

Healy, L. M. (1986). The international dimension in social work education: current efforts, future challenges. *International Social Work, 29,* 135-147.

Healy, L. M. (1988). Curriculum building in international social work: toward preparing professionals for the global age. *Journal of Social Work Education, 24*(3), 221-228.

Healy, L. M. (1990). International content in social work educational programs worldwide. Unpublished raw data.

Hilliard, J.F. (1965). AID and international social welfare manpower. Proceedings of the Conference on International Social Welfare Manpower, 1964. Washington, D.C.: U.S. Government Printing Office.

Hokenstad, M.C. (1984). Teaching social policy and social work practice in an International context. In Sanders, D. S. & Pederson, P. (Eds.). *Education for International Social Welfare.* Manoa: University of Hawaii.

Hokenstad, M. C., Khinduka, S. K., & Midgley, J. (1992). *Profiles in International Social Work.* Washington, D.C.: National Association of Social Workers Press.

International Highlights. (1968). *Social Work Education Reporter, 16*(1), 11.

Interprofessional training goals for technical assistance personnel abroad. (1959). Report of the Interprofessional Conference on Training of Personnel for Overseas Service, Itasca, New York, 1959.

Joint Working Group on Development Education. (1984). *A Framework for Development Education in the United States.* New York: InterAction (ACVAFS and PAID).

Kendall, K A. (1967). Highlights of the new C.S.W.E. program of international cooperation in social work education. *Social Work Education Reporter, XV*(2), 20-23,37,42.

Kendall, K. (Ed.). (1969). *Teaching of Comparative Social Welfare: A Workshop Report*. New York: Council on Social Work Education.

Kendall, K. (Ed.) (1971). Population dynamics and family planning: A new responsibility for social work education. Proceedings of an international conference on social work education, population and family planning, Hawaii, 1970. New York: Council on Social Work Education.

Khinduka, S.K. (1971). Social work and the third world. *Social Service Review, 45*(1), 62-73.

Kimberly, M.D. (Ed.). (1984). *Beyond National Boundaries: Canadian Contributions to International Social Work and Social Welfare*. Ottawa: Canadian Association of Schools of Social Work.

Kojima, Y. (1988). Japan's national report on international content in social work curricula. *Year Book of Social Work Education* vol. 9. Japan Association of Schools of Social Work. City unknown.

Konopka, G. (1969). Introduction to workshop on teaching of comparative social welfare. In Kendall, K. (Ed.). *Teaching of Comparative Social Welfare: A Workshop Report*. New York: Council on Social Work Education.

Mendoza, T. L. (1987). Peace and social work education in the Asia-Pacific Region. In Kojima, Y. & Hosaka, T. (Eds.). Peace and social work education. Proceedings of the 23rd International Congress of Schools of Social Work, August 1986, Tokyo. Vienna: IASSW, 28-29.

Midgley, J. (1981). *Professional Imperialism: Social Work in the Third World*. London: Heinemann.

Miller, P. (1968). Social work education and the international education act. *Social Work Education Reporter, 16*(2), 34-37.

National Council on Foreign Language and International Studies. Explanatory brochure. Undated. (This organization has disbanded and been replaced by the American Forum for Global Education, 45 John Street, New York, New York.)

Pettis, S. (1964). American social workers abroad. *Social Work Education, 12*(2), 14-15.

President's Commission on Foreign Language and International Studies. (1979). Strength Through Wisdom: A Critique of U.S. Capability. Report to the President from the President's Commission on Foreign Language and International Studies. Washington, D.C.: U.S.D.H.E.W.

Prigmore, C. (1968). Special report: a brief overview of international activities sponsored by schools of social work. *Social Work Education Reporter, 16*(3), 23, 48.

The professional education of students from other lands. (1963). Proceedings of the Interprofessional Conference on Professional Training in North America for Students from Other Countries. Boston, 1961. New York: Council on Social Work Education.

Rogers, G. & Ramsey, R. (1989). A curriculum planning model for international social work education. Paper presented at the Annual Meeting of the Canadian Association of Schools of Social Work/Learned Societies, Quebec City, June, 1989.

Sanders, D.S. & Pederson, P. (Eds.). (1984). *Education for International Social Welfare*. Manoa: University of Hawaii School of Social Work.

Sikkema, M. (1984). Crosscultural learning in social work education. In Sanders, D. S. & Pederson, P. (Eds.). *Education for International Social Welfare*. Manoa: University of Hawaii.

Stein, H. (1957). An international perspective in the social work curriculum. Paper presented at the Annual Meeting of the Council on Social Work Education, January, 1957, Los Angeles, CA.

The time is now. (1965). Proceedings of the Conference on International Social Welfare Manpower. Washington, D.C. : U.S. Government Printing Office.

United Nations. (1950). *Training for Social Work: An International Survey.* UN Sales No. 0. IV. 11. City unknown.

United Nations. (1955). *Training for Social Work: Second International Survey.* UN Sales No. 55.IX. 9. City unknown.

United Nations. (1959). *Training for Social Work: Third International Survey.* UN Sales No. 59. IV. 3. City unknown.

United Nations. (1965). *Training for Social Work: Fourth International Survey.* UN Sales No. 65. IV. 3. City unknown.

United Nations. (1971). *Training for Social Welfare: Fifth International Survey.* UN Sales No. E.71.IV.5. City unknown.

Younghusband, E. (1963). Tasks and trends in education for social work: an international appraisal. *Social Work* (London), *20*(1), 4-11.

INDEX

ABOUT THE EDITORS
AND CONTRIBUTORS

Marian A. Aguilar School of Social Work, The University of Texas at Austin, Austin, Texas, U.S.A.

A.K. Ahmadullah Institute of Social Welfare and Research, University of Dhaka, Dhaka, Bangladesh.

Yvonne W. Asamoah School of Social Work, Hunter College, New York, New York, U.S.A.

L. Diane Bernard Visiting Professor. Resides in Panama City Beach, Florida, U.S.A.

Hans-Jochen Brauns Der Paritatische, Brendenburgische Str. 80, D-1000 Berlin 31, Germany.

Ben-Zion Cohen School of Social Work, University of Haifa, Haifa, Israel.

David Cox Department of Social Work, La Trobe University, Bundoora Campus, Bundoora, Victoria, Austrialia.

Otto H. Driedger Faculty of Social Work, University of Regina, Regina, Saskatchewan, Canada.

Doreen Elliott School of Social Work, The University of Texas at Arlington, Arlington, Texas, U.S.A.

Willy F. Frick Department of Social Work, University of Umea, Umea, Sweden.

David Guttmann School of Social Work, University of Haifa, Haifa, Israel.

Charles Guzzetta School of Social Work, Hunter College, New York, New York, U.S.A.

Joseph Hampson, S.J. Jesuit Province of Zimbabwe, Harare, Zimbabwe.

Frank R. Hawkins School of Social Work, Memorial University of Newfoundland, St. John's, Newfoundland, Canada.

Lynne M. Healy School of Social Work, The University of Connecticut, West Hartford, Connecticut, U.S.A.

Estelle Hopmeyer School of Social Work, McGill University, Montreal, Quebec, Canada.

Katherine A. Kendall Residing in Mitchellville, Maryland, U.S.A.

M. Dennis Kimberly School of Social Work, Memorial University of Newfoundland, St. John's, Newfoundland,   Canada.

David Kramer Sybelstrabe 45, 10629 Berlin, Germany.

John Lawrence The University of New South Wales, Kensington, New South Wales, Australia.

Joe C.B. Leung Department of Social Work and Social Administration, University of Hong Kong, Hong Kong.

Kei Kudo Maeda Japan Lutheran Theological College and Seminary, Tokyon, Japan.

Kalyan Sankar Mandal Indian Institute of Management-Calcutta, Calcutta, India.

Nazneen S. Mayadas School of Social Work, The University of Texas at Arlington, Arlington, Texas, U.S.A.

Tembeka Ntusi University of Transkei, Umtata, Transkei, South Africa.

Irene Queiro-Tajalli School of Social Work, Indiana University, Indianapolis, Indiana, U.S.A.

Ibrahim A. Ragab Department of Social Work, Al- Imam University, Riyadh, Saudi Arabia.

Rosa Perla Resnick Distinguished Visiting Professor, Seton Hall University, South Orange, New Jersey, U.S.A.

Abdul Hakim Sarker Institute of Social Welfare and Research, University of Dhaka, Dhaka, Bangladesh.

Paul V. Taylor Department Carrières Sociales, Institut Universitaire de Technologie, Tours, France.

Ronald G. Walton School of Social Work, University of Wales, College of Cardiff (formerly with), United Kingdom.

Thomas D. Watts School of Social Work, The University of Texas at Arlington, Arlington, Texas, U.S.A.

ISBN 0-313-27915-2